REVOLUTION

Volume 8

THE CUBAN REVOLUTION AND LATIN AMERICA

THE CUBAN REVOLUTION AND LATIN AMERICA

BORIS GOLDENBERG

LONDON AND NEW YORK

First published in 1965 by George Allen & Unwin Ltd

This edition first published in 2022
by Routledge
4 Park Square, Milton Park, Abingdon, Oxon OX14 4RN

and by Routledge
605 Third Avenue, New York, NY 10158

Routledge is an imprint of the Taylor & Francis Group, an informa business

© 1965 George Allen & Unwin Ltd

All rights reserved. No part of this book may be reprinted or reproduced or utilised in any form or by any electronic, mechanical, or other means, now known or hereafter invented, including photocopying and recording, or in any information storage or retrieval system, without permission in writing from the publishers.

Trademark notice: Product or corporate names may be trademarks or registered trademarks, and are used only for identification and explanation without intent to infringe.

British Library Cataloguing in Publication Data
A catalogue record for this book is available from the British Library

ISBN: 978-1-032-12623-4 (Set)
ISBN: 978-1-003-26095-0 (Set) (ebk)
ISBN: 978-1-032-13005-7 (Volume 8) (hbk)
ISBN: 978-1-032-13007-1 (Volume 8) (pbk)
ISBN: 978-1-003-22721-2 (Volume 8) (ebk)

DOI: 10.4324/9781003227212

Publisher's Note
The publisher has gone to great lengths to ensure the quality of this reprint but points out that some imperfections in the original copies may be apparent.

Disclaimer
The publisher has made every effort to trace copyright holders and would welcome correspondence from those they have been unable to trace.

The Cuban Revolution and Latin America

BY BORIS GOLDENBERG

LONDON · GEORGE ALLEN AND UNWIN LTD

FIRST PUBLISHED IN 1965

This book is copyright under the Berne Convention. Apart from any fair dealing for the purposes of private study, research, criticism, or review, as permitted under the Copyright Act, 1956, no portion may be reproduced by any process without written permission. Enquiries should be addressed to the publisher.

© *George Allen & Unwin Ltd, 1965*

Published under the auspices of the Congress for Cultural Freedom

PRINTED IN GREAT BRITAIN
in 10 point Times Roman type
BY C. TINLING AND CO. LTD
LIVERPOOL, LONDON AND PRESCOT

FOREWORD

Latin America is one of the critical areas of the present day world and the Cuban revolution—in itself a most interesting phenomenon of modern history—one of the most important happenings in the subcontinent south of the Rio Grande. This book tries to describe and to analyze the Cuban developments, its origins and consequences for America, especially Latin America.

The original manuscript was written in German while the author was living in London. The present English version, brought up to date wherever possible and changed according to recent experiences, has been finished in Cologne. The first impulse to write it arose out of the author's impression that there was a general lack of knowledge about Latin American affairs in Europe and out of the fact that so many inaccurate descriptions and interpretations of what happened in Cuba, were published after 1959.

As no book of this sort can be 'objective', each one depending on the sum total of experiences and background of the author, a few words have to be said on this topic.

Born in Russia, having spent the formative years of school and university in Germany, the author became a socialist in 1924 and a Communist some years later. After having been expelled from the Communist party in 1929, and having joined some opposition Communist and radical socialist groups, he was arrested in 1933 by the Nazis. After fleeting to France where he lived until 1941 he then went on to Cuba where he arrived in September of that year. In 1946 he became a Cuban citizen and in 1946/47 participated, for the last time in his life, in revolutionary groups of a pseudo-marxist character. After that he became a teacher at the 'Ruston Academy' —a Cuban-North-American high-school in Havana. He left Cuba in July 1960.

As a naturalized Cuban of European extraction he may claim to share the advantages which Georg Simmel ascribed to the '*Fremde*' (the alien)—the one who does not come today to leave tomorrow, but who comes and stays at least for a time—thus combining the 'inside' knowledge of the citizen with the 'detachment' of the foreigner. His marxist past—traces of which attentive readers will find all over the book—as well as his present non-marxist views have contributed to his interpretation and will, no doubt, arouse criticism from pro- and anti-Communists alike.

The author does not consider himself a 'Latin-America-specialist' in his view there is no such thing, just as there can be no 'Europe-specialists' or 'Asia-specialists'. Nobody can pretend to know *all* the essential facts about a big and heterogeneous area which is in a constant state of flux. Furthermore reliable *data* are hard to come by while many of the *facts* are subjective and uncertain. This explains many of the inaccuracies which this book will inevitably contain—inaccuracies which do not necessarily invalidate the generalizations. Nineteen years in Cuba and a number of brief trips to other countries of the subcontinent have given the author some experience, though others have, of course, a greater and more thorough knowledge of Latin America and the author has used their publications extensively.

Another difficulty which confronts all writers on Latin American affairs arises out of the inevitable application of sociological concepts and categories which have originated in the West and which only help to distort the analysis of countries and peoples with a different history. Although Latin America in so far as it can be considered as a single unit, is part of the 'Western world', it has numerous characteristics of its own. These constitute another source of errors, particularly grave, because Latin Americans many of whom have imported their ideologies from outside tend to classify their own problems within 'European' or 'occidental' categories.

The author hopes that readers who have not been deterred by these remarks, which are not just a *captatio benevolentiae*, will find this book of some value.

BORIS GOLDENBERG

CONTENTS

	page
Foreword	7

PART I: LATIN AMERICA: A CONTINENT IN FERMENT

1. Introduction	13
2. Underdevelopment	17
3. 'Misdevelopment' and 'Imperialism'	26
4. Problems of the Latin American Economy	29
5. Latin American Society: A Glance Through a Kaleidoscope	38
6. Remarks about the Latin American State	43
7. Militarism and Catholicism in Latin America	46
8. The Intellectuals	52
9. Latin American Revolutions Before Castro	57

PART II: BACKGROUND OF THE REVOLUTION IN CUBA

1. The Historic Roots of the Cuban Revolution	99
2. Cuba's Economy and Society	120
3. Castro's Road to Power	143

PART III: THE DEVELOPMENT OF THE CUBAN REVOLUTION

1. The Honeymoon of the Revolution	175
2. The Emergence of Contradictions	185
3. The Road to Socialism	193
4. Achievements of the Revolution 1959–61	214
5. Opposition and Invasion	236
6. Towards *Normalisation* of the Cuban Revolution	242
7. The Year 1962: Unplanned Events in the Year of Planning	255
8. 1963: At the Threshold of Socialist Construction	278
9. After Five Years—Past and Future	289
10. Analysis of the Cuban Revolution	292

PART IV: THE STRUGGLE FOR LATIN AMERICA

1. The Impact of Castro   305
2. The United States Between Monroe and Moscow   323
3. 1962–1963: Years of Indecision   337
4. Reform or Revolution   344

Bibliography   361

Index   369

PART I

LATIN AMERICA:
A CONTINENT IN FERMENT

1. Introduction

'There are two Americas: the visible and the invisible. The visible America, that of the presidents and embassies, finds its expression in the official organs of a controlled press. It sends its representatives to the Pan-American Union and it has many voices in the United Nations. But there is also an invisible, suppressed America, and this forms a big reservoir of revolution.'
(Germán Arciniegas)

This reservoir of revolution is formed by the people of the twenty republics south of the Rio Grande, collectively referred to here as Latin America.

Even the name of this subcontinent is in dispute: some people prefer South America, Ibero-America or even Indo-America.[1] Close to the small, racially homogeneous Costa Rica, inhabited by Spanish-speaking *mestizos*, lies the French-speaking, negro republic of Haiti. High in the Andes there is Bolivia, where two-thirds of the rural population, often living in primitive autarchy, still speak Indian dialects; diagonally opposite it, so to speak, across the Andes, lies the small, modern welfare state of Uruguay in which the lives of about 40 per cent of the inhabitants of the vast city of Montevideo are controlled by state capitalism. To the north of Uruguay lies the racial 'melting pot' of Portuguese-speaking Brazil where all levels of civilization are represented, from tribal Indians to ultra-modern town dwellers.

Five Latin American countries (Venezuela, Argentina, Uruguay, Cuba and Chile) have *per capita* income figures of over $330 a year; two (Haiti and Bolivia) reach barely a third of this. According to official figures in three republics (Argentina, Costa Rica and Uruguay) four-fifths or more of the adult population can read and write; in three others (Guatemala, Bolivia and Haiti) less than 30 per cent are literate. In four states (Panama, Argentina, Uruguay and Cuba) there is one doctor for every 1,000 inhabitants, whereas in the Dominican Republic there is one for every 5,600, in Colombia one for every 9,960 and in Haiti one for over 10,000.[2]

Nevertheless, Latin America must be regarded as a whole, if only because all its countries have many important problems in common,

[1] The countries of Latin America, according to size of populations, are (the figures are approximate estimates in millions for 1963): Brazil 71, Mexico 38, Argentina 24, Colombia 16, Peru 12, Chile 8·2, Venezuela 8·1, Cuba 7·2, Ecuador 4·6, Guatemala 3·8, Bolivia 4·0, Haiti 3·9, Dominican Republic 3·3, Uruguay 3, Salvador 4, Honduras 2, Paraguay 2, Nicaragua 1·5, Costa Rica 1·2, Panamá 1·1 (UN Comisión Económica para América Latina, *Boletín Económico de América Latina*, Vol. VI, Santiago de Chile, November 1961, Suplemento Estadístico.)

[2] *Statistical Yearbook of the United Nations*, 1959.

and because Latin Americans are increasingly aware of these.

This feeling of solidarity is directed against 'North America' that is to say, the United States. The Latin Americans regard themselves as united by their Catholic and Ibero-Indian traditions against the Protestant Anglo-Saxons. Their countries are dominated by US capital, they all export raw materials and import industrial goods, and each of them can on the face of it regard itself as the victim of foreign capitalist exploitation. They are weak states which nevertheless, in the name of freedom and independence, resist the political pressure of their northern neighbour.

Until well into the twentieth century, America for many people meant the United States. The people south of the Rio Grande were objects rather than agents of world history, and, behind the big landowners and generals, the growing, seething masses, the invisible America, tended to be forgotten. They first made themselves felt in the Mexican revolution of 1910 and, after the revolutions and rebellions of the 'thirties, finally appeared on the historical scene with the victory of the Cuban revolution. Now the whole subcontinent threatens to become, metaphorically speaking, a chain of erupting volcanoes.

Basically the upheaval is the result of capitalist change which was introduced from outside mainly after the first world war, and has progressed unevenly ever since.

The fast growing, rootless masses are no longer resigned to their poverty; new ideas have reached them, and find expression in the 'revolution of growing expectations'. The breath of the Cold War fans the incipient glow.

If the transition to the twentieth-century welfare state, dimly desired by millions and strongly advocated by angry young intellectuals, cannot be achieved by democratic means, these countries will take the totalitarian system of the East as their model.

Like Asia and Africa, Latin America belongs to the underdeveloped world and its protest movements have much in common with the national revolutions of these two continents. But there are features which distinguish the Latin American subcontinent from the rest.

The *per capita* income figures given above only show the degree of variation in wealth between the different states. In fact they have little meaning: first, because the statistics are unreliable;[1] secondly,

---

[1] To give but one example: according to the *Informaciones de Venezuela* (Oficina Central de Coordinación y Planificación, Carácas, 1963) the 1961 *per capita* income was $1,115; according to the International Bank for Reconstruction and Development (*The Economic Development of Venezuela*, p. 3, Baltimore, 1961) it was about $1,000, though if account were taken of the high price-level this corresponded rather to $600; according to R. Vekemans and J. L. Segundo's *Essay of a socio-economic typology of the Latin American countries* (in UNESCO *Social Aspects of economic Development in Latin America* Vol. I, p. 77, Paris, 1963) it was $540.

INTRODUCTION

because the averages hide the fact that there is great inequality of income inside the various countries; thirdly, because in almost every one of these countries large sections of the population are outside the money economy, and, finally, because income figures have little meaning unless one takes into account the purchasing power of money in each country as well as certain climatic, psychological and cultural factors.

In general Latin America is much more highly developed than Asia and Africa. No Latin American country is overpopulated. In most of them there has been some economic progress, and the whole area progressed rapidly between 1945 and 1957. But even the richest Latin American states are considerably poorer than the poorest states of the USA. National incomes are rising only slowly, and the majority of the population has no share in the increase. Meanwhile, the population, its political awareness and its expectations are growing rapidly.

True, natural conditions do not favour rapid development. Latin America is full of mountains, deserts and jungles; it is short of roads and railways. Only a small proportion of the whole area is suitable for agriculture.[1] But all such obstacles can be overcome. It is not nature which is responsible for Latin American poverty, but the people. The subcontinent is poor because it is underdeveloped and misdeveloped.

It is underdeveloped because potential wealth is not realized. Much fertile land is not used or is used badly. Millions are unemployed or underemployed. Savings are not converted into capital and capital is used unproductively.

South America is misdeveloped in the sense that everywhere there are super-modern economic enclaves dependent on the world market within backward economies which are not, the conflict between which aggravates divisions inside all its nations. It is misdeveloped in the sense that almost all these countries live from the exports of a few products whose prices fluctuate on the world market. It is misdeveloped in the sense that foreign capital plays a central role everywhere.

These facts require historical explanation. Until recently most African and Asian countries were colonies and in almost all of them there existed deep-rooted traditional cultures and forms of life which stood in the way of modern development. But most Latin American states achieved independence 150 years ago—under the leadership of classes who had come from Western Europe, were

---

[1] 'Less than 5 per cent of the total land area of Latin America has the combination of climate, topographical and soil conditions necessary for agricultural production. This compares with 37 per cent for Europe and 10 per cent for the US and Canada.' *Problems of Latin American Development*, University of Oregon. A study prepared for the Committee on Foreign Relations of the US Senate, 86th Congress, 2nd Session, February 11, 1960.

influenced by Western Europe, and controlled economic and social life. When they became independent there was little of what today is called imperialism: no external forces seemed to stand in the way of modern development. That stagnation was not inevitable, even later, is shown by the example of Japan where foreign encroachments provoked the Meiji revolution, and the development of a modern, highly industrialized country.

Why was there no comparable development in Latin America? It is possible that misdevelopment was caused by modern imperialism, but the 'underdevelopment' which alone made misdevelopment possible can only be understood by examining the history of the individual countries.

2. Underdevelopment

(*a*) *The Iberian Tradition*
The Iberian Europeans who, in the name of their kings, advanced into the spacious regions of the continent in the course of the sixteenth century differed completely from the Anglo-Saxons who opened up North America: they were *conquistadores*—conquerors rather than colonizers. They came from countries where the centuries of Christian *reconquista* had only just ended—the voyage of Columbus coincides in time with the capture of Granada—and where its values were still alive. They came from countries in which the middle classes of the Middle Ages had been destroyed or weakened, and where absolutism had been established.

During the Middle Ages the Iberian Peninsula had possessed powerful towns with strong 'fraternities', had produced the first European 'parliaments' (the Cortes of Aragon had been in existence many years before King John was forced to sign the Magna Carta), and had been the birthplace of first-class universities. Its economic life had flourished under the control of the Moors and the Jews. All this came to an end when Castile established its hegemony and the Habsburgs came to the throne of a united Spain. The towns lost their privileges, the Moors and Jews were suppressed, the 'parliaments' ceased to exist, and the Inquisition ruled intellectual and social life.

The *conquistadores* did not come from the middle classes, they were neither traders nor settlers who came to establish new homes in self-administered local communities in the name of religious freedom. They were military leaders acting in the name of their kings, who were filled by greed for precious stones and treasure, and who sought adventure and an existence befitting their station in life. They came accompanied by priests whose task it was to convert the infidel by whatever means were necessary. Manual work to the *conquistadores* was dishonourable, thrift degrading, a peaceful middle-class way of earning a living despicable. They encountered a sizeable Indian population, partly organized in what had once been highly developed states, which in earlier centuries had produced remarkable cultures. They also found the treasures they desired. They destroyed the Indian states, divided the land between themselves and, with the help of religion, enslaved the natives. Then they began to send home the precious metals which contributed both to the rise of capitalism and the decline of Spain. The new society continued as it had started: as a society of overlords based on the exploitation of unfree labour. Two vast vice-royalties, divided into extensive territories, were ruled by a large number of increasingly greedy officials from Spain and inhabited by a growing number of *peninsulares*, (whites from Spain), and a minority of creoles (whites born in America). Together, with the *peninsulares* at the top, they formed an upper class consisting of landowners, senior officials and the higher clergy. New classes developed around this oligarchy as immigration grew and the number of creoles and people of mixed blood, the *mestizos*, increased. At the same time negro slaves were imported in places where the Indian population was dying out or proved unsuitable for work.

In the beginning the gold and silver mines were the main source of wealth. Around them, big towns sprang up, like Potosí in Bolivia, which in the sixteenth century is said to have had more than 150,000 inhabitants. When the mines began to dry up these towns declined and agriculture came to the fore.

But without labour, mines and land alike would have been useless. The natives were therefore divided among the new masters. Although the distribution of men (*encomiendas*) was at first strictly distinguished from that of land (*mercedes*), the systems eventually merged in the common goal of production. The result was that the natives were reduced to serfdom and a kind of feudal system developed that could be maintained the more easily because the Indians themselves had already developed a similar system—the *cacigazos*—in which the *cacique* represented the counterpart of the European feudal overlord.[1]

These fiefs of estates and mines differed from those of Europe in the Middle Ages. 'There was no question of "autarky" and the economic system in the colonies was organized to suit the economic demands of the mother countries and of the colonial market.'[2]

The exploitation of the natives led to protests, particularly from the Church, so that laws were soon passed prohibiting all private 'slavery' and proclaiming the natives to be 'free vassals of the King'. But these laws, which were contrary to the interests of the ruling classes, were not enforced. The 'trustees' continued to be the masters, and those under their care remained slaves. In many areas the royal officials—*corregidores* or *alcaldes mayores*—appointed to maintain the law became entrepreneurs, who administered their territories in the interests of their own pockets, and lent or sold Indians to landlords and mineowners. This was all the easier because the native chiefs, the *caciques*, took part in the exploitation.

Thus, as the enslavement of the natives progressed, a parasitical upper class developed, and new immigrants were quick to adopt the values and ways of life of this society. A complaint addressed to the Emperor Charles V in the first half of the sixteenth century is typical.

[1] Julio Ycaza Tigerino, *Sociología de la Política Hispanoamericana*, Madrid, 1950, p. 58.
[2] Sergio Bago, *Economía de la Sociedad Colonial*, Buenos Aires, 1949, p. 103.

UNDERDEVELOPMENT 19

'If in any of your domains . . . it was [ever] necessary to prescribe the manner of life of your subjects and vassals, here it is even more necessary for, since the land is rich in food and in mines of gold and silver, and everyone becomes swollen with desire to spend and possess, by the end of a year and a half, he who is a miner, a farmer or a swineherd, no longer will be so, but wishes to be given Indians, and so he spends everything he has on ornaments and silks. In like fashion other mechanics cease the pursuit of their trades and incur heavy expenditure and do not work . . . in the belief that they will be given Indians to serve them and support their families in gentility.'[1]

Those who could not reach the status of *hidalgo* in this manner tried to get government positions or to join a great lord. Others went into trade, but only few became artisans or working farmers. It was vital to have good relations with the mighty. 'Personalism', patronage and idleness characterized the upper classes of the new continent, as they had characterized the *hidalgos* in the Iberian peninsula.

All this is, of course, greatly simplified and a word of warning must be added here. The Indian cultures were based no less on the exploitation of the masses than Spanish society and were characterized by great cruelty towards the masses. In the fifteenth century they had long passed their peak and were already in a state of decline. Although in some areas the Spaniards destroyed the old agriculture they also introduced new methods, new tools (the wheel and the cart), new draught-animals (horses, mules and oxen), and new crops (wheat, rye and barley) into the countries of the continent. The Spanish kings tried, though without much success, to protect the Indians. Priests and religious orders worked towards the same end. Except in Brazil[2] the towns were the centre of social life—particularly since government decrees for the protection of the natives had forbidden the owners of the estates to live among their serfs.[3]

In the towns a colourful mixture of people who served the rising oligarchy gathered round lords, high government officials and Church dignitaries. These towns had no special privileges, and their population did not consist of more or less autonomous producers and traders; they were consumers' towns with a feudal upper class administered by appointed officials. Town councils (*cabildos*) did exist but historians still do not agree on their rôle or the extent to which they represented a form of democracy. The fact is that the

[1] Quoted in L. Byrd Simpson *Many Mexicos*, University of California Press, 1959, p. 227.
[2] In Brazil 'the cities did not count—they were servants of the plantations. The people of the cities packed and shipped the sugar, cotton, hides, chocolate and tobacco that the fazenda produced. Cities furnished errand-boys, hucksters and no more. The lords of Brazil lived inland.' H. Herring, *History of Latin America*, New York, 1955, p. 236.
[3] Sergio Bago, *op. cit.*, p. 108 ff.

cabildos met only irregularly and consisted of representatives of the small oligarchical upper class, while the *cabildos abiertos* (to which representatives of the lower orders were admitted) met even less frequently and had no real power.

After independence it was the new masters of the Latin American republics who dealt the death blow to these organs of local self-administration.[1] 'The *cabildo*, the town council, failed as a local unit of government to maintain its representative character... there was little real comparison between the Spanish *cabildo abierto* ... and the New England town meeting, there was none at all between the government of an English colony and the organization of a Spanish vice-royalty.'[2]

It would certainly be wrong to describe the colonial and post-colonial structure of Latin American society simply as 'feudal', if only because the economy was tied to the world market with the result that a colonial capitalism developed.[3]

But colonial capitalism did not promote the growth of a prosperous and active middle class. The 'feudal' *haciendas* remained *the* centre of life; they were the vital institution behind the towns, which made town life possible and gave society its characteristic form.

'The hacienda is not just an agricultural property, owned by an individual. It is a society, under private auspices. The hacienda governs the life of those attached to it from the cradle to the grave and greatly influences the rest of the country ... an isolating and a conservative influence. It lived by routine share-cropping methods which prevented the use of improved machines, methods or seeds. It tied its labour force to the property and kept mobility down to a minimum. It hampered commercial development by buying little in the open market and selling ... little. Its huge areas and internal system of paths leading to the big house discouraged road building. It established and maintained a system of dependence between the hacendado and his peons which perpetuated an authoritarian tradition ... It prevented the accumulation of capital, required no investment, called for no change, did nothing to prevent soil erosion ... The tradition of the hacienda opposed preoccupation with the material world, business, industry or even agriculture.'[4]

The Church, and particularly the religious orders, played an important economic rôle in colonial Latin America. In contrast to the methods of the big landowners and managers of mines the

[1] H. Portell-Vilá in *The Carribean*, edited by A. Curtis Wilgus, University of Florida, Gainesville, Vol. VI, 1956, p. 211.
[2] R. A. Humphreys, *The Evolution of Modern Latin America*, Oxford, 1946, p. 32.
[3] Sergio Bago, *op. cit.*
[4] Frank Tannenbaum, 'Towards an Appreciation of Latin America' in *The U.S. and Latin America*, The American Assembly, Columbia University, December 1959.

Jesuits in particular understood how to make use of the natives in a rational manner.

They founded hundreds of Indian settlements—at times, in Paraguay even a whole state—which they ran in a systematic fashion. The Jesuits protected the Indians from the slave merchants and at the same time employed them paternalistically and methodically for useful work. The best fields, orchards and plantations were in the hands of the followers of Loyola. The Jesuits also extended their activities to trade and industry: they monopolized the medicine trade, built ships, founded bakeries and became important bankers; in what is now Chile they founded and directed the meat industry and ran abattoirs and potteries. They shared many privileges with other Orders and became increasingly rich; but as they looked after the interests of the Indians they naturally aroused the growing opposition of the ruling classes.

Amongst the ruling classes there emerged a group of factory owners producing both for a relatively narrow local market and for export. It was neither a very large nor a powerful class but one which had grown out of local needs: Spain was unable to produce at reasonable prices all the required goods, although in accordance with mercantilist principles the Spanish viceroyalties were required to import industrial products from the mother country. The colonial factories were mostly small enterprises which used Indian labour and talent to make textiles, leather goods, furniture and food.

The official mercantilism was undermined by the pressure of internal forces and the influence of 'illegal' external competitors—Dutch, English and French. Similarly official centralism, corruption, evasions of the law,[1] was undermined by the growth of local powers and *caudillos*.

In the second half of the eighteenth century the wind of the Enlightenment blew across the ocean. Spain and Portugal had entered the period of Enlightened Despotism. The colonies were to be rationalized, modernized and cleaned up. But what was done helped to weaken the mother states and was of doubtful value for America.

The idea was to fight corruption, to prevent the sale of offices, to rid the administration of unreliable elements, to replace the viceroys, captains-general and *corregidores* by administrators, to prevent smuggling and to destroy the Jesuits as a state within the state.

The attempt met with strong opposition: there were violent objections from the corrupt elements, the dismissed officials, the smugglers and particularly from the many creoles who had bought

---

[1] The Spanish government was anxious to regulate every detail of life. In 1681 there were 6,400 laws for America. But this represented already a big advance in systematisation and abridgement, it is said that there had previously been as many as 400,000 laws (Herring, *op. cit.*, p. 157). But most of these laws had no more importance than did later the detailed legal documents and constitutions of the South American states.

their way into high government positions and who were now to be replaced by *peninsulares*. The ideas of the Enlightenment undermined religion and the expulsion of the Jesuits had catastrophic consequences.

'Their disappearance left a vacuum that no others were able to fill. The orderly Indian communities fell into decay and many of the well-tilled fields and orchards reverted to tropical jungle or barren wasteland. Other of their confiscated properties came into the hands of rising creole and *mestizo* families. Those who were fortunate thereby secured a better economic footing from which to oppose the peninsular Spaniards who had dominated the political and economic scene in the colonies from the days of the conquest. Schools and colleges were shut down or deprived of their ablest teachers and education in the colonies, limited and imperfect as it had been, received a setback from which it had not recovered by the time of independence'.[1]

Then, at the end of the century, there followed a series of wars involving Spain, France and England. The colonies were cut off from the mother country for years: goods intended for export rotted away in the ports. At the same time, however, Latin American industry received a considerable impetus, although it was still much less developed than that of North America. The conditions for Latin American independence developed at a time when the United States of America had already been established.

(b) The Period of Independence

'There is no good faith in America. Treaties are scraps of paper, constitutions are printed matter, elections battles, freedom anarchy and life a misery... America cannot be ruled and the revolutions have ploughed an ocean.'

(Simon Bolívar)

The Latin American revolutions had their heroes and martyrs who gave expression to the resentment dimly felt by the masses: in Peru, Tupac Amaru, a descendant of the Incas, who was hanged, drawn and quartered in 1780; the Brazilian dentist, da Silva Xavier (*Tiradientes*), who in 1792 suffered the same fate as Amaru; the Spartacus of the New World, the negro leader Toussaint L'Ouverture, whose fight against France first ended in defeat but then, in 1804, led to the independence of Haiti; the priest, Hidalgo, who in 1810, at the head of an excited, unruly mob, proclaimed the independence of Mexico, and his abler successor, Morelos, who was executed in 1815, four years after Hidalgo. The last two are now

[1] D. E. Worcester and W. G. Schaeffer, *The Growth and Culture of Latin America*, New York, 1956, p. 286.

fêted as the founders of Mexican freedom, but they were then the harbingers of a distant future, the victims of the creole-*mestizo* upper class which supplanted them and assumed power. At the beginning of the nineteenth century Napoleon overran the Iberian peninsula and thus became the involuntary father of Latin American independence.

For Brazil this had no immediate revolutionary consequences. The King of Portugal moved to Rio de Janeiro, and his son, without a struggle, later became ruler of the Brazilian Empire which continued to exist as an independent monarchy until 1889.

But in Spanish Latin America a vacuum was created out of which new states crystallized after many years of chaos, confusion and war. Out of the viceroyalty of New Spain came Mexico and the United Provinces of Central America, which in 1838 broke up into the states of Guatemala, El Salvador, Nicaragua, Honduras and Costa Rica. After the failure of Simon Bolívar's unification attempts, the viceroyalty of New Granada broke up into Venezuela, Colombia and Ecuador. The viceroyalty of Peru gave birth to the Republics of Peru, Chile and, together with the viceroyalty of La Plata, to Bolivia. The remainder of the viceroyalty of La Plata broke up into two states, Argentina and Paraguay. The Republic of Uruguay developed only later as a buffer state between Argentina and Brazil. (The Dominican Republic gained its independence from Haiti in 1844 and the Republic of Panama broke away from Colombia in 1903 in a revolution supported by the United States).

The political fragmentation of Latin America was largely the result of the social and intellectual structure of its upper classes. In South America there were undoubtedly many more geographical obstacles in the way of political unity than in North America. But the North American States also had overcome great distances, deserts, forests and mountains, on their road to national expansion and unity. This however was brought about by the pioneering activities of trappers, hunters and settlers working for themselves; the problem of the 'expanding frontier' dominated whole epochs of North American history and formed the North American character. With minor exceptions such as the *bandeirantes* in Brazil there was nothing similar south of the Rio Grande. In general the ruling classes had nothing to gain from a unification of the continent. The *hacienda* is not an expansionist institution and the South American town did not become the starting point of a movement to unify the continent. The ruling creoles preferred to live in the dozen or so towns—with a head of state, a court and a bureaucracy in each capital.[1]

Side by side with the creoles there were the *mestizos* who now were free, influential and often factious citizens. But for the mass of the

[1] W. S. Woytinsky, *The U.S. and Latin America's Economy*, The Tamiment Institute, New York (no date), p. 13.

people nothing changed. Independence was not accompanied by social revolution. The rich creoles—and *mestizos*—who replaced the *peninsulares*, even where they called themselves liberal, were socially and economically conservative.

Big landowners continued to predominate and increased their powers through conquest, confiscation of church estates and the expulsion of Indians.[1] The *hacienda* remained—as did the plantation tied to the world market, and, on poor land and usually in impassable regions, the Indian community based on a subsistence economy. Almost everywhere the oligarchies were supported by armies with numerous generals, greedy for booty and power. Regional *caudillos*, often but not always in close co-operation with the oligarchies, ruled over vast, thinly populated and inaccessible territories.[2] Politics were not concerned with principles but with people, not with ideas but with sinecures. Party struggles became civil wars, governments were changed by *coup d'état* and behind the facade of liberal-democratic constitutions there were rigged elections, corruption and dictatorship.

It is true that a bourgeois sector did gradually grow up in the nineteenth century. It consisted, however, of immigrants who were numerous only in a few countries, and many of whom returned to Europe.[3] The development of a true middle class was hindered by circumstances. Modern capitalism could not develop properly where *haciendas* and Indian communities predominated, where the purchasing power of the population remained weak, where Iberian traditions prevailed and where there was no political or legal stability.

From time to time modern entrepreneurs appeared in Latin America, for example in the 1870s Ireneo Evangelista Souza in

[1] In Argentina, for example, after the extermination of the Indians, twenty million acres of land were divided among a small number of white settlers. (J. Orden, *La burguesía terrateniente en Argentina*, Buenos Aires, 1936, pp. 141 ff.) In Peru, the Spanish Crown had introduced a tax ('impuesto de cabezón') on unused land of big landowners. A decree of 1826 abolished it and resulted in 'riots of the peasants, specially in Arequipa, where the Indians were forced to give land back to the big owners'. (E. Romero, *Historia Economica del Perú*, Buenos Aires, 1949, p. 273.) In Mexico, a period of land-concentration began after independence and reached its apogee under Diaz. Villagers were driven from their holdings or incorporated into large estates without having any longer the advantages of protection by the Spanish crown and its legislation. (Frank Tannenbaum: *The Mexican Agrarian Revolution*, New York, 1929, p. 13).

[2] Sometimes the *caudillos* struggled against the oligarchs and enlisted in the lower classes even in very backward countries; for example, General Belzú, who in the 1850's was the idol and champion of the people of Bolivia. But it seems, to this writer, an exaggeration to consider most of the leaders as belonging to this type, as Victor Alba does in his *Le mouvement óuvrier en Amérique Latine*, Paris, 1953.

[3] Between 1850 and 1814 18 million persons immigrated to Latin America, about 6 million of whom returned to Europe. Of those who remained in America 6 to 7 million were in Argentina, 4 million in Brazil and about 2 milllion in Chile. In some countries, especially in Chile, there arose a group of active, indigenous entrepreneurs which, however, loses its importance after 1860 see A. Pinto Sanchez Cruz, *Chile: un caso de desarrollo frustrado*, Santiago, 1962).

Brazil, who is somewhat reminiscent of J. P. Morgan. But such individuals were exceptions and outside Argentina, Chile, and parts of Brazil, industrial capitalism still hardly existed at the start of the twentieth century.

Modern capitalism cannot flourish without internal markets, developed credit systems, transport and political security. In the absence of these conditions for profitable investment the rich will 'waste' their money, transfer it abroad, or buy more land with it. If it is difficult to look ahead nobody will make long-term plans, everybody will try to make large, quick profits. Where social progress cannot be achieved through methodical work, where there is no visible correlation between rational effort and success, people will search for contacts, government posts, look for unproductive work or pin their hopes on lottery gains.

3. 'Misdevelopment' and 'Imperialism'

'For Europe imperialism is the *last* stage of capitalism, for Latin America it is the first.'
(Haya de la Torre)

'We are wrongly developed rather than underdeveloped.'
(Ernesto (Ché) Guevara)

If Latin America's underdevelopment is due to indigenous causes its misdevelopment must be attributed to external factors: together they are responsible for its present economic problems.

Latin Americans pejoratively sum up the external factors as 'imperialism', meaning that foreign capital plays too great a part in their economies, that their nations are, economically and politically, too dependent on developed countries and that they are 'exploited' by foreign capitalists.

There is nothing new in the dependence of Latin American economies on the world market or in the excessive part played by foreign capital, and modern imperialism cannot therefore be held responsible for these facts and their consequences. What a Brazilian writer says, applies to many of the South American countries: 'Within the free play of the world economic forces that have shaped the course of various countries, it has been the lot of Brazil, ever since colonial times, to organize its economy in such a way as to serve foreign interests rather than those of its own population. The tenacious and carefully planned action of those who colonized our country at an early stage, and of foreign investors in more recent times, took full advantage of a complex of natural resources ... and thereby completely distorted the normal expansion of Brazil's economy.'[1]

Nineteenth-century capitalism and incipient imperialism merely increased the already existing tendencies towards misdevelopment.

Towards the end of the nineteenth century the expansionist tendency of the industrially developed countries increased. The search for raw materials, markets and later also for investment opportunities drove their nationals across the earth. Japan was the only non-European country where the external challenge produced an endogenous modernization of society. The other backward countries merely became objects of attack, victims of a partial transformation produced from outside which served the interests of foreign powers.

---

[1] Thomas Pompeu Accioly Borges, 'Relationship between Economic Development, Industrialisation and the Growth of Urban Population in Brazil,' in UNESCO *Urbanization in Latin America*, edited by Philip M. Hauser, Paris, 1961.

Latin America's minerals, raw materials, and agricultural products gained new importance. New mines were opened, new plantations established and the production of copper, nitrates, wheat, coffee, tin and sugar grew. Harbours and railways were built, foreign firms moved in and loans were given. The subcontinent was 'opened up'.

The foreign capitalists were not philanthropists: investors were out for large gains: consumers in the developed countries looked for cheap food and raw materials and producers for sellers' markets. They were economically stronger and their interests won the day; not, or not only, because they used non-economic means of pressure, but because they were favoured by the free play of the liberal world economy.[1]

What was more, liberal economic theory appeared to prove that the interests of those who were doing the 'opening up' coincided with the interests of those who were being 'opened up'. Inevitably, monoculture was encouraged, the industrialization of Latin America made more difficult (though not prevented), and its dependence on the world market increased. But this was claimed to be in the interest of both parties. It was said to be most advantageous for each country to specialize in what it could most easily produce. The Latin American countries could produce raw materials and the developed countries industrial products. If such a country needed machines or even shoes or textiles it should not establish its own industries, which could only produce inferior and expensive goods, and would have to be protected by high tariffs, at the expense of the Latin American consumer. These countries should produce more wheat, coffee, sugar or copper and exchange them for industrial goods from foreign countries. According to this theory there could be no conflict between the interests of foreign investors and those of the economies being developed with their aid.

It is true that without 'imperialism' Latin America would be much less developed today. But this does mean that there is necessarily a predestined identity of interests. What may be justified from a purely economic point of view can have undesirable social consequences.

Before the First World War external influences had produced an economic structure described by an expert in the following words:

'A substantial part of the income from exports was earned by plantations, large cattle farms or mines. Much of it flowed straight out again. Some of it was remitted as profits to foreign companies or absentee landowners; the rents and profits received by local property owners were mostly spent on imports. The remainder entered the

[1] Gunnar Myrdal, *An International Economy*, New York, 1956, and John Strachey, *The End of Empire*, London, 1959; New York, 1960, contain critical accounts of the consequences of the free play of forces for underdeveloped countries.

local economy by two main channels; namely, taxes on foreign trade and profits of export and import merchants. These sustained civil service bureaucracies and commercial life in the large cities, where some manufacturing activities could be found, such as food processing and the clothing industry. A considerable proportion of the population, especially those of Indian or Negro stock, worked on estates or on smallholdings, or on communal land for very little remuneration, so that they hardly counted as part of the consumer market.'[1]

In general imperialism led Latin America to specialize in the export of a few products; it resulted in greater dependence on price fluctuations in the world market, in a lack of industrialization and diversification, in the formation of ultra-modern enclaves in the middle of backward economies, in the drain of considerable profits and interest, and at the same time awakened desires for modern comforts in the rapidly growing populations.

As protectionism gained ground in the highly developed countries, as immigration barriers, protective tariffs and quotes were introduced, Latin America began to suffer from a combination of the disadvantages of liberalism and protectionism.

Misdevelopment could of course have been avoided—if the Latin American states had been willing and able to avoid it. The will was absent because they were ruled by minorities interested in preserving the *status quo*; but there was also a lack of experts and government machinery able to carry out a progressive economic policy. The imperialists and their influence were incidental to this. The economic power of foreign groups almost inevitably assumes a political character and behind the interests of private individuals stood their governments. Despite this, only the small, weak states close to the US became protectorates, in which American ambassadors usually played the part of proconsuls. Latin America as a whole consisted of sovereign states, which in theory could have reacted in more or less the same way as Japan. Responsibility for their failure to do so rests largely with their ruling classes who today sometimes blame the *Yanquis* in order to hide their own guilt.

---

[1] *Inflation and Growth—A Summary of Experience in Latin America*, UN Economic and Social Council (ECLA), Caracas, May, 1961.

4. Problems of the Latin American Economy

(a) Delays and Obstacles

'An unprecedented development is taking place in Latin America. There is no previous example of countries wanting to transform their agriculture technically and at the same time to start industrializing—and this while they are faced with a demographic rate of growth unique in world history.'

(Raúl Prebisch)

The modern world is a child of the industrial revolution which began in England at the end of the eighteenth century. Half a century later it also became effective in France: shortly before the middle of the century it crossed the Atlantic and some years later it caught hold of the countries on the other side of the Rhine and the Alps. In the last quarter of the Victorian age it reached the distant island empire of Japan and around 1890 it penetrated into Russia.

The economic historian W. W. Rostow gives the following dates for the start, or 'take-off', of modern economies:[1]

Great Britain	1783–1802
France	1830–1860
United States	1843–1860
Germany	1850–1873
Japan	1878–1914
Russia	1890–1914
Argentina	1935–?

The only Latin American country mentioned by Rostow is Argentina and he adds that in some respects it had 'taken off' already before the First World War, but that this take-off had been so slow and irregular that before 1935 one can hardly speak of the final arrival of a modern industrial economy. Since then, however, Argentina too has got stuck. Mexico and Brazil have become the two countries of the subcontinent which are now industrializing at the fastest rate.

The late arrival of progress is usually connected with irregular development. In Britain, politically and economically united as she was, the rise of modern capitalism was an organic progression. In Germany, it occurred under the leadership of a strong state, influenced by the upper middle class, but led by the Junkers. In Japan, modernization demanded an almost revolutionary change which

---

[1] *Stages of Economic Growth*, New York, 1960, p. 38.

took place under the leadership of the transformed Samurai and was based on an extraordinary exploitation of the masses. In Russia, industrialization was one of the causes of the revolution, and was completed by a totalitarian tyranny.

In Latin America the rapid growth of population preceded the economic transformation which would have made it tolerable. South America is the continent with the highest rate of population growth, and this in turn continues to rise: it has now reached about 2·9 per cent a year.[1] In 1900 the population of Latin America was about 63 million, approximately 4·1 per cent of the world's population. In 1961 it rose above the 200 million mark, overtaking North America. In 1975 there will probably be more than 300 million Latin Americans who will make up 7·9 per cent of the world's population, compared with only 240 million North Americans.[2] As infant mortality has fallen considerably while birth rates have remained constant there is a growing number of people who are economically unproductive. Apart from the vast expenditure on education which such a demographic structure places on his feeble shoulders, the Latin American must also feed more mouths than his North American or European brother; and he must do this while working much less productively.

About 50 million Latin Americans, that is 25 per cent of the population, live on 200,000 square miles, that is 2·5 per cent of the total territory. This rather densely populated area consists of twenty widely separated zones, and only in these do the amenities of modern society exist.[3]

There is a lack of transport facilities between the densely populated areas, and even inside the various countries. There are few railways, and most of them were built by private companies to carry goods to the ports, not for internal transport. Brazil, for example, has no more railway track than Belgium. Railway rates are usually high and gauges vary from one railway to another: in Brazil there are five different gauges and in Venezuela twelve.[4] Construction and upkeep of roads, particularly in the mountains, is very costly. There are only a few, and most of them are in bad condition. A Peruvian,

---

[1] *Boletin Económico de América Latina*, Santiago, October 1962, Vol. VII, No. 1, Suplemento Estadistico. Between 1800 and 1850, the population of North Western Europe grew at an average yearly rate of 0·811 per cent; during the second part of the 19th century at 0·861 per cent. The decade with the highest increase was that of 1820–30; 1·142 per cent. (A. M. Carr-Saunders, *World Population*, Oxford, 1936, p. 21, Fig. 3.)

[2] United Nations. *The Future Growth of World Population*, Population Studies, No. 28, 1958. Sometimes the population increase seems so extraordinary that it may be due, in part, to statistical deficiencies: the census of Venezuela of 1961 shows an increase of not less than 4·1 per cent per year in the last 10 years!

[3] Roman Perpina, 'Determinantes Económicos del Desarrollo Iberoamericano' in *Revista de Política Internacional*, Madrid, 1961, No. 56/57.

[4] Arturo Uslar-Pietri, *Sumario de la Economia Venezolana*, Carácas, Universidad Central, (no date), p. 38.

for example, who wants to get from Lima to the provincial town of Cajatambo, situated in the same department, must spend at least eight hours in a car and another sixteen on horseback; a voyage of over seven weeks round Cape Horn or through the Panamá Canal is needed in order to get from Lima to Iquitos on the upper Amazon.[1]

The establishment of an 'economic community' might greatly accelerate the economic development of the whole subcontinent. But, apart from the enormous distances between centres of population and the inadequacy of transport facilities, there are other formidable obstacles in the way of economic co-ordination. The various states are not economically complementary to begin with, and competition between them must grow as they independently develop identical industries.

Latin America suffers from a lack of productive capital. The economic development of a country depends primarily on the quantity and productivity of the capital invested. If capital is not imported—and in the long run the development of an economy could hardly be based entirely on imports of capital—investment has to be financed from domestic saving. In countries where the masses are poor the rich upper classes must do the saving. But rich Latin Americans like luxury and are accustomed to spending a large part of their income, in contrast to the European and North American bourgeoisie in the early days of capitalism. What is not spent is used unproductively, savings are kept in the form of cash, exported or used for the purchase of land, construction of luxury houses,[2] or lent to consumers at extortionate rates of interest.

A North American author[3] rightly explains the low level of investment in part by the attitude of the rich, which was an understandable reaction, to general underdevelopment and to political and social insecurity.

The State could of course counteract these tendencies by taxation. In Latin America at present a smaller percentage of the national income is paid in taxation than in the developed countries: 10 to 20 per cent as compared with 25 to 35 per cent.[4] Indirect taxes play a greater part than direct taxes and 'most taxes bear proportionately more heavily on people with low incomes than on those with high incomes. For example, taxes on ordinary food are high, while those on expensive jewellery are not'.[5]

---

[1] L. Hanke, *South America*, New York, 1959, p. 21.
[2] 'In Latin America a fixed capital investment of $100 generates on an average a production amounting to $40–50 per annum. The same $100 invested in residential building generates only $10–12 annually' (UN, ECLA *Economic Bulletin for Latin America*, Vol. VI, No. 2, October 1961, p. 31).
[3] W. S. Woytinsky, *op. cit.*, p. 16-18.
[4] *Economic Survey of Latin America, 1955*, New York, 1956, p. 131 ff.
[5] V. Salera, 'Government and the Economic Order', in *Government and Politics in Latin America*, edited by H. E. Davis, New York, 1958, p. 448.

Income tax is of secondary importance[1] and much less steeply progressive than in modern welfare states.[2] Tax evasion is normal. It is doubtful whether any rich South American ever pays his taxes in full. A substantial percentage of the taxes finds its way into the pocket of corrupt officials and a large part of the rest is used unproductively, for example to pay the salaries of an inflated bureaucracy.

A vital factor of the Latin American economies is that the majority of workers are still employed in agriculture, in which badly run, often semi-feudal *latifundia* predominate.[3]

The extent to which land ownership is concentrated emerges from the following figures: in Argentina 500 families own 19·8 per cent of the land in use; in Guatemala 43 per cent of the land is in the hands of one fifth of one per cent of all landowners;[4] in Chile 1·5 per cent of the owners hold 49 per cent of the land. In Brazil 1 per cent of all landowners possess *latifundia* more than 25,000 acres in size, and between them own 19·4 per cent of the land under cultivation.[5] But there is another highly important social and political aspect involved in the existence of the *latifundia*:

'Land ownership in Latin America is more than just the control and ownership of the land resource. It is the web on which the existing economic, social and political structure rests ... In a sense, ownership of land carries with it ownership of government, the right to tax, the right to enact and enforce police regulations and the

---

[1] 'Income Taxes, Personal and Corporate, which account for nearly two-thirds of federal revenues in the United States, average roughly one-quarter of the total in Latin America.' Salera, *ibid.*, p. 447.

[2] An income which is a hundred times the average income attracts tax at the rate of 67 per cent in the US and of 80 per cent in Great Britain. The corresponding figure for Chile is 37 per cent, for Argentina 29 per cent, for Brazil 17·4 per cent, for Mexico 13·1 per cent. (*Economic Survey of Latin America, 1955*, Table 30.)

[3] A good if somewhat impressionist description is found in René Dumont's *Terres Vivantes*, Paris, 1961.

[4] L. D. Mallory in *State Department Bulletin*, Washington, November 28, 1960.

[5] D. Lambert, 'La estructura agraria de Iberoamerica', Cuadernos, Paris, No. 42, 1960. In *Latinskaya Amerika*, Moscow, 1960, p. 66, M. B. Danilevich gives the following figures on land distribution:

	Estates of under 50 acres		Estates of over 50 acres	
	% of all landowners	% of area under cultivation	% of all landowners	% of area under cultivation
Brazil	51·1	3·4	3·4	62·3
Colombia	81·5	11·9	0·9	40·2
Nicaragua	51·5	5·6	1·6	41·9
Uruguay	42·0	1·8	8·3	70·8
Ecuador	89·9	16·6	0·4	45·1

'Roughly 90 per cent of the land belongs to 10 per cent of the owners. This degree of concentration is far greater than that in any other world region of comparable size.' T. F. Carroll, 'The Land Reform Issue in Latin America,' in *Latin American Issues*, ed. A. O. Hirschman, New York, 1961, p. 164.

right to judge ... On the surface, the landless of South America look to land reform to assure them food and shelter. Actually they seek something much broader and quite different. They want relief from a feudalism which we North Americans find hard to understand.'[1]

Then there are the *minifundia*—extremely small holdings whose owners have neither the money, the know-how, nor the implements to make rational use of their tiny, often infertile, plots of land. In 1950 it was estimated that of all those engaged in agriculture 88 per cent owned no land. They led a miserable existence as small tenant farmers or as farm labourers, employed for a few months in the year. Many of them were heavily in debt and became the virtual slaves of landowners, traders and money-lenders.[2]

As a result agricultural productivity is low: in Latin America, according to responsible estimates, output per man in agriculture is only 40 per cent of what it is in other branches of the economy. This represents an obstacle to economic development, first because as a result of rural poverty there are no adequate markets for local industries, and secondly because food must be imported to feed the continually increasing population, and there is therefore a shortage of foreign currency to finance other imports required for industrialization.

Latin Americans today place their hopes of solving their economic and social problems on industrialization, and land reform is often seen as a necessary preliminary.

The obstacles to this transformation are not only lack of capital, narrow local markets, transport difficulties and a shortage of modern entrepreneurs and qualified technicians. There are other difficulties. Modern industries are 'capital-intensive': they need heavy investment and at the same time employ fewer workers than will need employ-

[1] R. J. Penn statement before a Committee of the US Congress, May 1962 in *Economic Development in South America*. Hearings before the Subcommittee on Inter-American Relationships of the Joint Economic Committee—86th Congress—2nd Session, May 10/11, 1962.

[2] Miguel Mejía Fernandez, *El Problema de Trábajo forzado en América Latina*, Mexico, Universidad Nacional, Instituto de Investigaciones Sociales, 1953, p. 41.

[3] One writer paints the following picture of Central America: 'In general ... the land holdings are either quite large or extremely small. The large holding is the latifundio, frequently thousands of acres large. The owner of the latifundio usually keeps out of production large portions of land, and he rarely re-invests much of his income in improvement. Labour is paid a beggarly sum, and its efficiency is correspondingly low ... On each latifundio the owner is absolute ruler. His word is law, and those who defy it find themselves without home, job or food. At the other extreme is the small holding, the minifundio. This is usually a poor chunk of land. It may be on a mountainside where the problem of erosion must be dealt with but never is. There is barely enough space to cultivate the staples with which the owner must feed his family ... Planting and harvesting methods are primitive, time-consuming and ineffective. Even ploughing is often done by hand ... Such an existence is almost as complete an economic slavery as that to which the latifundio laborers are subjected.' John D. Martz, *Central America*, University of North Carolina Press, 1959, p. 9/10.

B

ment given the population increase. But even when they have been built, modern factories are usually unable to survive without state protection against competition from the industries of developed countries. Protection, however, leads to price increases which the local consumer must bear[1]. Prices are also increased by workers' claims, often encuoraged by democratic politicians, which usually go far beyond what these countries can really afford. High prices in turn restrict markets, inhibit the development of industries, and retard the absorption of the growing army of unemployed.

(b) *Slow, irregular, uneven progress*

'Only a rather substantial and stable rate of economic progress in the underdeveloped countries will enable political disaster to be averted. Retarded, slow and uneven progress may actually be equally or more conducive to ... cataclysms than continued total stagnation.' (G. Myrdal, *An International Economy*)

Latin America's present economic development is not only retarded, it is also, in relation to the growth of population and expectations, slow, irregular and uneven. According to rather optimistic expert estimates the total products of the continent increased from 1948 to 1958 at an average rate of 4·3 per cent per annum; bearing in mind the increase in the population this means an annual increase in *per capita* products of scarcely 2 per cent. In 1959 the gross national products of Latin American countries together amounted to roughly $67,000 million, or about 15 per cent of the GNP of the United States.[2] The rate of growth was lower than that recorded for the countries of the Eastern bloc, for Japan, and for most Western European countries. In other words, the gap between the

[1] 'What every observer notices are on the one hand the courage, spirit of enterprise and the dynamism with which new industries are created and, on the other their organizational short-comings, the plethora of under-employed labour ... the high costs with which they can work only under the protection of tariffs, the absence of planned investments ... the multitude of medium-size and small factories which can only exist because of protectionist measures.' G. Friedmann, *Problèmes d'Amérique Latine*, Paris, 1959, p. 27/28. This author mentions the vicious circle in which industrialization is caught: the inadequacies of production methods and the poor quality of products are in part due to a lack of capital—but capitalists refuse to invest in badly-run enterprises.

[2] *Studies of Latin-American Economic Development*. Study prepared by the University of Oregon for the Committee on Foreign Relations of the US Senate, 86th Congress, 2nd Session, February 1960. Some estimates are higher, especially if the years 1945–1950 are taken into account. J. Ahumada estimates that the annual rate of increase in gross domestic income from 1945 to 1958 reached 5·2 per cent yearly. UNESCO *Social Aspects of economic development in Latin America*, Vol. 1, Paris, 1963, p. 117. However, B. Higgins' contribution in the same volume contains the following statement: 'Yet if one regroups Dr Ahumada's figures for 1950–1958 ... a less satisfactory picture emerges. Per capita production for Latin America as a whole rose by 2·1 per cent per year during this period, as compared to the 3 per cent Dr Anuhada himself sets as a minimum target. Moreover, only 4 of the 19 Latin American countries ... had growth rates above 3 per cent ... Moreover, a good many Latin American countries seem to be developing less rapidly in recent years.' op. cit., p. 159/160.

developed and the underdeveloped countries actually widened during the 'fifties. The figures for 1960 were no more encouraging:[1] the *per capita* product, even in the more developed countries,[2] seems hardly to have changed.

Nor should the progress of Brazil and Mexico, the two states which are industrializing at the fastest rate, be over-estimated. Their annual rate of growth is no higher than that of some Western European countries, while their populations are growing at more than twice the rate. In Brazil, progress is accompanied by dangerous inflation; in Mexico, the annual average rate of growth of the national product is showing a downward trend: in the years 1945–49 it averaged about 8 per cent and in 1955–59 approximately 5 per cent —with a rate of growth of population of 3·1 per cent per annum.[3]

The irregularity of economic progress in most Latin American countries is explained by their dependence on the export prices of a few major products. In thirteen of them over half the total exports consist of a single product; in fourteen more than two-thirds of exports are accounted for by only two products.[4] Not only are the prices of these goods subject to large fluctuations, but since the end of the Korean War they have shown a downward trend—so that ever greater quantities are exchanged for the same or smaller quantities of imported industrial goods. The question of how to stabilize and raise the prices of these products is therefore of vital importance to the Latin American economies.

Coffee, for example, makes up more than one-third of the total exports of fourteen Latin American countries and more than three-quarters of the exports of five countries. The vital market is North America, particularly as Europe's consumption of African coffee has been increasing. In 1950 the price for top quality coffee was over 80 cents (US) a pound: today it is between 40 and 45 cents. The average price fell from over 50 cents in 1957 to 31 cents in 1960.

---

[1] 'Economic Survey of South America', *New York Times*, January 12, 1961.

[2] Argentina is only recovering slowly from the Perón era. Uruguay is hardly developing. Of Chile, an economist living there reports 'that it has not progressed for years'. (Louis Escobar Cerda in *Tremestre Económico*, Mexico, October-December 1960). From 1900 to 1929 the per capita production of Argentina had grown by 1·2 per cent per year, from 1930 to 1948 by only 0·6 per cent, while there has been a decrease since 1948 (N. Unidas, CEPAL, *El Desarrollo Económica de la Argentina*, Mexico, 1959, p. 3). In Peru the national production per head, calculated in constant values, increased in 1950 to 1960 by a bare 1·3 per cent. (Union Panamericana, *Integración Económica y Social del Peru Central*, Washington, 1961, p. 5.)

[3] Expressed in real terms (i.e. after correcting for price-changes) the national product of Mexico increased in 1960 by 5·7 per cent. During the previous five years the average rate of annual growth was barely 4·2 per cent. (Bank of London and South America. *Quarterly Review*, October, 1961).

[4] International Commodity Consultants, 'Commodity Problems in Latin America', in *U.S.-Latin American Relations*, Compilation of Studies, US Senate Committee on Foreign Relations, 86th Congress, 2nd Session, Document 125, 1960.

The ex-President of Costa Rica, José Figueres, made an interesting calculation: if the North American consumer were prepared to pay *one* cent more for every cup of coffee it would mean an extra annual income of $400 million for Brazil, $150 million for Colombia and $20 million for Costa Rica. In other words, a price increase of one cent a cup would give these three countries $70 million more than the annual financial aid promised by the United States to the *whole* of Latin America in 1961.[1]

The economic development of Latin America is not only slow and irregular, it is also uneven, and this unevenness widens the gap between town and country, between rich and poor, between class and class.

The average family income in the city of Caracas in 1957 was estimated at $4,200 a year as compared with $430 in the rural areas of Venezuela.[2]

UN experts estimate that the inequality of income distribution in Latin America is greater than in all other underdeveloped countries.[3] A Latin American economist has calculated that during the last 150 years at the most 20 per cent of all Latin Americans received not less than 60 per cent of the total income of the region[4] and other experts estimate that in Mexico for example, after ten years of progress only a tenth of the population is noticeably better off than before, a fifth is worse off and the situation of the remaining 70 per cent had remained almost unchanged.[5]

But it would be an oversimplification to say that the 'rich' have become richer and the 'poor' poorer. Firstly because it is not simply a question of differences between 'rich' and 'poor', but also of growing contrasts between different economic interests existing side by side, secondly because it ignores the fact that a new class between 'rich' and 'poor' has developed in most South American towns, whose members are much better off than their fathers; and finally because it is important to point out that income differentials within the lower classes have also grown. In almost all countries the regularly employed part of the proletariat forms a minority—and there are very big differences in wages and salaries among workers and employees: there is a wide gulf between the wages of an oil worker in Venezuela and his colleague in other industries, and in Chile the weekly wage of a worker in the copper mines is $90 as compared with the average weekly wage of $14.[6]

[1] J. Román, 'Café – Sangre negra de América Latina', in *Bohemia Libre, Puertorriqueña*, No. 57, November 5, 1961.
[2] UN *Report on the World Social Situation*, New York, 1961, p. 61.
[3] *Ibid.*, p. 58.
[4] Jorge Ahumada, 'Economic Development and Problems of Social Change in Latin America,' quoted in UN *Report on the World Social Situation*, p. 58.
[5] *The Economist*, London, April 22, 1961.
[6] *ibid.*

5. Latin American Society: A Glance Through a Kaleidoscope

'Although it is very popular to apply the term "structure" to social realities one must have some scruples about using it with reference to Latin American societies. The word "structure" gives the impression of stable conditions. But a continent such as Latin America shows more symptoms of change than of stability.' (Paul Arbousse Bastide, *Les Structures Sociales de L'Amerique Latine*)

(a) Society and Institutions

Modern society is an *objective*, functional structure, with prescribed rôles for its individual members. Doctors are needed, and those who want to become doctors must follow a certain training and act in a certain way. Modern traffic demands roads, experts to build them, policemen to regulate them, and means of transport which require to be staffed, and so on. The objective functions, arising from requirements, come first—the man must adapt himself to them. The worker knows more or less exactly what he must do to fulfil his function, and what his chances of work, promotion and pay are. For the members of the society life assumes an impersonal and, in theory, predictable character.

In 1944 the Havana bus workers demanded a wage increase as well as shorter hours. But at the same time they refused to agree to the introduction of mechanization which would have resulted in a cut in staff. The only solution was, of course, to increase fares, which was naturally very unpopular. There were demonstrations and burnings of buses—not unusual in Latin America on such occasions—and transport workers put up notices in every bus saying: 'Fellow-citizens: remember that six Cuban families are dependent on this bus.'

This illustrates the difference in attitudes between Latin American and Western European societies. In a subjective, personalistic society, buses are looked upon not in terms of economic rationality, but of individual needs and wishes. In the extreme case, a particular job exists not because it is needed but because it has been created as a source of income for a relation or friend. Similarly a student may attend medical lectures not because there is a demand for doctors' services or because he has a sense of vocation, but primarily because this occupation gives him the *entrée* to social positions which have nothing to do with medicine. The great number of students, doctors and teachers in some Latin American countries is therefore not necessarily an index of the social needs of their level of development, but on the contrary often reveals an absence of economic opportunities, an inflated government apparatus, and an unsatisfied intellectual proletariat.

Accordingly if positions and promotion in these societies do not depend on objective requirements neither do they depend on real qualifications. What is important is personal contacts with a protector. As it is uncertain and unpredictable whether these favours will continue to be bestowed, economic existence becomes a game of chance in no way dependent on the requirements of society. This has important effects on moral concepts and the whole way of life. People do not accept institutions as something objectively given. To the extent that such institutions exist at all they are regarded as arbitrary and impermanent emanations of the will of some ruler. Conversely, where there are objective barriers in the way of subjective desires they are regarded as the expression of malevolent personal forces. In Latin American countries there are far too many lawyers, and little faith in the rule of law.

(b) *Fragmentation and Rootlessness*

Latin America is not composed of homogeneous nations but of heterogeneous, fragmented groups of people without internal unity. This is the basic characteristic of their social life.

To begin with, in many states large sections of the population live primitively, cannot speak the 'national' language, and stand outside the official economic and social structure. This applies to many of the Indo-American countries where ethnic and cultural contrasts exist in addition to the contrasts between town and country and rich and poor.[1] 'In Ecuador one cannot speak of one society but only of a variety of societies, not of one culture but only of a variety of cultures. Therefore it is impossible to regard the Ecuadorian population as a nation.'[2]

About a ninth of the Mexican population are Indians who live in closed communities isolated from the rest of the nation, and from each other, and who know only their own languages, of which there are almost a hundred. Moreover, the fragmentation of the country is so great that a French observer writes: 'There is not one Mexico, but a variety of Mexicos which differ from one another in soil, in climate and in their demographic, economic and cultural characteristics ... I know of no generalization which could be applied to all the Mexicos.'[3]

[1] Nobody knows how many Indians live outside the official society. One author estimates that there are in Latin America at least 35 million 'natives' (*indigenas*) of whom only 25 per cent speak Spanish while the remainder uses 133 Indian languages with more than 3,000 dialects. A. Eduardo Beteta, *Apuntes Socio-Economicos del Peru y Latino-America*, Lima, 1959, p. 14.

[2] O. Antonio Diaz, 'Análisis expectral de la sociedad equatoriana,' *Cuadernos*, Paris, No. 44, 1960.

[3] G. Friedmann, 'Signal d'une troisième voie?' *Problèmes d'Amerique Latine*, Vol. II, Paris, 1961, p. 33.

In Brazil all stages of civilization can be found, from the primitive barbarism of wild Indian tribes and the feudalism of the *fazenda*-ruled districts to the highly developed capitalism of the state of São Paulo.

'The state of Colombia comprises worlds as different from one another as Belgium and the Belgian Congo', remarked a Colombian minister.[1] It contains urban districts around Bogotá, Medellin and Cali, each filled with separatist local pride, and rural territories where millions are living outside modern society. Conditions akin to civil war have existed for years in the mountain regions, where, between 1948 and 1960, more than 250,000 people became victims of the *violencia* of armed bands. There are also two *de facto* independent 'communist' republics, Tequendama and Summapaz, where no central government official can go.

Even the most highly developed of these countries lacks the basic unity which underlies the class and group conflicts of modern nations. Nor are there any more or less clearly defined, more or less homogeneous social groups. A North American writer says: 'Socially and politically Argentina is a highly fragmented country. Its fragmentation is different from the pluralism which many of us think is one of the best attributes of society in the USA. In Argentina, the divisions are sharper, deeper and more numerous, and the several fragments either do not communicate with each other at all or else do so mainly to quarrel and fight.'[2]

The process of urbanization helps neither to unify the urban population nor to reduce the contrasts between town and country. On the contrary, it results in a sharpening of all conflicts. The cities grow more rapidly than the opportunities for work which they provide. Recent experience in Latin America shows that, in countries where the population is increasing fast, the manufacturing sector—even if it is expanding—cannot absorb the natural growth of the urban labour force and is even less able to absorb redundant rural workers.[3] Immigrants from the country feel lost in the cities. Families or individuals torn from the communities and large family groups of the villages and small towns, or from the often paternalistic, feudal *patrón-peón* relationship became social driftwood in slum districts. Many become domestic servants, sell lottery tickets and so on, and together with others who live more or less parasitically, appear in official statistics as part of the 'services' sector. Such a classification also helps to distort Latin American reality. In the developed countries the so-called tertiary 'services' sector developed after the sectors of 'agriculture' and 'industry' and fulfils a socially and economically necessary function. In Latin America 'the appearance

[1] Quoted in R. Dumont, *Terres Vivantes*, Paris, 1962, p. 1.
[2] A. P. Whitaker, 'The Argentine Paradox', *The Annals*, March 1961.
[3] *Economic Bulletin for Latin America*, VI, No. 2, October 1961.

of a substantial tertiary sector has preceded rather than followed the development of an important secondary or manufacturing sector. Indeed, in terms of persons employed, the share of the tertiary sector is excessive'.[1]

In Latin America this sector consists mainly of disguised unemployed and social parasites whose activities are not determined by the necessities of economically productive development.

If, however, classification by 'sectors' cannot reveal the real problems of the Latin American economies, division by occupation is no more satisfactory. People frequently change jobs and in the towns they often have two or more occupations, and sometimes extra earnings which do not appear in any statistics.

In short, Latin American society cannot be analysed in conventional, sociological terms. It is difficult to discuss the 'structures' of such fluid societies, in which the rootless masses form a continuously growing sector.

(c) *Social Classes*

Many writers regard the rise of the middle classes as the decisive factor in the social and political development of Latin America. Although there is some truth in this interpretation it is so vague that it is almost useless.

Most authors[2] seem to employ the concept 'middle classes'—in itself imprecise and unclear—as a collective name for all urban groups between the landowning oligarchy and the industrial workers, though there are even some observers who include in the middle classes some sections of the industrial proletariat.[3] Some emphasise that in Latin America the way in which money is spent is more important for class differentiation than the extent and sources of wealth.[4] One writer believes that the heterogeneity of this 'middle stratum'[5] makes it necessary to speak of 'middle sectors' and their 'rise'. But this vague concept leaves doubts about *who* is rising.

At the other extreme there are the communist writers who try to force Latin American realities into the categories of their system.

---

[1] 'Report of the Expert Working Group on Social Aspects of Economic Development in Latin America', *Economic Bulletin for Latin America* (UN), Santiago de Chile, March 1961.

[2] For example, most members of the *Oficina de Ciencias Sociales* of the Union Panamericana, and the editors of the *Materiales para el Estudio de la Clase Media en América Latina*, 1950. The same is true of F. Debuyst, *Las Clases Sociales en América Latina*, Fetes, Bogota, 1960.

[3] Haya de la Torre, *Treinta Años de Aprismo*, Mexico, 1956, p. 133.

[4] 'Socially and economically the groups dealt with are highly fluid and widely disparate . . . their membership ranges upward from the poorly paid white collar employee in government . . . to the wealthy proprietors of commercial and industrial enterprises.' John J. Johnson, *Political Change in Latin America*, Stanford University Press, 1958, Preface.

[5] J. Ycaza Tigerino, *Hacia una Sociología Hispanoamericana*, Madrid, 1958, p. 153.

They distinguish a feudal oligarchy, a bourgeoisie, an urban lower middle class, a peasantry and a proletariat with urban and rural elements. The bourgeoisie is subdivided into the *'comprador* bourgeoisie' closely associated with the 'imperialists', the 'national bourgeoisie' which produces mainly for the domestic market and is therefore opposed to imperialism,[1] and (according to some authorities) a 'bureaucratic bourgeoisie', whose wealth is derived directly or indirectly from 'politics'.

As far as the lower classes are concerned an East German expert on Latin America claims that in the countryside there are sharp distinctions between the rural bourgeoisie, the middle peasants and the poor peasants, that the rural proletariat predominates in the working class and that the 'aristocracy of labour' is of no importance.[2]

In all this there is a mixture of truth and falsehood, of relevant and irrelevant facts. 'Classes' in the Marxist sense can of course be identified in Latin America as elsewhere, but an analysis by class reveals only *one* aspect of society. One must neither ignore those characteristics which cannot be classified nor overlook the fact that the various classes in Latin America are not clearly differentiated and have not become finally consolidated.

A capitalist bourgeoisie has grown up alongside the big landowners, but the two classes merge into each other. The big landowners lose some of their feudal characteristics and often become capitalists, while capitalists invest their profits in land and sometimes assume feudal attitudes.

Some of the oligarchs and *compradores* also put their money into local industry and trade, thus transforming themselves into a national bourgeoisie. The national bourgeoisie as a whole, however, must not be identified with modern, progressive entrepreneurship. It consists in part of small capitalists clamouring for protection and subsidies so that they can continue to use outdated methods and to sell at excessively high prices. Its members are no less interested in tax evasion and more interested in low wages than most *compradores*, and they too invest their money in land and buildings.

But modern entrepreneurs are, though still a minority of the upper classes, developing in Latin America. Some are recruited from the bureaucratic bourgeoisie which made its money from politics and corruption. Other members of the bureaucratic bourgeoisie occupy leading positions in the many state and semi-state enterprises, some as parasites but others also as modern managers.

[1] 'The contradictions between the national bourgeoisie and foreign imperialism bear a permanent character,' claims W. G. Spirin, 'Na puti k natsionalnomu osvobozhdeniu in *Latinskaya Amerika v Proshlom i Nastoyashchem*, Moscow, 1960, p. 19.
[2] Manfred Kossock, 'Klassenlage und Befreiungsbewegung in Lateinamerika', *Deutsche Aussenpolitik*, Sonderheft II, 1961, Berlin (Ost).

If one talks about a 'bureaucratic bourgeoisie' one must also talk about a 'bureaucratic middle stratum'. The fairly numerous government, provincial and municipal officials and holders of a variety of sinecures, together with the shopkeepers, tradesmen, middle-grade employees, members of the liberal professions and so on, form an urban middle stratum which is even more heterogeneous in Latin America than elsewhere.

In the countryside the independent peasant who tills his own soil and supplies his own needs, but is nevertheless in close touch with the market, forms an exception. The rural population in the main consists of small and very small tenant farmers, farm labourers who are often treated like serfs,[1] and Indian communities which are really outside the national economies.

The urban proletariat is split. Only 5 to 8 per cent of all proletarians are factory workers.[2] Many workers (and especially immigrants from foreign countries) cannot find permanent employment, and a group of experts has described them as the marginal population. 'Marginal labour may be defined as all those who live at the lowest income level—approaching subsistence levels—either because of the unproductive and non-essential nature of their occupations or because work is irregular and unobtainable. Marginal labour, plus dependents, forms the marginal population.'[3] Most of these people between the proletariat and the *lumpenproletariat* lack class consciousness, expect improvements to come from politicians, from the state or from the trade unions, which are almost always dependant on the state, and dream of a future independent, lower middle-class existence.[4]

The other extreme of the proletariat is represented by a minority of permanently employed, highly paid workers in modern factories who form a privileged stratum remote from the urban masses and from the half-starved agricultural labourers.

---

[1] Miguel Mejia Fernandez has convincingly shown how many different forms of forced labour exist and how they are rooted in serfdom and slavery of the pre-colonial period. (*El Problema del Trabajo Forzado en América Latina*.)
[2] Economic Commission for Latin America, 'Creation of Employment Opportunities in Relation to Labour Supply', in UNESCO *Urbanization in Latin America*, 1961, p. 121.
[3] *ibid.*, p. 123.
[4] G. Friedmann, *Problèmes d'Amérique Latine*, Paris, 1959, pp. 32–40, and Juarez Rubens Prandao Lopes, in UNESCO *op. cit.*, p. 241 ff.

6. Remarks about the Latin American State

'The acceleration of economic development cannot be a spontaneous phenomenon resulting exclusively from operations of the market forces. A combination of private enterprise with vigorous state action is necessary ... This need for State intervention in economic development is due in Latin America to institutional, economic, political and social circumstances very different from those prevailing in some other countries when they passed through a similar stage of their evolution.'
(UN/ECLA *International Cooperation in a Latin American Development Policy* [1954])

The state must play and plays in Latin America a much bigger rôle than it played in Western Europe more than a century ago. But its progressive action is impeded by a number of factors:

In Latin America the state lacks a clear principle of legitimacy, the free allegiance of the citizens, stability and continuity. It lacks sufficient financial means and spends those available in a highly unproductive fashion. The personal composition of the public administration remains highly defective and it finds itself under constant pressure from social forces which hinder the task of development.

A modern state can only function if it appears legitimate, and it appears so in so far as the state is considered to represent the nation in the fulfilment of necessary tasks, and if it embodies a suprapersonal rule of law. Only then can it count on the allegiance of its citizens and enjoy a measure of continuity and stability.

In Latin America this is made impossible by fragmentation and personalism. There is neither a fundamental national unity, nor a healthy pluralism based on this unity. Most countries are very far from a 'rule of law', the law, and all state-action, appears rather as an emanation of the will of a powerful *caudillo* who rules primarily in his own interest and that of his followers.

True: almost all these countries pay lip-service to democracy and enjoy attractive, elaborate constitutions which sometimes describe almost perfect welfare states. The 1940 constitution of Paraguay expressly prohibits 'the exploitation of man by man'.[1] All constitutions establish a division of power, contain guarantees of individual freedom and many guarantee all citizens the right to work, an adequate income, old-age pensions, free education, paid vacations, etc. All the 200 constitutions enacted in the course of the last 140 years are based on imported ideas and very few of them have any-

[1] A. M. Lazcano y Mazón, *Las Constituciones de Cuba*, Madrid 1952, p. 259.

thing to do with the social reality of their countries.[1] No wonder that, as one British writer puts it, 'Nowhere are constitutions more elaborate—or less observed.'[2] A North American author writes: 'It is probably true that no constitution anywhere functions exactly as written. It is also probably true that the divergence between written constitutions and actual political systems is wider in Latin America than in most areas of the world.'[3] In Latin America a constitution is rather a poetic than a political document. It does not determine what exists—but what ought to exist if it had any force; it is almost a utopia influencing the minds and hopes of men.

The division of powers is habitually disregarded and power is concentrated in the hands of a president-*caudillo* who dispenses all the favours. No real local government, or other self-government, exists. The welfare provisions remain mostly a dead letter. A large part of the population remains outside the nation and the struggle between 'ins' and 'outs' takes all too frequently the form of *pronunciamientos*.

Because of the deficient tax-system and corruption of all kinds, the governments in power lack the financial means necessary for progressive development action, while the means available to them are spent on enormous sprawling bureaucracies and sinecures, costly armies and, all too often, on showy but inessential public works.

The administration consists of hosts of civil servants who are unskilled, inefficient, underpaid and prone to corruption and who rarely have any security of tenure, since each change of government involves a change of civil servants. This is inevitable in countries where the 'spoils' system belongs to the essence of political life and where politics itself becomes, because of the scarcity of other available jobs, one of the main industries. This is the most important fact about Latin American corruption—not that it is bigger than it is elsewhere, but that it belongs to the sinews of life, because of the essential function of politics in countries plagued by unemployment and under-employment.

Finally, the growing Latin American state finds itself under the constant pressure of antagonistic social forces. On the one hand there is still, in many countries, the braking power of the old oligarchy which effectively prevents not only the realization of measures favouring the lower classes but also, and particularly, of those necessary for rapid development.

[1] 'It is our idiosyncrasy that we leave out all traces and suggestions of those complexes which control our national life.' P. Jaramillo Alvarado, *El regimen totalitario en América*, Guayaquil, 1940, p. 73.
[2] R. A. Humphreys, *The Evolution of Modern Latin America*, Oxford, 1946, p. 79.
[3] G. I. Blanksten, 'Constitutions and the Structure of Power', in *Government and Politics in Latin America*, ed. H. E. Davies, New York, 1958, p. 251.

On the other hand there are the pressures arising out of the wishes and hopes of the under-employed masses with their rising expectations, which are increased and exploited by power-hungry, more or less irresponsible politicians and demagogues. Out of these forces emerge the welfare state prescriptions enshrined in so many constitutions and laws, which go far beyond anything an underdeveloped (or even developed) economy can afford. The mere existence of many of these formulae closes the eyes of the people to reality, and creates the belief that welfare is entirely unrelated to productivity and the lack of it must be the result of the working of some malevolent power. Insofar as such measures are put into effect, they tend to create small privileged minorities and a kind of 'worker-aristocracy', and they frequently contribute to declining productivity, higher prices and inflation. Insofar as they remain on paper—as they must —they foster corruption,[1] increase disillusion and despair, and produce a cynicism which pervades the whole of political life.

So there is a vicious circle. Underdevelopment cannot be overcome without an efficient state, and an efficient state cannot arise out of underdevelopment.

---

[1] Because the employer has to pay some official for not complying with the laws.

7. Militarism and Catholicism in Latin America

Two institutions which play a particularly important rôle in Latin America must briefly be analyzed: The Army and the Catholic Church. The Army has always represented a state within the state, and the Church has long had close links with the state.

(a) The Armed Forces

To the general public Latin America is the classic continent of military dictatorships and *pronunciamientos*, of *coups d'état* in which one military tyrant is replaced by another.

In fact, in nearly every Latin American state the Army remained the decisive force until well into the twentieth century. During the wars of liberation, the armed gangs gathered around the *caudillos*, although at first badly trained and undisciplined, soon became the only coherent force capable of governing. Often they had close links with the landowning oligarchy and ruled in its interests. Later, when the old oligarchies became weaker and new classes sought power, the armies became the guardians of order: 'The environment in Latin America invited military rule. The decadence of the oligarchy, the political immaturity . . . not to mention the poverty and illiteracy of the new groups aspiring to power, the lack of any strong, well integrated group aside from the armed forces—all these combined to encourage militarism.'[1]

The armies served less to defend countries from external enemies than to preserve the *status quo* at home. A man chose a military career, not because he wanted to die a hero's death for his fatherland, but because he wanted to lead a secure and privileged existence; moreover, an army career often meant social advancement. Although the higher ranks of the army were normally reserved for sons of the ruling class, in turbulent times non-commissioned officers sometimes became colonels or even generals. In the process they also became rich and this helped to transform a revolutionary rebel into a guardian of peace and order. Almost everywhere, whether as the supporters of civilian governments or as the actual rulers, the armies had political control, and they exercised it to preserve the *status quo*. This is still the position in many Latin American countries.

'The tradition of *pronunciamientos* has given the army the privilege of exercising a right of veto over the decisions of the electors and the

[1] Edwin Lieuwen, *Arms and Politics in Latin America*, New York, 1960, p. 123.

plans of the civilian authorities... Should one minister be replaced by another? Be careful! The army might take it amiss!... Should the wages of certain groups of workers be increased? Beware! The employer might turn to the army to stop it!... Should there be a land reform? That is out of the question because the big landowners have so much influence with the army. Thus there is almost no social problem, almost no decision of the civilian authorities which does not depend on the preliminary question: "And what will the army think about it?" [1]

It is impossible today to generalize about the character, rôle and further development of the armies of Latin America. There are still a number of smaller and less developed states where they rule the country as the pretorian guards of some general (in Paraguay, Nicaragua and, until the beginning of 1961, also in San Domingo); in others, for example in Peru,[2] they still have very close links with the oligarchy, while elsewhere they have become less political and are more nearly an integral part of the state, as in Uruguay, Chile and Mexico; finally, there are countries in which the institution of an army has been abolished (Costa Rica) or where new revolutionary armies have been created after the destruction of the old (Bolivia, Cuba). Brazil occupies a somewhat special position: 'Traditionally the army rather than being truly aristocratic and controlled by the landed gentry has been a means of upward mobility and has been dominated by the middle class'.[3] But generally the political rôle of the armies has not diminished since the 'forties, though it has changed in an extremely complicated manner.

These changes are the result in part of military reorganization, and in part, of the social and political transformation of Latin America.

Technical progress and modernization have affected the armies. Officers are becoming experts in a complicated profession. Their careers are beginning to depend more on ability than on knowing the right people. An increasing number of them now come from the middle classes. The officers' attitudes are changing: they are beginning to think like managers and to favour a policy of modernization, industrialization and centralized, economic planning. Even the older generals and colonels are sympathetic towards state capitalism because its development often gives them a chance of finding well-paid positions.

[1] Victor Alba, 'El Militarismo en la Historia de Iberoamerica', *Combate*, San José, Costa Rica, No. 1, 1958.
[2] But even in Peru the higher officers have lately been influenced by radical, even communist ideas, through the communist-influenced teachers and consultants attached to the Peruvian Centre for Advanced Military Studies (*see* Richard W. Patch, *The Peruvian Elections of 1962 and Their Annulment*, American Universities Field Staff—Reports Service—West Coast South America Series, Vol. LX, No. 6, p. 15–16.
[3] Charles Wagley, 'The Brazilian Revolution', in *Social Change in Latin America Today*, Council on Foreign Relations, New York, 1960, p. 217.

Latin America's social crisis has given the armed forces renewed political importance. Whereas formerly the armies, as the only organized force in a social vacuum, operated in the interest of the oligarchies, they are now pushed into the position of arbiters in the growing struggle between a variety of contending forces. In situations of acute crisis, when Latin American democracy ceases to function, the armed forces, which have so much more power because they are equipped with modern weapons, have again become politically decisive factors. Either their representatives take over the government themselves, or they become the vital support of nominally democratic governments.

The establishment of a classic, military dictatorship without an ideology has become difficult. Somehow military dictatorships must find mass support and appear as the defenders of social justice.

In this the generals and colonels are encouraged by the 'socialist' ideas of many younger officers. (It is not without interest to mention that one of the officers' lodges in Argentina bears the name of Gamal Abdel Nasser.) But even the younger officers are usually unwilling to be active radical revolutionaries. Unlike the young, unemployed intellectuals they enjoy secure positions and many privileges; unlike the radical civilians, who in Latin America are usually strongly anti-militarist, they neither want to abolish the special privileges of the armies, nor to reduce inflated military budgets. Frequently, they tend to be much less 'anti-imperialist' than the civilian radicals, if only because supplies of arms and equipment depend largely on good relations with the United States.

New military dictatorships are inclined to develop into a kind of 'Bonapartism', the clearest example of which was Perón's alliance between the army and the workers. Similar tendencies would be observed in a few, mostly very backward countries in which the officers sought to play the rôle of 'intellectuals in uniform', for example in Bolivia and Venezuela and, in a somewhat different form, in Colombia, where General Rojas Pinilla tried for a time to pass for a social reformer.

However, the most recent manifestations of neo-Bonapartism have shown that it is unlikely to succeed in Latin America. The armies are therefore now more inclined to support and influence civilian governments. Almost everywhere their aim is to circumscribe the radicals while preserving the outward forms of civilian constitutionalism.

However, it is impossible to speak of a clear army policy in any South American country. In Argentina the armed forces brought Perón to power—and later overthrew him. The officers brought democracy to Venezuela in 1945, put an end to it in 1948, and took a leading part in overthrowing the Pérez Jiménez dictatorship in 1958.

It is impossible to generalize about armies and politics in Latin

America if only because the armed forces do not represent a homogeneous force. In addition to the latent conflicts between army, navy and air force which are partly, but only partly, due to their social composition, there are the struggles between the generations —every successful rebellion gives the younger officers a chance of promotion—as well as purely personal conflicts among the all too numerous colonels and generals. In periods of acute political crisis these conflicts are intensified by external influences and regularly split the armed forces.

(b) *The Catholic Church*

The other coherent force in Latin American countries used to be the Church, which is still influential in some republics, even in Mexico with its anti-clerical government. But modern social, political and ideological changes are undermining the Church in Latin America and the danger to its position is all the greater because the clergy are numerically extremely weak.[1]

In 1960 there were 33,000 priests in Spain and 37,600 in South America: Spain has 30 million inhabitants and Latin America 200 million. In Chile, Ecuador and Colombia there is one priest for every 3,000–3,500 inhabitants:[2] In Uruguay, Bolivia and Argentina one for every 4,000–4,500; in Venezuela Mexico and Peru, one for every 5,000–6,000; in Brazil one for ever 6,500; in Cuba one for every 9,500; in Guatemala one for 11,000 and in Honduras only one for ever 12,000 inhabitants. It is important to note that in some countries most of the clergy are foreigners.

The Latin Americans are Catholics, but their 'Catholicism is theatrical, sensual, superficial, in a word: childish'.[3] Many town dwellers go to Mass on Sundays and the women go to Confession. The upper and middle classes send their children to Catholic schools, often with unexpected results, as is shown by the example of Fidel Castro, who was educated at one of the biggest Jesuit schools in Cuba. But anti-clericalism has always existed among intellectuals, and the influence of the Church on the urban proletariat has long been weak and is becoming progressively weaker.

In the countryside the Church was usually more powerful, although in Cuba and elsewhere most of the rural population were not under the influence of the Church, and there were large areas without priests. The Indians, in particular, are often fanatically religious, perhaps because their Christianity contains strong non-Christian elements. But the 'revolution of growing expectations' has reached the rural population; outmoded ways of life are breaking down and

[1] For a presentation of the rôle of the Church in present-day Latin America as seen from a Liberal Catholic standpoint, see Gary MacEoin, *Latin America— the Eleventh Hour*, New York, 1962.
[2] All figures are taken from A. Garrigos Meseguer, 'La Iglesia Católica en Iberoamerica', *Revista de Politica Internacional*, Madrid, 1961, No. 56/57.
[3] L. Barahona Jiménez, *El Ser Hispanoamericano*, Madrid, 1959, p. 209.

the process of urbanization is undermining the power of the clergy. The growing masses in the towns are being 'de-christianized' as social radicalism reinforces traditional anti-clerical tendencies.

During the wars of liberation the hierarchy was on the side of Spain and thus became the enemy of nationalism. The politically ambitious creoles were strongly influenced by freemasonry and the ideas of the Enlightenment, and many of them had an eye on the big Church estates. Anti-clericalism became the political war-cry of the 'liberal' parties against their 'conservative' opponents. In countries where the liberals were in control the position of the Church was often precarious; it lost wealth and influence. In twelve out of twenty Latin American states the constitution has separated Church and state.[1] But the struggle between liberals and conservatives took place within the ruling upper classes, and they both generally understood the value of religion as 'opium for the people'. A *modus vivendi* between priests and politicians was reached almost everywhere. The clergy became the closest ally of the oligarchy. They had to pay for this in the twentieth century when they were attacked by radical democrats and social revolutionaries as well as by anti-Spanish nationalists and anti-clerical liberals. In the 'thirties the Church began to realize the need for a transformation, even though a new social reformist attitude was bound to lead to tension within the hierarchy.[2]

A Soviet writer says of the Church's need for political reorientation: 'Faced with the growing national liberation movement of the Latin American people the Church can no longer behave as before. It must take account of the wish of the toiling masses for social change and the democratization of public life.'[3]

An article which appeared in the semi-official *Informations Catholiques Internationales* on September 15, 1957, accused the Latin American Church of having been too long and too closely associated with oligarchies and dictators, while a Chilean archbishop has said: 'Social reform will come about, whether through our efforts or in spite of them. But in the latter case it will be anti-Catholic.'[4]

During the last few years the Church has not only reorganized itself—since 1954 there has been a Latin American Episcopal Council with headquarters in Bogotá—but has also tried to separate itself somewhat from the oligarchies and to take a 'Christian Social' road. It has taken a more or less firm stand against the dictatorships of Perón, Rojas Pinilla, Pérez Jiménez, Batista and Trujillo. Christian circles are in favour of land reform and today a Catholic can write:

[1] Brazil, Chile, Cuba, the Dominican Republic, El Salvador, Guatemala, Haiti, Honduras, Nicaragua, Panama, Uruguay and Mexico.
[2] J. J. Kennedy, 'Dichotomies in the Church', *The Annals*, March, 1961.
[3] I. P. Lavretski, 'Katolitsism v Stranakh Latinskoy Ameriki', in *Problemy Latinskoy Ameriki*, Moscow, 1959, p. 231.
[4] Quoted in L. Hanke, *Mexico and the Caribbean*, New Jersey, 1959, p. 114.

'To aim at a land reform based on the principle of avoiding any damage whatsoever to the present owners would mean making it impossible.'[1]

In most countries 'Catholic Action' and 'Christian Working Youth' groups have begun to be active in the field and to mobilize the Catholic students. A catholic Trade Union movement centralized in the CLASC (Confederación Latino Americana de Sindicalistas Cristianos) is very active and many of the young leaders can only be classified as social revolutionaries. In Colombia the strongest Trade Union Centre (UTC) is inspired by the doctrines of social catholicism and the same is true of the strongest Trade Union organization in Costa Rica, although the Colombian and the Costa Rican organizations do not belong to the CLASC but to the ORIT the regional organization of the ICFTU. In Chile and Venezuela the Christian-Democratic parties have a growing influence inside the Trade Unions.

In several republics there are Christian Social or Christian Democratic parties, some of which were founded only after the Second World War. In Argentina 'rural missions', composed of priests, doctors, veterinary surgeons, agronomists, and social workers, look after the spiritual and physical well being of the countryfolk. A similar rôle is played by the 'Institute for Rural Education' in Chile. In Colombia, the 'Radiophonic Schools' at Sutatenza have placed broadcasting for the first time systematically at the service of Christian propaganda and education.

This reorientation is not easy, nor is it without danger for the Church. In most South American countries the hierarchy still sides with the oligarchies and fears the consequences of the radical social reforms advocated by many priests whose views bring them into close contact with more or less communist-influenced circles. The 'radical' priests come mainly from the secular clergy or the Jesuits, while the other religious orders, whose members are mostly foreigners, regard radicalism with suspicion and hostility.

The position of the Church remains difficult because in many South American countries it maintains its connections with the upper classes and because urbanization and secularization are working against it. It is doubtful whether and to what extent radicalized masses whose hopes are focused on this world will be sympathetic towards the 'transcendental' ideology of an institution which they suspect of inveterate conservatism. A European who during a visit to Latin America talked to many priests and active Catholics summed up their mood as follows: 'These people smart under the de-Christianization of the Latin American nations which they face almost impotently.'[2]

[1] A. Garrigos Meseguer, *op. cit.*
[2] Raymond Scheyven in *Le Monde*, Paris, November 12/13, 1961.

8. The Intellectuals

'Radical reform-movements appear to be inexorable forces in Latin America, which cannot be exorcised by ostracism and are, probably, the major political instrument by which various indigenous obstacles to Latin American economic development may be broken through.'
(*U.S. Business and Labor in Latin America*, Study by the Research Center in Economic Development and Cultural Change of the University of Chicago)

Radical reform movements particularly in underdeveloped countries are led and encouraged by intellectuals. This was so in pre-revolutionary Russia and is so in Asia and Africa today. It is equally true in Latin America although in most Latin American countries capitalism is more highly developed, the middle class stronger, and the proletariat better organized than in nineteenth-century Russia, or the Asian, and particularly the African, countries of today.

The social character and attitudes of the revolutionary intelligentsia are similar in all underdeveloped countries. But it seems worthwhile to point out some of the special characteristics of this group in South America.

What distinguishes the intellectuals of this subcontinent from those of other countries and periods above all is that they are numerically more important. Statistics comparing the numbers of university students in different countries need careful interpretation, but they are of some illustrative interest. If we confine ourselves to university students and exclude further training establishments, such as teachers' training colleges, we find that in India for every 1,000 inhabitants there are about 2·0, in Ceylon 0·8, in Pakistan 1·2, in Tunisia 0·5, in Syria and in Burma 0·5 students.[1] But in Latin America the average figure is 2·6 students for every thousand inhabitants, and in four countries—Argentina, Uruguay, Cuba and Mexico—there are over 3·8 students for every thousand inhabitants. These figures resemble those for some highly developed countries. In Latin America the young represent a larger percentage of the total population than in Europe or the United States, but the number of students is remarkably high, particularly because many children do not go to school at all. Moreover, the student population of the universities is growing more than twice as fast as the population. In 1951 the National University of Mexico built a new university town for 45,000 students—in 1960 there were already 58,000. In 1957 Buenos Aires had fewer than 60,000 students, in 1961 there were more than 70,000. In 1944 the San Marco University in Lima had 4,000 students,

---

[1] The figures are taken from the UN *Statistical Yearbook*, 1959.

four years later there were 8,000, and in 1960 as many as 13,000.[1] Whereas Russia in the nineteenth century suffered from underproduction of intellectuals, Latin America suffers from overproduction, and this is an important factor in the radicalization of the intelligentsia.

Hugh Seton-Watson has stressed[2] that in pre-revolutionary Russia the intelligentsia were isolated, from the masses, from the state and from the bourgeoisie. In many underdeveloped countries today there is a gulf between the small minority of 'modern' intellectuals and the majority of the people. In Latin America this gulf is beginning to disappear even in those countries in which the Indian sector of the population lives in archaic social formations, whereas in others it does not exist at all. The intellectuals are much less isolated from the masses. Nor are they isolated from the bourgeoisie: a few students belong to the upper classes, but most of them come from the middle and lower-middle classes and remain closely connected with these classes. Finally, intellectuals easily get into the civil service and often influence government policy.

In many underdeveloped countries the younger army officers play the rôle of an 'intelligentsia-in-uniform'. This phenomenon existed, and exists, also in Latin America—for example, in Brazil in the nineteen twenties and at the beginning of the 'thirties, and in Bolivia and Venezuela in the 'thirties and 'forties. But the importance of this class is small, even though radical ideas often penetrate into the armed forces. The prestige of the academic is greater than that of the soldier; the revolutionary movements are anti-militarist and the spread of revolutionary ideologies among the officers' corps is strictly limited.

In nineteenth-century Russia and in Asian countries with ancient traditions the conflict of Western ideas with indigenous cultural values reflected itself in the ideology of the intellectuals. Analogies exist in Latin America, but they are relatively unimportant.

Historically, Latin American societies are young, they are predominantly European and the Indian element in them is of little or no ideological importance. Even those movements which stress the Indian characteristics of the subcontinent and speak of Indo-America, like the APRA,[3] have programmes which derive mainly from European ideologies. The Indian land commune in Mexico, the *ejido*, can be regarded as a positive achievement, but nowhere did it ever play the same ideological rôle as, for example, the Russian *mir*.

[1] Luis Alberto Sanchez, 'La Universidad en Latinoamerica', *Cuadernos*, Paris, No. 53, October, 1961.
[2] *Neither War nor Peace*, London and New York, 1960, pp. 170-1—My comments in this section are made partly with regard to the chapter 'The Intelligentsia' in Seton-Watson's book.
[3] A good account is found in H. Kantor's *The Ideology of the Peruvian Aprista Movement*, Berkeley, California, 1953.

The spiritual conflict in Latin America does not arise from the contrasts between Western and non-Western values but from the differences between North American and traditional Iberian values. Even quite non-revolutionary, elderly and often wealthy members of the educated classes regard themselves as the guardians of European culture against *Yanqui* utilitarianism and materialism. But the Iberian way of life is saturated with pre-capitalist elements. The *hidalgo* tradition with its emphasis on honour, its individualism and its contempt for manual work is combined with a high regard for human diversity and a dislike of empirical rationalism.

Latin American writers claim that in contrast to Europe's scientific orientation and North America's technical utilitarianism the character of South America's culture is essentially aesthetic,[1] and that poets are best able to understand it.[2] Rhetoric is valued highly; words are often used not to express ideas but to hide their absence, and more importance is placed on elegance than clarity.

This intellectual atmosphere gives rise to curious conflicts. On the one hand the young intellectuals are influenced by antiquated values and use them in the ideological battle against the *Yanquis*; but on the other hand they sense that these values are 'reactionary' and represent obstacles to quick modernization. This results in ambivalence, bad conscience, increased resentment and a tendency towards nihilism which helps the import of foreign or revolutionary ideas.

The revolutionary intellectuals are university students and secondary school pupils. Their influence on politics is so great that in Latin America one can speak of a 'paidocracy'. The universities are not primarily places for education but centres of national reform movements, bastions of radicalism, temples where the goddess 'Revolution' is worshipped. The universities are poor. In the United States a college education costs about $1,000 a student, a year. Everywhere in Latin America the figure is below $300; in Mexico it is $200, in Peru and Buenos Aires $170. Whereas the US student pays about half the cost of his education himself, the South American students are so poor that they can hardly pay 20 per cent.[3] University teachers are underpaid and most of them have other jobs. Lecture rooms would be overcrowded if students in fact attended lectures. According to Argentinian university statistics for 1957 only 30 per cent of all registered students in Buenos Aires university went at all regularly to lectures and seminars. As many as 64 per cent were unable to concentrate on their studies, because, like their teachers, they had other jobs.[4]

[1] Gil Tovar, *Visión breve de Ibero América*, Bogotá, 1956, p. 63.
[2] J. Ycaza Tigerino, *Hacia una Sociología Hispanoamericana*, Madrid, 1958, Prologue.
[3] Luis Alberto Sanchez, in *Cuadernos, op. cit.*
[4] W. Benton, 'The Voice of Latin America', in *Britannica Book of the Year*, 1961.

THE INTELLECTUALS

Academic training also suffers from the fact that students usually have an important influence on the methods of teaching and examination and that their representatives often have a place and voice in the university administrations. Examinations must not be too strict because the professors would otherwise be liable to threats and strikes. In an agricultural country like Argentina schools are crowded while only 2·1 per cent of all students study agronomy or veterinary medicine.[1]

Graduates have few opportunities for exercising their professions, not only because the Latin American economies are developing slowly but also because they could not in any case absorb tens of thousands of lawyers, doctors and journalists. The overproduction of intellectuals explains both their desire for government jobs and their rebellious attitude, which is the result of frustration.

These angry young men are radical nationalists. A sense of Latin American solidarity shows itself mainly in their hostility to the common imperialist enemy, the United States. If they cannot always be proud of their countries in their present state, they want to become proud of them and are inclined to put all the blame for existing grievances on foreign forces. In the name of national unity they protest against the fragmentation of their nations, in the name of social justice they fight against oppression and poverty, in the name of culture they attack illiteracy, and in the name of national sovereignty they battle against imperialism. In addition some of them are motivated by a more or less conscious desire to become influential themselves so that they might change their societies quickly and radically.

What Seton-Watson wrote, applies also to them: 'It is the intelligentsia that clamors most loudly for short-cuts to Utopia, to complete social justice ... The poverty and squalor of the labourer in the field and factory is more keenly resented by the intelligentsia than by the labourer himself ... It is seldom that (the intellectuals) have any appreciation of the relevance of law to social progress. Observance of the law involves delay ... It is equally seldom that they understand what is meant by free institutions. The word 'democracy' has their enthusiastic approval, but this normally means the triumph of the people, which by definition is the triumph of themselves'.[2]

With the help of the intellectuals, and not least as a result of their propaganda, the rootless urban masses and the starving rural

---

[1] In 1957/58 about 40 per cent of all students at Western and Central European universities studied scientific and technical subjects. The same was true of the Soviet Union. In Spain the corresponding figure was about 17 per cent while the average for the eleven Latin American states which provided information was 12·5 per cent. Therefore only one out of every eight graduates from South American universities is an engineer, scientist or agronomist. (The figures are taken from UNESCO, *Basic Facts and Figures*, 1960–61, Paris.)

[2] H. Seton-Watson, *op. cit.*, pp. 182–3.

populations are becoming aware both of their misery and of the fact that it can be remedied. These people are much less concerned with democracy—their experience of which has not been very satisfactory—or with personal freedom, which often means in practice freedom to starve, than with a quick and fundamental improvement of their material position. This is the moment when radical reform movements develop revolutionary tendencies; if expectations outstrip opportunities, if people want to run but democratic methods only permit them to crawl, then they will be tempted to look for a short cut by the totalitarian road.

9. Latin American Revolutions Before Castro

Castro's victory in Cuba began the most radical revolution in the history of the American continent. It took place against the historical background of past Latin American political and social crises, five of which are of special importance: the two victorious social revolutions in Mexico and Bolivia, the successful political revolution in Venezuela, the unfinished social revolution in Guatemala, which was interrupted by outside intervention, and Argentina's years of political and ideological crisis, associated with the name of Perón.

Five short, greatly simplified historical sketches of these phenomena follow.

(a) From Zapata to the 'Thermidor'

'The Mexican revolution can perhaps best be characterised as an emerging nationalism. It was directed toward identifying the people of Mexico with the Mexican nation and toward giving unity to a people who had, from time immemorial been divided by language, race, culture, and class. In that sense it aimed at giving the coherence to what had always been a conglomerate, even a contradictory pattern.'
(Frank Tannenbaum, *Mexico*)

'We can look at Mexico today and thank the Lord its revolution occurred and matured before Sino-Soviet imperialism had become militant and powerful.'
(L.D. Mallory, in *U.S. Department of State Bulletin*)

The Mexican Revolution was the first and most famous of the revolutions of modern Latin America. It was also the most contradictory and the longest. Its two great names were Emiliano Zapata at the beginning and Lazaro Cárdenas at the end. The fact that its most lasting effects can perhaps be summed up in the words of Frank Tannenbaum quoted above, and that it seems merely to have created the pre-conditions for a capitalist 'take-off', is due to a large extent to that circumstance for which the State Department spokesman quoted above thanks his maker.

The Revolution arose out of the conditions prevailing at the end of the thirty-five-years long dictatorship of Porfirio Díaz, who used to get himself constantly and fraudulently re-elected to the presidency. Superficially, this period was one of stability—before his time, from independence onwards, Mexico had been characterized by constant turmoil and government changed, on the average, once a year. Díaz's dictatorship was also a period of economic progress. Mexico City was rebuilt into a modern capital, the state of the finances was highly satisfactory, foreign capital poured into the country, and industrialization was encouraged. At the same time, however, the whole economy came under foreign domination and the trend towards concentration of land in huge *haciendas* was accentuated. The situation became worse than it had ever been in colonial times 'because the conquerors were in part compelled to respect the land of the Indians, while under the Diaz régime these were completely at the mercy of their new masters, not even having the protection of the Spanish colonial legislation'.[1] The mass of the Indians had indeed become landless serfs on the newly formed, huge, often foreign-owned *latifundia*; so that the new capitalist industrialization was based on a 'feudal' structure of agriculture.

The birth-pangs of growing, foreign-directed industrialization with the concomitant appearance of a miserable proletariat, was thus complicated by agrarian unrest arising out of the feudal state of the countryside, the dictatorial straightjacket of political institutions, and the struggles of mighty political bosses for power inside the Díaz establishment. When the revolution began, in 1910, it started under a rich liberal bourgeois, Francisco Madero, who defeated Díaz under the banner of '*Sufragio efectivo!—no reeleccion*' ('Effective suffrage, no re-election'), a slogan Díaz himself had used a generation earlier to acquire power. Madero was victorious because of the forces of revolutionary agrarianism, anti-imperialist nationalism, and anti-capitalist socialism which he unleashed, and because of the *caudillo*-personalism of power-hungry political bosses. The struggle between these contradictory and confused forces characterized the Mexican revolution[2] led to the downfall and murder of Madero himself, and to a time of troubles reminding one of a Shakespearian tragedy, with corpses of the protagonists filling the scene: Madero, Zapata, Carranza, Villa, Obregón ... to mention only some of the most important victims. The Indian leader Emiliano Zapata, disappointed with Madero, rose against him, proclaiming in his *Plan de Ayala* an agrarian revolution, demanding the restitution of the stolen land to the villages. After Madero had been deposed (and killed) and replaced (with the active help of the United States ambassador, who was disavowed by his own government) by the counter-revolutionary General Huerta, what appeared

[1] F. Tannenbaum, *The Mexican Agrarian Revolution*, The Brookings Institution, Washington, 1929, p. 13.

[2] 'If from the beginning the Mexican revolution had possessed a concrete plan it would have been of greater importance than the Russian ... it would have become the guide for the liberation of many millions of people. But at the beginning was action and only then came ideology. At first, the rejection of the re-election of political dignitaries, the protest against the lack of freedom, against the extreme subservience to imperialist capital, against the oppression of the Indians, against Porfirist centralism. Only after years of incessant bloodshed there developed the core of a coherent constructive doctrine.' (Luis Alberto Sanchez, *Historia General de América*, Santiago de Chile, 1944, Vol. II, p. 375.)

to be a united front of avengers rose against the new victor. It consisted of the opportunistic and power-hungry governor Venustiano Carranza, whose main asset proved to be his able military commander, Alvaro Obregón, a farmer turned general. Allied with them were workers and artisans influenced by anarcho-syndicalism, especially those of Mexico City, who had formed a central organization, *La Casa del Obrero Mundial*. They forced Carranza to make promises in favour of the workers, signed a pact with him and fought under Obregón in special 'Red Battalions'. Never on good terms with Carranza, and soon in active struggle against him, were Zapata and his ally, the 'Mexican Robin Hood', Pancho Villa. Huerta was driven from power, and Villa and Zapata were conquered by Obregón who, however, promised agrarian reforms. Carranza was the victor, only to be driven from power[1] and killed in his turn. He was succeeded, in 1920, by Obregón who ended the first chaotic period of the revolution.

In the meantime, a Constitutional Assembly had been summoned by Carranza to Querétaro, and it elaborated the Constitution drafted in February and proclaimed in May 1917. It was, and is, one of the most extraordinary documents of modern history; a mixture of radical liberalism, nationalism, democracy, socialism, and positivism, and it established the first 'welfare state' of the twentieth century.

In this utopian document—so at variance with Mexican realities— we find together both liberal and social revolutionary principles. On the one hand, the proclamation of legal security, the guarantee of private property, free elections, division of power, recognition of the freedoms of the press, of speech and of religion; on the other hand the subordination of private property to the requirements of social justice and national sovereignty. In it we find the principle of 'nationalization' of land side by side with that of the division of *latifundia*; the striving for rapid modernization together with welfare state provisions which would hinder such a process and which went far beyond any possible realization, while the political system arising on this fundament had, in turn, hardly any similarity with the proclaimed principles.

The fundamental articles were article 27, dealing with agrarian questions, and article 123, enshrining the imprescriptible rights of the workers. The first one was by no means clearly formulated. In its first paragraph we find the statement that all property of land 'rests originally with (*corresponde originariamente*) the nation', but the nation was entitled to give land into private ownership, which, however, was conceived as having a social function and as being subordinated to the national interest. There are attacks on the *lati-*

---

[1] 'One can say that he fell from power because of the absolute lack of any support by the workers and peasants of the Republic who considered him as their enemy.' (Rosendo Salazar, *Líderes y Sindicatos*, Mexico, 1953, p. 47.)

fundia, but not a definition or general prohibition of *haciendas*; there is an emphasis both on communal property and *ejidos* and on the creation of a peasantry consisting of independent farmers. Not surprisingly a lot of conflicting interpretations arose. Some, arguing that the Constitution had promised something like agrarian socialism, felt betrayed and began to preach a new revolution. Some had thought that the *latifundia* would disappear, although one of the interpreters of article 27 writes that the rules laid down in it do not by any means liquidate the *latifundia*.[1] The confusion was inevitable because apart from 'nationalism' out of which came the prohibition of foreign ownership of land and nationalization of the subsoil, there were three strands of reforming thought interwoven: the collectivistic, agrarian ideas which had in great part inspired Zapata, the wish for individual ownership and distribution of land among independent small farmers and, finally, the ideas of technicians which favoured a productive agriculture and wanted to modernize the *haciendas* instead of abolishing them, while at the same time giving small plots to peasants. 'The Revolution, early and late, has never fully reconciled these divergent points of view, swinging from one to another. Agrarian reform has thus been confused, uncertain, difficult to assess. At all times the three main strands have been the bases for action.'[2]

Article 123 has become the Magna Carta of the workers. It expresses ideas which, in 1917, had never been introduced into any modern constitution:

'The social and economic order created by economic liberalism subjected man to things ... transformed him into an object of the free play of economic forces ...

'The Mexican Constitutionalists revolutionized the doctrine of the natural rights. They blended the individual rights which guarantee the formal liberty of man with the social rights which guarantee him the material conditions without which formal liberty becomes a chimera.'[3]

The article establishes *de facto* an ideal welfare state: the right to form trade unions and the right to strike are laid down; child labour is prohibited, female labour restricted, minimum wages laid down, an eight-hour day established and a system of social insurance promised. Employers have to give workers annual paid holidays, provide them with decent housing and medical care, and share profits with them.

[1] V. Manzanilla Schaffer, *ibid.*, vol. II, p. 244.
[2] H. F. Cline, *Mexico: From Revolution to Evolution*, Oxford University Press, 1962, p. 210.
[3] E. Alvarez del Castillo, M. de la Madrid Hurtado, Raul Cordero Knocker, *La Legislación obrera en México—50 Años de Revolución*, Vol. III, p. 205.

With Obregón a period of stabilization began which ended with Cárdenas' rise to power in 1934. Obregón himself died a big landowner and successful monopolist. Calles, who came after him, made a considerable fortune out of casinos. Hordes of revolutionary profiteers grew up; *Mordidta* (*literally* 'a bite'), bribery and corruption became national institutions. Not very much land was distributed, and the newly founded *ejidos* with their peasants were subjected to the strict control of the new ruling class and its political apparatus. As the villages depended on financial and technical assistance given by the state and as any particular *ejidatario* could, if considered inefficient, be deprived of his plot, the peasant was in the power of the local or regional boss, who, defending himself from the President and making himself rich, forced the *ejidatarios* to vote always for the official candidate in the elections. The labour movement was strictly supervised and directed by trade union bosses who were set in their places by the government and became themselves senators, deputies and profiteers.[1]

At the same time, the Calles era was filled with a violent struggle against the Church, which erupted in horrible bloodshed and led to an anti-religious terror. The state party, which, since its foundation in 1928, has changed its name several times and is today aptly called *Partido Revolucionario Institucional*, had the monopoly of political power. Consisting originally of four, today of three, sectors—the worker's sector, the peasant sector, the military sector (which has disappeared) and the so-called 'popular' sector (for those who did not fit in the other three)—it was firmly in the hands of the President. The functioning of opposition parties was legally recognized and public political controversies took place, particularly before elections. But it was not possible for any opposition candidate to obtain any important political or administrative position, while in Congress the opposition party was conceded a small, previously determined number of seats, quite unrelated to the number of votes it might have obtained. A famous anecdote tells of a North American who bragged that in the USA technical progress was so far advanced that one knew the result of an election a few hours later. 'That is nothing,' replied a Mexican, 'we know the result long before the election takes place.'

This was Mexico's 'guided democracy' in which state capitalism arose side by side with a new private sector of business. The state indeed played a central, independent role. This was recognized in 1926 by Vicente Lombardo Toledano, who was to become the supreme boss of the trade unions under Cárdenas and afterwards the

[1] A very good history and analysis of the Mexican labour movement up to 1950 is given by Alfonso Lopez-Aparicio, *El Movimiento obrero en Mexico*, Mexico, 1952.

main representative of the 'Red Trade Union International' in the Western Hemisphere. He wrote,

'The Mexican state recognizes the division of society into oppressed and oppressors—but does not regard itself as belonging to either group. It considers it necessary to protect the proletariat and to improve its position, so that it can obtain as strong a position as Capital in the class war. The state wants to preserve its own freedom of action and its pre-eminence and does not want to join either of the fighting classes, in order to remain the mediator and judge of social life.'[1]

However, the mediator seemed to lean more and more towards the rich and the powerful. Then a change occurred: Calles had handpicked Lazaro Cárdenas as his successor, but Cárdenas, once elected (1934), turned against his former protector and proved to be a real revolutionary. He was also very much influenced by Marxist and even Leninist ideas and, after helping in the creation of a new Trade Union centre, which remained as much subject to him as the former one had been to Calles, he inaugurated a policy favouring the workers as against the capitalists. As he stated himself in a speech in 1936, 'The Labour Department must not be a ministry which maintains an equilibrium between Capital and Worker but an organism dedicated to the protection of workers'.[2]

Under Cárdenas the distribution of land among the peasants began in earnest. Between 1917 and 1932 the government had distributed, in all, an area of about 18 million acres. In the six years of the Cárdenas régime it distributed 45 millions. In 1934 there were 4,000 *ejidos*; their number grew to 20,000 in 1940.

As far as he could, Cárdenas cleaned up the civil service and subordinated the Army to civil government.

He nationalized the railways and also expropriated the most powerful of the foreign capitalist groups—the oil companies—when they refused to carry out the rulings of Mexican courts in favour of their employees. All protests against this act (described in the USA as 'communist') and all subsequent boycott measures against the newly established Mexican nationalized oil company, 'Pemex', remained unsuccessful. Roosevelt's popularity in Latin America was enhanced by the fact that he refused to intervene in the companies' favour, accepted their expropriation and insisted only on the payment of a compensation which turned out to be very much inferior to that for which the companies had asked: 24 instead of 450 million dollars, finally paid in 1942. Touching scenes took

[1] V. Lombardo Toledano, *La libertad sindical en México*, Mexico, 1926, pp. 84–5.
[2] Quoted in A. Lopez-Aparicio, *loc. cit.*, p. 216.

place: workers and poor Indians from the countryside sent their small savings to the President and even the clergy allowed collections to be made in the churches so that the expropriated owners could be compensated.

Cárdenas had a very personal style of governing.

'He tried to do it all himself. Each little detail, no matter how small, came to him and was handled through him. People flocked around him by the thousands wherever he went, each with a petition in hand, a demand, a need. Something that they could get in no other way they would now receive from the hands of the President. Cárdenas would spend hours and days visiting, listening, and then, in the night, classifying the innumerable papers he had collected, writing on each one of them what was to be done, and forwarding them to the cabinet-ministers, many of whom he dragged along much against their will in his constant travels over the country. In fact, he played the rôle of a great father to the people, a rôle that taxed his energy and time, but gave him the loyalty and support of the common people.'[1]

As suddenly and peacefully as the revolution had reached this climax in 1934, it entered, in 1940, a period which seemed to be the Mexican Thermidor. It was symptomatic that, in 1940, the newly elected President, Avila Camacho, declared, '*soy creyente*' (I am a religious believer). The revolution slowed down and, not only in the religious sphere. 'Mexico is turning to the right' was the general impression and a recent American author, looking back, writes,

'Decision-making in Mexico has been dominated by the urban middle sectors since the early 1940s. The members of the present leadership were able to assert themselves only after the socio-economic elements they represented had waged a prolonged and tenacious holding action against the forces of radical agrarianism born out of the revolution.'[2]

The new trend became conspicuous under the Presidency of Miguel Alemán (1946-1952), the first civilian since Madero to hold power. Land distribution slowed down and new *latifundia*, frequently modern and efficient enterprises, arose: foreign capital streamed in. Native capitalists were encouraged, the private sector began to grow, industrialization went forward under the sign of capitalism albeit inside the framework of a 'mixed economy'. The workers were tamed, and the courts no longer decided almost exclusively in their

[1] F. Tannenbaum, *Mexico, op. cit.*, p. 75.
[2] John J. Johnson, *Political Change in Latin America*, Stanford University Press, 1958, p. 128.

favour. A new class of entrepreneurs arose which included the 'bureaucratic bourgeois', the profiteers of the revolution.

The result was partially inevitable: the agrarian reform with its *ejidos* may have been socially progressive, but it also lowered productivity without satisfying land-hunger.[1] Besides, the technicians of the United Nations were sure that no amount of land distribution would satisfy the land hunger of a continuously growing population.[2] Mexican economists have estimated that the yields of private farms are 30 per cent higher than those on the *ejidos*.[3] The nationalized firms ran into huge difficulties; particularly Pemex, and Mexican petroleum production went sharply down. It therefore seemed rational to give more emphasis to the private sector everywhere.

The new economic policy was accompanied, till 1958, by a spectacular growth of the GNP. It seemed that all that had happened before had just been a prelude to capitalism. In 1954 a Mexican economist wrote:

'The agrarian revolution and the industrial revolution are not two opposed facts, but rather, two aspects of a single phenomenon. The agrarian revolution had the objective of destroying the feudal and slave system under which the country was living in order to establish capitalism. The objective of the industrial revolution is to establish the capitalist regime throughout the length and breadth of the country.'[4]

These developments brought with them new contradictions and also new sufferings for the masses. The industrialization was not considerable enough to absorb the population growth; a majority of all Mexicans lived, in 1957, hardly better than they had before 1934. The income inequalities were growing and, it was calculated that in 1957 46 per cent of all families with an average of less than 500 pesos (about $40) a month shared 14 per cent of the total national income, while 37 per cent of it went to the upper 5 per cent of the people.[5] As inflation set in the real wages of the majority of workers and employees began to sink.

According to Oscar Lewis, the Mexico of 1959 was still exhibiting many characteristics of an agrarian, colonial and underdeveloped country, with predominant foreign investment, lagging moderniza-

[1] In 1946 there were 1·6 million people who were recognized as *ejidatarios* and therefore had the right to a plot inside an *ejido*. But of these, 378,000 did not have any plot of their own, and a further 460,000 had plots but were unable to cultivate them because they lacked the necessary means.
[2] Naciones Unidas, *La Reforma Agraria*, New York, 1951, p. 66 ff.
[3] *Hispanic American Report*, Stamford University, January 1957.
[4] Manuel German Parra, quoted by Oscar Lewis, 'Mexico since Cardenas', in *Social Change in Latin America Today*, published by the Council on Foreign Relations, New York, 1960, p. 285, footnote.
[5] J. M. de Navarrete, *La distribución del ingreso y del desarrollo económico de México*, Mexico, 1960, p. 88.

tion of the transport system, and dependence upon the export of raw material. He adds:

'Even more serious, in terms of potential political consequences, is the failure to realize fully many of the social objectives of the Mexican Revolution. In 1960, over 60 per cent of the population are still ill fed, ill clothed, and ill housed, over 40 per cent are illiterate, and some 45 per cent of the nation's children are not schooled. The national wealth has greatly increased since 1940, but the disparity between rich and poor is even more striking than before.'[1]

This failure to reach the promised land is certainly not to be wondered at. Mexico could hardly be expected to achieve in half a century what it took progressive countries of Western Europe 150 years to achieve, since Mexico was in a much more difficult position to start with. Still, the disillusionment is there, as are the comparisons with the utopia promised in 1917, and the reinforced 'demonstration effect' transmitted from the big neighbour in the North. The official ideology remains revolutionary; anti-imperialism and anti-capitalism are still strong potential forces acting on a social volcano.

(b) *Guatemala: John Foster Dulles' Fall from Grace*

Guatemala, the 'Land of Eternal Spring', former home of the highly developed Maya culture, lies at the southern end of Mexico, two hours flight from the Panamá Canal. Today it is inhabited by 3·5 million people, two-thirds of whom are Indians. Until 1944, it was ruled exclusively by more or less 'progressive', more or less blood-thirsty dictators, in the interests of the landowning oligarchy and of foreign capitalists.

Guatemala's main problems were summed up in the following comments by a group of North American experts:[2]

'It must be apparent to the most casual observer that Guatemala possesses natural advantages which, if properly utilized should make it possible for the republic to achieve a relatively favourable position ... both in living standards and in financial stability. Yet actual economic development down to the middle of this century barely scratched the surface of these latent possibilities ... In the long view, however, the basic poverty of the Indian highland agriculture permanently hampers both agricultural progress and the whole economic growth of Guatemala, for the Indian population com-

[1] Oscar Lewis, *op. cit.*, p. 343.
[2] International Bank of Reconstruction and Development, *The Economic Development of Guatemala*, Washington, 1951, pp. 3 and 8.

prises the bulk of the potential internal market without which industry cannot develop.'

The Indians did not really constitute a 'nation within the nation', but an assortment of separate community groups who regard all governments with suspicion and hostility. If one could speak of a Guatemalan nation, the term could only refer to the minority of the *ladinos* (whites). The country was ruled by and in the interest of a small group of landowners who were often in league with the army officers and supported by foreign corporations and the Catholic Church. The small but growing class of businessmen, members of the liberal professions and employees had little influence.

The country lived by the export of coffee, (70 to 75 per cent of total exports), and bananas (15 per cent). Coffee production was largely in the hands of local landowners, 2·2 per cent of whom owned over 70 per cent of the area under cultivation, which was worked by Indians while the owners lived in the towns. The 'free' Indian peasants on the other hand produced, on tiny, primitively cultivated, infertile mountain plots, what they required to cover the bare necessities of life. In addition they were drawn upon for unpaid 'public works' and forced by the vagrancy law of 1933 to work at least 150 days a year, for payment in kind, or for a ridiculously low wage, on the estates of big landowners.

The bananas came from the vast plantations of the United Fruit Company, which possessed the best harbour, monopolized the shipping of exports from Guatemala and controlled the only railway in the country. Another American company had a monopoly of the electricity supply.

Various dictators gave these companies a variety of privileges: they paid almost no taxes, were 'masters' on their own plantations and in their own works, fixed railway and electricity tariffs at high levels, and with the help of the government, prevented the establishment of independent trade unions. Their profits were correspondingly high, and went into the pockets of shareholders who were usually North Americans. The economic domination of foreign companies, their privileges and profits, and their alliance with the local oligarchy and successive dictators were bound to produce strong anti-imperialist feelings among those small sections of the urban population which were becoming politically conscious. The positive contribution of foreign capital to the development of the country, of course was overlooked. Few people bothered to ask themselves whether the country would have been developed without the 'imperialists'. No account was taken of the fact that foreign employers paid twice or three times as much as local capitalists. Nor was any attention paid to the fact that the workers of the United Fruit Company had better working conditions, better houses, and schools for their children and that the only hospitals in the country were built and maintained by foreign firms.

In 1944 there was a revolutionary protest movement against the dictator, Ubico, who had been in power since 1931. It was an urban middle class movement led by students and joined by members of the liberal professions and businessmen. A memorandum, signed by 211 prominent citizens, demanded the introduction of democratic reforms. A strike broke out and there were clashes with the army and the police. The army began to split. On July 1, 1944, Ubico resigned and an officers' junta took over control. In an atmosphere of uncertainty a number of political organizations tried to put the presidency into the hands of a democratic professor, Juan Arévalo, who had emigrated and was teaching at the university in Argentina. Arévalo returned home and was fêted as the future head of state. But the military was opposed to this plan. One of the generals wanted the presidency for himself, in the name of the traditional Liberal Party, whose liberalism was confined to its name. In September of the same year a state of emergency was declared and a wave of terror swept the country. But the people, particularly the urban middle classes joined by such workers as there were, protested with increasing vehemence. They were assisted by discord among the officers. Major Francisco Araña and Captain Jacobo Arbenz established contact with the democratic leaders and students. A *coup d'état* was prepared and successfully executed on October 20, 1944. Tanks advanced against the would-be dictator, who fled. This October Revolution was the start of a new stage in the history of Guatemala. A provisional junta consisting of Araña, Arbenz and the trade unionist, Jorge Toriello, took over control and prepared elections. In an atmosphere of freedom and confusion five candidates fought for the votes of those citizens who had the franchise, which was restricted to the literate 20 to 25 per cent of the population, Juan Arévalo was elected President of the Republic for six years. He described himself as a 'spiritual socialist' and sometimes also as a 'humanist'. It is not easy to say what exactly he meant by this. 'We are not materialist socialists. We do not believe that man is primarily stomach . . . man is above all a will for dignity . . . Our socialism does not . . . aim at an ingenuous distribution of material goods, or the stupid economic equalization of men who are economically different. Our socialism aims at liberating men psychologically, granting to all the psychological and spiritual integrity denied by conservatism and liberalism.'[1]

On the whole his period of government can be described as democratic. He wanted to make the Indians into full citizens, to promote popular education, to introduce new social legislation for the workers,

[1] Quoted by Ronald M. Schneider, *Communism in Guatemala, 1944–1954*, New York, 1959, p. 17.

to free the country from foreign domination and to guarantee freedom of speech and association. He dreamt of social democracy, of a modern welfare state in his primitive country.

A new democratic and 'social' constitution was adopted. Parties became legal, trade unions were recognized and became powerful, protected by socialist labour legislation which in 1947 found expression in the *Codigo de Trabajo* and in 1948 in social insurance legislation.

The conduct of education was improved and teachers' salaries, which had been extremely low, were raised. 'Before 1944 a teacher earned less than a general's horse. Then an end was put to generals and their horses—but some teachers received generals' salaries.'[1]

New schools were set up, the universities became autonomous and a state institute for the development of production—the first swallow of state capitalism—was created. That was all—but it was something.

'To overthrow a tyrant is only the prelude. The new political freedom creates problems which have their origins in the sad heritage of the Spanish colonial system.'[2]

In parliament the government relied on a loose coalition of the new revolutionary parties which lacked unity and whose leaders sought after government positions.

'In the course of ten years it was impossible to produce a healthy social climate ... the parties could not agree, they were full of internal conflicts, opportunism, demagogy and personal rivalries. To make a career in politics became the basic aim of many of their leaders.'[3]

The old oligarchies felt threatened; the foreign companies were suspicious and the majority of the urban upper classes looked anxiously at the mixture of freedom and pro-labour laws. New conflicts broke out in the army and the press became hostile.

In the course of six years Arévalo had to survive no less than thirty plots. The first dangerous crisis started in 1949. The chief of staff of the army, Araña, a former member of the triumvirate, who had all along put a conservative brake on Arévalo's policy, seemed to be preparing a *coup d'état* and was assassinated. Nobody ever found out who was responsible, but many signs pointed to Captain Arbenz, Arévalo's Minister of Defence, who was in close touch with left-wing radical groups.

A year later the middle classes began to move abainst Arévalo. The original unified front started to break up according to classes. With the help of the army and the organized workers, Arévalo survived again, but for the first time he was forced to declare a state of emergency.

[1] Guillermo Toriello, *La Batalla de Guatemala*, Mexico, 1954, p. 34.
[2] William Krehm, *Democracia y tiranias en el Caribe*, Mexico, 1949, p. 105.
[3] Luis Cardoza y Aragón, *La Revolución Guatemalteca*, Mexico, 1955, pp. 56–7.

At the election in November 1950—at which illiterate persons were allowed to participate by casting an open vote—Captain Jacobo Arbenz was elected as the new president. With Arévalo's help an energetic campaign was conducted for him in the whole country by the revolutionary coalition parties and the newly created peasant organizations. In the fight against the other three candidates he received about three-quarters of all votes; only in the city of Guatemala did his conservative opponent receive more votes.

Captain Arbenz was strongly influenced by Marxist ideas and surrounded by leading Guatemalan Communists. The official leader of the Communist Party, which later called itself *Partido Guatemalteco de Trabajo*, Manuel Fortuny, was one of his closest friends. Arbenz' government took a radical line, but its programme and actions did not go beyond progressive bourgeois ideas. Arbenz nationalized some harbour installations, built a road to the Atlantic to break the transport monopoly of the railways, began the construction of a harbour in Santo Tomás to compete with the harbours of the United Fruit Company and planned a water works to put an end to the monopoly of the North American electricity company. But his main act was the proclamation of a land reform law in June 1952. The most important points of this law were:[1]

Article 1: 'The agrarian reform of the October revolution has the aim of destroying feudal land ownership and its conditions of production and of developing capitalist methods in agriculture.'
Article 2: 'All forms of serfdom and slavery and with them unpaid personal peasant services ... shall be abolished ...'
Article 3: 'The land reform shall achieve the following essential aims:

(a) A capitalist peasant economy shall be established and capitalism shall be promoted in agriculture generally;

(b) Peasants, tenant farmers and farm workers who have no land or only a little land, shall be given land;

(c) New capital investments in agriculture shall be made available by letting nationalized land to capitalist tenants;

(d) New forms of cultivation shall be introduced and less well-off peasants shall be provided with cattle, fertiliser, seeds and technical assistance;

(e) More agricultural credits shall be made available to all peasants.'

Farms of under 225 acres were not broken up or confiscated; estates of 225 to 675 acres which were farmed by their owners or under their instructions and in which at least two-thirds of the land was cultivated were also exempt from confiscation. Uncultivated *latifundia* on the other hand, were confiscated and compensation

[1] Luis Cardoza y Aragón, *op. cit.*, pp. 85–6.

was paid according to their listed value, in long-term, low-interest bonds. In addition state-owned land was also distributed. A special office, the *Departemento Agrario Nacional* (DAN) was entrusted with the execution of the land reform. Two years later the government had distributed two and a half million acres to about 10,000 peasants and farm labourers.[1]

It need hardly be said that the landowners raised strong protests. More serious was a ruling of the supreme Court that the land reform was contrary to the constitution. At Arbenz' instigation parliament dismissed the judges by forty-one votes to nine with six abstentions, although under the constitution a judge could be removed only if shown to be guilty of a criminal offence, flagrantly immoral or grossly incompetent.

The main sufferer as a result of land reform was of course the United Fruit Company. Thousands of acres of its land were not under cultivation. There were economic reasons for this: banana cultivation impoverishes the soil, which must accordingly be left fallow for longer or shorter periods, depending on its quality. There are also banana diseases which make it necessary to vary the sown area. A large reserve of land is therefore required. This reserve was regarded as unused land and was therefore subject to confiscation.

The United Fruit Company was furious about the confiscations, both accomplished and threatened, and about the inadequacy of the promised compensation. As it was pointless to appeal to the purged courts the Company turned to the State Department. On March 23, 1953, the USA addressed a note to the Guatemalan government firmly demanding speedy and adequate payment of compensation to the victims of confiscations. Two months later the Arbenz government rejected the demand as an attempt to intervene in the internal affairs of the country and an attack on Guatemalan sovereignty. A second, more strongly worded, American note remained unanswered. At the same time many Guatemalan newspapers and the radio embarked on an increasingly violent anti-imperialist campaign. In the USA more and more was being written about the threat of Communism in Central America while Guatemala represented the anti-communist campaign as a cover for an impending attack by *Yanqui* imperialism.

Communist influence in Guatemala was undoubtedly increasing. The Communists had been helped by the government's incompetence, by internal tensions, a certain amount of corruption, an absence of ideological clarity, and not least by the organizational weaknesses of the other revolutionary parties. Members of the Communist party occupied the most important positions, controlled the trade unions, dominated the peasant organizations and were strong in the growing bureaucracy. Communists were in control of

[1] Guillermo Toriello, *op. cit.*, p. 45.

the department of agriculture, ran the most important newspapers and were in close touch with the President for whom they organized mass demonstrations, and with whom they were always in agreement. Through Cruz Wer and J. Rozenberg, the Communists gained control of the Civil Guard, which came increasingly to resemble a secret police force. It is true that the official aims of the government never went beyond democracy and anti-imperialism; the agrarian law emphasized, one might almost say over-emphasized, the importance of capitalism. Was not the creation of an independent peasantry a bourgeois aim which ran counter to communism? Did not opposition parties exist in the country? Would it not have been contrary to democratic principles to remove the Communists from all government positions, particularly in view of their contribution to reform? Was it not obvious that all these accusations from the north were only being made to prevent an improvement in the living standards of the people and to advance the interest of greedy imperialist monopolists?

Guatemalan propaganda could be sure of a sympathetic audience in Latin America. It had a ring of truth—and there was indeed a measure of truth in it.

In isolated, backward countries the aim of the Communists cannot be to steer straight towards socialism; their first task is to bring democratic anti-imperialism to a head. In agriculture their fight against big landowners must start with the distribution of the land, not with collectivization.

A book on Latin America which appeared fairly recently in Moscow contained the following passage:

'The Communist parties do not press for nationalization of the land; they restrict themselves to the demand that land owned by big landowners must be confiscated and handed free as private property to the peasants. In this the Communists start from the assumption that the idea of private ownership of the land is so firmly fixed in the minds of the peasants that land reform is impossible if the confiscated land does not become the private property of the peasants ... The programmes of the Communist parties also lay down that the property of rich peasants must be protected by law. The Communist parties assume that in the *present* (my italics) stage of the struggle the rich peasants can be brought on to the side of the national front.'[1]

The leader of the Guatemalan Communist Party said that his party recognized that because of Guatemala's special development the country would first have to go through a capitalist period—

[1] *Problemy Sovremennoy Latinskoy Ameriki*, published by the Institute of World Economy and World Politics of the Academy of Sciences of the USSR, Moscow, 1959, pp. 345-6.

although it was historically no longer inevitable that this capitalist period would last a long time.

As far as the leading rôle of the Communists was concerned the Party naturally fought for it with all 'bolshevist' means at its disposal, but in certain situations it disguised the fact that it had acquired this leading rôle and even changed its name.[1]

By March 1954 the situation was increasingly tense and the Conference of American States was specially convened in Carácas to discuss the communist threat. Dulles succeeded in pushing through a resolution endorsed by a majority of 17 to 1, to the effect that Communism was incompatible with freedom and that its infiltration into the Western hemisphere was regarded as a threat to interAmerican security.

The basis for a possible American intervention had thus been established, but it would have to be carried out discreetly and indirectly. The voting on the American resolution was misleading. As one delegate said in a private conversation with the correspondent of the *New York Times*, 'if the United States wanted it badly enough it could have a resolution passed declaring that two and two make five'.[2] Earlier in the proceedings, the Guatemalan delegate's attack on *Yanqui* imperialism had been favourably received by some Latin American representatives. A strongly anti-Communist expert on Latin America wrote that Dulles on this occasion badly misunderstood the climate of opinion.

'He failed to realize, despite repeated warning, that the Republics of Central and South America were relatively unconcerned with communism and wanted a small-scale Marshall Plan, or at least some form of increased assistance ... The United States gained no prestige in Latin America from the conference. In addition much good will was lost. A Brazilian delegate claimed that the US had reached its lowest ebb in its rôle as leader of democracy in the hemisphere.'[3]

The Arbenz government had sought in vain to buy arms from the United States. Now it obtained what it needed from the East. On May 17, 1954, a ship from Stettin arrived in Guatemala with war materials. It was unloaded the same night under the personal supervision of the Minister of Defence. In Washington the news acted like a bombshell; two hours' flying time from the Panamá Canal, a revolutionary country was becoming a Russian stronghold. It was impossible to wait any longer. Arbenz saw the danger, tried to stop it and to save what could still be saved. His Foreign Minister,

[1] The Party theoretician of the Guatemalan Communists said later that the change of name had been decided in order to avoid the emotional and legal difficulties presented by the word 'Communist'. (J. D. Martz, *op. cit.*, p. 35.)
[2] *ibid.*, pp. 53 and 56.
[3] *ibid.*

Toriello, flew to Washington and tried to see Eisenhower. After many difficulties he succeeded. The report on his efforts read like a tragi-comedy.[1] The President of the United States appeared to know little about the situation in Guatemala; with 'devastating naïvety' he kept on repeating that Guatemala was a communist country. Toriello's account is reminiscent of Hindenburg's dismissal of Brüning after the latter had aroused the enmity of the Prussian Junker landowners by legislation against them. Brüning tried to explain the true situation to the *Reichspräsident*, but Hindenburg could only repeat: 'No, I have been told that you want to introduce Communism'.

The main parts in the last act were played by the energetic US Ambassador Peurifoy and the emigré Guatemalan Colonel Castillo Armas, who had already tried to organize one *putsch* and, in the course of 1954, assembled a small army in neighbouring Honduras for an invasion of Guatemala.

Castillo Armas and his band of 500 to 1,000 men were given money, arms and four aircraft and began to march in the middle of June. Meanwhile Peurifoy established contact with dissatisfied elements in the Guatemalan army. In Guatemala the Arbenz police began to make mass arrests of 'suspects'; the torturing of the victims aroused both fear and hatred against the government. Toriello tried to mobilize the United Nations and the Organization of American States. But the State Department succeeded in foiling this defensive maneouvre by delaying tactics.

Whereas Castillo Armas hardly made any progress, Peurifoy's scheme was a brilliant success. The Chief of the Army, Colonel Díaz, asked him for an audience and volunteered to throw out Arbenz, to suppress the Communists and to form a military junta; in return Peurifoy should help to arrange a cease-fire; the pro-consul agreed. Thereupon Díaz and two of his officers called on Arbenz and succeeded in making him resign. They promised that they would continue to fight against Castillo Armas and to defend the achievements of the revolution. Arbenz stood down and many of his collaborators fled abroad or went underground. When Peurifoy heard that many Communists had managed to escape, he 'withdrew his confidence from Díaz' and insisted that he should be replaced by Colonel Elfego Monzon. The latter flew to Honduras for discussions with Castillo Armas, and, when these did not go smoothly, Peurifoy himself went and managed to achieve a compromise.

At the beginning of July Castillo Armas entered Guatemala City and was warmly welcomed by the crowds. He promised justice, elections and the preservation of 'justified reforms'. When he was elected President, he began to undo the results of the revolution.

[1] G. Toriello, *op. cit.*, p. 80.

After the murder of Castillo in 1958 his successor, the former Ubico officer Ydígoras Fuentes continued his policies.

In June 1954, Dulles had promised greater financial aid to Guatemala. 'The United States undertakes ... to assist in improving ... Guatemala's material position ... which favours Communism.' Promised aid from the US was slow in coming. The expected flood of financial assistance was a bare trickle. The words of shining optimism from Secretary Dulles in June 1954, were not followed by actions.[1]

The Communists had obviously made mistakes. The masses did not rise—not even the workers. The army had not been purged or made to toe the line. The peasants remained passive. There was no peoples' militia.

'Thus when the Arbenz regime was attacked, although the forces or rebel chieftain Castillo Armas had been unable to advance more than 10 miles into the country, the Guatemalan army stepped in and ousted the revolutionary government, which had been in power almost ten years, with no more expenditure of energy than was necessary to march into the Presidential Palace and announce to Colonel Arbenz that he was no longer president.'[2]

The Communists no doubt drew their lessons from these experiences. Most Latin Americans on the other hand believed that Roosevelt's Good Neighbour Policy had come to an end, that the United States had once more embarked on its traditional policy of active imperialism. People are not motivated only by 'facts' but by their interpretation of these facts. The United States still suffers from the effects of the Guatemala incident.

(c) *Perón and his Justicialism*

'Argentina showed the world for the first time that a totalitarian government can be overthrown by a nation's love of freedom and its readiness to make sacrifices.'
(General Lonardi, speech of October 23, 1955)

On September 16, 1955, there occurred an event which all well-informed people, including such outstanding foreign observers as Herbert L. Matthews of *The New York Times*, had only a few weeks earlier considered impossible: Perón was overthrown by generals, in alliance with the Church, liberal democrats and democratic socialists. Yet Perón's régime was neither totalitarian nor—despite some similarities with Hitler and Mussolini—really 'fascist'. And the 'liberation' of which General Lonardi, one of the anti-*Peronista* leaders, spoke looked suspiciously like the beginning of a period of reaction.

From 1916 to 1930 Argentina had been ruled by the 'Radicals'

[1] J. D. Martz, *op. cit.*, pp. 65, 66.
[2] Norman A. Bailey in 'Latin America Since the War', in *Journal of International Affairs*, Columbia University, Vol. XIV, No. 2, 1960

who came to power after the introduction of universal franchise in 1912. They were a middle-class party with a rather confused programme of anti-feudalism, anti-clericalism and social democracy. They wanted to end the power of the landholding oligarchy of the *estancieros*, to further industrialization, and to introduce social legislation favouring the workers. Middle class people, workers and nationalistic intellectuals had given them their votes. But the Radicals failed miserably. This was not entirely their own fault: they could hardly have succeeded.

In spite of a spurt of industrialization during the First World War, Argentina had hardly any class of modern entrepreneurs. Its middle class consisted of small industrialists, merchants, artisans, shopkeepers and intellectuals. The real power lay with the *estancieros*, with British capitalism (which owned the railways, the meat packing houses, and the important banks, while Britain constituted the most important market for Argentina produce), and the '*comprador*-bourgeoisie' allied with both these forces.

Although it seems exaggerated to state that 'A modern industrial proletariat did appear in our country only after 1930',[1] agricultural and workers in small factories and shops predominated. The trade unions of Argentina were the oldest and numerically the strongest of Latin America—and the First World War gave their numbers a big boost: according to their own affirmations the number of the, then most important, trade union centre (the FORA of the ninth Congress) had grown from 20,000 in 1915 to 488,000 in 1919.[2] But if Latin American statistics are not particularly reliable, those of Latin American trade unions are even less so, beside these unions included many members who were not proletarians at all. In reality, the trade union movement had for two decades been plagued by doctrinal squabbles between anarchists, anarcho-syndicalists and socialists, and by numerous splits.

Very many of those who joined during the war and the immediate post-war period disappeared as rapidly as they had come in. During the 1920s, and even later, the trade unions contained but a rather small minority of proletarians, and were recruited in two vastly different camps: on the one hand among rather high paid and privileged groups like the railwaymen who were strongly unionized in two federations which tended towards 'reformism'; on the other hand, among workers of the construction industry and employees of small factories and shops, which lacked security and permanent work. Another characteristic of the trade unions was the numerical preponderance of the foreign born. In 1914, 30 per cent of all

[1] Jose Abelardo Ramos, *El Partido Comunista en la Política Argentina*, Buenos Aires, 1962, S. 20.
[2] Rubens Iscaro, *Origen y Desarrollo del Movimiento Sindical Argentina*, Buenos Aires, 1958, p. 98.

inhabitants of Argentina were foreign born, but in the trade unions this percentage rose to 59 per cent.[1] The majority of Argentine-born proletarians worked as agricultural workers or in the big meat packing houses; they were outside the trade unions as were the huge number of domestics and workers in small enterprises—and all the 'rootless' people who began to come to the cities from the countryside. They might occasionally participate in the violent strikes which fill Argentine social history, but they had neither 'class-consciousness' nor the capacity and will to organize themselves. They looked to a *caudillo*—as did much of the small middle classes. They found him in the Radical leader Irigoyen. Irigoyen, it is true, tried to introduce democracy—although of so 'personal' a sort that his followers inside the Radical party, which later split, called themselves *'personalistas'*—and introduced some social reforms in favour of the (urban) workers. But he was unable to break the power of the 'conservative' *estancieros* and British capitalists, nor to realize 'nationalism', to achieve the industrialization of the country, or to change the balance of power in favour of the 'left'. On the contrary, the big strikes that occurred in the immediate post-war period and the first appearance of a 'communist threat'[2] caused him to attack the workers' organizations and to reduce, very considerably, the power of trade unionism. When in the middle of the world crisis of 1929-30 the Radical régime was toppled by General Uriburu, the 'reformist' trade unions offered the new government their willing collaboration. But the future *'descamisados'*—that is to say, the unemployed, the underpaid, the unorganized workers—participated in 1933 in huge masses at the funeral ceremony of the same Irigoyen, whom they still considered as their 'father-figure'. In many senses, Perón would be his successor.

From 1930 to 1943 Argentina was again under the dominance of the Conservatives ruling in alliance with some minor parties—and maintaining themselves in power largely by means of rigged elections. From 1935 on, a new process of industrialization began. New middle classes appeared and the number of impoverished proletarians who had neither socialist nor trade unionist traditions increased. The Conservatives were losing their grip and voices in favour of democratization became stronger.

At the beginning of the Second World War, Argentina remained neutral. But the forces who wanted to enter the war on the Allied side steadily grew in strength. They were a mixed lot: landowners, bankers and exporters with close links to British and United States interests, politicians supporting democratic ideals, communists clamouring for an 'anti-fascist' crusade, and, above all, the Navy,

[1] Alberto Belloni, *Del Anarquismo al Peronismo*, Buenos Aires, 1960, p. 29.
[2] The Argentine Communist party is a founder-member of the Communist International.

with its traditional associations both with Britain and with the ruling oligarchy. Against these stood the majority of the Army, apparently with the support of the industrial bourgeoisie and the workers. Some generals were frankly pro-fascist, and favoured the Axis. Others were authoritarian, and simply disliked democracy. Among the colonels, the radical nationalist group in the GOU Lodge was of particular significance. Influenced by the ideas of the German geopolitical school of Haushofer, they wanted Argentina to become the leading power of Latin America, to destroy the predominance of British and United States interests and to industrialize the country, preferably in alliance with the bourgeois, but if necessary even with the workers.

In 1943 a military dictatorship was established, political parties were prohibited, freedom of the press was abolished, the trade unions were put under government control and the rebel students were severely dealt with. Many of these measures were supposed to be temporary, but there was no doubt about the authoritarian character of the new government. The generals fully realized that they could not always rely on bayonets; they found an ally in the Church. Since 1880, when it lost control over education, the Church had watched its influence dwindle. Now the new government announced that henceforth religious instruction would be compulsory in all state schools.

But one of the younger members of the government at any rate thought this alliance insufficient and realized the precariousness of an authoritarian régime without an ideology. He was Colonel Juan Domingo Perón, who had spent some years in Mussolini's Italy, and was influenced by Fascist ideas. His plan was to win over the workers and thus to form a holy (or unholy) trinity of power in which the proletariat would join the army and the Church as a third force.

He managed to have himself appointed chief of the newly created Secretariat for Labour and Social Welfare, and from this key position he began to carry out his plans.

Until then the trade unions had derived their main support from skilled workers; in the 'forties they had just over 300,000 members. In many urban and provincial factories the owners had enforced their 'master-in-their-own-house' attitude with such success that whole industries had no trade unions and in the countryside the mere thought of such organizations was out of the question. The wages of most workers were extremely low, there was hardly any social insurance and the right to strike was not recognized.

Perón set to work. He made friends with the workers' leaders and initiated new legislation which met with angry resistance from the employers. Social insurance was introduced, conditions of work were improved, wages were raised through government intervention, annual paid holidays became compulsory, and trade unions were established even in industries in which such an innovation was strongly opposed by the management. Government arbitration organs were created which enabled Perón to do away with independent trade unions. The 'official' unions grew rapidly; in 1939 they had included only 10 per cent of all workers, but by 1955, more than 75 per cent of the workers were organized, and the total number of union members was almost six million. All key positions were filled by 'friends' of Perón who was praised everywhere as the father and patron saint of the *descamisados* (the 'shirtless' workers became the *sansculottes* of the Perón revolution). Small wonder that many workers were prepared to exchange their 'democratic' freedoms, which were of no practical value to them, for the opportunity of economic improvements offered by Perón.

When in the Second World War the scales began to come down in favour of the Allies a growing number of Argentinian citizens, intellectuals as well as workers, started to turn against the military dictatorship, while many capitalists attacked Perón's reforms. As a result of these pressures, differences emerged in the army.

At the beginning of October 1945 several garrisons rose in rebellion. A provisional government, consisting of members of the army, was set up; it announced an amnesty, reintroduced freedom of the press and legalized all parties, including the Communists, but did not dismiss the President of the Republic, General Farrell. A chaotic situation ensued. While those parts of the army which had remained loyal to Farrell marched against the rebels, the democratic opposition announced that it would not work together with a military government. When it became known that Perón had been arrested by the rebels the workers began to prepare for battle. A wave of strikes began on October 15 and grew into a workers' march on Buenos Aires. The liberation of the 'Father of the Workers' became the war-cry of most classes, in spite of some hesitations on the part of many old workers' leaders. On October 17 the capital was taken over by the workers, and Perón appeared, enthusiastically received, at the side of President Farrell. The rebellion was over. One of the trade unionists calls this day the most important revolutionary deed in the history of the Argentinian proletariat.[1] The 'Patron of the Workers' stood as presidential candidate for the forthcoming elections. His programme? Social justice, national sovereignty, economic independence of the country; nationalization of the railways, telephone and electricity companies; abolition of trusts and monopolies; preservation and extension of his social legislation.

A paradoxical electoral battle ensued: on the one side there was the democratic Bonapartist, Perón, with his programme of nationalism, anti-capitalism and social reform. On the other there was the

[1] Belloni, *op. cit.*, p. 51.

'anti-Fascist', but inevitably also anti-socialist, bourgeois-led Democratic Union, which united such different groups as the Radicals, Socialists, Progressive Democrats, Communists and some conservative elements. Its candidate was the radical leader, Tamborini, for whom the American ambassador, Braden, worked behind the scenes, which enabled Perón to make full use of his anti-*Yanqui* propaganda. 'Perón or Braden' became a *Peronista* slogan.

The election was fixed for February. In November, in the middle of the electoral campaign, a government decree, prepared by the Secretariat for Work and Social Welfare, ordered all workers and employees to be paid a Christmas bonus of 25 per cent of their annual salary. The employers protested and some lock-outs of workers occurred. There was an appeal to the Supreme Court and at the beginning of February both the decree and the Secretariat for Work and Social Welfare were declared to be contrary to the Constitution. 'The judges are protecting the oligarchy'—soon afterwards they were rewarded with dismissal.

The election was held on February 24. It was conducted in such an orderly fashion that when the first results came in even the opposition leaders praised its 'cleanness'. They were convinced of their victory: how could the people in a free election vote for bondage?

Their shock was all the greater when Perón was victorious. He did not get a big majority: 1,480,000 against Tamborini's 1,220,000. But in Argentina, as in the USA, the President is elected by an electoral college, and there the majority was overwhelming: 304 for Perón and 72 for his opponent.

In the parliamentary elections the newly established *Peronista* Party received two-thirds of the seats in the lower house and all but two in the Senate. Perón could therefore have governed in a parliamentary and legal manner. That he did not do so; that his government became increasingly characterized by the *Führer* principle, was for ideological and political reasons. As Mussolini's pupil he had little love and even less respect for the parliamentary system. 'Democracy,' he wrote later, 'was used by the powerful class as a tool for the suppression of the poor. The whole system was based on the equality of individual rights; but if economic circumstances are unequal, equality before the law is an empty phrase.'

Moreover, parliamentary government would have been difficult. The *Peronista* Party soon began to disintegrate and lost something of its *descamisado* character. But the opposition was subjected to increasing pressure which quickly ceased to bother about constitutional limitations. The courts were purged and freedom of the press disappeared. Most public associations and organizations were made to toe the line, and such opposition parties as continued to exist were deprived of all opportunity for active propaganda. A secret police was established which arrested and tortured people. But incense rose from radio and press around the saviour of the fatherland, and particularly around his wife, Evita, who directed the propaganda, looked after popular welfare and filled the trade unions with her own followers. She was presented to the masses almost as 'Saint Evita', and in 1951 an attempt was even made to elect her as Vice-President of the Republic.

Fascism? Totalitarianism? Hardly. To begin with the ideology was different. Mussolini and Hitler never made such markedly socialist speeches and neither of them would have dreamt of calling one of his biggest party newspapers *Democracia*. But the essential difference was that the opposition parties were not dissolved and could take part in relatively free elections in which the Argentinian constitution, which had never been set aside, gave them a right to one-third of the seats in parliament. The fact that at Perón's re-election in 1951 the opposition parties received 25 per cent of the votes shows that they, particularly the Radicals, were not without influence. In addition there were of course also the Church and the Army which Perón was never able to purge completely and which later brought about his downfall.[1]

As long as Perón was able to combine his noisy anti-imperialism with rapid industrialization, extension of state capitalism, social welfare for urban[2] and rural workers, growing bureaucratization of state and economy and support of the Church, most people were satisfied. Many capitalists made big profits, the army was content, and even more so the workers, who had *panem et circenses*. The Church supported Perón's régime. The nationalists were able to boast about Argentina's leading rôle and the Communists, who at times openly supported Perón, could look upon him as a comrade-in-arms against *Yanqui* imperialism.[3] But the economic policies of the régime doomed it to instability.

The strain showed itself first in the agricultural sector, which was exploited by a state trading monopoly: the state bought wheat at a third of the price at which it resold it. At the end of the Perón régime, agriculture, the country's most important export industry, had sunk

[1] In passing it might be said that not only was there no persecution of Jews under Perón—there are many Jews in Argentina—but that in his book, published in 1956, Perón proudly mentions the fact that he had taken action against anti-semitism. (*La Fuerza es el Derecho de las Bestias*, Lima, 1956, p. 55.)

[2] The following words of the leading economist of the country show the extent to which industrial workers benefited under Perón, and at whose expense: 'While from 1945–1955 the *per capita* income of the population rose only by 3·5 per cent, that of industrial workers increased by 47 per cent. But this increase was not accompanied by an increase in productivity. It took place at the expense of the rural population and had serious consequences.' (Raúl Prebisch, *Informe preliminar acerca de la situación económica*, Buenos Aires, October 26, 1955.

[3] Later and in between times the Communists fought him as a Fascist. But it is curious that two large works on Latin America which appeared in Moscow in 1959 and 1960 make no mention of Perón: this is probably due to the fact that since Perón's fall, Peronistas and Communists have been making common cause.

so low that there was not only no money for imports, but there was even a meat shortage in Argentina.

Once the country had used up its accumulated capital, the system of subsidies, growing bureaucracy and irrational industrialization together produced increasingly serious inflation. In the years 1950–1952 the cost of living rose by 73 per cent and wages only by 35 per cent. At the end of April 1953 Perón himself admitted that during the two preceding weeks prices had increased by 50 per cent.

As its difficulties grew the régime became more demagogic and more dictatorial. Perón was forced to try to remove all opposition. One of his potential opponents was the Church, which since the end of 1950 had become increasingly hostile and had provoked the government by organizing a Christian Socialist movement. The régime became more markedly anti-clerical, introduced compulsory 'patriotic' lessons in schools and planned to legalize divorce and prostitution.

In the course of 1954 tension mounted. A change in economic policy seemed to be in the air: both Socialists and Nationalists were apprehensive. A draft law was prepared giving concessions to the American Standard Oil Company. Argentina's pro-American foreign policy went to such lengths that in March 1955 the US Secretary of the Navy, Charles Thomas, on the occasion of receiving a high Argentinian decoration, called Perón a pioneer of the Argentinian struggle for freedom against world communism!

Nationalist protests were heard accompanied by communist complaints, and at the same time Perón's struggle with the Church broke out. In October, Perón had warned the Church against interfering in political or trade union affairs. The Church protested against the government's increasingly Hitlerian methods. While the government published a law giving illegitimate children the same legal rights as children born in wedlock, the *Peronista* press accused the Catholic hierarchy of communist tendencies. In November and December priests were arrested. Then one of the biggest Catholic schools was placed under government supervision. When the bishops protested a new law was published legalizing divorce, and a draft law was introduced in the Senate to end all subsidies for religious education. In April 1955 religious instruction in schools was abolished and in May it was decided to hold elections for a national assembly to prepare a new constitution—one of the articles of this new constitution was to provide for the separation of Church and State. Almost at the same time, on May 9, Perón submitted to parliament the draft law for a forty-year concession to the Standard Oil Company.

Meanwhile the conflict had reached the streets. The Church, never very strong in a country in which only 15 per cent of the population were churchgoers, became the focal point of all anti-*Peronista* elements. In June, in spite of a police prohibition, big

Corpus Christi processions took place. There were bloody clashes and *Peronista* counter-demonstrations in which elegant cafés and luxury shops, as well as churches, were attacked. When the Church protested Perón had two bishops deported. On June 16 the Pope replied by excommunicating Perón. On the same day sections of the armed forces, particularly the fleet air arm, rose. The last, confused and complicated act had begun.

Aircraft dropped bombs, some of which fell on government buildings, others on *Peronista* masses demonstrating in the biggest square of the town. There were several hundred dead. But the army still remained loyal to Perón and it was the army, assisted by civilian *Peronistas*, which suppressed the rising.

Nevertheless Perón seemed impressed and declared himself ready to make concessions. He dismissed a number of radical, anti-clerical ministers, praised the army and in two big speeches on July 5 and 15, offered reconciliation. The revolution, he said, was over—now it was a question of developing the country together. He was prepared to stand down as leader of the party—henceforth the President should be the leader of the nation. He offered the Church compensation for material damage and greater liberty to the opposition.

On July 28 the opposition leader, Frondizi, made a speech over the radio. Instead of accepting the outstretched hand he sharply attacked the President and his whole policy, in particular his law betraying the nation to the Standard Oil Company. On the next day, Frondizi was brought before a court for showing disrespect to the President. But Perón's counter measures were of no avail: at the beginning of August the associations of teachers, lawyers, doctors and engineers raised their voices and demanded the return of their democratic freedoms. The leader of the Conservatives made a strong opposition speech; an alleged attempt on his life was discovered. Fifty-six dismissed trade union leaders published a statement condemning state control of the workers' movement.

When attempts at reconciliation failed, Perón opened his counter-offensive: on August 31, the Secretary-General of the unions read a letter from the President expressing his readiness, in the interests of national harmony, to resign if the workers so desired. This provoked wild protests, oaths of loyalty to the President, mass strikes, and demonstrations. On the evening of the same day, Perón made his strongest speech and declared that under pressure from the masses he would remain at the head of the state in order to lead his *descamisados* into battle against reaction. The struggle, he said, would have to become universal and 'for every one of us who falls, five of our opponents shall fall'. On September 1 a state of siege was declared. On September 7 the trade union leadership suggested to the government and the army that the workers should be armed and transformed into a militia. The army leaders protested. A new rising began on September 16, exactly three months after the June rebellion, in three widely separated northern centres; in the agrarian district of Cordoba where rebel troops under ex-General Lonardi received substantial help from the civilian population, in the trading and harbour town of Bahia Blanca, situated almost 1,000 miles south of Cordoba, and in the naval base of Rio de Santiago. Many army units fought for Perón. The battle was long and hard. But when the *Peronista* army started to go over to the rebels and the fleet threatened to bomb Buenos Aires, Perón fled.

The dream of the demagogic 'Justicialism', as Perón called his confused 'doctrine', was over. A leading member of the christian trade unions can still write today that Perón's revolution was 'the first popular-industrial (sic!) revolution in the whole of Latin America'.[1] And he came to this opinion after having witnessed himself how 'liberating' revolution was jubilantly received in the rich quarters of Buenos Aires while the workers' quarters lay in obscurity and silence, full of evil forebodings and sadness.[2]

(d) Bolivia: The Revolt of the Beggar on the Golden Throne

'Since April 9, 1952, Bolivia has been trying to catch up with history. The national Revolution which began at that date, and which is the most profound movement for social change which has swept any Latin American country since the Mexican Revolution of 1910, has attempted to lay the foundations of a twentieth century society.'

(Robert J. Alexander, *The Bolivian National Revolution*.)

Bolivia is as big as France and Spain together but is inhabited only by a little over three and a half million Indians, *mestizos* and whites. This land-locked mountain state is the poorest South American country. The *per capita* income of the population is estimated at less than $100 a year. In 1952 80 per cent of the population were illiterate. The vast majority of Bolivians are undernourished, public health is deplorable and infant mortality high. The first railway was built in 1903. There are only a few roads, 'usually incredibly bad and most often dangerous'.[3]

Two-thirds of the population are Indians most of whom speak only Quechua and Aymaro, Indian dialects. The majority live on the *Altiplano*, a plateau some 10,000 to 12,000 feet above sea level and one which resembles a lunar landscape. There they scrape a miserable living, as miners or 'peasants', scratching at an exhausted soil, living in primitive huts on dried potatoes, maize and beans, and chewing coca leaves. The rural minority in the fertile valleys were, until 1952, subject to the *pongaje* system, a form of serfdom. They were given a piece of land, in return for which they had to work for its owner.

[1] Emilio Máspero, *América Latina: Hora Cero*, Buenos Aires, 1962, p. 27.
[2] *op. cit.*, pp. 59–60.
[3] H. Osborne, *Bolivia*, 2nd edition, London, 1955, p. 25.

They had no protection because the state was the instrument of the ruling class, and, in an officially parliamentary country, those who could neither read nor write had no vote.

Bolivia was a state but its inhabitants did not form a nation. 'The various groups which inhabit Bolivia, many of whom are pure Indian communities, have never been able to develop a feeling of national unity', writes a US specialist on Latin America.[1]

Until the beginning of the twentieth century the small upper class of whites and *mestizos* in the towns consisted of landowners, owners of silver mines, a few wholesalers, senior officers, and members of the clergy, around whom there was a small middle class.

In the sixteenth century this country had been the source of Europe's growing wealth: masses of silver crossed the ocean from Potosí. In addition to silver, which is still found today, though only in small quantities, there is tin, lead, tungsten and oil. There are also large areas of fertile land. The eastern provinces with their tropical vegetation and untapped wealth cover 70 per cent of the country. The semi-tropical valleys on the foothills of the Andes, the *yungas* . . . 'are a different world from the Altiplano. The vigor and variety of plant life there are incredible; yet vegetables, fruit and other crops are largely unexploited because coca, from which cocaine is derived, yields such good returns that all else is neglected.'[2]

As so often in Latin America a poor people lives on rich soil. Not for nothing did a French nineteenth-century explorer remark that the Bolivian population resembled a beggar sitting on a golden throne.

The beggar was aroused from his sleep for the first time when the tin mines were opened up at the beginning of the twentieth century. A few tin barons joined the urban oligarchy of big landowners, and several thousand Indians became miners, unpaid outcasts who worked under incredibly bad conditions. After 1914, the output of tin and the greed of Bolivia's governments grew. Some of the sources of public revenue were pawned and Bolivia became increasingly dependent on New York bankers. In the course of a few years the government's external debt increased from $6 to $60 million.[3]

Then came the world economic crisis: in 1927 Bolivia had exported 47,000 tons of tin and received $96 per ton: in 1933 it exported 21,000 tons for which it received $33 per ton. The crisis coincided with the disastrous Chaco war against Paraguay (1932–1936). The Chaco war provoked a prolonged revolutionary crisis. In the country there were peasant disorders and in the towns there was unrest among the intellectuals, particularly the junior officers.

Rural Indians, mobilized as soldiers from the Chaco war, awoke

[1] P. E. James, *Latin America*, revised edition, 1950, p. 174.
[2] L. Hanke, *op. cit.*, p. 33.
[3] H. Herring, *History of Latin America*, New York, 1955, p. 528.

from their age-old lethargy and began to protest against their misery. In 1936 in the Cochabamba valley the first peasant syndicate was set up, which took up the struggle against the landowners. Years of armed clashes followed. The landowners with their heavily armed mercenaries managed to suppress the peasant revolt, for the time being. But under the surface the ferment continued and in 1947, José Rojas, a peasant's son influenced by Marxism, founded the *Sindicato Campesino de Ucureña*, which became the organizing centre of the peasant revolt.[1]

In the towns the feeling of shame over the military defeat led to revolutionary unrest among the officers. Bolivia had only few civilian intellectuals and to begin with the main part of the revolt was taken by the uniformed intelligentsia. The army had been trained by German officers and the revolutionary movement therefore started under the ideological banner of a far-western Hitlerism. A few colonels and majors founded a National Socialist Party. In 1936 a *coup* brought them to power. A 'Socialist Republic' was proclaimed, a Ministry of Labour was set up, social reforms were initiated and the US Standard Oil Company was expropriated. The small class of civilian intellectuals was in a state of ferment. Fascist, socialist, communist and democratic ideologies appeared, not always very clearly formulated, in many combinations. In 1939 Presidential elections took place for which the franchise had been considerably extended. Lieutenant-Colonel Germán Busch, a revolutionary influenced by socialist ideas, received a majority and became the head of state. A few months later he was murdered by unknown assassins. The forces of reaction began a counter-offensive. The revolution was stopped and the country entered upon a period of reaction. The revolutionaries split: on the right there was a fascist movement, the Falange, which took a firm stand against Socialists, Communists and Democrats; on the left there were radical-socialist, communist and Trotskyite groups and a new radical-nationalist, pro-socialist movement, the *Movimiento Nacional Revolucionario*, led by Victor Paz Estenssoro and Hernan Siles Suazo. In the unions the Trotskyist-influenced Juan Lechin emerged as the leading personality. In the armed forces radical officers set up a revolutionary lodge called 'Radepa' (*Razón de Patria*).

At the beginning of the 'forties a Zionist official visited South America to collect money for European Jews. He came to La Paz and was received by the tin baron Dr Hochschild, who lived in a fenced-in palace, guarded by his private police, while Indian women sat outside the gates delousing their children. 'Dr Hochschild,' said the visitor in the course of the conversation, 'you are a European intellectual from Germany. People in the know estimate your fortune

[1] R. W. Patch, 'Bolivia', *Social Change in Latin America Today*, New York, 1960.

at over $70 million. Your colleague, Patino, who was once a Bolivian peasant, prefers to spend his life in Paris. But you live here, all alone, among poor Indians who are hardly likely to have much sympathy for you. Why?' Hochschild was silent for a moment, then he said: 'Tell me, do you know what it means to have the feeling of power?'

When he made this remark his power had already begun to collapse. In December 1942, there was a bloody clash between government troops and striking miners in Oruro. There were many dead. This 'Massacre of Oruro' was the curtain raiser to a new revolt. The civilian revolutionaries made contact with the 'Radepa' lodge. A *coup* was carried out a few months later and Major Villarroel formed a government in which Victor Paz Estenssoro was given the Ministry of Finance.

But the political line of the new government remained unclear: Fascist and democratic ideas conflicted and Perón's influence made itself felt. The administrative abilities of the new men were not great and they had little contact with the revolutionary peasants. Social reform could not overcome the economic difficulties. Terrorist acts against members of the opposition increased and there was disagreement among the victors. There was renewed unrest, some army officers, backed by big mine-owners, began to conspire, and, when in July, 1946, an angry mob moved towards the government palace, the army remained neutral. The government fell, Villarroel ended his life on a street lamp, Paz Estenssoro fled to Argentina and the revolutionary groups were declared illegal.

This was the beginning of a confused period of counter-revolution. The MNR tried to organize a revolt but failed. Yet the revolutionaries, unable to establish themselves firmly by terrorist methods, preserved democratic forms and made concessions. At the presidential elections in 1951 Paz Estenssoro, the candidate of a united front consisting of the MNR, the Communists, Trotskyist and other groups, received most votes, but an army junta briefly assumed control. The armed forces split again and the head of the military police, in a bid for power, supplied arms to the workers whom the revolutionaries had mobilized. With the help of these arms and dynamite, provided by the miners, a successful mass rising took place on April 9, 1952. Paz Estenssoro became President and—a unique event in Latin America—the army was disbanded. Armed workers' militia were formed. A change, both social and political, began. Universal suffrage was proclaimed: for the first time illiterate Indians became full citizens. But no dictatorship was established, parliament continued to exist and although pressure was put on them,[1] opposition parties were not prohibited, nor were their papers suppressed.

[1] An admirer of the revolution writes: 'There is no doubt that the Paz Estenssoro administration mistreated many of its opponents, keeping many in jail and concentration camps, where they were sometimes tortured, keeping others in exile.' P. G. Alexander, *The Bolivian Revolution*, New Brunswick, 1958.

The victory of the revolution had been won in the towns—the peasants only came into the picture afterwards. They had little contact with the urban groups and José Rojas, for example, was full of suspicion towards the MNR. The fall of the old ruling classes opened the way for the Indian peasants: 'The unexpected and irreversible feature of the revolution was the organized emergence of the *campesinos* as a political and social force'.[1]

The leaders of the MNR were basically radical reformers, not wild revolutionaries. But now, without a strong civil service and without an army they were under pressure from the masses whose wishes frequently conflicted with the objective requirements of economic development.

In October 1952, the tin mines were nationalized. A government mining enterprise, *Compañia Minera de Bolivia*, was set up whose management included representatives of the workers as well as of the government. The nationalized oil industry was reorganized. Other foreign-owned enterprises were nationalized too and this often reduced their efficiency and placed additional burdens on the government budget. Paz Estenssoro was aware of the fact that Bolivia needed foreign capital and tried to maintain a favourable climate for investment, but found it extremely difficult.

With the active participation of the population—particularly the rural Indian population—schools, hospitals and new roads were built. Comprehensive social legislation was enacted. Most important was the land reform law of 1953, promulgated after the peasants themselves had already illegally redistributed land in several places. The law was intended only to liquidate feudalism and create an independent peasantry. Small and medium farms were not touched, only *latifundia* were to be confiscated and broken up. But not every big farm was regarded as a *latifundium*: 'An estate is not regarded as a *latifundium* if the owner has invested capital in machinery and modern methods', said Paragraph 35 of the land reform law, and Paragraph 12 defined a *latifundium* as an estate 'of a size varying with the geographical situation, which remains unexploited or insufficiently exploited by an extensive system, with antiquated methods and implements . . .'

The state encouraged voluntary co-operatives and a special credit bank was set up to assist them. In the Cochabamba valley the *campesinos* were allowed to choose between continuing on an individual basis or setting up co-operatives, and the majority opted for the first alternative.[2]

The fact that all citizens were given equal political rights, that the army and the old bureaucracy were broken up, that important

[1] R. W. Patch, 'Bolivia: The Restrained Revolution', *The Annals of the American Academy of Political and Social Science*, March, 1961.
[2] Robert J. Alexander, *The Bolivian National Revolution*, New Brunswick, N.J., 1958, p. 75.

industries were nationalized, that there was a land reform and that the unions and peasants' associations played an important rôle showed that a profound social revolution was taking place. This revolution had socialist characteristics but scarcely went beyond the limits of a mixed economy. Bolivia lacked the prerequisites for quick changes which would satisfy the masses. There was a shortage of capital, experts, patience and discipline. Under these conditions the united revolutionary front was bound to break up. Those who wanted to take the capitalist road with assistance from the US started agitating on the right, while on the left there were those whose inclinations were anti-imperialist and socialist.

The revolution took place in a predominantly Indian country. The Indians were gradually integrated into the nation, but a Minister of Education in the revolutionary government, Fernando Díaz de Medina, could still say, 'The Indian is a sphinx. He inhabits a hermetic world, inaccessible to the white and the *mestizo*. We don't understand his forms of life, or his mental mechanism.'[1]

Those Indians who were politically conscious and organized often resist the wishes of the government and, as many of them were armed, various parts of the country were repeatedly in a state of civil war.

Extensive areas of the country are underpopulated although extremely fertile. Considerable funds would be needed to develop them and many Indians of the Altiplano could not stand the valley climate.

The country needed foreign capital but the revolution took place in a country in which the workers had control of the arms. Their behaviour deviated substantially from the ideals of their leaders. Discipline declined and productivity fell. The miners successfully resisted all attempts at rationalization as well as all government efforts to deprive them of some of the privileges which they enjoyed at the expense of the economy as a whole—particularly their special government-subsidized shops in which goods were sold below cost price. Moreover, the means for modernization of the mines were lacking, at a time when most mines were becoming uneconomic or petering out. Within a few years most nationalized industries had to be subsidized, and in a number of nationalized firms the workers asked that they should be returned to their former owners, as for example in the case of the Cochabamba-Oruru and Antofagasta-Bolivia railways formerly owned by the British.[2]

Agriculture fared little better. The distribution of land proceeded very slowly and productivity failed to rise.

A large, unproductive bureaucracy developed and with it new corruption. This applied not only to the civil service but also to the trade unions in which, in 1955, according to the then President of

[1] Quoted in P. G. Alexander, *op. cit.*, p. 17.
[2] *Hispanic American Report*, Stanford University, Vol. XIII, 1960, Nos. 3 and 7.

Bolivia, Siles, there was one trade union official for every three members.[1]

These difficulties were aggravated by the fall in the price of tin on the world market, which was a catastrophe for the country. Bolivia had long been unable to manage without substantial US financial help. The $160 million from public funds made available by the United States for Bolivia up to 1960[2] represented more per head of population than the United States has ever given to any other Latin American country. But a large part of these funds was apparently wasted, and in any case they were only a drop in the ocean of needs. Anti-American feeling remains, even if the official communist party is weak.[3]

Richard W. Patch, who spent 1959 in Bolivia, summed up his impressions as follows:

'The MNR pushed the most ambitious program of social and economic reforms in the Western Hemisphere since the Mexican revolution. It has attempted in seven years to reach a goal that Mexico is still pursuing after forty years. Bolivia's agrarian reform, nationalization of the mines, citizenship for the Indians, universal vote, and elimination of army influence in politics have brought the country more critical problems than most nations have to deal with in a generation. The force-fed changes, many made because of political, not practical, necessities, have brought the country to a state of chaos which must be seen to be believed.'[4]

(e) Venezuela: An Incomplete Revolution

'Venezuela described over a century ago as a "barracks" by its founder, General Simon Bolivar, has remained pretty much a barracks ever since. The history of the nation would be told in the lives of its military dictators, the unchallenged supremacy of the armed forces has been the chief characteristic of the nation's politics.'
(E. Lieuwen, *Arms and Politics in Latin America*)
'There has been no real revolution here!'
(Interruption by a Venezuelan member of parliament during Castro's visit in January 1959.)

There are 'political' and there are 'social' revolutions. The most recent Venezuelan revolution stopped short of a fundamental transformation of society. This was partly due to the decisions of its leaders and partly to the wish of the army.

[1] *Hispanic American Report*, Stanford University, Vol. XIII, No. 8.
[2] *Time Magazine*, December 19, 1960.
[3] In the election of June 1960 in which the bourgeois opposition parties refused to take part, the MNR received 74·5 per cent of the votes, the right wing splinter group, the MNRA, 14·3 per cent, the Fascist Falange 8 per cent, and the Communist party 1 per cent.
[4] New York. American Universities Field Staff, April, 1959, quoted in L. Hanke, *op. cit.*, p. 29.

The character of the armed forces has certainly changed over the years: they have become specialized, modernized and also more democratic. But their political influence remains, even if the way in which it manifests itself is difficult to define. It was the army which for years supported the paternalistic, 'reactionary' dictators; it was the army which in 1945 put an end to the long period of dictatorships and which a few years later terminated the short-lived democracy. The democratic period after 1958 began with an army *putsch* against the dictator Pérez Jiménez, and since then the same army has prevented any radical development. Today there is no shortage of prophets who predict a new military dictatorship.

Modern Venezuela is a monster born of the union of oil and backwardness. Oil production began in 1918 and by the 'thirties had transformed the country. Until then Bolivar's creation had been poor and sparsely peopled. A small class of big landowners, mostly *mestizos* and creoles, ruled an impoverished illiterate rural population which raised coffee, cocoa, tobacco and cattle; and whose rate of increase was very slow.[1] This society was ruled by paternalist military dictators. Oil made the last of these powerful tyrants, General Juan Antonio Gómez (1908–1935), one of the richest men in Latin America. Those who were anxious to legitimize the traditional despotism called his form of government 'democratic Caesarism'. But the need for an ideological façade was itself a sign of social change. New classes with new aspirations were rising from the petrol-sodden soil. During the last years of the Gómez régime the prisons were filled with the opponents of the dictator, and students demonstrated in the streets. Gómez died in his bed. His two successors, General Lopez Contreras and General Isaias Medina were forced to make democratic concessions which weakened the old régime without satisfying the opposition. A modern nation was developing, thanks largely to imperialism.

'It is a fact that Venezuela is no longer what it was under Gómez— when the country had barely two million inhabitants, when it was a backward, agrarian nation without industries which, because of the absence of means of transport lived cut off from the world ... Today we are a modern nation experiencing an industrial revolution; we have 5 million inhabitants, half a million of whom are workers. Large sections of the population are educated, a middle class has

---

[1] 'From 1810 to the first quarter of the twentieth century the rate of growth of the Venezuelan population remained below that of all other American countries. This phenomenon is explained by the absence of immigration, frequent civil wars, a decline in births and a growing mortality rate.' Arturo Uslar-Pietri, *Sumario de la Economía Venezolana*, Universidad Central, Caracas, (no date), pp. 28, 29. Since 1920 the population has grown as follows:

| 1920 | 2·8 million | 1950 | 5 million |
| 1940 | 3·75 million | 1960 | 6·9 million |

developed and we are no longer isolated from the world,' wrote Rómulo Betancourt at the beginning of the 'fifties.[1]

Parties developed, and corrupt politicians flourished. Before long the word politician had become a synonym for 'embezzler of public funds'.[2]

Outstanding among the democratic radical opposition parties was the *Acción Democrática*, led by Rómulo Betancourt, a former Marxist. It had the support of a group of senior officers who wanted neither the old tyranny nor the new corruption. On October 18, 1945, a bloodless, almost peaceful, revolt took Venezuela across the threshold of the twentieth century. Democratic elections were held after which control passed to the candidate of the *Acción Democrática*, the writer Rómulo Gallegos. Behind him as a dynamic force stood his leading minister, Rómulo Betancourt.

An era of far-reaching changes began, all of which took place within the framework of democratic legality. A land reform was announced and actually prepared; trade unions, led by the *Acción Democrática*, and containing active Communist minorities, were legalized. Welfare legislation was enacted and wages were raised. Houses were built for the poor and schools were set up. At the same time new taxes were imposed on the rich and on the oil industry. Plans for partial nationalization of this industry were also prepared. Inevitably, the resistance of the upper classes and the foreign oil interests stiffened. Discontent spread to the army. The situation was all the more dangerous in that the pre-revolutionary civil service had not been purged, because, as Betancourt explained with some pride, the government did not want to do anything illegal.

Ten months after President Gallegos had officially assumed power, senior officers presented him with an ultimatum: they demanded influential positions in the government and a slowing down of radical reforms. Among them were some of the same officers who had, in 1945, brought the *Acción Democrática* to power, but who had not wanted radical change, however peaceful. Gallegos rejected their demands—and thus put an end to the democratic experiment. A military junta took over and in a manifesto dated November 28, 1948, said among other things: 'A radical fraction of the *Acción Democrática* had obtained positions of power and was beginning to sow dissension in the army through a series of manoeuvres aimed at bringing the armed forces under its control... they planned a general strike to establish their undisputed rule. This led the army to take over the government in order to avoid political chaos and economic collapse.'[3]

[1] Rómulo Betancourt, *Venezuela: Política y Petróleo*, Mexico, 1956, p. 768.
[2] Rómulo Betancourt, *Trayectoria Democrática de una Revolución*, Caracas, 1948, p. 17.
[3] Quoted in Lieuwen, *op. cit.*, p. 86.

The new junta naturally promised to preserve all democratic and social achievements and to hold early elections. The *Acción Democratica* was suppressed and its leaders went into exile, the trade unions were, more or less, made to toe the line, but a modicum of public freedom was preserved, and new opposition parties developed, including the Christian Democratic Copei, and the left-wing URD. The November 1952 elections, however, led not to a broadening of democracy, but to the re-establishment of personal dictatorship. The first published election results showed that the army's candidate, Colonel Marcos Pérez Jiménez, had received only a bare third of the votes. Thereupon a state of siege was proclaimed and Pérez Jiménez was declared 'elected'.

The new régime returned to 'democratic Caesarism' and the Minister of the Interior, Valenilla, the son of one of Gómez' chief collaborators, said that in a backward country like Venezuela democracy was nonsense. The activities of the surviving opposition parties were restricted, the trade unions became state organizations and civil liberties were abolished. But the new 'Caesarism' had to be different from its predecessor; nationalist phraseology, social demagogy and state-capitalism now became part of a policy which favoured the industrialization of the country and which promised tempting profits to foreign capital. The rule of the new 'strong man' coincided with the Korean War and the Suez crisis. The production of crude oil grew from 40 million tons in 1945 to over 120 million tons in 1957, the national income rose by 90 per cent in nine years and foreign investment in the oil industry increased. Venezuela became the country with the highest *per capita* income in Latin America, and at the same time the most expensive country in the world.

It also became a country in which differences in wealth were most obvious, in which differences in wages between various classes of workers were bigger than anywhere else and in which urbanization proceeded at a rapid pace. Between 1931 and 1950 the number of town dwellers rose from 22 per cent to 50 per cent of the population, and kept on increasing; this flight from the countryside manifested itself primarily in the growth of an urban *lumpenproletariat*.

The official slogan of Venezuelan economic policy had long been *'Sembrar el Petróleo'* ('sow the oil'). In fact it seemed sensible to use the growing wealth from oil production for a general diversification of the economy. Pérez Jiménez developed the country, but in a way which heightened its contradictions. Within a few years Caracas became the most luxurious town in Latin America, and the shanty towns also grew. First class motorways were laid, but they passed through villages without water, schools or hospitals. No expense was spared in building elegant clubs, houses and swimming pools for officers and creating highly paid positions for them. The palaces of the upper classes were filled with servants and luxury cars.

In 1953, before luxury reached their climax, an American professor wrote:

'Though tremendous tax wealth has come in, the program of "sowing the oil" has accomplished surprisingly little. The mass of the people in Venezuela today are poor, unhealthy, illiterate and live in the most primitive surroundings. The economy is still shockingly backward ... Too much goes to the army and the huge government bureaucracy ... The amount of funds peculated by dishonest officials has been tremendous. The state becomes more and more opulent; the populace continues to live in misery.'[1]

On May 1, 1957, the Archbishop of Caracas said that 'nobody could say that the wealth of the country was distributed in such a way that the majority of the population had a share in it'. 'While the upper classes live in great comfort,' continued the Archbishop, 'the mass of the people live under conditions which cannot be regarded as human.' According to semi-official calculations 50 per cent of the national income went to 10 per cent of the population.[2]

There was some modest economic development outside the oil industry, but local industry suffered because of the distortion of the economy caused by the predominance of oil and because of high production costs.[3] New enterprises financed by foreign capital, were established and protected by duties which increased the prices of all products; they competed with Venezuelan industries and this naturally led to the development of anti-imperialist feelings among Venezuelan citizens and traders. The conflicts grew and discontent spread to the armed forces.

Meanwhile, Pérez Jiménez, whose rule was becoming increasingly terrorist, began to prepare a fraudulent plebiscite which would give him an excuse to retain power after his term expired.

In the spring of 1957, came the news of the fall of the Colombian dictator, Rojas Pinilla, a close friend and ally of Pérez Jiménez. There was a noticeable increase of opposition. In August 1957 an underground 'patriotic Junta' was established in Caracas. It circulated propaganda against the government in large quantities and organized

---

[1] Edwin Lieuwen, *Petroleum in Venezuela*, 1954, quoted in L. Hanke, *Mexico and the Caribbean*, New York, 1959, p. 166.
[2] *Venezuela Up to Date*, Publication of the Venezuelan Embassy in Washington, April 1960.
[3] At the beginning of the 'fifties *Investment in Venezuela*, US Department of Commerce, had already pointed out that the quick development of the oil industry had created new problems. The high wages and salaries paid by this industry and revaluation had pushed up production costs, and this had an adverse effect both on traditional exports and on production for the home market.

student strikes operating so efficiently that the police were unable to break it or even to discover the names of its leaders.[1]

The only prominent opposition leader still in Venezuela, Rafael Caldera, was arrested, but soon managed to go into exile where he formed an alliance with Betancourt of the *Acción Democrática* and Jovito Villalba of the URD. Thereafter the incipient revolution had two heads: an 'official' emigré leadership, and an underground centre of which the Communists formed part, in Venezuela itself. In November 1957 students and school children demonstrated in Caracas and there were bloody clashes. The legal 'official' Catholic newspaper, *La Religión*, took the side of the students and democracy and came out against the proposed plebiscite.

The plebiscite took place in December 1957, and resulted in the expected majority for Pérez Jiménez, but the obvious faking of the election results brought the crisis to a head.

Early in January 1958 disturbances in the armed forces provided encouragement for the opposition and further demoralized a government already divided against itself.

The lack of unanimity showed itself in a change of government and in the flight or arrest of a number of leading officials. Pérez Jiménez oscillated between those who were in favour of compromise and those who wanted more terror. Street demonstrations became more numerous every day, although government forces opened fire on them. A leaflet of the 'Patriotic Junta' called for a general strike on January 21. Many workers, employees, students and pupils struck, shops closed, church bells were rung, police stations were attacked and buses were set on fire. The general strike spread to the whole country and soon transformed itself into a rising. The streets were filled with barricades, the revolutionaries succeeded in finding arms and some troops remained neutral. Fighting went on for two days and the outcome of the struggle was still in the balance when a new military junta emerged on the evening of January 22. It was led by Admiral Wolfgang Larrazábal, who had recently been appointed commander of the navy. The junta presented an ultimatum to Pérez Jiménez, who fled abroad in the early hours of January 23. The news of the tyrant's flight, however, did not bring peace. Strikes and fighting continued, the garrisons of the hated security police were stormed and chaos seemed imminent.

The revolution was a many-headed hydra: there were the rebel officers and the leaders of the popular revolt which itself had double leadership: the 'Patriotic Junta' of young men in the country and the less radical alliance of democratic parties in exile whose leaders were now rushing back to Venezuela. The 'Patriotic Junta' regarded the military with suspicion and even hostility and had no feelings of

[1] Later it was discovered that it was led by a little-known journalist and member of the URD, Fabricius Ojeda.

friendship for the 'old' parties. It demanded that the military junta should dismiss some of its members and replace them by reliable civilian revolutionaries. The military gave way. On January 26 the revolutionary officers' junta was transformed into a provisional government of officers and civilians under Larrazábal's chairmanship. The civilians belonged to the three emigré parties. The new government promised extensive reforms and early elections. Peace returned to the country and the revolt seemed to have been directed into democratic channels.

In December 1958, elections were held in which three candidates fought for the votes of the electorate: Rómulo Betancourt for the *Acción Democrática*, Wolfgang Larrazábal for the URD (and also the Communists) and Caldera for the Copei. All three promised that they would respect the democratic result of the election. Betancourt received 49·2 per cent of the votes, Larrazábal 34·6 per cent and Caldera 26 per cent. The lower house now contained 73 members of the *Acción Democratica*, 33 of the URD, 20 of the COPEI, and 7 Communists. The Communists received only 6·2 per cent of all votes. On February 13, 1959, Betancourt became President.

Rómulo Betancourt had long ceased to be a Communist, but members of the upper classes continued to suspect him of Communist tendencies. He stood for social reform within the framework of democracy, but the masses with their great expectations, particularly the urban masses in the slums, regarded steady slow and law-abiding progress as a betrayal. Betancourt embarked upon his policy of reform: in February 1960 a land reform was initiated which had been prepared by specialists and was mainly aimed at the creation of an independent peasantry. State-owned land was used to resettle 30,000 families a year. They had to pay for their allotments by instalments, but received help in the form of credits, and roads, houses and schools were built for them.

The execution of such a land reform demands substantial funds and much time. Not all peasant families were able to farm their land successfully. Delays in implementing the reform caused discontent. On the right, growing opposition from the big landowners found sympathizers in the armed forces.

The flight from the land did not stop. The slum districts around Caracas continued to grow even while the luxury building activities of the Pérez Jiménez period ceased. Unemployment in mining rose. Tens of thousands of houses were needed every year, if only to push back the slums and to restrain the radicalism of their inhabitants. This required an annual expenditure of $250 million.

Progress was made in the sphere of education. According to official statistics the number of teachers more than doubled in the course of two years (1958–1960) and the number of primary school pupils grew from 400,000 to over 700,000. But the Venezuelan population continued to increase at a rapid rate and illiteracy hardly declined.

Encouragement was given to local industry. But its costs were very high and duties had to be raised with the result that the prices of all goods rose.

Even such gradual progress requires vast funds, but foreign and local capitalists were put off by the fear of 'radicalism'. More and more capital left the country. At the same time there was increasing over-production of oil and the USSR began to undercut 'Western' producers. Prices fell and with them the revenue of Venezuela at the very moment when its government needed more funds for its radical reforms.

When Castro won in Cuba opposition had already begun to grow from the left and the right. Disappointment was spreading among the enthusiastic revolutionaries of 1958 and there were signs that their unanimity of purpose was beginning to vanish.

PART II
BACKGROUND OF THE REVOLUTION IN CUBA

1. The Historic Roots of the Cuban Revolution

'Be quick! We have lost 50 years!' This slogan was displayed in many offices of the Cuban revolutionary government in 1959. It explains many things, particularly the tremendous dynamism of the transformation which was not only the result of youthful enthusiasm and utopian longings, but also expressed the awareness of having lost decades and the will not to fail again, not to come to a stop half way, not to be disappointed again, and not to give breathing space to the enemies of the revolution. It had been the fate of the three preceding generations to fail in their efforts, to be disappointed in their wishes and to see progress come to a full stop.

(a) Unsuccessful Rising

The emblem of Cuba—the blue, white and red flag with the white star—was first hoisted on Cuban soil in 1848 by the Venezuelan-born Narciso Lopez. He had landed at the head of a band of invaders, mostly American, to liberate the island from Spanish overlordship. What he wanted was not, however, freedom, but annexation to the USA. Earlier in the 1840s a secret Club of rich Cubans with representatives in New York had even tried to hire the American General William J. Worth to conquer Cuba for the USA—a plan which was frustrated by President Polk.

Annexation was the slogan of some of the big landowners, who wanted to get rid of Spanish colonialism without incurring the risk of a slave war like that of Haiti. An unsuccessful rising of negroes had occurred in Cuba itself in 1812. These upper class 'annexationists' were, however, opposed by 'autonomists' and the first 'independentists', both recruited mostly among the Creole intellectuals.

This opposition abated during the 1850s. Economic conditions were favourable. Spain embarked on a policy of reform, and former annexationists, autonomists and independentists became 'reformists'. Their hopes reached a peak in 1866 when a *Junta de Información* was formed with the task of elaborating principles of the new colonial policy. It came to nothing. Disillusion followed, and out of it grew the first great national rising of Cuba—the War of Independence[1].

On October 10, 1868, the main leader of the movement, the rich lawyer and landowner Carlos Manuel de Céspedes called to Cubans to conquer their freedom. This *'Grito de Yara'* is still a Cuban national holiday. Céspedes freed his own slaves and it was from

[1] Cuba had then about 1·4 million inhabitants, 750,000 of them white, and more than 80 per cent of them Cuban-born creoles. More than half the negroes were free. There were also some 32,000 Chinese.

them, and from the ranks of other Cuban planters, freed negroes, students and intellectuals, that the first batallions of liberation were formed. They won some victories, and even captured the city of Bayamo, which became the provisional capital of Free Cuba. While risings in other provinces took place, a provisional government was set up which included the future first President of the Cuban Republic, Tomás Estrada Palma. A constitution was promulgated, which, among other things, abolished slavery. But the Spaniards proved to be stronger than had been thought. The war against them degenerated into guerilla warfare which became more and more hopeless. It took the Spaniards ten years, however, to overcome the rebels, and that only after they had made a promise of reform embodied in a virtual peace treaty, the *Pacto de Zanjón* of February 1878.

Again a feeling of despair and bitter disappointment spread. The torch of freedom was passed on to the next generation, whose leader became José Martí, poet, writer and philosopher, to whom the Cuban people owes many of its political ideas and whom they call the 'Apostle of Independence'. José Martí, an indefatigable fighter, organized the final part of the war of liberation, but was killed in battle in 1895 to become a martyr of Cuban independence.

(b) *Unsuccessful Independence*

At the beginning of 1898, when the eastern part of the island was in the hands of the rebels and Spain's rule over the rest of the country was shaky, the United States intervened in the war. Genuine sympathy for Cuba's struggle for independence was mixed with the imperial ambitions of the young power. The excuse for intervention was the still unexplained explosion of the battleship *Maine* anchored off Havana. The Spanish Government, though not responsible, immediately declared its readiness to give satisfaction to the *Yanquis*. But the United States wanted war. In April 1898 Congress passed a resolution in favour of Cuba's independence, although in fact many Americans wanted to annex the island.

The Americans landed. There was heavy fighting, but after a few weeks everything was over. In the Treaty of Paris, Spain transferred sovereignty over Cuba to the United States. This was the beginning of a period of occupation by American generals, characterized by uncertainty and Cuban anxiety.

The country had been laid waste. Almost 400,000 people had died, many in the big 'concentration' camps into which the Spanish General Weyler, had collected a large part of the population. The 1899 census showed a population of 1·5 million inhabitants—60,000 less than ten years earlier. The number of cattle had fallen by 80 per cent and tobacco production by about the same amount. The sugar harvest of 1895 had amounted to one million tons: now it was hardly more than 300,000. The health of the population was causing anxiety for yellow

THE HISTORIC ROOTS OF THE CUBAN REVOLUTION 101

fever claimed many victims. Bridges and roads had been destroyed. The Americans had to lay the foundations for a better future. On the whole they worked quickly and thoroughly: everywhere repairs were carried out and new projects started. Yellow fever was checked.[1] Roads were laid, schools and hospitals were built, modern streets were planned. It was not easy to lay the foundations of a democratic state—and not only because of war damage to the economy. There was no democratic tradition in Cuba, no local self-government, no popular education, no experts, and few people who could form an effective and honest administration. Small wonder that some of the imposed reforms could not be carried out, or were only of short duration, as, for example, the introduction of juries, the attempt to set up local self-government, and the abolition of lotteries. In the end the educational reform introduced by Varona and encouraged by the Americans also failed. Its aim had been to change the purely 'oral and rhetorical' form of traditional education, to base it on active co-operation of the pupils, and to develop independent thought. University education should also have been adapted to new requirements: 'A few writers', as Varona said, 'are enough for Cuba. What it needs in order to exist is engineers.'[2]

Other reforms proved double-edged. The Cuban élite was anticlerical. At first the American authorities fell in with their wishes and introduced civil marriage, but soon afterwards clerical pressure forced them to legalize religious marriages. For this and other concessions the clergy showed its gratitude and—in the opinion of many Cubans—developed from a pro-Spanish into a pro-American force. 'The alliance which the Catholic hierarchy and the Americans, formed at that time, has continued until the present day', wrote an anti-communist Cuban historian.[3]

For an unprejudiced outside observer there can hardly be any doubt about the positive effects of the American occupation,[4] but nationalists tend to take a negative view of reforms carried out by an occupying power. This view is held all the more strongly because such reforms are often dictatorially imposed.[5]

[1] The cause of yellow fever had been discovered some years earlier by the Cuban doctor, Finlay, but the results of his researches were not recognized by his own people. Only the American doctor, Reed, took them seriously and carried out the necessary reform.
[2] R. Portuondo del Prado, *Historia de Cuba*, Havana, 1957, p. 410.
[3] H. Portell-Vilá, *Historia de Cuba en sus Relaciones con España y los Estados Unidos*, Havana, Vol. IV, p. 53.
[4] 'It is beyond question that the US left in Cuba an immeasurably better and surer foundation for a Cuban Republic than any upon which the Cubans could have built had they succeeded without American aid in expelling the Government of Spain.' Charles E. Chapman, *A History of the Cuban Republic*, New York, 1927, p. 148.
[5] 'The exigencies of the times and the Latin temperament probably called for something of the iron hand even if the velvet glove was not always in evidence.' Russell F. Fitzgibbon, *Cuba and the USA 1900–1935*, Menasha, Wisconsin, 1935, p. 32.

In 1902 political control was handed over to a freely elected Cuban government. Cuba achieved *de jure* independence, but was transformed *de facto* into an American protectorate.

The Cubans were encouraged to incorporate into their constitution a clause drawn up by Congress and known, in honour of the Senator responsible for it, as the Platt Amendment. The Cubans had to agree never to incur any foreign debt which might exceed their capacity to pay, to give up until further notice sovereignty over an island (*Isla de Pinos*) which had always been considered part of Cuban territory, and to allow the United States to establish naval bases on Cuban territory. What is more, the United States was given the right to intervene in Cuba in order 'to protect life, property and personal liberty'. The Platt Amendment was thus both the birth certificate and the gravestone of Cuban independence. In 1928 an American historian could with reason publish a book entitled *Our Cuban Colony*, and in 1935 a group of American observers could note the paradox that Cuba 'as a consequence of its struggle for political independence lost control over its economic resources'.[1]

In fact hordes of American businessmen now invaded the country, where land was fertile and absurdly cheap. New sugar mills were founded with American capital, existing refineries were bought up and modernized, vast areas of land were taken over, banks came under American control and American influence penetrated into all branches of the economy.

'The banks were in American and British hands—so were the railways. Electricity and Telephone Services were monopolies of North American companies, while the most important (and many of the small) commercial enterprises were owned by Spaniards, who preferred to employ their compatriots. No wonder that "politics" became for the Cubans the most important "industry".'

(c) Unsuccessful Republic

In 1900 the American governor, General Wood, had announced that American administration would end only when the Cubans had acquired the necessary maturity to govern themselves. 'When that time comes,' he said, 'we shall have to go. But to do so now would be senseless and would only lead to a state where we would soon have to return under unpleasant conditions.'[2]

His words were prophetic. When the Americans did leave, conditions were not propitious for the existence of an orderly, democratic republic. Large sections of the upper class had close connections with American interests. The big traders—most of them Spaniards—the high clergy, the Cuban landowners and all wealthy people

[1] Foreign Policy Association, *Problems of the New Cuba*, New York, 1935, p. 1.
[2] H. Portell-Vilá, *op. cit.*, p. 84.

regarded the Platt Amendment as a guarantee of their well-being. Many politicians who had taken part in the liberation movement honestly shared this view. The first President of the country, Estrada Palma, in his own words, preferred personal freedom and order in the country to independence: the poverty and ignorance of the masses, the corruption of the politicians, the absence of any tradition of self-government, and the lack of a widespread sense of national identity made any democratic order difficult.[1]

Estrada Palma's régime soon assumed the characteristics of a dictatorship. In 1905, when he systematically falsified election results in order to retain power, civil war broke out in the course of which *both* sides demanded American intervention. It is a curious fact, recognized by Cuban historians, that the 'imperialist' President Theodore Roosevelt, was entirely opposed to intervention but was forced into it by pressure from President Palma and his opponent, the 'Liberal' Gomez. When Roosevelt urged him at all costs to make American intervention unnecessary[2] the Cuban head of state said that he was incapable of maintaining order without American help.

On September 28, 1906, the Americans landed. Portell-Vilá writes bitterly:

'Thus ended the first Cuban Republic, mortally wounded by the Cubans themselves. But the climax of the disaster was that those responsible for the catastrophe on both sides were not *ipso facto* disqualified but reached the highest positions in the state ... This is the origin of our crises, of our disappointment, the reason why there has been no normal development and the cause of the lack of morals in government and administration.'[3]

The new American governor, a civilian named Charles E. Magoon, wanted to replace his predecessors' authoritarianism by different methods. In avoiding the Scylla of dictatorship, however, he foundered on the Charybdis of corruption, because he could get local support only by giving politicians and their followers a chance of gaining power and wealth. The ironic result was that this apparently honest and conciliatory[4] man has, to the Cubans, become the 'inventor' of corruption.

[1] Portell-Vilá is shocked by the 'annexationist' mood of the upper class and of those politicians and businessmen for whom 'the interests of the fatherland were subordinated to the interest of exporting duty-free sugar to the US' (*op. cit.*, p. 232). He quotes two remarks by Estrada Palma: 'To me freedom is more important than independence' and 'For my beloved Cuba I would a hundred times rather have political dependence which guarantees freedom than independence which is characterised by periodic civil wars'. (pp. 215, 569).
[2] Portell-Vilá, *op. cit.*, pp. 493, 483.
[3] Portell-Vilá, *op. cit.*, p. 510.
[4] 'In all the thousands of charges against Magoon, not one has ever been proved.... At his death in 1920 he left an estate of $86,000—less than he had when he went to Cuba.' (Charles E. Chapman, *op. cit.*, p. 233.)

The second occupation lasted about two years. Thereafter open military intervention became less frequent and the United States normally relied on economic[1] and diplomatic pressure. 'Consequently, the term 'intervention' became a much more elastic one after 1909. Whether or not the US 'intervened' upon a particular occasion is a question of definition and to arrive at an objective determination of the whole number of US interventions in Cuba might be as difficult as for the mediaevalist to determine the number of crusades.'[2]

The Platt Amendment was revoked in 1934, but American influence still remained so strong that the American ambassador (under Batista in 1958) could say, with some exaggeration as we shall see: 'Before Castro took over the influence of the United States in Cuba was so great that the American ambassador was the second most important man in the country—at times even more important than the President.'[3]

(d) Unsuccessful Revolution

In 1924 the 'Liberal' Gerardo Machado was elected President after promising among other things not to stand again when his term of office expired. He was responsible for building the road across the country which remains Cuba's most important traffic artery and also for the erection of the costly and large 'Capitol' in Havana. To spite American export interests he raised duties, which made possible a modest programme of industrialization. But his dictatorial tendencies soon became clear. A packed Congress decided to prolong his presidential term from four years to six. The collapse of the sugar market in 1929 was the biggest catastrophe in Cuba's history. Faced with growing opposition Machado banned newspapers and organizations, imprisoned his opponents or had them murdered and established a brutal secret police.

There was a variety of opposition. On the 'right' were the conservatives under the former President Menocal, and further to the 'left' the liberals led by Mendieta who was respected on account of his personal honesty. The students of the *Directorio Estudiantil*, led by, among others, Carlos Prío Socarras and Eduardo R. Chibás, were more radical. A terrorist organization, called *ABC*, developed, consisting mainly of intellectuals organized in highly conspiratorial cells. The workers organizations, leading a semi-legal existence, were strongly influenced by anarcho-syndicalists and communists.

---

[1] Including an unofficial embargo on deliveries of goods to Cuba in 1918 in order to force the Cuban government to make concessions to American interests. (Leland Jenks, *Our Cuban Colony*, New York, 1928, p. 199.)
[2] Russell H. Fitzgibbon, *op. cit.*, p. 146.
[3] August 30, 1960, *Communist Threat to the U.S. Through the Caribbean*. Hearings before the Sub-Committee to Investigate the Administration of the Internal Security Act, Committee of the Judiciary, US Senate, 86th Congress, 2nd Session, Washington, D.C.

THE HISTORIC ROOTS OF THE CUBAN REVOLUTION 105

In 1931 Machado succeeded in suppressing a revolt. But the revolutionary mood spread to the poverty-stricken masses in town and country. Disturbances, strikes and bomb outrages became normal occurrences in 1932/3.

The majority of Americans in Havana supported Machado, although he preferred to import from Europe and had reduced American tariff preferences. Banks exerted pressure in Washington in favour of the dictator, because he promised to continue to pay interest on loans punctually.[1] When increasingly loud protests were heard from Cuba against Machado's government the Americans tried to get him to compromise with the opposition for the sake of 'peace and order'.[2] But Machado proved stubborn and the opposition leaders urged Washington to intervene.[3]

In May 1933, the new American President, Franklin D. Roosevelt, sent Sumner Welles to Cuba to act as mediator. The opposition, particularly the ABC and the Liberals, approved of his mission, but Machado protested against American interference in the name of 'national sovereignty'. Welles intervened on behalf of arrested opposition leaders and even insisted on the removal of a notoriously brutal police chief. Machado began to waver, declared himself ready to make concessions and then went back on them.

On August 3, 1933, a strike of bus workers broke out in Havana which soon developed into a general strike. The correspondent of the *New York Times* wrote: 'The general strike is a marvellous thing. An entire nation folds its arms and quits work... There is no leadership to this strike: it is entirely spontaneous'.[4] The movement also spread to the countryside. Sugar mills and plantations were occupied by farm workers. In some places 'Soviets' were formed and took over power.

Welles, impressed by the strength of the movement, explained to Machado that he would have to resign. But the President held out until August 11, when senior army officers turned against him because they feared that American intervention would damage their own positions and result in a reduction of the military budget—then amounting to 25 per cent of all public expenditure.[5]

At dawn on August 12 Machado fled. With Welles' aid his place was taken by a liberal minister, Céspedes; he was acceptable to the

[1] Ruby Hart Phillips, *Cuba: Island of Paradox*, New York, 1959, pp. 7, 46.
[2] 'Political reforms and democracy in Cuba were only stressed by the US during times of crisis as concessions to keep opposition groups from starting trouble.' Robert M. Smith, *The US and Cuba: Business and Diplomacy 1917–1960*, New York, 1960, p. 137.
[3] Robert M. Smith, *op. cit.*, pp. 127, 131.
[4] Ruby Hart Phillips, *op. cit.*, p. 30. Later the communists claimed to have led the strike. A highly exaggerated claim to say the least, but later repeated by Batista also. (Fulgencio Batista, *Respuesta*, Mexico, p. 390, cf. the digression below on the Communists in Cuba.)
[5] Charles E. Thompson, *The Cuban Revolution*, Foreign Policy Reports, New York, Vol. XI, No. 21, December 18, 1935.

officers, the upper class and most of the politicians, but the masses, the students, the anarchists and communists thought differently. In the villages and towns law and order had disappeared. *Machadistas* were persecuted and killed, houses looted, newspapers burnt: anarchy seemed to have broken out and the new government was powerless. Welles was desperate. On September 4, a *coup d'état* unique in the annals of Latin America took place. With the support of the lower ranks of the army and with the agreement of some student leaders and of the *ABC*, a non-commissioned officer, Fulgencio Batista, drove out the officers and took over military control without loss of life. A mulatto from the lower classes, with Indian features, an army stenographer who as a sideline taught commercial subjects at a private school, thus became the central figure, without either his superiors or most politicians, or even the Americans, knowing anything about his plans.

After four days of interim government by five men, the *pentarchy*, a little-known professor of medicine at the university, Ramón Grau San Martín, was appointed by the students to take over control. The government was a radical nationalist-democratic-social reformist student government, without clear ideology, without a sense of realities, without experience, and without real roots in the people. In desperation Welles cabled to Washington on September 18: 'It is quite on the cards that the social revolution which has begun can no longer be stopped'.[1] Roosevelt sent a squadron to Havana but refused to land troops. At the same time he refused to recognize the new government until it could guarantee peace and order and fulfil its international commitments. But this the new government was unable to do. The chaos in the country grew: no rents or taxes were paid, strikes broke out everywhere and bombs were thrown. Members of the government made strong speeches against the *Yanquis* and against the rich, and published a flood of revolutionary laws. One of the most important of these was the Law of Nationalization of Labour, ordering that all workers should be Cuban nationals and that at least 50 per cent of all employees should be Cuban-born. There were large-scale protests and demonstrations in the streets against this both by the many Spanish-born citizens and by the Communists, who accused the Grau government of 'chauvinism'. Other decrees forced the American electricity company and the telephone company to lower their rates. When the companies refused to raise wages at the same time they were put under temporary government control. The government decided to raise wages and suspended the payment of interest on foreign loans. While opposition increased—Conservatives, Liberals, Communists and the *ABC* were all, if for different reasons, against Grau and the existing anarchy—and while disagreements were beginning to appear among

[1] Robert M. Smith, *op. cit.*, p. 144.

government supporters, the presidential palace presented the following picture:

'Visiting the palace is like visiting a lunatic asylum with all the inmates turned loose to do as they please ... In the press room ... soldiers sitting on the desks, smoking ... on the second floor ... another crowd in the cabinet room where President Grau receives everyone. He sits at the head of a table surrounded by the *Directorio Estudiantil* ... No one around the President pays the slightest attention to him, nor has the courtesy to stop talking long enough for him to make himself heard.'[1]

Behind Grau's back a struggle began between the young radical Minister of the Interior, Antonio Guiteras, and the army leader, Batista. The Conservatives and the Americans soon put their money on the latter. He showed himself capable of restoring order when in November 1933 his troops suppressed an uprising organized by the *ABC*, and in action against communist demonstrators. In December 1933—after Welles had been replaced by Jefferson Caffery—almost all political groups began to demand Grau's resignation and on January 6 a student meeting withdrew 'its confidence' from Grau in protest against Batista's growing influence.

On January 15, Grau resigned and a few days later Carlos Mendieta became President. The students were furious and the Communists attacked the new President no less violently than his predecessor, but the remnants of the *ABC*, the Liberals, the Conservatives and the Americans expressed themselves in his favour. There was remarkable popular enthusiasm for him in the capital. 'The town is celebrating the removal of the students' government with almost the same enthusiasm as when Machado fell.'[2]

The revolution was over, but to restore order was difficult, although the Americans made the new government an important gift in the form of the revocation of the Platt Amendment.[3] Strikes, assassination attempts, and demonstrations continued. Martial law was proclaimed more than once. Behind the back of the President, Batista established his military dictatorship. The dying revolution reached its last climax in March 1935 when a mass strike broke out which lasted nearly ten days and in which about half a million Cubans took part. The trade unions, the new *Partido Revolucionario Cubano Auténtico* (*Auténticos* for short), founded by Grau and his friends, the *Jóven Cuba*, the organization led by Guiteras, the *ABC* which had again changed front, the Communists and others took

[1] Ruby Hart Phillips, *op. cit.*, p. 73.
[2] Ruby Hart Phillips, *op. cit.*, p. 150.
[3] This was no real sacrifice for the US which had already long indicated the wish to give up open intervention. American bankers were dissatisfied with restrictions on loans to Cuba, whereas the new 'Treaty of Mutual Assistance' gave American exporters big opportunities on the Cuban market.

part. Batista broke the strike. A few weeks later Guiteras was shot 'trying to escape'. 'Normalization' began. In December 1935 Mendieta resigned and Batista began his unchecked rule, sheltered by a series of powerless presidents.

At the end of 1935 an American correspondent wrote:

'The fall of Machado initiated two revolutions in Cuba—one political, the other social. The first sought to supplant dictatorship and to return to constitutional democracy. The second envisaged such social reconstruction as would restore control of land and economic life to the Cuban people. To date, both revolutions have failed in their objectives ... The forces of protest have been driven underground but whether to disappear or to reappear in more aggressive form the future alone will decide.'[1]

(e) *Unsuccessful Democracy*

Batista was less anxious than most other Latin American dictators to do without democratic phraseology and democratic institutions. Abraham Lincoln and Franklin D. Roosevelt were his heroes. He wanted to go down in the history of his country as having preserved order *and* having founded a democracy. His thoughts were directed towards social reforms, and towards enriching himself.

After 1937 he set course towards 'democratization'. Laws which favoured the workers were passed. Full of hatred against the *Auténticos*, he legalized the Communist Party and entrusted Communist leaders with the direction of the newly established trade unions. In 1939 there were more or less *free* elections for a national constituent assembly. This body drew up the 1940 Constitution which continued to exist until 1961 as a more or less platonic manifesto of social democracy.

Human and civil rights and all forms of freedom were guaranteed, the death penalty was abolished, the inviolability of the home and of correspondence, freedom of the press and of association, equality of class and race were proclaimed. Paragraph 37 prohibited all political organizations opposed to representative democracy. Paragraph 40 recognized the right of the individual to resist illegal actions by the state. The independence of the judiciary, local self-government, the appointment of officials on merit and their immovability thereafter, were provided for.

In an under-developed country with chronic mass unemployment work was recognized in Article 60 as the 'inalienable right' of every citizen, and an obligation was placed on the state to provide it.

The constitution promised the establishment of minimum wages, compulsory social insurance, a 44-hour working week with wages for

[1] Charles E. Thompson, *The Cuban Revolution*, Foreign Policy Reports, Vol. XI, No. 22, January 1, 1936.

48 hours, and an annual four weeks' holiday with pay. The right to strike was guaranteed and the dismissal of employees without a labour court ruling prohibited. Compulsory free education for all children up to the age of fourteen and free means of instruction become basic rights—Article 52 even laid down that all primary school teachers must get a monthly minimum wage equal to one millionth part of the total budget. If this had ever been put into practice Cuba in the 'fifties would have had the best paid primary school teachers in the world, receiving about $450 a month.

Property was declared to be a 'social function' and mineral resources the inalienable property of the nation. Article 89 prohibited *latifundia* and envisaged further legislation on this subject (which never appeared).

According to Article 24 the state could expropriate only on the basis of laws and court decisions and after paying adequate compensation.[1] Article 271 made it the duty of the state to run the economy in the interest of the people so that 'every citizen is guaranteed a decent existence . . .'

The document was signed among others by Grau San Martín, Prio Socarras, Eduardo Chibás, by Liberals and Conservatives, by Communists, such as Juan Marinello and Blas Roca, and by Eusebio Mujal, who had begun as a Communist and become later an *Auténtico* trade union leader.

In Cuban conditions, this Utopian manifesto was bound to work against democratization. Those of its social and economic promises which were realized acted rather as a brake on progress; those which were not gave any demagogue an opportunity to accuse the government of treachery.

In 1940 a coalition, which included the Communists, elected Batista as President under this Constitution. In 1944, at the end of Batista's term of office, his candidate, Dr. Carlos Saladrigas, the former leader of the ABC, who also had the support of the Communists, was surprisingly defeated. The elections really had been free—and the *Auténticos* and their 'historic' leader, Grau San Martín, emerged as victors. At first a new day seemed to be about to dawn, but disillusionment and disappointment was soon to set in.

The *Auténtico* administrations of Grau (1944–48) and Carlos Prío Socarras (1948–March 1952) were marked by the introduction of important social reforms, extensive public works and the foundation of such important institutions as the National Bank and a supreme Court of Audit (*Tribunal de Cuentas*). The position of the lower classes improved, particularly that of urban workers and sugar

---

[1] It is interesting to note that the Communist delegates were opposed to this compensation obligation, among other reasons because, in their opinion, it made radical agrarian reform impossible.

workers.[1] But achievements nevertheless fell short of expectations—and during this period almost complete freedom of expression made it possible to accuse the president and his ministers in the press or over the radio of every possible misdeed. Revolutionary terrorist groups openly went about their activities and their members were given official positions. Corruption was rife and oppositionist propaganda represented it as being far worse than it was in fact. Leading politicians were often justly accused of embezzlement, of smuggling narcotics, and of other shady transactions. In a legal case—the files of which later 'vanished'—the Grau government was accused of having embezzled about £60 million ($174 million), and the Finance Minister of the Prío government was said to have allowed 160 million old bank notes, which had been withdrawn from circulation in order to be burned, to continue to circulate and to have made an enormous profit from the transaction. The number of persons on the government pay-roll increased from 60,000 in 1943 to 131,000 in 1949.[1]

During its first years the *Auténtico* government enjoyed the support of the Communists, whom Grau left for a time in charge of the trade unions. Then, under pressure from the *Auténtico* trade unionists, Eusebio Mujal, who had meanwhile become an *Auténtico*, was allowed to take them over. The Communists would in any case have gone into opposition when the 'cold war' began.

More important was the growth of a new opposition party, the 'Party of the Cuban People' popularly known as the *Ortodoxos*. This group had split from the *Auténticos* under Eduardo Chibás' leadership and was extremely active in its protests against corruption. Chibás was an outstanding speaker who could rouse the masses. In 1951 he shot himself at the microphone to 'wake up' the people. It was unfortunate that the microphone had already been switched off because he had exceeded his speaking time. The official leadership of the party went to Professor Robert Agramonte, who became presidential candidate for the elections due to take place in June 1952.

In 1948, Batista had returned to Cuba from 'voluntary' exile and had been elected senator of a new party led by him. He also became a presidential candidate. It soon became clear that his chances were small and that he would probably take third place behind the *Auténtico* candidate, Hevia, who though not very popular was known for his honesty, and Agramonte.

[1] 'While the government continued to cling to the policy of high wages it also began to intervene in private enterprises. Such intervention usually took place if owners refused to raise wages. When this failed the government looked for other solutions which would not result in a reduction of wages ... tax reliefs, payment of subsidies.' (Economic Commission for Latin America 1951, *Economic Survey of Latin America 1951*, quoted in Gustavo Gutiérrez, *El Desarrollo Económica de Cuba*, Havana, 1952, p. 223.

[2] Gustavo Gutiérrez, *op. cit.*, p. 98.

On December 16, 1951, the Cuban weekly *Bohemia* published a public opinion poll which aroused great interest. In answer to the question, what did they think of the government's policy, 29·8 per cent said that they agreed with it, 33·2 per cent replied that they were against the government, 26·6 per cent approved of some aspects of the government's policy while disapproving of others, and 10·4 per cent had no opinion. (The chances of the *Auténticos* had improved considerably because one year earlier less than 18 per cent had been for the government.) An interesting fact was that oppostion was much stronger in the towns than in the country.

As far as the candidates were concerned—at the time the *Auténticos* had not yet settled on Hevia—33·8 per cent were in favour of an *Auténtico* candidate, 30 per cent supported the *Ortodoxo* candidate and only 14·2 per cent were in favour of Batista. Twenty-three per cent were still undecided.

Equally interesting was the 'social' analysis of the survey showing from what classes the candidates derived their support. A comparison of the opinions of the upper classes (big landowners, directors, senior officials and the cream of the liberal professions) with those of the lowest classes (unskilled workers, domestic servants and unemployed) shows the following picture. (The 'middle classes' are omitted):

	Upper Classes	*Lower Classes*
For Agramonte	34·8 per cent	21·8 per cent
For Hevia	19·7 per cent	14·6 per cent
For Batista	11·5 per cent	18·9 per cent

The organizer of the survey, Raul Gutiérrez Serrano, commented: 'As in all preceding surveys it is noticeable that the percentage of votes for the Orthodox candidates becomes smaller as one descends the social scale, whereas there is more sympathy for General Batista among the lower than among the upper classes'.

(f) Unsuccessful Dictatorship

In the early hours of March 10, 1952, Senator General Fulgencio Batista appeared in front of a heavily guarded entrance to one of Cuba's most important garrisons, Camp Columbia, outside Havana. He was allowed to pass. A few hours later the population of the island awoke to learn that General Batista had taken over the government. He said that he was doing so with a heavy heart in order to save democracy, which was threatened by corruption, the terrorism of revolutionary bands, and a *coup d'état* planned by President Prío. All the democratic achievements which he—friend of the people, father of the constitution, organizer of the free elections of 1944—had taken such a prominent part in bringing about would be preserved, as would all social reforms. This was the beginning of an adventure the end of which could not have been foreseen by anybody.

The *coup* took place almost without bloodshed. Prío, surprised and confused, sought sanctuary in the Mexican embassy together with his Minister, Aureliano Sánchez Arango, and, like other political leaders, fled abroad a few days later. The trade union leaders tried unsuccessfully to call a general strike. After two days under arrest Mujal came to an agreement with the new ruler, who declared his readiness 'to respect the rights of organized labor and to allow the CTC (the Cuban Trade Union Confederation) to resume its leadership provided it did not try to undermine the government'.[1]

Batista continued to enlist the sympathies of the workers. In December 1952, when as the result of an unfavourable situation on the world market it was decided to harvest very much less sugar in 1953, the government, in spite of protests from the sugar mill owners, decreed that sugar workers' wages should be maintained at the high 1952 level. In September 1953, the government interfered in the affairs of the country's big artificial silk factory and forced it to give way to the workers' demand. In December 1955, after a strike of sugar workers, the government intervened in their favour.

Officialdom supported Batista, particularly the army and the police whose pay was raised considerably immediately after the revolution; the agricultural population remained passive. The opposition parties were unable to fight and their leaders seemed very susceptible to corruption. The press which in any case depended on government subsidies—in Havana alone there were sixteen daily papers—could hardly be expected to offer resistance. Democratic promises (including the promise to hold early elections), the maintenance of 'peace and order', and measures to stimulate economic development rendered the opposition impotent and satisfied the United States—the more so as Batista allowed diplomatic relations with the Soviet Union to lapse[2] and made anti-Communist statements.

But everything did not go as smoothly as Batista had hoped. Many of the bourgeoisie continued to express democratic sentiments. Not all the opposition leaders were prepared to sell themselves or to emigrate. And the emigrés began to form an active opposition abroad. The *Auténticos*, the *Ortodoxos* and the Communists came out against the new dictatorship. Even the press made repeated protests: in October 1952 all newspapers published a joint manifesto demanding the restoration of the constitution and of

[1] US Department of Labor, *Foreign Labor Information: Latin American Labor Legislation*, Comparative Summaries [Cuba], Washington, December, 1956.
[2] On March 21, 1952, two Soviet diplomatic couriers coming from Mexico were stopped at the airport and refused the right to take away their luggage without customs examination. When the Cuban government failed to react to a Soviet protest, the USSR broke off diplomatic relations with Cuba.

democracy. Highly critical speeches were often made on the radio. Above all there were the students, who had voiced the loudest protests immediately after the *coup d'état*. Havana University became the breeding ground of conspiracies, and of fighting units.

It seemed impossible to do without repressive measures. There were all kinds of prohibitions, arrests and police brutalities. There were limited periods of press censorship and of 'suspension of constitutional guarantees'. Police terror became particularly severe in the summer of 1953 after Castro's first unsuccessful rising, at which time the Communist Party (*Partido Socialista Popular*) was banned. But the terror did not reach Machadist dimensions until 1957.

In 1954–55 Batista seemed to have been successful. The economy was developing. His rule was formally legalized in elections which of course were anything but free. Opposition appeared to be decreasing. Batista also began to make concessions which had a soothing effect. A general political amnesty was proclaimed— Castro and his friends, among others, came out of prison. Most of the emigrés, including Prío, came back, began a new legal opposition campaign and even held mass meetings at which demands for free elections were heard. 'Peace negotiations' began in January 1956 in the form of a so-called *Dialogo Cívico* at which opposition delegates met members of the government under the chairmanship of a generally respected patriarch of the Cuban war of liberation. Batista however soon felt himself strong enough to refuse serious concessions. The 'dialogue' dragged on. There was renewed unrest. Revolutionary terrorist acts grew more frequent, and the government replied with counter-terror, which cut the ground from under the feet of the 'legal' opposition. People were killed, there were demonstrations, political strikes, attacks on garrisons and armed clashes. Most of the opposition again went into exile, or were arrested. The 'constitutional guarantees' were repeatedly suspended and the prisons began to fill again. In December 1956 Fidel Castro and his followers landed from Mexico in Oriente Province to take up armed resistance. This was the end of the plan for a 'democratic' dictatorship . . .

(g) *Digression: Cuba's Communists*

On January 22, 1961, the following allegedly true story was published by the weekly journal *Bohemia*, which after the flight of its proprietor and publisher was made to toe the line: 'Fidel was talking to a group of peasants. He asked them: "Are you happy about the agricultural reform?" The peasants replied: "Of course, it's wonderful". "Are you happy about the nationalization of the big factories and the sugar refineries?" "Of course, we are happy about all those things!" The leader of the revolution then asked them what they thought about other government measures and received nothing but favourable answers. Finally he said: "Does that mean you are in favour of communism?" whereupon they replied with one voice: "No, no, we don't want communism".'

The journalist who reported this conversation said of himself that he was neither a communist nor an anti-communist, but condemned the reaction of Castro's audience. 'This is a kind of phobia. They condemn communism because they have been told from birth that it is bad, because they believe that communists are hateful and bad people'. This does not completely explain the unpopularity of the communists. It is interesting to note that the author of the article, the most popular radio commentator of the revolution, the most violent enemy of *Yanqui* imperialism, Pardo Llada, fled to Mexico at the end of March 1961, only a few months after personally signing copies of the Russian translation of his book *Recollections of the Sierra Maestra*, saying that Cuba was now ruled by communists who left him no freedom ...

The Communist Party of Cuba was founded in 1925 by an old socialist, Boliño, and a young intellectual, Mella, who a few years later was expelled for 'lack of discipline', emigrated to Mexico during the Machado persecutions, was received back into the ranks of the Communists there, began to deviate again from the 'general line', and was assassinated in mysterious circumstances by a Machado agent in 1929.[1]

At the beginning of the 'thirties the Party had barely two thousand members though it had some influence among intellectuals and also in some trade unions, which increased during the revolution against Machado.[2]

Its rôle during the strike of August 1933 was strange. Official party circles maintain that they led the strike together with other groups, but the journal *Communist International* admitted that the Party was weak and its links with the masses quite inadequate at that time.[3] Another article in *Communist International*[4] stated that the fight against Machado had chiefly been led by bourgeois groups and landowners, and that 'in the August strike, the proletariat was not yet opposed to the ruling classes, because in practice the working masses did not yet see that essentially, in their class-hatred for the toilers, these bourgeois landlord groups in no way differed from Machado although they opposed him'.

The reason for this rather obscure language is found in the fact that during the strike the Communists made a tactical mistake which

[1] A number of informed people, including Mella's former wife and his daughter, suspect that the Communists had some part in this murder.
[2] For a short description of the history of the Cuban communists, written from their standpoint, see Jacques Arnault, 'Cuba et le Marxisme, Essai sur la Révolution Cubaine', *La Nouvelle Critique*, Paris, September-October, 1962.
[3] *Communist International*, October 15, 1934.
[4] *Communist International*, February 15, 1934.

THE HISTORIC ROOTS OF THE CUBAN REVOLUTION 115

lost them many sympathies. On August 8, Machado called in some Havana Communist union leaders in order to negotiate with them and to promise them concessions. Thereupon they appealed—quite unsuccessfully—to the masses to stop the strike, a move which the Communists themselves later singled out as a serious error.[1] The Communists continued to be reproached with this 'betrayal', for example at a student meeting in November 1934, at which the student leader and later founder of the *Ortodoxo* Party, Eduardo R. Chibás, declared: 'The so-called "revolutionary" leaders who after the massacre of August 7, 1933 ordered the proletariat which had tried to overthrow Machado to resume work, are today trying to speak in the name of the revolution. These are their old tactics, which are to attack revolutionaries more violently than reactionaries. The more revolutionary a person is the more the Communists attack him. Therefore they attack the *ABC* more strongly than the Conservatives, the *Auténticos* more strongly than the *ABC*, and if they could they would like to eat Guiteras alive. Therefore I am sure that I am a good revolutionary if I am attacked by these little leaders of tropical Communism.'[2]

After Machado's fall the Party became legal, and in conformity with the general line of the Communist International at the time, according to which 'Social-Fascism' was the main enemy, directed its main attacks in Cuba against those parties and groups which more or less corresponded to European Social Democrats. Immediately after the formation of the Grau government the party organ appealed to the masses to fight against Grau and his government of 'bourgeois and big landowners' and to work for the establishment of a workers' and peasants' government.[3] The government's most radical Minister, Guiteras, was 'unmasked' in the following terms: 'As the Communist Party of Cuba has correctly stated, what Guiteras with his "left" demagogy is preparing is a *coup d'état* in which a fraction of certain elements of the army that are antagonistic to Batista will take part'.[4]

The Communists even criticized Grau's foreign policy because they considered its anti-imperialism as too extreme, and this could make them only less popular among radical nationalists. The *Communist International* wrote: 'The Communist Party must take all steps to prevent a US intervention, making certain concessions to US imperialism ... The Communist Party directs its main blow against the local ruling classes in Cuba.'

[1] Robert J. Alexander, *Communism in Latin America*, New Brunswick, N.J., 1957, p. 272, and Charles E. Thompson, *Foreign Policy Reports*, Vol. XI, No. 21, December 18, 1935.
[2] Alberto Baeza Flores, *Las Cadenas Vienen de Lejos*, Mexico, 1960, p. 111.
[3] *Communist International*, February 15, 1934, and Robert J. Alexander, *op. cit.*, p. 274.
[4] Robert J. Alexander, *op. cit.*, p. 276.

If a 'government of workers and peasants' under Communist leadership were to take over it would 'start to negotiate with the US government in order to lay down conditions for the nationalization of American enterprises. It might be possible to buy them or to take over some of them in the form of concessions'.[1]

To the nationalists such views must have appeared all the more suspicious as the Communists had already expressed themselves against the 'nationalization of labour', that is to say the Grau laws compelling employers to use at least 50 per cent Cuban-born labour.

In the summer of 1933 the action programme of the Communist Party contained the following points: nationalization of big industrial enterprises, transport and banks, if owned by imperialists; expropriation, *without compensation*, of big estates owned by Cubans or foreigners to be distributed among peasants and agricultural labourers; repudiation of the national debt; formation of a workers' and peasants' army, the establishment of soviets.[2] In October 1933, a new action programme was adopted which favoured collectivization instead of distribution of land. But this was strongly criticized by the *Communist International*: 'The demand for collective cultivation of the land . . . is the most dangerous of mistakes because . . . it deprives the Party of the support of considerable sections (if not the majority) of the peasants and some of the farm labourers . . . who wish to cultivate their own farms.'[3]

Official communist writers later admitted that the Communists shared the responsibility for the fall of the Grau government: 'The old political parties, the *ABC*, the employers and the representatives of American interests were against Grau. These groups regarded the government as too 'left-wing'. On the other hand, elements of the workers' movement under the leadership of the Communists also fought against Grau, because they considered the government too moderate and incapable of fighting against the imperialists.'[4]

Meanwhile, the strategy and tactics of the Communist International changed and as early as 1935 the mistakes in the line of the Cuban communists were exposed: 'The Party failed to distinguish sufficiently between the national-revolutionary camp and the feudal-counter-revolutionary camp. This explains its hostile attitude towards Grau'.[5]

Just as the 'ultra left' line of 1933/1934 is a reflection of the general world line against 'Social Fascism', so is this quotation a

[1] *Communist International*, October 15, 1933.
[2] *Communist International*, September 15, 1933.
[3] *Communist International*, February 15, 1934.
[4] L. I. Zubok, *Imperialisticheskaya Politika SSh. v Stranakh Karibskogo Basseina* (Imperialist Policy of the USA in the Caribbean Countries), Moscow, 1948, p. 313.
[5] *Inprecor*, English edition, October 10, 1935.

THE HISTORIC ROOTS OF THE CUBAN REVOLUTION 117

reflection of the international change to a 'popular front' which had begun in 1935.

During the Popular Front period the Communist Party moved towards Batista. In 1937, the *Partido Unión Revolucionaria* under Juan Marinello was legalized, and all anti-Communist persecutions came to a stop. After May 1, 1938, the legal Communist daily, *Hoy*, began to appear. The 10th Plenum of the semi-legal Communist Party had already earlier decided to adopt a positive attitude towards Batista. In September 1938 the Communist Party amalgamated with the *Unión Revolucionaria*. A new trade union organization, the CTC (Confederation of Cuban Workers) was recognized by the government and the Communist Lazaro Peña was put at its head. The Communist Party joined the Batista coalition which was fighting the *Auténticos*. The short period of 'neutrality' which resulted from the Stalin-Hitler Pact made little impact on Cuba because the country only joined the war in 1941 after Hitler's attack on Russia, at the side of the United States.

When Batista became President the Communist press was full of praise for this 'great democrat' who 'has the heart of a true representative of the people' and the 'great exponent of our national policy, the embodiment of Cuba's sacred ideals'. 'General Batista is leading the country along the road of dignity and progress'.[1] In 1944 Batista was defended against *Auténtico* attacks: 'While Chibás has been attacking and slandering the work of the President of the Republic since 1933 we Communists have co-operated closely first with Colonel Batista and then with the President of the Republic'.[2]

During the war two leading Communists—Juan Marinello and Carlos Rafael Rodríguez—became ministers in the Batista government. Collaboration became so close that Batista himself repeatedly stressed the loyalty of the Communists, as for example in the curious letter of recommendation which he addressed to Blas Roca, Secretary General of the Party, published in *Hoy* on June 13, 1944:

'My dear Blas,
'With reference to your letter transmitted to me by our mutual friend, Dr Carlos Rafael Rodríguez, Minister without Portfolio, I am glad to be able to confirm that my government has received and continues to receive effective and loyal support from the *Partido Socialista Popular*,[3] its leadership and its masses.'

It is hardly necessary to say that the Communists were at that time in favour of lasting friendship with the United States.[4]

[1] Quoted in Yves Guilbert: *Castro l'Infidèle*, Paris, 1957, p. 82, *et seq*.
[2] *Hoy*, Havana, June 13, 1944. Quoted in Yves Guilbert, *op. cit.*, p. 83.
[3] The name adopted by the Communists during the Second World War after the dissolution of the Communist International. Quoted in Yves Guilbert, *op. cit.*, p. 83.
[4] The 1943 edition of the theoretical 'text book' of Cuban communists, Blas

In the 1944 elections the Communists were again members of Batista's coalition, and as candidate for the Presidency, supported by Dr Carlos Saladrigas, a former *ABC* leader whom they had attacked as a 'Fascist' during the 'thirties. They had even suggested this candidate to Batista: 'If our Party is asked why it was the first to suggest Dr Carlos Saladrigas for the highest office, the Party's reply is simply that for a thousand reasons Saladrigas means the continuation of Fulgencio Batista's progressive, democratic and popular course'.[1]

When Grau was victorious the Communists tried, successfully, to maintain friendly relations with him as well. After one of Grau's speeches, *Hoy* (December 10, 1946) commented: 'Dr Grau has spoken for the people and the people will not desert him in his march towards national development, towards the consolidation of democracy and in his activity for the improvement of the conditions of the masses.'

In 1947 the situation changed. Anti-Communist tendencies gained the upper hand in the *Auténtico* party and the Communists were pushed out of the leadership of the unions. This put them into a difficult position. The 'cold war' was beginning and both Batista and the *Auténticos* took the side of the West.

In 1952, collaboration with Batista thus became impossible. (Some former leading Communists went over to him, perhaps with the agreement of the Party leadership). On May 23, 1952, Blas Roca wrote in *Hoy* that the new government which had emerged after the *coup d'état* 'does not differ in character from the Prío government'. On June 1, 1953, another party leader, Anibal Escalante, said that the new government had been formed to stop the growing struggle of the masses, to oppose the fight for peace and to restrain the struggle against imperialism.[2] We shall see that the Communist Party (PSP) was much less active in the fight against Batista than many other groups. But the picture even up to 1952 shows that the Communists in Cuba were unable to gain much sympathy, particularly among anti-Batista circles.

In fact, although the Communists exerted some influence on the organized workers and were able to maintain their leadership of the trade unions as long as they enjoyed official favour, the party was never very strong anywhere. They reached ten per cent of the vote in the congressional elections of 1946. In the presidential

---

Roca's *Fundamentos del Socialismo en Cuba*, contains the following passage: 'The Cuban people need and desire close and cordial relations with the United States because they will derive innumerable advantages from these. They must continue after the end of the war also because they are indispensable to the favourable development of the Cuban economy, on which the progress of the nation depends.' (p. 111.)

[1] *Hoy*, May 13, 1944.
[2] Alberto Flores, *op. cit.*, p. 300.

elections of 1948 their candidate received seven and a half per cent of the poll. In 1950 they elected 8 out of 136 members of Congress. As far as their *membership* was concerned, a distinction has to be drawn between party 'backers' or 'sympathizers' (*afiliados*) on the one hand and dues-paying members organized in party cells (*militantes*) on the other. According to Cuban electoral law as it then stood each party had every two years to undergo a 'reorganization'. On these occasions citizens were required to put their names down on lists as *afiliados* of a party. In 1946 there were 152,000 such *afiliados* of the *Partido Socialista Popular*. But the party leader Fabio Grobart wrote in the monthly party journal *Fundamentos* of December 1946 that only ten per cent of these were *militantes*.

2. Cuba's Economy and Society

(a) *Myths and Facts*
In order to understand Cuba's real problems and also to judge the results of the revolution it is necessary to correct some general misconceptions.

All statistics in Latin America are unreliable, and each of the figures below really requires further explanation. But they can nevertheless convey a first impression. (The Roman figures give the 'rank' of Cuba among the twenty Latin American states):

1. Annual income *per capita* (1956–1958),—353 (V)[1]
2. Persons *not* employed in agriculture, 58 per cent (III)[2]
3. Life expectancy at birth, 56–62 years (III/IV)[3]
4. Electricity consumption (kilowatt hours *per capita*), 256 (IV)[4]
5. Energy consumption (kilos of oil or equivalent *per capita*), 799 (II)[5]
6. Railways: about 1 mile for 4 square miles (I)[6]
7. Private cars: 1 private car for every 40 inhabitants (II)[4,7]
8. Telephones: 1 for every 38 inhabitants (IV)[4,7]
9. Radio sets: 1 for every 6·5 inhabitants (III)[4]
10. Television sets: 1 for every 25 inhabitants (I)[4]
11. Literate persons over 10 years, 76·4 per cent (IV)[2,7]

[1] *Revista del Banco National*, March 1959, Vol. V, No. 3. This figure fluctuates with the sugar harvest. The number given above is the average of three years—but it is probably much too low. This was shown recently by investigations of the Cuban national product made by an independent author, see Harry T. Oshima, *The National Income and Product of Cuba in 1953* in Food Research Institute Studies, Vol. II, No. 3, Stanford University, November 1961. Felipe Pazos, former president of Cuba's National Bank accepts the criticisms directed by Oshima against the Cuban statisticians and estimates the *gross* income per capita in 1957 at $554. In *Cambridge Opinion*, 32, February 1963.
[2] Republica de Cuba *Censo de Población, Vivienda y Electoral*. Informe General, Havana, 1953.
[3] *Boletin Económico de América Latina*, Santiago de Chile, Vol. VIII, No. 1.— Suplemento Estadistico. The rate of infant mortality as given in 1949 was only 37·6 per mil and would have placed Cuba at the top of Latin America. (UN Department of Economic and Social Affairs, Statistical Papers, Series A, Vol. XIV, No. 1–1962). But this seems to be not very reliable. The same may be said with respect to the death rate of 4 per mil as mentioned in UNESCO *Social Aspects of Economic Development in Latin America*, Vol. I, Paris 1963, Tables pp. 83 and 84.
[4] UN Statistical Yearbook, 1959.
[5] UN Department of Economic and Social Affairs, *Energy in Latin America*, Geneva, 1957.
[6] US Department of Commerce, *Investment in Cuba*, 1956. Two-thirds of the railways are private railways of the sugar mills. Few countries are better served by railways than is Cuba. *op. cit.*, p. 107.
[7] Especially during the last seven years before the revolution.

12. Newsprints: 5 kilos per 1,000 inhabitants (III)[1]
13. University students: 4 per 1,000 inhabitants (III)[1]
14. Doctors: 1 per 1,000 inhabitants (IV)

As early as 1949 one expert noted that in relation to its population Cuba was more highly capitalized than any other Latin American country,[2] and another calculated that a higher percentage of the Cuban population had been brought into the money economy than in any other Latin American country.[3] Reverend Roger Vekemans and J. L. Segundo, in *Essay on a Socio-economic typology of the Latin American Countries*,[4] while seriously underestimating Cuban *per capita* income, still class Cuba as the fourth country of Latin America with respect to general economic and social development.

Cuba was therefore not underdeveloped in the same sense as most Asian and African countries. On the whole it compared favourably with Spain and living conditions in Cuba were better than in many Iron Curtain countries, as appears from a statement made by Guevara after a visit; 'This does not mean at all that we saw nothing but marvels in the [Eastern] countries. Naturally there are things that for a Cuban living in the twentieth century, with all the comforts that imperialism has accustomed us to surround ourselves with in the cities, might seem uncivilized.'[5]

It is true that even in 1955–1957 the country depended mainly on sugar. Although the income generated in the whole sugar sector (i.e., wages and salaries, profits of planters, producers and traders, rents of plantations) fell slowly as a percentage of the national income, to less than 25 per cent in the last two years before the revolution, sugar was responsible for about 80 per cent of all exports. But most of the facts mentioned below indicate that a certain diversification of the economy had taken place.

In 1950 only 22 per cent of rice consumed in Cuba was produced at home. In 1956–1958 the proportion had risen to 55·6 per cent.[6] Before the Second World War almost all the maize and black beans had been imported. At the end of the 'fifties the country produced nearly its total consumption.[7] Potato production grew from 125 million pounds in 1946 to over 200 million pounds in 1957,

[1] UNESCO, *Basic Facts and Figures*, Paris, 1961.
[2] H. C. Wallich, *Monetary Problems of an Export Economy: Cuban Experience 1914–1947*, Harvard University Press, 1950, p. 6.
[3] William Anderson in *Foreign Agriculture*, US Department of Agriculture, Washington, March 1961.
[4] UNESCO, *Social Aspects of Economic development in Latin America*, Paris, 1963, p. 67 ff.
[5] Ernesto (Ché) Guevara, *Obra Revolucionaria*, No. 2, Havana, January 6, 1961, p. 13.
[6] Antonio Núñez Jiménez, *Geografía de Cuba*, Havana, 1959, pp. 230–1.
[7] Rudolfo Arango, *Política Agraria*, Havana, 1958, pp. 17, 19.

and coffee production from 53·4 million pounds to 79·6 million.[1]
In 1946 there were about 4 million cattle; by 1957–1958 the number had increased to 6 million.[2] In 1950 Cuban hens produced 50 million eggs, in 1958 315 million.[3] Between 1949 and 1957 agricultural production for the home market increased at the rate of about 3·7 per cent per annum.[4]

Industry: From 1946–47 to 1957–58 cement production increased by 150 per cent.[5] In 1948 59,000 car tyres were produced; in 1958 the number had risen to 265,000.[6] Domestic shoe production covered more than 90 per cent of home demand.[7] The production of condensed milk and soft drinks was rising continuously. The development of the textile industry is illustrated by two figures: in 1924–1928 14·2 per cent of all Cuban imports were textiles; in 1957–1958 the figure was 2·7 per cent.[8]

A special index of industrial production, *excluding* the sugar sector, prepared by the Cuban National Bank reads as follows:

1947	81·8
1953	100·0
1958	120·1[9]

Some figures on the composition of Cuban imports are also of interest: in 1924–1928 41·5 per cent of all imports were foodstuffs; in 1949 the proportion had fallen to 26·2 per cent. and in 1956–1957 to 21·7 per cent. The import of 'fixed' capital goods on the other hand continued to grow: in 1949 it was 52·6 per cent of all imports, and in 1958–1960 60·9 per cent.[10]

Nevertheless far greater diversification could have been achieved and the country was developing much too slowly—particularly because from 1943 to 1953 the population had grown at the average rate of 2·3 per cent a year.

In the West (and probably also in Japan) the beginning of industrialization meant greater poverty for the masses, at least to the

---

[1] *Informe Técnico-Económico sobre la Reforma Agraria*, Havana, 1959, Instituto Nacional de Reforma Económica (in manuscript form).
[2] Antonio Nuñez Jiménez, *op. cit.* This estimate was probably on the optimistic side. American sources estimate the number of cattle at 4·4 million on the average for the years 1951–1955 and at 5·7 million in 1958. (*Foreign Crops and Markets*, US Department of Agriculture, Washington World Summaries, April 27, 1961.
[3] *Cuba Económica y Financiera*, Havana, May 1960.
[4] *U.N. Economic Survey of Latin America*, 1957.
[5] *Cuba Económica y Financiera*, February 1960.
[6] *ibid.*
[7] Antonio Nuñez Jiménez, *op. cit.*, p. 346.
[8] Foreign Policy Association: *Problems of the New Cuba*, New York, 1935, and *Revista del Banco Nacional*, July/October, 1959 (Vol. V, No. 7–10).
[9] *Informe del Ministro de Hacienda del Gobierno Revolucionario al Consejo de Ministros*, Havana, September 1959 (*Ministro de Hacienda*).
[10] 'Problems of the New Cuba,' *U.N. Economic Survey of Latin America*, 1975, and *Revista del Banco Nacional*, June 1959, Vol. V, No. 6.

extent that the rich were getting richer, while the majority of the poor did not benefit from the growing national income. In Cuba it was different: the lower classes shared, though to an insufficient extent, in the gradual improvement in living standards.

In 1950 an International Bank mission pointed out that 'living levels of the farmers, agricultural labourers, industrial workers, storekeepers and others, are higher all along the line than for corresponding groups in other tropical countries and in nearly all other Latin American countries. This does not mean that there is no dire poverty in Cuba, but simply that in comparative terms Cubans are better off, on the average, than the people of these other areas.'[1]

After Castro's victory an official booklet of the 26th July Movement was published under the title *Political, Economic and Social Thought of Fidel Castro*. Castro himself, as the introduction pointed out, had approved every section of the book, which said among other things: 'Since 1933 Cuban distributive policy has, as the result of wage increases, the introduction of the eight-hour day, paid holidays, social insurance etc brought about a juster distribution of the national income. Before it used to flow into the pockets of the few, now it reaches the hands of many.'[2]

In a speech to sugar workers in spring 1961 Guevara said that the Cuban people had lived in a state of colonial dependence, but had nevertheless been much better off than many other peoples.[3]

Asked in December 1960 whether it was true that the revolutionary government intended to confiscate all bank accounts of over 10,000 pesos, Castro denied it (only to do it after all in August 1961). On this occasion he said: 'Ten thousand pesos is not much. Such a sum represents the normal savings of a working man, which he uses at the end of his working life to build himself a house.'[4]

The Communist leader Anibal Escalante attacked the erroneous theory that revolution was only possible in countries where the misery of the masses was great: 'In reality Cuba is ... one of the [Latin American] countries where the standard of the masses was particularly high ... If the above mentioned theory were correct there would first have been revolutions in Haiti, Colombia, or even Chile, countries where the masses were poorer than in Cuba in 1952 or 1958.'[5]

In general urban workers were better off than most agricultural workers, and the latter were better off than the vast number of unemployed.

[1] International Bank, *Report on Cuba*, Washington, 1951, pp. 39–40.
[2] English edition, *Political, Economic and Social Thought of Fidel Castro*, Editorial Lex, Havana, 1959, p. 153.
[3] *Bohemia*, Havana, April 9, 1961.
[4] *Obra Revolucionaria*, No. 2, January 2, 1961. One Cuban peso was equal to one US dollar.
[5] *Verde Olivo*, July 30, 1961.

A remarkably high share of the national income, about 60 per cent, went to wage and salary earners, among whom there were enormous differences in income.[1] While the majority of wage and salary earners received less than 75 pesos a month there were many workers whose wages exceeded 250 pesos and even 300 pesos. It is impossible, and would be misleading, to work out an average wage. The basic daily wage of agricultural sugar workers was tied to the price of sugar and that of seasonal workers fluctuated with the number of days worked in the year.

In addition there were legally fixed supplements: 9·9 per cent of the basic wage because although the working week was 44 hours payment was made for 48 hours; and another supplement of 9·9 per cent for four weeks' paid holiday a year, which the employer paid in monthly instalments. In addition every worker had the right to nine days' sick leave with pay. Most employers also paid a Christmas bonus of half the monthly wage. Overtime was paid at higher rates (150 per cent or more of the normal hourly rate). Taxes were low: on a monthly income of 250 pesos they amounted to about 3 per cent, and with all other payments, including trade union contributions, they came to approximately 6 per cent.

In 1953 over two-thirds of the 750,000 people working in agriculture were farm labourers. Most of them were seasonal workers who were badly off because the sugar harvest lasts barely four months. A third of the seasonal sugar harvest workers was, however, employed from October to December on the coffee harvest. On the whole the families of seasonal workers lived very badly, although it must be borne in mind that in many cases more than one member of the family was earning and that there were various extra sources of income.[2]

The majority of the peasants were tenants or share-croppers. From the 1930's on their lot improved: the tenants got security of tenure and rents were fixed at a low level.

'At the time Fidel Castro took power, all the tenant farmers in Cuba were already assured of a security of tenure of their land for which they paid also very low rents. It appears ... that the Cuban tenant farmer had many of the rights which are normally associated with full ownership of land but without the obligations which are usually involved. Conversely, the Cuban system did not encourage the tenant farmer to make long-term plans to expand output and improve the soil.'[3]

---

[1] 'In Cuba with its relatively small number of industrial workers and its many unemployed and underemployed this high share in the national income can only be a sign of great differences, within the working class.' (Gustavo Gutiérrez, *El Desarrollo Económico de Cuba*, Havana, 1952, p. 60.)

[2] Revolutionary sources put the average income of seasonal workers in the sugar industry at 300 pesos. (Ed. Santos Rios in *Revolución*, August 28, 1961). But their actual income was probably considerably higher.

[3] *Cuba and the Rule of Law*, International Commission of Jurists, Geneva, 1962, p. 15.

In 1937 the sugar growing tenants—about 65,000 in 1958—were granted the Right of Permanence, i.e. of permanent possession of their plots, provided they filled a legally fixed quota of sugar-cane and paid a rent of 5 per cent of the annual product. They were even entitled to inherit, sell, and mortgage their plots. In 1950 this protection was broadened: the grower could no longer be expelled even if he failed to pay any rent for the land planted with sugar-cane. In 1952 the Right of Permanence was extended to all small tenants with plots up to 165 acres—including the 'squatters' i.e. those who had no legal title to the plot. 'The classic and dramatic dispossessions of farmers prior to 1937 were completely eliminated from rural Cuba from that year on. There were no more dispossessed sugar-cane growers, so that when Fidel Castro came to power the great private properties were more juridical properties than real ones. For example: the company named Atlantica del Golfo which owned 10,000 *caballerias*, only answered for, and had under cultivation, 300. The Tánamo Sugar Mills owned 3,000 and could cultivate only 100 (I cite these cases because I know them first-hand).'[1] The rents were in general fixed at 5 per cent of the land value as inscribed in the Municipal Land Register—which was usually less than the 'real' value. For these reasons there was, after 1937, no longer any violent unrest in the countrywide; the great majority of the peasants did not take part in the struggle against Batista after 1952.

An expert who visited Cuba at the end of the 'forties found that the situation of the share-croppers working on tobacco farms was not bad. In general he noted with surprise that the agricultural population was 'remarkably satisfied with its situation ... Paradoxically, discontent was greatest in those areas where living conditions were best.'[2] The most important demands listed by him in order of frequency were for roads, irrigation, schools, better houses and better tools. The demand for ownership of land came only sixth and the request for better hygienic conditions seventh.[3]

In spite of all this the majority of the agricultural population lived in extremely poor conditions, a part of it close to starvation level. This was not only due to the plight of the seasonal workers. In some sections of the country, especially the mountains, the protective laws remained a dead letter.[4] The average peasant lacked knowledge, credit, adequate instruments and tools. He was usually in debt to local traders and was exploited by middlemen.[5] There was still in

[1] T. Casuso, *Cuba and Castro*, New York, 1961, p. 197.
[2] Lowry Nelson, *Rural Cuba*, University of Minnesota Press, 1950, p. 205.
[3] *ibid.*, p. 249.
[4] *See* Wyatt MacGaffey and Clifford R. Barnett, *Cuba: Its People, Its Society, Its Culture*, published under the auspices of the American University, New Haven, 1962, p. 43. This book is a mine of information, although the authors seem to have drawn an all too pessimistic picture of the pre-revolutionary Cuba.
[5] In extreme cases, for example tomatoes, the consumer paid twenty-eight times as much as was received by the producer. The urban consumer had to

1958 a shortage of roads, of schools, of doctors, of piped water. Housing conditions were very poor: according to the official census of 1953, 75 per cent of all rural dwellings had no other floors but the naked earth, 80·9 per cent had no electric light, 85 per cent no running water and 54·1 per cent no lavatory.

American business interests were still playing an important part in Cuba's economic life. The Americans controlled the electricity supplies, the telephone system, the big oil refineries, parts of the mining industry—primarily nickel (in which Cuba is particularly rich) and manganese—tyre production, one of the three cement factories, some of the big banks, etc.

But the last twenty-five years had seen many changes. Wholesale trade was 'Cubanized' if only because most resident Spaniards adopted Cuban nationality. Important Cuban firms were set up, the railways became Cuban-owned. Many of the banks belonged to Cubans even if they had English names: in 1958 there were 156 insurance companies, 76 of which were owned by Cubans.[1] In 1939 only 56 sugar factories had been in Cuban hands, producing 22·4 per cent of the country's sugar: the corresponding figures for 1958 were 121 (out of 161) and 62·1 per cent.[2] In 1933, American companies still owned 5·7 million acres of sugar plantations: by 1958 it was only 1·9 million.[3] In 1957, American capital invested in Cuban industry and public utilities amounted to $879 million,[4] but a symposium on Cuba's resources, held in 1958, estimated the total capital employed in the country's industry and trade at over $3,000 million. Cubans continued to play an increasingly greater rôle in all branches of the economy. Some of the American companies' shares were also owned by Cubans: early in 1960 for example the revolutionary 'Ministry for the Recovery of Embezzled Property' justified the confiscation of one of the biggest 'American' sugar companies by saying that it had been discovered that the majority of the share holders were Cubans.[5]

(b) *Problems of the Cuban Economy*

Cuba was 'underdeveloped' to the extent that it failed to exploit its resources, and remained a poor nation on a rich soil. Progress could have been quick, but the country was always on the point of stagnation.

In fact Cuba had enough fertile land. About 30 per cent of the

---

pay 30 pesos for 100 pineapples for which the rural producer got only 3·12 pesos (INRE, *Carta publica Semanal*, No. 88, Havana, 1959).
[1] *Revista del Banco Nacional*, April 1959.
[2] *Anuario Azucarero 1959*, Havana, 1960.
[3] *Problems of the New Cuba*, 1935, and *Anuario Azucarero*, 1960.
[4] US Department of Commerce, *US Business Investments in Foreign Countries*, Washington, 1960.
[5] *Revolución*, March 12, 1960.

available land was not exploited,[1] and a large part of the cultivated area could have been more productively used.

Cuba had enough labour. We shall see later that in 'normal years' about one-quarter of the labour force was permanently unemployed, excluding 'disguised' unemployment.

Cuba also had substantial capital resources: every year 12 to 16 per cent of the national income was not consumed and was thus available for productive investment.[2] According to the calculations of an expert such an investment would have permitted an annual rate of growth of 4 per cent even without any capital imports.[3]

There was no reason why Cubans could not have acquired the managerial and technical skills required by modern development, but only a minority did acquire them. The less well-off did not find it easy to get educated and for the others it seemed more profitable to study law or education in order to obtain positions of higher status, if possible, government positions.

What were the reasons for this particular kind of backwardness? The main cause was that on the world market this small island was at the mercy of external forces. Its soil and climate made it particularly suitable for the production of sugar. The absence of many industrial raw materials and sources of energy—neither coal, oil, nor exploitable water power—the original lack of capital and of entrepreneurs, and the restricted size of the domestic market hindered industrial development. Most important, however, Cuba lay close to a highly developed country with a demand for sugar, wanting to export its industrial products and with plenty of capital.

During the period of liberalism Cuba thus became a sugar plantation, and later under protectionism all the advantages of such specialization turned into disadvantages. A doubtful blessing became an undoubted curse: as a result of quota restrictions on sugar production land was condemned to lie fallow and workers to unemployment.

Concentration on sugar prevented a diversification of the economy and preferential customs agreements with the United States tied Cuba to its northern neighbour. Those in Cuba who wanted to invest their money 'safely' invested it in sugar, with the result that a vicious circle developed: when sugar prices were high all money was invested in sugar, and when they were low, no money could be found for other investments.

---

[1] INRA, *Informe Técnico Económico*, 1959.
[2] In 1949, the International Bank mission estimated the percentage at 12 per cent. (*Report on Cuba*, p. 73.) Since then it has increased considerably.
[3] Felipe Pazos, 'Dificultades y Posibilidades de una Política de Industrialización en Cuba', *Humanismo*, Mexico, October 24, 1934.

Concentration on sugar encouraged idleness,[1] and the dependence of the economy on unpredictable fluctuations of the world market[2] produced a 'lottery' mentality. The well-being of the individual seemed to depend more on luck than on his own efforts, more on accident than on rational planning.

The country was tied to a seasonal industry whose cycle coincided with those of other industries, such as tourism or the tobacco industry. As a result the entire economy was subject to enormous fluctuations and there was a 'fantastic waste of factors of production',[3] since power stations, railways and other costly installations remained idle for long periods every year.

Concentration on sugar and dependence on the most important market, the United States, made Cuba dependent to an extraordinary degree on exports and imports.[4] The proximity of American manufacturers and the preferential tariffs which they enjoyed hampered the development of local industry, and many foodstuffs, which could have been grown at home, were imported.

Cuban agriculture, like that of most of Latin America, was characterized by big 'concentrations', the presence of landless masses and by *latifundia*.[5] *Latifundia*—mostly dedicated to cattle raising—existed as early as the eighteenth century, although their relative importance as compared to that of small and middle farmers is still a subject of debate. One of the experts writes: 'Cuba has never known an agricultural system based on small peasant farmers ... It has always been a land of *latifundia* and its agriculture has suffered from a shortage of credit'.[6] This was before sugar became king.

But the development of the modern sugar industry encouraged

[1] 'From the point of view of agricultural techniques sugar is particularly easy to grow and requires only a minimum of knowledge and work. Anybody can grow sugar.' Ramiro Guerra y Sánchez, *La Industria Azucarera de Cuba*, Havana, 1940, pp. 27, 28. Almost everywhere in the country, sugar can be grown without artificial irrigation or fertilizers. Cuba, with a much lower productivity per acre than its competitors, can produce sugar much more cheaply.

[2] Examples of quantity fluctuations: in 1923 production was 3·6 million Spanish tons; in 1925, 5·2 million; in 1928, 4 million; in 1932, 3 million; in 1952, 7 million and in 1954, 4·7 million.
Price fluctuations: 1920, 11·95 cents per pound; 1937, 1·76 cents; 1953-1958, 5 cents on the American market and 4¼ cents on the free world market. In 1952 the sugar harvest peroid (*zafra*) lasted 130 days, in 1955, only 76 days.

[3] Julián Akienis y Urosa, *Caracteristicas Fundamentales de la Economia Cubana*, Havana, 1950, p. 129.

[4] 'The importance of exports is striking, even for a small country ... the averate ratio of Cuban imports to national income appears to be among the highest in the world.' (International Bank, *Report on Cuba*, pp. 723 and 726.)

[5] According to the 1945-1946 census 1½ per cent of all landowners owned 46 per cent of the land under cultivation. Half of one per cent of all holdings (894) were bigger than 2,500 acres each and owned 36 per cent of the land. 84 per cent (135,000) were smaller than 125 acres and owned over 20 per cent of the land. In holdings over 2,500 acres only 10 per cent of the land was used as compared with 40 per cent in those of under 25 acres.

[6] Alberto Arredondo, *Cuba: Tierra Indefensa*, Havana, 1945, p. 230.

the growth of new big estates.[1] The industry is relatively concentrated (in the nineteenth century there were at times as many as 2,000 sugar mills: the number fell to 161 in 1958). The size of the sugar estates surrounding the mills grew and every establishment tried to own as much land as possible and to control as many sugar planters as possible. Railways were built for this purpose—most Cuban railways are private sugar railways—and the size of 'dependent' territories increased when steel rails were introduced. In order to restrict competition, to protect tenant farmers and to strengthen the country's position on the world market the entire industry was put under state control, and a Cuban Sugar Institute established. It decided every year how much should be produced, how much land should be used for the purpose and what prices, rents and wages should be. When quota restrictions were introduced a substantial area remained unused as 'potential reserve' and part of the sugar remained unharvested. In fact, the sugar requirements of the whole world could be grown on about a third of the land used for the purpose.

In addition to sugar estates there were cattle ranches which were even less productive. There was only one farmworker for every 1,600 acres, one head of cattle for every $2\frac{1}{2}$–$4\frac{1}{2}$ acres and cows produced a daily average of only 5 to 7 pints of milk.

Cuban *latifundia* were not, however, feudal in character. They had nothing in common with the big, almost self-sufficient *haciendas* of the other Latin American countries which hardly come into the money economy and are worked by serf-like peasants. The big Cuban estates worked mainly on a capitalist basis and employed paid labourers. Concentration of land ownership as well as extensive cultivation, unproductive from the point of view of the economy as a whole, were from the point of view of the private owner often entirely rational. In a country where land is cheaper than labour, and labour cheaper than capital there always exists a tendency towards *extensive* agriculture. It would have been unprofitable for the landowners to borrow large sums at high interest rates and to use them for machines, irrigation, etc., in order to compete on a narrow domestic market with fairly cheap imported products. But the result was that large areas were unproductively used, that large parts of the labour force remained unemployed or underemployed, that the peasants were tied to the land and that the low purchasing power

---

[1] The classic account of the development of sugar estates is found in Ramiro Guerra y Sánchez, *Azúcar y Población en las Antillas*, Havana, 1953. It refers mainly to Cuba, but deals also with the other islands. Against Guerra later critics maintain that even sugar *latifundia* had existed already in the nineteenth century and that Cuban agriculture was never characterized by considerable numbers of free and independent peasants. (Gerardo Brown-Castillo, *Cuba Colonial*, Havana, 1952, pp. 32 ff.)

of the agricultural population prevented the development of national industries.

The workers' main interest was to keep their jobs and they were opposed to any 'rationalization', which in turn made capital investment difficult.[1] While the workers with the help of various governments obtained the advantages of a welfare state which threatened all profits, the employers exerted successful pressure on the government to obtain tax reliefs, subsidies and protection. Many capitalists preferred to live in luxury, to keep their money liquid, to put a large part of such money as they did invest into land or into building flats—particularly for the rich and the middle classes—or to export their capital. It is a remarkable fact that in the mid-'fifties Cuban investments in the United States alone were estimated to amount to more than $312 million.[2]

In the last resort the distortion of the Cuban economy was due to the free play of world market forces. The necessary structural changes could be made only through government planning. But the Cuban state was hardly fitted to play this rôle. It was short both of revenue and of qualified officials, and it spared little thought to the long-term interests of the community.

Revenue was insufficient because taxes were lower than in the developed countries,[3] because there was the normal amount of tax-evasion and because a substantial proportion of public revenue was lost through corruption. The funds available were used irrationally. Too much was spent on expensive and unproductive projects, and a frighteningly high proportion of the budget—about 80 per cent in 1950[4]—was used to pay officials and holders of sinecures. In 1950 according to official figures, no less than 186,000 officials, about 11 per cent of the working population, were employed by the central government *and* the provincial and municipal administrations.[5]

To create government jobs thus became an important occupation for politicians. More-or-less parasitical officials, without qualifications, lived in a permanent state of insecurity because they were afraid of losing their positions whenever there was a change of

---

[1] 'The attitudes of both labor and capital, which are blocking development seem to be the effect of more basic causes—stagnation and instability—which in turn are the result of the excessive predominance of sugar and of the great difficulties which the sugar economy has undergone since 1925.' *Report on Cuba*, p. 528.

[2] *Investment in Cuba*, p. 15.

[3] In 1949/50 the average Cuban paid 15 per cent of his income in various forms of taxes; the comparable figure for the United States was 23·4 per cent and for the United Kingdom, 35 per cent. Direct taxes in Cuba amounted to only 21·5 per cent of the total revenue, as compared with 45·7 per cent in the United Kingdom and 51·7 per cent in the United States. *Report on Cuba*, pp. 666 and 669.

[4] *ibid.*, p. 683.

[5] *ibid.*, p. 453. The authors of the report describe government as the country's 'second largest industry'.

CUBA'S ECONOMY AND SOCIETY

government. This, together with totally inadequate salaries, forced them to have several jobs and to rely on corruption.

The government itself consisted of politicians most of whom put their own material interests first and who were subject to pressure from various groups. The classes who controlled the economy were opposed to any real reforms and had close ties with American interests; they were supported by the trade unions, the attention of whose members was focused on their short-term special interests.

Under pressure from various forces a strange 'welfare state' had developed in Cuba which exercised considerable control over the economy—without encouraging development. In view of the general position of the country *rapid* economic progress was hardly possible. It was astonishing that even the existing low rate of development was attained.

(c) *Individual and Society in Cuba*

Compared with other Latin American countries Cuban society was relatively homogeneous, which was partly due to the smallness of the country and its topography. There were no distant inaccessible regions, no linguistic diversity; no oppressed minorities.

There were no more Indians. Black and white Cubans shared the same institutions, values and ideas. Negroes—according to official figures only 12½ per cent of the population were negroes and 14½ per cent mulattos, although in reality the number of coloured people was much greater—were poorer than whites, and 'better class' private schools, fashionable clubs and bathing pools were closed to those whose skin was too dark. But officially there was no discrimination, and in many important spheres of life it really did not exist. For more than twenty years all jobs had been open to coloured people. They used the same cafés and the same means of transport as white people. They could attend public schools, universities, and places of entertainment and could become government officials. Some negroes penetrated into the upper classes. A leading general in the war of liberation was a negro, as was one of the presidents of the senate. In 1949 negroes commanded the army (General Querejeta) and the police (General Hernández Nardo). There were black members of parliament and ministers and one of the country's leading journalists, the very 'reactionary' engineer Gaston Baquero, who wrote leading articles for the conservative *Diario de la Marina*, was a negro. Batista himself, as already mentioned, was a mulatto.

It is true that there were differences between town and country, particularly between modern Greater Havana, with its 1·3 million inhabitants, and poor villages and settlements far from the main roads. But the vast majority of the population formed one nation and lacked all the taboos and traditions which in many underdeveloped countries stand in the way of modern development. In

Cuba there were no 'sacred cows', no 'ancestral tombs', no self-sufficient tribal or village communities.

Attitudes which can be described as 'pre-capitalist' were the result of the prevailing conditions and not of past tradition, as for example the 'idleness' to which reference has already been made, and the 'lottery' mentality.

As far as it is possible to generalize about national characteristics one can say that the average Cuban is extremely gay, friendly, unresentful, individualist, emotionally uncontrolled, and lives entirely in the present. Here as elsewhere the lower classes were more inclined towards superstition than towards 'faith', so that for the mass of the people religion was not very important. Since the disestablishment of the church the clergy had to be paid by the faithful, with the result that their power was considerably curtailed. There was only one priest for every 9 or 10 thousand Cubans and only the urban upper and middle classes, particularly the women, were regular churchgoers. Large numbers of rural marriages were solemnized without a priest—and often also without a civil ceremony—which had no unpleasant consequences as illegitimate and legitimate children had the same status. Patriarchal authority was not strongly developed in the family, with the result that there was little sexual repression, particularly among boys, who generally enjoyed great sexual freedom at an early age. All this resulted in the absence of any feelings of guilt and the lack of such feelings can prove an obstacle to the establishment of totalitarianism.[1]

The interest of the individual came before the interest of the community. In so far as feelings of loyalty and obligation existed they were concentrated on family and friends. This attitude corresponded to the economic interests of the individual: within an economy which offered little security, family relationships and the network of 'friendships'—particularly with influential people—served as protective armour.

The most recent social statistics were collected in 1953 and are, it must be stressed once more, not altogether reliable. At that time about 40 per cent of the population lived in towns of over 10,000 inhabitants. About 42 per cent of the economically active population was engaged in agriculture, some 20 per cent in services, less than 18 per cent in industry (including mining and building), 12 per cent in trade, the rest in transport, gas-water-electricity supply and free professions.

Another set of figures is more important: In 1957 the National Economic Council carried out an investigation into 'employment, underemployment and unemployment in Cuba'. It showed that

[1] The importance of feelings of guilt in this connection is admirably described in Robert J. Lifton's *Thought Reform—A Study of Brainwashing in China*, London, 1961.

out of a working population of 2·2 million (53 per cent of the population over 14 years of age) 16·4 per cent were chronically unemployed, 6·1 per cent were underemployed and 7 per cent worked for their families without remuneration.

Sixty per cent of those who worked a 40-hour week or more earned less than the minimum wage of 75 pesos (£27 approx.) a month and were therefore underpaid.[1] Only 35 to 38 per cent of all working Cubans received more than the bare minimum. About a quarter to one-fifth of the population were 'well-off', which included members of the upper classes, members of the liberal professionals, middle grade officials and salary earners and petty bourgeois—owners of restaurants, hotels, cafés, shops, petrol stations, and the workers' aristocracy. Some Latin American sociologists asserted that Cuba had a strong 'middle class'[2] but this is a highly ambiguous concept, especially since these authors include the better-paid proletariat in the 'middle-class'. But it is undoubtedly true that in Cuba 'the middle income group was among the largest in Latin America'.[3] This could be confirmed by anybody who walked with open eyes through the better quarters of the cities and saw the new middle-class suburbs which were shooting up like mushrooms.

The 'upper class' was no feudal oligarchy: it was based on wealth rather than status and, although to a big extent based on landownership, it was essentially a 'capitalist' class, where landowners mixed with factory owners, bankers, big traders, merchants, highly paid members of the professions and, last but not least, rich politicians. During the last decades a stratum of modern entrepreneurs and managers began to develop—although they still formed a minority inside the upper class. It was hardly possible to distinguish a *comprador* bourgeoisie, closely linked with foreign capital, from a 'national' bourgeoisie interested in the development of the home market and in economic independence. Some protective tariffs had made possible the rise of an independent, if numerically small, national class of entrepreneurs which profited from close links with American interests. This explains why anti-imperialist tendencies in the upper and middle classes were weaker in the 'fifties than they had been a generation before, even though there was considerable anti-*Yanqui* feeling among the educated and even though the students were the upholders of an anti-imperialist nationalism which, however, hardly affected the lower classes.

[1] *Consejo Nacional de Economía*, Havana, 1958; the Cuban peso was equal to the American dollar.
[2] Some of the Latin American authors maintain that the middle class in Cuba made up 33 per cent of the population (A. Diaz, 'Notas sobre la Clase Media de Ecuador', in *Política*, Caracas, No. 17, August–September, 1961. Others consider the Cuban upper and middle class as having, together, made up 22 per cent of the population (*see Cambridge Opinion*, p. 34, Table 3).
[3] Wyatt MacGaffey and Clifford R. Barnett, *Cuba*, p. 60.

Two characteristics of the Cuban economy and society which do not emerge from statistics seem to the author of great importance. They can only be described as 'rootlessness' and 'parasitism'.

More than most other Latin American countries Cuba lacks 'rooted' classes, land-loving peasants and tradition-bound urban artisans. Cuba has never been a peasant country. 'Cuban agriculturists are not subsistence farmers, except for a small minority. This is another very significant way in which Cuba differs from most of the so-called 'underdeveloped' countries.'[1]

Nor could a class of skilled craftsmen have developed. Strong historical traditions were lacking, partly because over a quarter of the population consisted of or were descended from, people who had come to the country only in the twentieth century. There was an absence of cohesive local and regional communities, as well as a lack of security of work and there were no firmly anchored political institutions.

Cuban society was, furthermore, to a certain extent parasitical: not only did a substantial percentage of the population do no work and have to be kept by those who did, but a remarkably large part of the national income came from activities which can hardly be regarded as 'productive' or 'socially necessary'. The wealth of the upper classes was largely derived from ground rents, excessive profits, tax evasion, usury and all kinds of corruption. Part of the income of the middle classes came from similar sources—from sinecures and lottery transactions. A large part of the labour force was engaged in underproductive agriculture. In relation to the size of the population there were 50 per cent more people employed in commerce and twice as many lawyers and (mostly underemployed) teachers than in the developed countries. Distribution was more strongly developed than production. The government machine was inflated. In economic life such activities as advertising assumed amazing dimensions: large sums and vast numbers of people were used, with the aid of dozens of radio stations, six television channels and many subsidized newspapers, to praise products which for the most part were imported. Domestic servants abounded. 'Featherbedding' was endemic in both public and private offices. Urban workers fought with such slogans as 'security of work'[2] and 'more pay for less work', and many of the members of the working class were able to procure various kinds of additional income. In Havana (one of the world's most expensive harbours) two dock workers were employed on every one-man job, and some ships were unloaded only in the evenings when overtime had to be paid. Bus drivers and conductors kept a substantial part of the fares.

[1] *Report on Cuba*, p. 44.
[2] It has been said ironically that it was easier and cheaper to get a divorce in Cuba than to dismiss a worker.

In conclusion I should like to quote from an author who knows both countries, a comparison of Cuba and Mexico:

'Instead of being reticent, quiet and melancholy, the Cuban people are gay, noisy, full of song and laughter, bubbling over with enthusiasm and the love of life and immersed in the present ... Having no Indian background, [Cuba] lacks Mexico's basis for traditional nationalism. The nationalism at the moment [1960—Author] is intellectually inspired and can only acquire popular support by constant propaganda—and may falter even then ... There is no tradition of communal land-holding in Cuba, no tradition of individual land-holding by the mass of the people, either as villagers collectively or as individuals. The elements that made and make Mexico an agrarian nation do not exist in Cuba ... The urban population of Mexico in 1910 was somewhere between 10 and 15 per cent of the total. Mexico was rural and lived by what it produced. The Mexican revolution was essentially a revolution of rural folk who wanted the land that had been taken from them ... The situation in Cuba is very different. The urban population is somewhere between 50 and 60 per cent of the total. The city folk have been fed from outside, have the standard of living, the outlook and attitudes of urban peoples the world over ... All of our social revolutions have been in agricultural countries ... The Cuban upheaval is an attempted social revolution in an urban society, for the sugar plantation is more like a factory than a farm.'[1]

(d) Reform or Revolution
A former member of the International Bank Mission and a joint author of the *Report on Cuba*, wrote in 1954. 'Cuba though developed enough to be in our "intermediate" rather than the "underdeveloped" group stays dead on center ... Though it has ample resources and opportunities it is caught in a vicious circle. It could find its way out if somehow improvement could be brought about in the organizing factors—government, business leadership, labor leadership—and if there could be a stronger sense of social cohesiveness and civic responsibility throughout the community.'[2]

In Marxist terms, this means that in Cuba there was a conflict between productive forces and the 'conditions of production', even if this was a conflict whose character had nothing in common with the one Marx had in mind. Cuba did not have too much, but too little, capitalism.

As we have seen, some progress had been made and the possi-

[1] Frank Tannenbaum, 'The Mexican and Cuban Revolution'. 29th Annual Couchiching Conference, August 1960, in *The Latin Americas*, Canadian Institute of Public Affairs, University of Toronto Press.
[2] Eugene Staley, *The Future of Underdeveloped Countries*, New York, London, 1954, pp. 209–210.

bility of peaceful evolution existed. This evolution would undoubtedly have demanded a bitter struggle, it would have taken a long time and would have needed the preservation and development of democracy as prerequisites. Batista's dictatorship had destroyed the forms of democracy. A democratic revolution against the dictator might easily have developed into a social revolution especially if it were to be led by radical intellectuals. Such a 'radical' revolution might, however, have assumed many forms, including those of totalitarianism. This was all the likelier because young, intellectual revolutionary leaders have little patience, because Latin American politicians do not know the spirit of compromise, and because Communist countries then appeared to offer the only formula for developing a country quickly. The revolution would take place under the banner of radical democracy, social justice, and—inevitably—nationalism and anti-imperialism. Because the Cuban upper classes had such close connections with America, anti-imperialism was bound to have an anti-capitalist core. As this revolution would fall into the period of the 'cold war' an eastern breeze would fill its sails ...

(e) *Yankee Imperialism as the Scapegoat*

'The normal process of capitalist development in Cuba was interrupted by the intervention of American imperialism ... At the end of the last century the Cuban economy had been pre-capitalist. Capitalism produces its own propelling force and one might therefore have expected that Cuba would prove no exception, and that it was destined to develop evenly according to the example of Western capitalism. This was prevented by imperialism.'[1]

These words were written by a theoretician of the Cuban revolution, who expresses a widely held view that is, however, fundamentally wrong. It is a fallacy that there are, or were, in all pre-capitalist economies compelling internal laws which push them towards the development of modern capitalism. The development of modern capitalism in Western Europe is a unique historical event (as Marx himself recognized)[2] and the fact that it did not occur in several countries with non-colonial economies, like those of the Iberian Peninsula, or that countries like Japan created it as a conscious reaction to Western pressure in the Meiji era, shows that it was unique—a fact which has long been recognized and has been the object of many works of research, from Max Weber onwards. Far

[1] Oscar Pinto Santos, *El Imperialismo Norteamericano en la Economía de Cuba*, Havana, 1961, pp. 9 and 11. Pinto Santos, presently Cuban Ambassador to China, had held a high position in Batista's National Economic Council up to December 1958.
[2] *See* especially his letter to the editorial board of *Otechestvenniye Zapiski* (November 1877) and to Vera Zasulich (March 8, 1881) in *Marx, Engels: Selected Correspondence*, Moscow, 1953, pp. 376–9 and 411–12.

from preventing the rise of capitalism, 'imperialism' represents one of those external stimuli which in colonial and semi-colonial countries promote the development of capitalism, although in ways which often do not correspond to the interests of the 'victims'. Without wishing to analyse the concept of 'imperialism'[1] we want briefly to examine the accusations made by Cubans about the economic consequences of American influence,[2] and to give some facts about the rôle of American capital in Cuba.

i. *Distortion of the Cuban Economy*. American capital turned Cuba into a sugar plantation and prevented the industrialization of the country. This is the first, basic accusation.

It is true that the country was distorted into a sugar country and it is true that American capitalists were responsible for this development. But it must be said that this, as we have already seen, was the result of a 'free play' of forces and not of a policy forced on the country, that development in the wrong direction is not identical with the absence of any development; and that it is very doubtful whether Cuba would have reached even the relative prosperity which it did in fact achieve had it not been for large American investments. Ernesto 'Ché' Guevara, the revolutionary leader, said: 'One wonders why it was that an underdeveloped country like Cuba could experience some economic development in the past. This was due to favourable climatic conditions and also to the development of a single industry—the sugar industry. Both factors produced a certain amount of prosperity. The sugar industry developed through the stimulus of North American capital.'[3]

As far as the 'prevention of industrialization is concerned, the most that can be said is that obstacles were placed in the way of possible development but not that it was prevented altogether. These obstacles were the result not *only* of the preferential tariffs granted to the US, but also of objective factors which favoured the powerful industrial neighbour. In spite of opposition from interested American quarters, Cuba was in a position after the second world war to grant its own industry a certain degree of customs protection

---

[1] Schumpeter rightly remarks that anti-imperialist propaganda along Marxist lines 'is particularly successful because the facts ... combine the virtues of being superficially known to everyone and of being thoroughly understood by very few'. *Capitalism, Socialism and Democracy*, New York, 1942, p. 52.
[2] The accusations mentioned here are taken from an official note of the Cuban government, *En Defensa de la Soberanía Nacional*, November 13, 1959.
[3] Proyecciones futuras del Orden Económico, Político y Social', Lecture at Havana University, March 7, 1960. Published by the *Comité Ejecutivo de la FNTA*, Havana, 1960. The development towards sugar monoculture precedes any influence of 'American imperialism': in 1862 the value of sugar production was estimated at 62·1 million pesos, that of tobacco at 15·3, of maize (corn) at 5·5, and that of coffee at 2·6 million pesos. (Gerardo Brown-Castillo, *Cuba Colonial*, Havana, 1952, p. 58.)

which led, for example, to a sharp fall in the import of American textiles and shoes and brought about the Cuban industrialization.

ii. *Steps to Prevent Imports of Cuban Sugar.* After the first collapse of the world sugar market in 1921, the Americans raised the duty on Cuban sugar from 1 cent to 1·6 cents per pound, and in 1930 to 2 cents.[1] Although Cuba still enjoyed preferential treatment (the duty on sugar imported from other countries was always higher than that on Cuban sugar) the Cubans were hit hard. In 1934, the quota system was introduced which, although it brought greater stability to the sugar market, had adverse effects on Cuba because it restricted sugar production. The annual quota was fixed by the American government, which in fact put Cuba in a defenceless position. On the whole Cuba's percentage share in the American market fell— which, however, was not of great importance in view of the increase in consumption. During the second world war the world market price was considerably higher than the American price and Cuba thus sold its sugar to the United States at a lower price than it could have got on the world market.

The facts are clear but require some explanation. (1) Sugar protectionism and quota legislation are not an expression of 'imperialism' but the result of pressure from North American sugar producers to which the government submitted—unwillingly at times. In addition there was the pressure from producers in other regions who continually complained about Cuba's excessively high share. (2) American sugar interests in Cuba tried regularly, and not without success, to obtain preferential treatment for their, that is to say for Cuba's, production. On this point their interests coincided with those of Cuba. (3) On the whole, prices on the American market were subject to fewer fluctuations than on the world market and were, during the last ten years, above world market prices: the average North American price from 1945–1958 was 5·3 cents a pound and the world market price 4 cents.[2] Recently the American price has been 2 cents above the world market price. From 1950 to 1959, Cuba delivered 54·5 per cent of its total sugar exports (over 27 million metric tons) to the United States. The price differential resulted in gain of about $780 million. The higher American price was not intended to provide the Cubans with advantages but was due to the higher costs of the American sugar producers. But this higher price was to the advantage of Cuba's sugar planters and workers whose income was tied to the sugar price. It was only because of these American prices that Cuban producers were able to make a profit since in 1957/58 average costs were about 3·8 cents.

[1] A detailed account of the rather complicated facts is found in a publication of the US Department of Agriculture, *Sugar Reports*, Commodity Stabilization Service, Sugar Division, No. 91, November, 1959.
[2] International Sugar Council, London, *Sugar Yearbook*, 1958, 1959.

In a televised speech of March 19, 1960, Guevara stated that the US sugar quota system was a form of 'economic slavery' imposed on Cuba. But this system made possible higher sugar prices on the American market and put Cuba apart from all other Latin American countries in one very important aspect: other countries complained about the worsening terms of trade, the discrepancy between the (decreasing) average prices of their exports to the USA and the (increasing) average prices of the goods they imported from the USA, and attributed much of their economic difficulties to this tendency. Cuba was the only Latin American country which, because of the quota system and the high sugar price, did not suffer from this trend. According to the calculations made by the UN Economic Commission for Latin America[1] the index for the terms of trade, taking 1955 as 100, developed in the following manner:

	1953	1958
All Latin America	103	95
Cuba	96	125

iii. *Balance of Payments Deficit with the US.* The balance of payments deficit was due to objective economic factors: apart from the profits which were drained off to the United States (see below) it was caused by the fact that Cuba had hardly any means of transport and that most industrial products and many foodstuffs were imported from America. Furthermore it was due not only to the preferential tariffs given to Americans but also to the efficiency and proximity of the American producer. Moreover, Cuba's balance of payments surplus with the rest of the world occurred in part thanks to the Americans, whose loans and aid enabled countries to buy Cuban sugar with dollars.

iv. *High American Business Profits in Cuba.* Nothing is more difficult than to calculate the profits of foreign firms, if only because 'book values' are usually well below true values. It is very probable that American profits were really high—not least because the investment of capital in Latin America represents a certain risk. According to one calculation, in 1948–51 the rate of profits on capital investments inside the United States averaged 12·4 per cent (before tax) and on investments in Latin America 18·8 per cent.[2] Other experts put the average rate of profit on American investment in Latin America at 13·8 per cent.[3] These figures include investment in oil production which was particularly profitable. According to official American

---

[1] *Economic Bulletin for Latin America*, Vol. IV, No. 1, October 1959.
[2] *Foreign Capital in Latin America*, UN Department of Economic and Social Affairs, 1955, p. 162.
[3] Committee on Foreign Relations. *US-Latin American Relations.* US Senate, 86th Congress, 2nd Session, Washington, 1960, p. 12.

statistics $849 million invested in Cuba in 1957 yielded a profit of $77 million—which is a little over 9 per cent.[1]

It is impossible to say to what extent these figures present the true situation. It may be that real profits were higher: the American-owned electricity company, for example, always claimed to be making extremely low profits, but a commission of Cuban specialists appointed in 1959 discovered that profits were considerably higher than the Company had maintained. It is possible that this was so: after all, big firms in the United States also try to make high profits and then to hide them—as has been demonstrated by many Congressional and governmental investigations. One might expect the same to happen in other countries.

Whatever the true facts, Cuban firms were also making very high profits: according to members of the revolutionary government the rate of return on capital averaged 23 per cent.[2]

v. *Drain of Profits.* From 1952–1958 there was an annual average drain from Cuba of approximately $50 million in the form of profits and interest. This represents about 2 per cent of the gross national product and 2·4 per cent of the Cuban national income. The figure includes interest on loans and profits of non-American companies. It is thus clear that substantial profits did not leave the country, but were reinvested. On the whole a drain of this size seems quite bearable. In this case it must be regarded only as payment for services rendered by foreign capital invested in Cuba.

vi. *Achievements of American Capitalists in Cuba.* At the beginning of 1960 the total North American investment in Cuba was estimated at $1,000 million. It had risen considerably since 1950 and was the second largest—after Venezuela—in Latin America.

It is interesting to note that the amount of capital invested in agriculture had declined whereas investments in industry had increased, as is shown by the following figures:[3]

American capital in Cuba (Direct Investment)

	1929	1950	1957
in agriculture	62·2%	41%	31·6%
in industry	5·0%	8·4%	11·9%

Eighty-five per cent of the production of American industry in Cuba was sold on the domestic market. In 1957, 160,000 people, of whom more than 90 per cent were Cubans, were employed by American firms in Cuba. Wages and salaries in these firms were

[1] US Department of Commerce, *US Business Investments in Foreign Countries*, Washington, 1960.
[2] Reported to the correspondent of the *Economist* by members of the Revolutionary Government. (*Economist*, January 7, 1961.)
[3] Figures calculated from *Investment in Cuba*, 1956, and *US Business Investment in Foreign Countries*, 1960.

considerably higher than in Cuban firms. In 1957 American firms spent $730 million in Cuba: $170 million in wages and salaries, $70 million in taxes—this amounted to almost 20 per cent of the Cuban budget—and the rest on purchases of local produce. In 1957, Cuba received a gross $361 million of foreign exchange through American capital investment ($273 million from exports and $88 million through capital imports from the US). Against this there was a foreign currency drain of $156 million ($56 million for profits and interest, $100 million for imports of raw materials and machinery).

The country derived advantages from direct investments which cannot be expressed in statistical form. To take one example: every firm established in an underdeveloped country, and recruiting its middle and senior employees locally, plays an important educational rôle in the development of the country.

vii. *The Credit Balance of Imperialism.* Altogether, there is a good deal more to be said for economic 'imperialism' than anti-imperialist circles are willing to concede. Where the Americans obtained greater benefits from their mutual relationship than the Cubans it was due to the advantage of a highly industrialized, large country over a small, less developed neighbour. This relationship produced what professor François Perroux has called the 'domination effect'.[1] But in this connection one might quote John Strachey's words: 'If ... we extend the term [imperialism] to mean any bargaining advantage which the developed countries can exert against the underdeveloped, then indeed it is entirely true that this is one of the factors which tend to keep the poor countries poor and the rich countries rich. But if we extend the term imperialism as widely as this it ceases to have any very clear meaning.'[2]

It was certainly not easy for Cuba to maintain its interests against its powerful neighbour. But it was not *impossible*, because the United States was not a single-minded opponent but a country with many forces whose contradictory interests Cuba could exploit. There were conflicts of interest between American industrialists *in Cuba*, and American industrialists in the United States who wanted to export, between American sugar producers, in Cuba, and the Louisiana or Florida sugar producers. The tariff concessions show what could be obtained and it must also be mentioned that the Cuban National Bank, which even revolutionary circles regard as important and

[1] F. Perroux, 'The Domination Effect in Modern Economic Theory', *Social Research*, June, 1950.
[2] John Strachey, *The End of Empire*, London, 1959, New York, 1960, p. 191. With reference to foreign capital investment, Myrdal rightly says: 'That the course of events took this "colonial" character was not mainly due either to the designs of those who provided the capital ... or to the international policies of their governments. It was much more the natural outcome of the unhampered working of the contemporary market forces.' *An International Economy*, New York, 1956, p. 100

progressive, owes its foundation in the last resort to proposals made by an official mission to Cuba in 1942, proposals which were opposed by many North Americans and Cubans.[1]

That there was a certain amount of progress has been reluctantly admitted by a Cuban communist who has already been quoted: 'During the 1940-45 war and in the course of the post-war years some changes of secondary importance took place in Cuba. Light industry developed; there was some slight improvement in workers' conditions of employment, the National Bank was established ... the dollar continued to circulate as currency ... The 1947 customs agreements ... permitted Cuba to protect some of its national industries.'[2]

But there was not enough development and it took place too slowly. Much more highly planned activity was needed, even in order to establish a secure local industry, which could only have been carried out by a government acting in the interest of the nation, with the advice of experts.[3] To the extent to which the revolutionary leaders realized this they were correct and found themselves in agreement with many economists (for example Myrdal)[4] and with the views expressed by Strachey elsewhere in his book: 'No underdeveloped country can become genuinely independent, in the sense of being able to develop its own resources, unless it can establish a government able and willing to interfere drastically first with its own internal economic life and second, and especially, within the free flow of international trade. For leaving the matter to the forces of market will produce stagnation and disaster'.

The author adds:

'But such conscious planning need involve neither communist methods nor communist aims.'[5]

---

[1] *American Technical Mission to Cuba on the Central Bank and Stabilisation Fund*, evidence by Spruille Braden in *Hearings before the Subcommittee to Investigate the Administration of the Internal Security Act*. Committee of the Judiciary, US Senate, 83rd Congress, March 25, 1954.
[2] Jose A. Tabares del Real, *La Revolución Cubana*, Havana, 1961, pp. 51, 52.
[3] Cuba's economy *was* controlled by the government, but not in such a way as to encourage fast development.
[4] Gunnar Myrdal, *An International Economy*, New York, 1956.
[5] Strachey, *op. cit.*, p. 203.

3. Castro's Road to Power

(a) Legends and Facts
Victors not only make history, they also influence the writing of history. Those who are anxious to show 'what really happened' must start by destroying legends.

Castro was victorious—and today it seems as if a lonely hero with a small band of armed friends achieved the remarkable feat of defeating Batista's strong army, trained and armed by the Americans.

During the fighting in the mountains of the Sierra Maestra the small band of guerilla fighters increased considerably. Most of those who joined the rebels were poor country dwellers. The rebel army thus seemed to have become a peasant army, and the revolution itself a radical agrarian revolution, supported by an impoverished peasantry.

Castro's victory led to a complete social revolution and to the abolition of all forms of representative democracy. Nothing seems more natural than to regard this as the realization of a programme existing from the beginning, put forward by the leader of the revolution and desired by the mass of the people.

The Cuban Communists also emerged victorious from this process. No wonder therefore that one of their leaders, Marinello, claims in a book published in the Soviet Union[1] that the Socialist People's Party (the Communists) leading the working classes had played a decisive rôle in helping Castro to achieve his victory over Batista.

From a synthesis of these claims grew, after 1960, the official legend which—in retrospect—must appear plausible, the more so because, before Castro, few people were interested in Cuba, and because many foreign journalists, often naïve enthusiasts ignorant of the language and of Cuban history, were prepared, after a few weeks in the revolutionary paradise at the invitation of the revolutionary government, to believe anything they were told.

The legend is based on the presentation of Cuba as an impoverished agrarian country with a stagnating monoculture exploited and oppressed by a small oligarchy and by American imperialists. We have already demonstrated the inaccuracy of such a picture.

This is the foundation on which the 'saga of the Revolution' is based; an exaggeration of Batista's terror is used to sketch in the background. Batista's police were forced by the revolutionary terrorism to adopt counter-terrorist methods, which gave the most

[1] Juan Marinello, 'Bol'shaya Pobeda Kubinskogo Naroda,' in *Latinskaya Amerika v Proshlom i Nastoyashchem*, Moscow, 1960, pp. 138–62.

sadistic elements an opportunity of playing a leading part. The official legend speaks of 20,000 dead. But this is a deliberately exaggerated figure: against such a black background the terrorist acts of the revolutionaries themselves will seem negligible. *Nobody knows the real number of victims.* A special edition of *Bohemia*, published soon after the victory of the revolution, contained a long list of the dead of recent years. There were just over 1,000 names.

The actual military operation did not cause heavy losses—certainly less than a thousand altogether. But many people were assassinated or became victims of the terror. The police tortured and murdered, the army competed with the police, and pro-Batista armed bands like Senator Masferrer's 'Tigers' vied with both. This must be stressed because pro-Batista elements are today trying to counter the Castro legend with a pro-Batista legend.[1] Nevertheless there can be no question of anything like 20,000 victims.

The aims of the revolutionary anti-Batista movement were primarily political and not social: to restore representative democracy and the 1940 constitution. Castro and his friends have said so repeatedly.

The revolutionaries were predominantly young intellectuals. The greatest sympathy with the movement existed among the middle classes, while the lower classes remained passive for a long time. The middle and upper classes also provided the revolution with financial support. The rising succeeded—and had the support of almost the whole population—only because it was *not* a class issue. As late as June 30, 1959, Raúl Castro said that the Cuban revolution had been an epic '... a wonderful process in which twelve lonely men, thanks to the support of the whole population, in collaboration with the workers, members of the liberal professions, intellectuals and businessmen who loved their fatherland, destroyed an apparently invincible army'.[2]

At that time therefore Raúl Castro did not regard the 'peasants' as the chief force of the revolution, and with regard to the workers it must be said that they took *less* part in the struggle than any other

---

[1] As for example in Batista's book *Respuesta*, Mexico, 1960, and the publications of Leopoldo Pío Elizalde and his organization, *Defensa Institucional Cubana*, Mexico. (Pío Elizalde not only published a book in Spanish, *La Tragedia de Cuba*, but also a short pamphlet in English, *Defamation*, Mexico, 1961.) A leading Batista officer, Colonel Barrera, writes that after the events of July 26, 1953, 'Colonel Río Chaviano made rivers of blood flow. Oriente experienced a terror the like of which it had never known before. Hundreds of people became victims of this barbaric repression.' He also reports that in 1957 during the fighting against Castro in Sierra Maestra the army burned down whole farms and villages and murdered dozens of innocent peasants. He quotes the report of an official investigation according to whom on another occasion 'over thirty peasants were brought aboard a warship, taken far off to sea at night, thrown overboard and shot at with machine guns'. (Pedro A. Barrera Pérez, 'Por qué el Ejército no derrotó a Castro', in *Bohemia Libre*, August 6 and 13, 1961.)

[2] *Revolución*, Havana, June 30, 1959.

class. Working-class strikes during the years of dictatorship almost all had *economic* and not political objectives. Such *political* movements and strikes as took place were supported mainly by students, pupils, shopkeepers, and, sometimes, office workers. On the occasions on which the revolutionaries tried to mobilize the urban workers their attempts were unsuccessful. The workers did not move either in March 1952 when Batista came to power or on April 9, 1958, when there was an abortive general strike. The only political mass strike took place after Batista's flight—in order to prevent the establishment of a non-revolutionary government by a weak military junta.

Leading Communists, like the Secretary General of the Socialist People's Party, Blas Roca, admit—or used to admit—that the workers played a passive rôle: 'The main form of opposition consisted in armed combat in the countryside whereas strikes, election boycotts and other actions by the working class and the urban proletariat played only a secondary part ... The armed struggle had been begun by the lower middle classes. For several reasons the working classes never played a decisive active part: the workers were split as the result of effective pro-imperialist, bourgeois activities; Mujal and his gang exercised bureaucratic control over the trade unions; 'economism' was important inside the workers' movement, together with a tendency to solve all disputed questions with the aid of the official union leadership.'[1]

These words show clearly how little the working classes did to overthrow Batista and also how small was the Communist influence on the proletariat.

As for the 'peasants' most of them also remained passive during the whole period. Since the fighting took place in the countryside it is natural that there were some rural elements in the rebel ranks.[2] But the leading elements of the revolution came from the towns. Moreover, those peasants who joined the rebels were by no means typical of Cuban agriculture. Guevara writes:

'The first part of the country which the rebels occupied was inhabited by a class of peasants completely different both culturally and socially from those country dwellers who predominate in Cuba's extensive and semi-mechanized agriculture ... The soldiers who formed the first guerilla army came from a class which is most aggressive in demonstrating its love for its own land, which is filled

[1] *World Marxist Review*, Prague, Vol. II, No. 8, August 1959.
[2] The reasons why the peasants took part in the rebellion in the Sierra Maestra are briefly mentioned by a Batista colonel who for a time commanded the troops fighting Castro: 'After the army began once again to maltreat and persecute the peasantry, which had taken no share whatsoever in the fighting, many peasants, particularly the young ones, fled to the mountains to join Castro.' Pedro A. Barrera Pérez, 'Por qué el Ejército no derrotó a Castro', *Bohemia Libre*, Puertorriqueña, August 27, 1961.

in classic fashion by a lower middle-class spirit: these peasants fight because they and their children own the land, because they cultivate it for themselves, sell it and want to enrich themselves through their work.'[1]

A very interesting remark which indicates also how little the subsequent *socialist* land reform corresponded to the wishes of those who had fought in the rebel army.

Castro's 26th July Movement was only *one* of several anti-Batista groups and historically it was not the first. As for the Communists: of all the active opposition groups they did least fighting and suffered the smallest losses, although they organized some small local guerilla bands during the autumn months of 1958 and infiltrated at the same time those of Castro. This was generally known in Cuba. As late as March 1961 an officer of the revolutionary army and a district leader of the agrarian reform said to a journalist: 'In all the countryside you won't find any Communists. They're all in Havana. Not one of them was with us in the mountains. They joined us at the last minute.'[2]

We must ask ourselves therefore how Castro succeeded in obtaining the leading position in the revolutionary movement, and why the Communists became the controlling force of the revolution.

It would be wrong to speak of a *military* victory by Castro. The truth is that the army became increasingly demoralized, having long been full of corruption and internal intrigues. Many officers and still more soldiers withdrew without a fight while other officers deserted to the enemy or were persuaded to retreat. This explains why there were so few casualties on either side. A French pro-Castro journalist rightly wrote: Fidel Castro's victory was no real military victory. It was primarily a moral victory of the people ... Castro did not destroy the enemy. The latter collapsed because he was rotten to the core.'[3]

(b) Beginnings of Revolutionary Opposition

The day after Batista's *coup d'état* black flags were flying over Havana University. Students addressed the population through loudspeakers to voice their protests. Shortly afterwards they organized a demonstration at which the 1940 constitution was symbolically buried. On May 20, 1952, students called a mass meeting which took place at the main entrance of the university. Students and professors made speeches against Batista and called for resistance. The first clashes with the police took place, the first bombs were thrown and the first secret groups were formed.

[1] *Verde Olivo*, Havana, April 9, 1961.
[2] G. Troeller-C. Deffarge, *Zwischen Kennedy und Castro*, Stern, Hamburg, May 7, 1961.
[3] Claude Julien, *La Révolution Cubaine*, Paris, 1961, p. 97.

From the ranks of the *Auténticos* emerged two illegal organizations, more or less independent of each other: the *Organización Auténtica* (OA) under the leadership of Prío and Antonio de Varona and the *AAA*, led by the energetic ex-Minister, Aureliano Sánchez Arango, who often came to Cuba on illegal visits. Catholic Action Groups consisting mainly of students, organized protest meetings which were dispersed by the police and began to take part in conspiratorial activities. Some of these Catholics were arrested, several were tortured, others driven into exile.

In January 1953, although prohibited by the police, a student demonstration took place in the streets of Havana. The police opened fire and killed a student who happened to be called Batista and who became the university's first official martyr.

In April 1953, the *Movimiento Nacional Revolucionario* led by a professor of philosophy, Garcia Barcena, organized an unsuccessful revolutionary *putsch*. Barcena was arrested with a dozen of his followers, severely maltreated and sentenced to imprisonment. Some of his friends and supporters later reappeared in leading positions in the Castro movement.

The actions which took place in 1952/3 were organized by small inexperienced groups of young impatient intellectuals, students and pupils, who had no connection with one another and who lacked any clear ideology. The Batista régime was too unsure of itself to adopt a 'totalitarian' course, and searched for 'democratic' solutions. The gaps in the façade of the semi-dictatorship revealed a motley assortment of 'legal' and 'illegal' opponents.

On May 26, 1953, Senator Pelayo Cuervo Navarro, of the *Ortodoxo* Party, said in a television programme that Batista must be overthrown by force. He was arrested on leaving the studio, but released again shortly afterwards.

During the same period members of various opposition groups met in Montreal to discuss the possibilities of concerted action. Some delegates came from Cuba and returned there without difficulty. The press reported the meetings and on June 2, 1953, published the anti-Batista manifesto drawn up in Montreal. The meeting had also decided to organize an insurrection and had prepared an exact plan. A few weeks later the plan fell into Batista's hands and the whole rising collapsed. Some rebels were arrested, others fled abroad.

In this atmosphere of general confusion, Fidel Castro emerged as the rising leader of the revolution.

(c) Fidel Castro: Pen Portrait of a Rebel
Men make history—and are at the same time the product of historical factors. Many aspects of the revolution can only be explained by the character of their leader. If ever there has been a

charismatic leader-figure blindly worshipped by the masses it was that of this young lawyer.

He was born in August 1926 on his father's estate in Biran in the Province of Oriente. His father, Angel Castro, came from Spain. When he arrived in Cuba he was poor and uneducated. In 1926 he was still uneducated, uninterested in 'higher' things, uncouth and tyrannical—but rich. To amass his wealth he seems to have used various, not always entirely unexceptionable methods. This, together with his lack of education and manners kept the doors of 'good society' closed to Angel Castro. He owned an estate, a minor *latifundium* in a region whose inhabitants were particularly poor. The family which consisted of an elder brother, Ramón, several daughters, Fidel and later also a younger brother, Raúl, lived in a large house on the estate. Eye witnesses claim that the house was remarkably primitive and had neither a bathroom nor an indoor lavatory.

Angel Castro had two children by his first marriage. After his wife's death he lived with his cook, Lina Ruz. Then he married her. She was Fidel's mother. The Castros do not seem to have had any real family life. It is said that the father bothered little about his children and ill-treated his wife. Later considerable conflicts developed between Fidel and his father: some say because of the father's behaviour towards his wife, others claim that old Castro exploited his farm labourers in a particularly merciless way and that Fidel spoke up for them. But Fidel's relations with his mother do not seem to have been very good either; when Fidel was already fighting in the mountains and ordered sugar cane plantations to be set on fire (including those belonging to his family) his mother was shocked. She had not seen her son for years but had heard that a group of Cuban revolutionaries in Mexico had radio communication with the rebels in the mountains. She flew to Mexico and without enquiring about the well-being of her son demanded that Fidel should be told over the radio to stop burning his mother's sugar cane. Teresa Casuso, to whom Lina Ruz de Castro made this request, writes: 'I was more than astonished: I was indignant. While Fidel was risking his life and suffering privations of every kind her only concern was for her cane fields.'[1]

Fidel was sent to a Catholic boarding school in Santiago de Cuba. Later he went to the Jesuit school, Belen College, near Havana, where he became noted as an athlete, a debater and a rebel. He is supposed on one occasion to have threatened a teacher with a pistol, and in contrast to most of his contemporaries he is said to have been defiantly dirty and unkempt. It is difficult to discover today how much truth there is in all this. In 1945, Fidel began to study law at Havana University, but took more interest in politics. He tried to

---

[1] Teresa Casuso, *Cuba and Castro*, New York, 1961, p. 130.

become chairman of the student federation, but only managed to become Vice-President of the students of the law faculty. Soon he established contact with the numerous revolutionary 'terrorist' organizations springing up at that time, and also with the Communists, whose sympathies he needed for his aspirations. At that time gunfights between the three large revolutionary 'activist' groups were a frequent occurrence. They fought for political favours and for official posts, or to pay off personal scores, or sometimes for even more sinister reasons. The line dividing gangster from revolutionary was ill-defined, pistols hung from the belt, revolutionary phrases echoed from all corners, and victims died in the streets.[1]

Fidel was in close touch with the *Union Insurreccional Revolucionaria* which in spite of its hair-raising name led a legal existence. Its members were given police posts by the Grau government, as were those of the two other activist groups, the MSR and the *Acción Revolucionaria Guiteras*. It seems probable that Fidel himself took part in two political assassinations. One victim was the former student leader and 'Sport Commissar' of the Grau government, Manolo Castro. All this may seem appalling to Europeans but it was part of the 'normal way of life' of a Creole revolutionary.[2]

In spite of his strained relations with the MSR Fidel participated in the summer of 1947 in their attempt, which the Grau government just managed to prevent, to send an armed expedition against Trujillo in San Domingo.

In April 1948 as Cuban student leader he went, together with other revolutionary delegates, to Bogotá in Colombia, where an anti-imperialist congress had been convened by various revolutionary organizations, including both Communists and *Peronistas*. It was intended to coincide with the Pan-American Conference which was meeting there, and its purpose was to protest against *Yanqui* imperialism. Shortly after the arrival of the delegates the radical,

---

[1] The author must confess that he himself—unaware of the true background of Creole revolutionary activities—belonged for some months to the leadership of one of these organizations, the MSR (*Movimiento Socialista Revolucionario*) and that he helped to edit its paper, *Tiempo en Cuba* and even wrote a draft programme. This was in 1946/47 when the organization was led by Rolando Masferrer, a veteran of the Spanish civil war, who had just left the Communist party and later became first an *Auténtico* and then a Batista Senator.

[2] To give a character sketch of the mentality of these groups: The author vividly recalls a discussion with Masferrer about India's impending independence. Masferrer regarded this as an imperialist trick, on the part of Great Britain, and refused to believe that there were real differences between Hindus and Moslems. When the author tried to convince him and expressed the fear that there would be chaos and bloody struggles between the religious groups in India, Masferrer said: 'I can't understand you. Chaos is a wonderful thing for a revolutionary!' The leader of the *Acción Revolucionaria Guiteras*, Jésus Gonzalez Cartas, had to make a ceremonial speech and begged one of the author's close friends to write it for him: 'You know, Roberto, I find public speaking very difficult. To do away with somebody is nothing, but a speech ... I can't do it. You must help me, please!'

extremely popular leader of the Colombian Liberals, Gaitán, was murdered by unknown assassins. The murder resulted in demonstrations, armed clashes, looting and destruction and a communist attempt to assume control. There were hundreds of dead. Castro's rôle in this remains unclear to the present day, but there is no doubt that he took part in street fighting, was hunted by the police, and fled to Cuba with the aid of the Cuban Ambassador.

Shortly after his return he joined the *Ortodoxo* Party, made public speeches for them and was nominated as an *Ortodoxo* parliamentary candidate in the 1952 elections. In October 1948, he married Mirta Díaz Balart by whom he had a son, Fidelito, in 1949. In 1950 he received his doctorate in law and started to practise, mainly with the idea of advancing his political career. He was on the left of his party and unlike the leader of the party, Chibás, did not object to collaborating with the Communists.

A few days after Batista's *coup d'état* the young lawyer brought an action in the Supreme Court against the usurper, which naturally ended up in the wastepaper basket. When the *Ortodoxo* Party split into several sections, he supported a revolutionary policy and tried to form his own group. At first, the police did not bother him, partly because his brother-in-law, Díaz Balart, played a leading part in the Batista Party and once even arranged a personal interview between Fidel and Batista—which yielded no result.

(d) 26th July 1953

For months Castro had been harbouring revolutionary plans. Arms were procured, a farm was rented for use as arsenal and training ground, and activists were trained. The *coup* was to take place in the Province of Oriente during the July carnival celebrations. It was a mad adventure, with little chance of success from the start. The intention was to capture the Moncada barracks in Santiago, in a surprise attack, 'take over' the town and make a radio appeal to the population to revolt. For this purpose Castro had about 160 young people who had army-type uniforms and arms, and were ready for anything. Even if the *coup* failed it would have historic consequences.

Some of the rebels did not even get to the scene of the fighting: they had got lost in the streets. Others succeeded in entering the barracks and overpowering the guards. There were dead and wounded on both sides. Many rebels were captured, tortured and murdered. Fidel Castro managed to escape the terrible fate of some of his friends, several of whom were castrated or blinded before they were killed. The exact number of dead is unknown: between 60 and 80 young people, including some who had nothing whatsoever to do with the affair, had been arrested in the streets.

The authorities found a proclamation which was supposed to

have been read over the radio after the victory. It was a strange, moving document written by Castro himself.

'Motivated by the noblest Creole values the revolution comes from the soul of the Cuban people,' he wrote. 'Its vanguard is formed by a youth that wants a new Cuba, a youth that has freed itself from all the faults, the mean ambitions and the sins of the past.'[1]

The revolution, it continued, would cleanse Cuba and provide freedom and prosperity for all. Basing itself on the 'honour and virtue of the Cubans' it appealed to all who are pure in heart to collaborate. It wanted to achieve the 'final victory of social justice' through planned changes in the economy which was to be diversified and industrialized. The revolutionaries proclaimed their loyalty to the ideals of José Martí, their agreement with Guiteras' programme of 1934 and also with the programme of Chibás' *Ortodoxo* Party. They promised to restore immediately the 1940 constitution.

In September 1953, the trial of the rebels began before a special court. In the middle of the hearing the government decided to try Castro separately *in camera*, which was done in October of the same year. It was during his imprisonment that Castro wrote the long speech which under the title *History will absolve me* has become the basic document, the birth certificate of Fidelism.

The rising against Batista is explained and justified by reference to many legal authorities and to the relevant articles of the 1940 constitution. Batista is accused of high treason, murder and theft. The accused tells the judges with irony:

'Once upon a time there was a Republic. It had its Constitution, its laws, its freedoms; President, Parliament, Courts; everyone could go to meetings, associate with others, speak and write with complete freedom. The government did not satisfy the people, but the people could change and this was not many days off. There was a public opinion which was respected and observed and all problems of collective interest were freely discussed ... This people had suffered much ... They had often deceived it and it looked in horror at the past. It believed, blindly, that this could never return ... it wanted a change, an improvement, an advance and it saw it coming ... Poor people! One morning the citizenry woke up with a shock. During the night the ghosts of the past had conspired while it was sleeping and now they had it bound hand, foot and throat.'

(As we shall see later, Castro has since changed his rather favourable attitude to the pre-Batista democracy, nor would he now

---

[1] This account and the quotations are taken from Cuban publications, private information and Jules Dubois' book, *Fidel Castro: Rebel—Liberator or Dictator?* New York, 1959, which Castro at the time admitted to be accurate.

admit the possibilities of a peaceful transformation of society). However the aims of the revolution were not solely political. In his speech Castro said that immediately after victory he would have promulgated laws:

1. Restoring the 1940 Constitution. (Until the elections, which would take place at an early date, the revolutionary government would hold all power in its hands and would immediately carry out a purge of the judiciary.)
2. Conferring full title to their holdings on all tenant farmers holding less than 165 acres, with compensation to the former owners.
3. Granting workers and employees of all big firms the right to a 30 per cent share of their profits.
4. Reserving to sugar cane planters 55 per cent of the gross receipts from sales of raw sugar and establishing a guaranteed minimum quota for all small sugar cane planters.
5. Confiscating property acquired unjustly at the expense of the people, after adjudication by special courts.

Later the revolutionary government would carry out a thorough purge of the civil service. It would initiate a policy of industrialization. It would take steps to solve the land problem; in accordance with the 1940 constitution a maximum would be established for each type of agricultural enterprise, *latifundia* would be broken up and the land set free would be distributed among landless workers and peasants. The government would encourage 'the formation of agricultural co-operatives for the collective use of expensive machinery, storage facilities, etc.'

Credits would be available to the new landowners and machinery and experts would be put at their disposal.

All house rents would be reduced by 50 per cent and a government building programme would help every family to acquire its own home. The electricity and telephone companies would be nationalized. There would be a basic reform of the educational system and teachers' salaries would be raised so that no primary school teacher would receive less than 200 pesos a month and no secondary school teacher less than 300 pesos. (The Cuban peso was equal to one US dollar.)

Although this represents a programme of far-reaching social changes, it cannot be described as socialist. Private ownership of the means of production is not abolished: on the contrary it is extended so that the majority of the nation would consist of property owners. The land reform then planned differs basically from that carried out in 1959; in particular, co-operatives mentioned in the speech have little in common with those established later.

Castro was sentenced to fifteen years imprisonment and taken to the 'model prison' on the *Isla de Pinos* where he met Garcia Barcena and other revolutionaries.

CASTRO'S ROAD TO POWER

After the official proclamation of the Marxist-Leninist character of the Cuban revolution its history was re-interpreted by Castro. This was done in great detail in his speech of December 1, 1961. According to the new version, Castro was at the time already a Marxist, influenced by Leninism. However, he was not a complete and mature Marxist, because he still had many petty bourgeois prejudices and confused ideas. But it had supposedly been clear to him that victorious revolutions are made by the masses and that *putschs* must be condemned. The attack on Moncada, however, had not been a *putsch*. Its purpose had been to obtain arms to start a guerilla war which would have mobilized the population. The only mistake had been to think that a large supply of arms was needed at the beginning and to attack Moncada rather than a smaller garrison. His subsequent speech had been carefully prepared, partly to hide his Marxist radicalism and to make it possible to set up a broad, united anti-Batista front.

But in spite of the new version, Moncada seems in fact to have been a *putsch*, and was regarded as such by the Communists. The whole action, including the proclamation which was to have been read, is evidence of Fidel's petty bourgeois confusion rather than his Marxism. On the other hand it is quite possible that his feelings and ideas were more radical than appeared from his speech.

(e) Castro's Strategy

In May 1955, Batista proclaimed a general amnesty. Fêted as heroes, Castro and other revolutionaries returned to Havana. But to take up the threads of revolutionary activities again was difficult—Castro lacked clear ideas, money and an organization. The régime seemed to be getting more democratic. Emigrés were returning: it looked as if political problems might be solved without revolution. The *Ortodoxo* Party had become united again under the chairmanship of Raúl Chibás—Eduardo's brother—and Castro expressed his confidence in him.

But Castro realized, maybe subconsciously, that there must be no 'peaceful' solution. In Havana he felt restricted, unable to act, supervised by the police. At the end of the year he emigrated to the United States. Soon he began to collect followers and financial support. Early in 1956 he announced the independence of his 26th July Movement, thus breaking with the *Ortodoxo* Party. At that time he could hardly be said to have had any clear plans. *On s'engage —puis on voit*, Napoleon said . . . Castro might have said the same.

By 1956 the prospect of peaceful change had receded. Castro's aims were now clear. There must be a campaign of assassination and sabotage in the country, but above all he must land in Cuba with an armed band and start civil war from the mountains in collaboration with *his* supporters in the towns. The other groups? They could not be relied upon: they were unimportant, or cowardly, or compromised by their past—but also they were or might become, dangerous rivals. Tactical collaboration with them was possible, but Fidel himself must emerge as leader in the struggle.

While he was reaching these conclusions the situation in Cuba deteriorated. The 'Civic Dialogue' broke down. In April, a serious army conspiracy was discovered, led by Colonel Ramón Barquín, probably the most capable professional soldier in the country. Barquín was no social revolutionary, but he was opposed to the new Batista dictatorship and also to the corruption which was destroying the army. He went to prison together with other officers: that nothing worse happened to him was partly due to the Americans, who had come to respect him when he was military attaché in the United States. Barquín was brilliantly defended in court by the chairman of the lawyers' association, Miró Cardona, who thus incurred Batista's hatred and soon had to emigrate.

At about the same time a trial of revolutionary students and teachers took place in Santiago. There were demonstrations and the police murdered some young people with the result that there was another school strike in the whole country. At the end of April, a group of dare-devils loosely connected with the *Auténticos*, tried to storm the Goicuria barracks in the town of Matanzas, only to die as heroes. A new wave of emigration began; a new struggle was about to start.

(*f*) *Fidel's Landing*

Castro had moved to Mexico and had collected a group of young people and arms. Among his new comrades was an interesting young professional revolutionary from Argentina, the physician Ernesto (Ché) Guevara. He was intelligent, very brave, asthmatic and a Marxist. Far from the Mexican capital a big estate was rented as training ground and a military teacher hired, an ex-colonel of the Spanish Republican army, Alberto Bayo. In September 1956, Castro even had a meeting with ex-President Carlos Prío who provided him with money, though only a short while before he had been the object of Castro's attacks. With this money Castro bought the yacht *Granma* on which he and eighty-two armed and trained expeditionaries set off to sea from Mexico in the second half of November. He had already openly announced in advance that he would land soon.

The landing was supposed to coincide with risings in several towns in the Province of Oriente where the young teacher Frank País was acting as the main leader of the 26th July Movement. Contact had also been established with other groups, for example the student organization (*Federación Estudiantil Universitaria*) with whose chair-

CASTRO'S ROAD TO POWER

man, Echevarría, Castro had recently concluded an agreement[1] to ensure collaboration.

Once again nothing went according to plan. The small yacht battled with the ocean and unknown to the revolutionaries on the island did not arrive on time. On November 30 the rising began: in Santiago the army at first withdrew in surprise and for a short period the town fell into the hands of the small band of revolutionaries. Shortly afterwards the army received reinforcements and attacked. The dream was soon over, and risings in several other towns in the eastern province suffered the same fate. Very few people were actively engaged in these actions: about 200 young men, directed by Frank País in Santiago de Cuba, even smaller groups in several other towns.[2]

On December 2, 1956, Castro landed. Most of the expeditionaries were sick, many had lost courage. They were discovered, attacked from the air and dispersed. Several were killed, others were arrested and tried. (During their trial a judge stated that the revolution was justified. This man was Manuel Urrutia Lleó, and, as a reward for his behaviour, Castro made him President of revolutionary Cuba until he was dismissed in July 1959). Fidel Castro, his brother Raúl, Ché Guevara and nine others managed to escape. With the help of a group of 'revolutionary' inhabitants of the Sierra Maestra they reached safety. In Havana, Batista was told that the whole affair was unimportant and that Castro was dead.

The Sierra Maestra is a wooded mountain region of about 3,000 square miles, poor, sparsely inhabited, and with few roads. Its foothills extend to the town of Santiago. Castro's problem there was more how to survive than how to protect himself against Batista's soldiers, most of whom were not anxious to fight even if they could find him in this impassable region. He needed the confidence of the local inhabitants, quite a few of whom were engaged in smuggling, or growing marijuana, or had escaped from the authorities for one reason or another. There were also many very poor peasants living on land which they did not own and from which they were frequently evicted. Some of these gathered round Castro and they were joined by young intellectuals and unemployed from Santiago and other neighbouring towns. In order to take the offensive Castro needed more people and more arms. Only military successes—however small—would give him the sympathy and confidence of most of the local peasantry. But for all this he needed publicity: it had to become generally known that he had survived and begun the fight.

[1] This 'Pact of Mexico' was concluded in September 1956. Among other things it said: 'The FEU and the "26 July" regard Colonel Barquín, Major Boreonnet and the other officers who have been dismissed and imprisoned as the worthiest representatives of our army ... and declare that an army led by these officers, observing the constitution and serving the people, will have the respect and the sympathies of the Cuban revolution.'
[2] V. Cubilla, 'La Carga Heroica del Granma', in *Bohemia*, December 4, 1960.

Decisive help came from outside in the shape of the North American journalist, Herbert Matthews, of the *New York Times*. Led by Javier Pazos, a student who had played an active part in the 26th July Movement in Havana, Matthews reached the Sierra Maestra and had, on February 17, 1957, an interview with Castro the publication of which caused a tremendous sensation. Soon afterwards Pazos also provided Castro with arms and with the help of these and additional men Castro was able to win his first 'battle' near the village of Uvero. It was a small skirmish in which only one army patrol was destroyed. But it was important from a moral point of view and increased Castro's prestige in the eyes of the local inhabitants who had been intimidated by the army.

A few weeks after Matthews' interview freedom of the press was re-established for a short time. In May 1957, *Bohemia*, the biggest weekly, published Matthews' interview with the bearded hero and also the words which Castro had spoken for 'The Story of Cuba's Jungle Fighters', an American television film. 'What is your programme?' the American journalist asked. Castro replied: 'To restore the 1940 constitution and to hold free elections . . .'

(g) *The Other Militant Groups and March 13, 1957*

Later on Castro criticized the use of terrorist methods and that foolhardiest of all revolutionary attempts which took place on March 13, 1957, in Havana.

An organization called *Directorio Revolucionario*, together with a group of *Auténticos*, former independents, and members of the student association, had attacked the presidential palace in broad daylight in order to assassinate Batista. The adventure was led by the former *Auténtico* member of parliament, Menelao Mora, and the student leader, Echevarría, who in spite of his pact with Castro apparently intended to play a leading rôle in the revolution and who was used by the *Auténticos* against Castro.

The members of this conspiracy were in contact not only with Prío, but also, strange though it may seem, with the Dominican dictator, Trujillo, who had long regarded Batista as an enemy. Some of the arms intended for the attack on the palace and also those which Javier Pazos delivered to Castro in the Sierra Maestra, came originally from Trujillo.

The plan was that the majority of the conspirators, led by Mora and Carlos Gutierrez Menoyo, should attack the palace, while Echevarría and his friends would occupy a radio station, inform the people of the death of the dictator and appeal to them to fight. The rebels really did succeed in entering the palace, and after some shooting reached Batista's office on the second floor. Echevarría also succeeded in occupying the radio station. But that was all.

Batista had known all about the impending attack. 'The authorities were busy discovering the details ... At midnight on March 12 I sent word to Candido Mora, the member of parliament ... that he should persuade his brother to abandon his plan. Thus we hoped to avoid any bloodshed.'[1]

The hand-grenades thrown by the rebels did not explode, the reinforced palace guard counter-attacked and tanks appeared in the streets. The final result was more than fifty dead, including Menelao Mora, Gutierrez Menoyo, and Echevarría who was shot down as he left the radio station. In his pockets the police allegedly found a document proclaiming the *Ortodoxo* senator, Pelayo Cuervo Navarro, provisional president of the Republic. Pelayo Cuervo was arrested, and next morning his body was found near the little lake of the Country Club district.

Why did Castro criticize the March 13 adventure? Hardly because he condemned *coups* or terror on principle: like others, members and sympathizers of the 26th July Movement had taken part in bomb attacks and terrorist acts. What was important to Castro was his leading position in the revolutionary movement. This was in danger because at the time he had very few fighters in the mountains and other groups had begun the fight independently of him.

In May 1957, the *Auténticos* attempted a landing under the leadership of Calixto Sanchez. The whole party—there were about twenty-five—fell into the hands of the Batista army and were murdered without trial. The *Directorio Revolucionario* began to plan its own landing. The Church started to criticize Batista and young Catholics again became active. Trade union opposition against the official leadership grew; the leader of the electricity workers, Cofiño, stood against Mujal and was soon forced to take refuge abroad. In June the murder of Frank País and some of his friends led to unrest and demonstrations in the Eastern Province. The new American ambassador, Earl T. Smith, after visiting Santiago openly expressed his horror at the brutal behaviour of the police against women demonstrators. In September 1957 there was a rising in the town of Cienfuegos, in which some naval officers took a leading part.

It seemed essential that all fighting groups should join forces. On July 12, 1957, in a 'Manifesto of the Sierra Maestra' Castro had called for the formation of a united front, and in October the delegates of various revolutionary opposition groups met in Miami. The ex-President of the National Bank, Felipe Pazos (father of Javier) represented the 26th July Movement, Manuel Bisbé the *Ortodoxos*, Prío and Varona the *Auténticos*, Prendes the student federation, Cofiño the revolutionary trade unions and Faure Chomón the *Directorio Revolucionario*. The Communists had not been invited.

A programme was drawn up which corresponded in all important

[1] F. Batista, *Respuesta*, Mexico, 1960, p. 57.

points to the 'Manifesto of the Sierra Maestra', but also contained 'secret' paragraphs. A 'Liberation Council' was established.

At first Castro was silent and then, to the surprise and dismay of all participants, rejected the newly established unity. He thus disowned his own representatives. His reasons were given in a letter dated December 14, 1957.

Castro was now in an optimistic frame of mind and considered himself strong enough to achieve victory with his own forces, without having to make any compromises. He was unwilling—he wrote—to obey any 'order or directive from outside'. The 'Liberation Council' consisted only of prattlers and inefficient people who instead of concentrating all armed assistance on the Sierra Maestra pursued their own aims and bought arms which either fell into the hands of police or remained hidden away; 'For us there can be no more the defeat, that will be suffered by those who are not here with us'.

He said that the 26th July Movement was in control of substantial parts of the country and that it was the only tried revolutionary organization.[1] With the help of its newly established 'movement of civil resistance' (Manuel Ray was one of its most important organizers) and its own revolutionary trade unionists (first under Salgado and then under David Salvador) the 26th July Movement would organize a mass movement and mass strikes.

He also raised ideological and political objections to the Miami programme. Why did it not reject any possible North American 'mediation action'? Why did it not expressly condemn North American military supplies for Batista? Why did it not expressly reject any possible provisional military junta? It was senseless to keep the Liberation Council as a 'supreme government' side by side with the revolutionary government which would be officially established, to start a 'double rule' which could only end in anarchy and open the door to 'old politicians'. Unacceptable too was the decision to incorporate the 'revolutionary forces' into the reorganized army after victory. The 26th July Movement—the only serious revolutionary organization—would have to reorganize the armed forces of the nation and take responsibility for the maintenance of order.

But these open claims to political supremacy are apparently contradicted by the following words: 'The 26th July Movement, and no other, has stated that it does *not* wish to participate in the provisional government and that it will put all its moral and material forces at the disposal of the citizen who will become President ... We have declared that we do not want to hold any government office.'

In the same document Castro proposed that Judge Manuel Urrutia should become President after Batista's fall.

[1] In fact, as Castro later admitted, his total force at the time was a mere 120 men. (*El Mundo*, Havana, December 2, 1961.)

In other words: the 26th July Movement, that is, Castro—because the 26th July Movement never existed as a definite party with officials and a programme and never held any legal or illegal party conference —wanted to monopolize the revolution. Suspicion against the 'old politicians', against everybody who is not sufficiently revolutionary or anti-imperialist is mixed up with a lack of willingness to compromise, a rejection of any form of collective discipline above party lines, a desire to achieve power, an exaggerated estimate of his own strength and an undeniable Machiavellianism. Castro himself would choose the President; but behind the obscure and unpolitical judge in whom all state power was nominally vested, would stand the real holders of power, the leaders of the 26th July Movement, who had no desire for government office but wanted only to reorganize the armed forces and maintain peace and order in the country.

(h) *From April 9, 1958, to the 'Pact of Carácas'*

In February 1958, the *Directorio Revolucionario* successfully landed a few dozen armed men. Soon their numbers began to grow but then this 'second front' split into two groups. In March 1958, Fidel sent his brother with about fifty men to the Sierra Cristal, a mountain region in the Province of Oriente. In order to belittle the importance of the group in Central Cuba calling itself the 'Second Front of Escambray' (Menoyo and Morgan) Raúl Castro's detachment was also known as the 'Second Front'. After the collapse of the government offensive in Spring 1958, he had a mere 180 men,[1] and in June, under 300.[2] Reliable sources say that on the day of victory the whole Castro army consisted of 803 men, which together with all other groups made up a force of 1,000 to 1,500. It was only after December 31, 1958, that he was joined by thousands who wanted to be able to say after the victory that they had played an active part in it. The number of fighters rose very quickly to over 40,000,[3] with the result that a thorough purge soon proved necessary.

Altogether there were up to October 1958 fewer than a thousand fighters in all organizations but the army was full of corruption and intrigues and incapable of destroying these groups. Terror ruled the country. Torture became an everyday event, corpses of young people appeared in the streets and in the plains bodies could be seen hanging from trees. The young fled to the mountains because they were safer there than in the towns. In February when a group of the 26th July Movement kidnapped the famous racing driver, Fangio, world attention was drawn to conditions in Cuba. Pastoral letters were read in churches against the dictatorship. The press published an

---

[1] Speech of February 1, 1961.
[2] Speech of February 24, 1959, published in *Discursos para la Historia*, Vol. I, Havana, 1959, p. 140.
[3] Castro's speech at the Production Congress, August 1961.

appeal from a 'Committee of Civic Institutions', signed by the associations of doctors, lawyers, dentists, engineers, teachers, freemasons and the organizations of catholic and protestant youth. It demanded a return to democracy and the restoration of the 1940 constitution.

Batista was not prepared to give way, although the American ambassador urged him not to proclaim another state of emergency but to organize really free elections. American public opinion was shocked: in March 1958, the United States put an embargo on all arms deliveries to Batista.

Castro was now certain of victory. On March 12 he published a new manifesto which was read over the rebel station (Radio Rebelde) and also over Radio Carácas in Venezuela where the dictator, Pérez Jiménez, had meanwhile been overthrown. Castro ordered an unlimited school strike for April 5, all public transport in the Province of Oriente was prohibited, all government employees were told to resign on April 5 and all taxpayers were asked to refuse to pay their taxes. A general strike was planned for April 9.

But Castro had overestimated his strength. Civil servants remained at their posts, taxes continued to be paid and all attempts to call a general strike failed miserably. It was a total fiasco: Batista triumphed, the revolutionaries were demoralized. In view of this an offensive in the mountains was out of the question, although arms had reached the Sierra Maestra from Figueres in Costa Rica, largely thanks to the work of the pilot Díaz Lanz and the rebel captain, Hubert Matos.

Castro realized that a united front had become essential. It was established without the Communists on July 20, 1958. Its basic document is the 'Pact of Carácas' written by Castro himself. It says among other things:

'Since the treacherous *coup d'état* on March 10, 1952 which interrupted the normal democratic development of the nation the Cuban people have fought unceasingly, heroically and with determination against tyranny. For six blood-stained years all forms of resistance were used and all sections of the Cuban people, filled with true heroism, have resisted Batista's dictatorship.'

After enumerating the most important revolutionary actions of the various groups, which this time were neither criticized nor belittled, the document goes on:

'Realizing that only by co-ordinating all human and material resources, only by ensuring the collaboration of the political and revolutionary sectors of the opposition, by uniting civilians and soldiers, workers, students and members of the liberal professions, businessmen and all citizens will it be possible to overthrow the dictatorship, the undersigned promise to collaborate to achieve the fall of the criminal Batista dictatorship and to bring Cuba domestic peace and a return to democracy.'

This united front rested on three pillars:
A joint strategy which covered an armed rising, the strengthening of all fronts, mass mobilization of the workers and all bourgeois forces and the preparation of a general strike.

Determination that once the tyrant was overthrown and 'after a short period during which power shall rest in the hands of a provisional government', the nation would return to the normal conditions of constitutional democracy.

A minimum programme to ensure the punishment of the guilty, the rights of the workers, the fulfilment of international treaties, the preservation of public peace and order and economic, social and political progress for the Cuban people.

This official programme of the revolution was signed by Fidel Castro, by Prío and Varona for the *Auténticos*, by members of the *Ortodoxo* Party, by delegates of the students, and the *Directorio Revolucionario*, by representatives of the trade unions (*Auténticos*, followers of Cofiño, and the 26th July Movement) by the ex-banker Justo Carillo of the *Montecristi* organization (to which the imprisoned Colonel Barquín also belonged), by Miró Cardona as representative of the 'civil resistance groups', and even by a member of the 'Democratic Party', a small old-established parliamentary party.

The programme was democratic rather than social revolutionary in character; for Castro it can hardly have meant more than a tactical move as a result of which he no longer appeared as a 'splitter' and which would enable him to achieve power. Miró Cardona was active on his behalf in Washington, he received increasingly more financial support, including regular contributions from the sugar magnates who regarded this as a kind of reinsurance which saved *their* sugar cane from being burnt by the revolutionaries.

Behind the backs of the other signatories Castro also came to an agreement with the Communists who had realized that his group was more important than they had originally thought. For many years they had had 'their' men in Castro's group, and as far as the leadership of the 26th July Movement was concerned, Raúl Castro and his future wife, Vilma Espin, had probably long been in close touch with the Communists. The same was true of Guevara, whose fighting unit in the Sierra Maestra was largely supplied by the Communist Party organization of the town of Bayamo, and who was himself a Marxist with such close links with international communism that in private conversations in the Sierra Maestra he even supported Lysenko's (the Stalinist geneticist) theories.

During August the Socialist People's Party sent its leading theoretician, Carlos Rafael Rodriguez, to the Sierra Maestra where he spent some time and concluded an agreement with Castro which was never made public.

(i) The Last Struggle

It was Batista's intention to hold elections in November at which his candidate, Rivero Aguero, would be chosen to succeed him as President. But before that Castro had to be finished off. The 'final offensive' began in the summer only to end a few weeks later in complete failure. On August 20, 1958, Castro announced the collapse of Batista's attack and the start of his own offensive. On August 24 he sent off two columns, together there were only about 200 men, under Guevara and Camilo Cienfuegos: they were to march through the Province of Camaguey and appear in the central province of *Las Villas* where Guevara incidentally would take over the supreme command of the troops of the *Directorio* and Escambray's 'Second Front'. The march was successful, although Camilo Cienfuegos' diary clearly shows[1] that at the time these columns were still completely isolated from the agricultural population, that they were in constant fear of betrayal and defeat and therefore had to move slowly and carefully. Only after both columns had reached their destination in late autumn did Castro start his final offensive. It is difficult to say exactly how strong the rebels were at that time.

In December 1961 Castro revealed that in the early summer months of 1958 his whole armed force had consisted of 180 men. In his speech of July 26, 1963, he claimed to have won the war against Batista with less than 500 soldiers. In February 1959 I myself was told that the total number of officially recognized soldiers of Castro (*barbudos*) had been 803 in December 1958. Certainly there can hardly have been more than 1,000 men in all the different fighting groups in June–July 1958. When Castro began his offensive and most of the troops retreated without a fight and appeared to be completely demoralized, the rebel army naturally began to grow—and the Communists organized some small guerilla groups in the Eastern and Central provinces.

In the Batista camp everything during the last December weeks was in a state of collapse. Various generals were openly engaged in conspiracy. One of them, Cantillo, even flew to Fidel Castro for discussions. The leader of the army, Tabernilla, tried to persuade the American ambassador to mediate. In the middle of November, after the elections at which Rivero Aguero was, as expected, 'elected' President the situation seemed hopeless. The bomber pilots—who after the American embargo received their supplies from the United Kingdom—used their bombs only occasionally (on the civilian population) but usually dropped them where they would do no damage. Junior and senior officers gave themselves up or fled.

[1] Extracts were published in a French translation in *Esprit*, Paris, April 1961.

Cantillo and others were planning the establishment of a military junta on December 26. At the end of December, before the plan could be put into operation, the 'battle of Santa Clara' took place in the Central Province, ending in a total fiasco for the government troops and causing little bloodshed. An armoured train hastily sent to the spot—its commander fled before there was any fighting— was put out of action and taken over by the rebels. Then Castro went from the mountains to Santiago, after the commander of the Moncada garrison had gone over to him. Allegedly, Cantillo had undertaken to stop all opposition, to prevent Batista's flight and to give up any plan of a military junta government. But this did not happen: during the night of December 31, Batista and many of his collaborators fled. There was an attempt, helped by Cantillo, to establish a 'provisional government' under the chairmanship of an elderly judge. From Santiago, Castro called for a general strike which put a quick stop to the adventure and also enabled the workers to identify themselves with the revolution. With the tumultuous support of the people the bearded victor proclaimed the new President Urrutia, and his ministers. He appointed the former commander of the Moncada fortress, Colonel Rego Rubido, as supreme commander of the army. This was an intelligent tactical move intended to neutralize the remains of the old army. A few days later nobody remembered this colonel. Cantillo was arrested. Castro declared that he would be tried but this in fact never happened.

The doors of the prisons were opened. In the name of the revolution Colonel Barquín assumed command in Havana and tried to get Castro, who was slowly moving through the country, to confirm him in his position. Instead, Castro rushed Camillo Cienfuegos to the capital where he took Barquín's place without difficulty. At the same time Guevara and his rebels occupied the fortress of *La Cabaña*, the capital's second most important military strongpoint.

Castro had been victorious. He, and he alone, now held all power in the country. The future would show how he would use it.

(*j*) *Castro's Ideology*

On March 25, 1961, Castro said:

'The revolution was a long process which developed step by step. At the beginning the revolution had its weaknesses, particularly as far as ideology was concerned. The leaders of the revolution had much support among the people; the revolution produced enormous sympathy, but its ideology was weak.'[1]

From Castro's standpoint in 1961 this was correct: before 1959 he had been a long way from Marxist-Leninism.

The contents of the 'Manifesto of the Sierra Maestra' referred to above are of interest in this context. Point 1 demands the formation

[1] *Revolución*, Havana, March 26, 1961.

of a united front. Point 2 makes it the task of this united front to appoint a provisional president. Point 3 demands Batista's immediate resignation. Point 4 condemns American arms deliveries to the dictators. Point 5 rejects all foreign mediation. Point 6 rejects the establishment of a 'military junta'. Point 7 'promises that the provisional government shall hold general elections within a year, in accordance with the 1940 constitution and the electoral law of 1943 and that it shall hand over control to the elected candidates immediately afterwards.' Point 8 promises the liberation of all political prisoners and guarantees 'the complete freedom of the press and the preservation of all individual and political rights laid down in the constitution'.

Other points promise reform of the civil service, punishment for all who acquired wealth through unlawful methods, the establishment of democracy in the unions, a campaign for the elimination of illiteracy, complete educational reform, a sound financial policy to safeguard the currency and an economic policy aimed at industrialization and the removal of unemployment. Point 14 deals with land reform: 'A basic agrarian reform aimed at transforming all tenant farmers into owners, in which unused or state-owned land shall be distributed and the former owners compensated'.

In January 1958, Castro gave an interview to the American journal *Coronet*. With reference to the nationalization of private firms he said:

'I have come to the conclusion that at best "nationalization" is a clumsy instrument. While it weakens private enterprise it does not seem to strengthen the state. What seems still more important to me is that an extensive policy of nationalization would delay the realization of the most important point of our programme, namely quick industrialization. Therefore we shall welcome foreign investment and shall give it complete security.'

In May 1958, Castro replied to questions by the American journalist Jules Dubois.[1] He said that he was not thinking of nationalizing all foreign firms, nor of any kind of socialization. After victory he would not accept a post in the government.

The 26th July Movement would become a normal political party and compete for power in elections.

During the years of fighting two economists closely associated with Castro, Felipe Pazos and Regino Boti, had prepared an economic programme approved by Castro and published in a large edition in 1959. Industrialization, government planning, land reform, greater participation of Cuban business and the state in foreign enterprises

[1] Jules Dubois, *Fidel Castro*, p. 264, *et seq.*

and a juster distribution of the national income—these are points which are more reminiscent of Keynes than of Marx.

All these ideas must be considered in conjunction with the documents already referred to. However radical they may seem, they can certainly not be called 'communist' nor even 'socialist'. It might be said that Castro concealed his real views and that he has really always been a communist. We must, therefore, cast a brief glance at Castro's relations with the Communists under the Batista regime.

(k) Castro and the Communists

In the summer of 1953, after the official prohibition of the 'Socialist People's Party' a police department was established to counteract Communist activities; however, it had little money and only a small staff. There was a suspicion that the Communists had taken part in Castro's Moncada adventure, but no proof of any such collaboration has ever been found. An adventure like the attack on the garrison was contrary to the tactical ideas of Marxist-Leninism. The Communists—five of their senior officials had joined the Batista Party—suffered less interference than other opposition parties. Leading party members like Marinello were able to live in Havana throughout the dictatorship. The party even published four illegal journals, some of which were sent through the post. The *Carta Semanal* allegedly had a circulation of 16,000 which corresponded more or less to the number of party members.

Characteristic of the policy of the Party was an appeal issued on June 1, 1954, 'for unity in the fight against the Truslow Plan' (the proposals of the International Bank Commission in the *Report on Cuba*), 'for free elections with guarantees for all parties, for a democratic solution of the Cuban crisis, for the formation of a government of the national democratic front.[1]

During the united opposition mass meeting on November 19, 1955, the Communists tried—apparently jointly with Castro's sympathizers—to interrupt speakers, an activity which could only be welcome to the police. A *Carta Semanal* of February 1956 contained a protest against the arrest of some Communist leaders and a reiteration of the slogan about 'free elections'. In the same year Communist delegates travelled without hindrance from Cuba to the Soviet Union.[2]

But none of this is very informative. Naturally the Communists were against Batista *and* against his anti-communist orientated opponents. They were bound to regard Castro and other young

[1] Quoted in Alberto Baeza Flores, *Las cadenas Vienen de Lejos*, p. 339.
[2] An anti-communist French journal commented: 'Apparently there was a sort of tacit agreement between Batista and the Communists'. (*Est et Ouest*, Paris, No. 208, January 1959. It is unlikely that anything will become known about this, because it is in the interests of both the Communists and Batista to keep silent.)

'*putschists*' from the middle classes with the greatest suspicion, which did not prevent them from trying to infiltrate and to influence such movements. On April 9, 1958, the Communists were *against* the strike which they regarded, not without justification, as an 'adventure'. After its collapse the Communist leader Carlos Rafael Rodriguez—who was also able to live unmolested in the Cuban capital—said to the French journalist Claude Julien that the failure of this strike might teach Castro that he could not act alone. He criticized Castro 'from the right' because he had refused to come out in favour of a big united front of all opposition forces which, in the opinion of the Communists, should have included even the *Auténticos* of ex-President Grau San Martin. Furthermore, Castro's exaggerated anti-imperialist propaganda was dangerous because it indirectly strengthened Batista. In a letter dated June 5, 1958, addressed to the same Frenchman, Carlos Rafael Rodriguez said: 'If there were any forces in the country which could conquer Batista and bring a progressive anti-imperialist government to power everything would be easy. But unfortunately the position is different.'[1]

On March 17, 1957, the Communist leader Juan Marinello wrote a letter to the *New York Times* correspondent, Herbert L. Matthews, in which he expressed himself against attacks on barracks and government buildings, against any expedition from outside, any *putsch* or military rising, but in favour of a solution through 'democratic elections'. He went on: 'Our attitude to the 26th July Movement is conditioned by these basic ideas of ours. To us that group seems to have noble aims but to use the wrong tactics. Therefore we do not approve of its activities but appeal to all to protect the movement from the blows of tyranny and not to forget that the members of this movement are fighting against a government hated by the whole Cuban people.'[2]

No wonder the participation of the Communists in the struggle against Batista was negligible, as Guevara confirmed in an interview with Latin American visitors, published in *Hoy* on August 24, 1963.

'In Cuba,' he said, 'the Communist party did not lead the revolution, but its influence made itself felt and its participation was important in the present socialist stage ... The Communist Party did not see clearly, it did not properly understand the methods of struggle, it erred in its estimation of the movement's chances of success. Here, this extremely serious mistake was not costly, because we had Fidel and a group of real revolutionaries.'

We shall see that even *after* the victory of the revolution the Com-

[1] Claude Julien, *La Révolution Cubaine*, Paris, 1961, pp. 82–5.
[2] Herbert L. Matthews, *The Cuban Story*, New York, 1961, pp. 51, 52.

munists were less radical than Castro whom they distrusted in spite of the pact which they had concluded with him in August 1959.[1]

This agrees with an interesting remark made by Castro to the correspondent of *l'Unità*, in January 1961: 'It is true that at the beginning the Communists were suspicious of me and of the rebels. This suspicion was quite justified because we guerilla fighters in the Sierra Maestra were still full of lower middle class ideas in spite of all our Marxist courses. We lacked ideological clarity and only wanted to destroy tyranny and privilege with all our strength'.[2]

In November 1959 a member of the American Central Intelligence Agency, General Cabell, said before a Senate Investigation Committee: 'Our information is that the Cuban communists do not regard Castro as a member, or even as pro-Communist... but as a representative of the bourgeoisie... Our conclusion is that Fidel Castro is no Communist, but certainly also no anti-Communist.'[3]

Although many other statements to this committee express the opposite view, they cannot be relied on because they betray confusion and ignorance of the situation, wrongly describing as 'Communists' a number of other revolutionary leaders who soon emigrated.

But it all depends what is meant by a Communist. Castro, though never a member of the Communist Party (PSP) had in fact long been much closer to 'Communist' ideas than appears from his utterances at the time. But Marxist-Leninist and petty bourgeois *putschist* ideas co-existed in Castro's mind, so that he was often to the 'left' of the official Communists, and was no less suspicious of them than they were of him. This 'angry young man' was a typical revolutionary intellectual of the 'populist' and 'voluntarist' kind. His aims and methods were far removed from those of the official Communists. He never considered himself to be a proletarian leader or the industrial workers to be the main force of the revolution. He did not envisage a socialization of the means of production, the establishment of a proletarian dictatorship, the destruction of personal freedom and representative democracy, or any subordination of Cuba to the whims of Moscow. He did not believe in the 'rôle of the party' and the necessity to submit himself to any collec-

[1] Yves Guilbert in his book *Castro l'Infidèle*, Paris, 1961, p. 86, quotes the view of an Italian Communist expressed in the *Cahiers du Communisme*, Jan./Feb., 1959, according to which Castro is a 'man of the Church, who has received political, financial and military help from the United States'.
C. Wright Mills reports that young Cuban revolutionaries told him in the summer of 1960: 'For over five years, in fact—before we won—the Communists, when they didn't ignore us, were political rivals of our movement. We owed them nothing when we triumphed over Batista's tyranny. They didn't help.' *op. cit.*, p. 105.
[2] *L'Unità*, Rome, February 1, 1961.
[3] *Communist Threat to the US through the Caribbean.* Hearings before the Subcommittee to Investigate the administration of the Internal Security Act, etc., of the Committee of the Judiciary. US Senate, 86th Congress, First Session, November 5, 1959.

tive discipline. Pushed forward by the idea of social justice, as well as the urge to get power for himself, he was a radical, anti-imperialist nationalist and regarded himself as champion of all the disinherited, frustrated, and poor, the '*humildes*'. He aspired to a new Cuba, free of oppression, social injustice and corruption, in which people would enjoy 'freedom as well as bread'. Filled with impatience, he would come out against opportunism, against compromises with a recalcitrant reality. He chose the way of direct action by a small group of insurgents which hoped to unleash a mass struggle in the cities but could also win by itself. This ideology was never clearly elaborated—and it was diluted in 'official declarations'—for tactical and strategical reasons. But it was profoundly revolutionary. Those who tended to consider Castro merely as a champion of 'political democracy' and of the Constitution of 1940, overlooked the revolutionary, utopian implications of that famous document, which, precisely because of those implications, had hitherto remained largely on paper.

Castro himself described his original ideology in the speech of December 1, 1961, in which he, for the first time, espoused Marxist-Leninism. It is not easy to summarize Castro's speeches. This one, like the rest, was diffuse and extremely long—it lasted six hours. To interpret it correctly we must look at it in the context of the revolutionary process. Until the beginning of 1961 it was important for Castro *not* to be taken for a communist; but, by the end of that year, the opposite was true. He had become the official leader of a socialist revolution, and the designated head of a Marxist-Leninist unity party in the process of formation. In this situation he had to represent himself as an old Marxist-Leninist, and his declarations must therefore be taken with a pinch of salt.

In this speech, and in the important speeches of December 20, 1961, and March 26, 1962, Castro said that when he left secondary school he had been still 'politically illiterate'. He had first come into contact with communist literature and with communists during his university years. By the time he had finished his studies, he claimed, he was practically a 'Marxist', though still full of petty bourgeois prejudices, and distrustful of the Communist whom he regarded as 'sectarians'. That was where he stood in 1953. At that time his ideas had been more or less the same as today and he was influenced mainly by Lenin's *State and Revolution*; but he still had many illusions and did not 'understand Marxism as well as later'. In his famous speech 'History will absolve me' he had deliberately toned down his radicalism so that nobody would be too put off.

On March 26, 1962, he attacked 'old Communists' who had described 'History will absolve me' as 'reactionary' and said: ' "History will absolve me" is not a classical Marxist text. Certainly not! It expresses progressive, revolutionary ideas in the process of development; they are not yet Marxist ideas, but the ideas of a young man who is moving towards Marxism and who is beginning to act as a Marxist.'[1]

He had not been a 'mature Marxist-Leninist' in 1953, nor even when the fighting began in the mountains. But he had moved closer towards Marxism-Leninism and had virtually accepted it. This fact he had been forced to disguise for tactical reasons: 'We were acting in the Marxist-Leninist sense, that is to say we took account of objective conditions. Naturally if we had stood on the top of Pico Turquino [the highest mountain in the Sierra Maestra—Author] when we only had a handful of men and said that we were Marxist-Leninists we might never have got down into the plain.' (Speech of December 20, 1961).

During the years in the Sierra Maestra he, in contrast to his bourgeois comrades-in-arms, had become convinced of the need for a socialist revolution, and dissatisfied with the exclusion of the official Communists from the united front. When he came to power the objective balance of forces still did not allow him to come out openly as a Marxist-Leninist. Moreover he had remained somewhat suspicious of the official Communists: 'There were differences between us which may have arisen from the fact that we did not see eye to eye in some things, but which can mainly be attributed to the fact that we did not speak to each other'. (Speech of December 1, 1961.)

Lack of contacts, and old prejudices, were responsible for the fact that in the early period after he had assumed power he had blamed the Communists for incidents and difficulties for which they were not in fact responsible. The subsequent development of the revolution had helped to remove all these misunderstandings and shown the need for bringing the Communist cadres into the revolution. That at that time he was already a clear Marxist-Leninist is illustrated by the (alleged) conversation with his closer friends which he describes: 'I remember that people came and said: "When shall we draft the programme of the 26th July Movement?" and I replied: "What kind of programme could that be? It could only be a Marxist-Leninist programme and why should there be two Marxist-Leninist programmes?"' (Speech of December 1, 1961.)

This conversation was very probably invented: in 1959 and later, Castro's closer friends and the sympathizers of the 26th July Movement were definitely anti-Communist and put forward their 'humanism' against 'Marxism-Leninism'. Otherwise the self-portrait, though slightly inaccurate, is not false. Castro was silent about many events in his past, including the reasons for his difficulties with the Communists: on the one hand his emotionalism, his intolerance of discipline, his desire to dominate, and on the other the opportunism of the Communists and their collaboration with Batista.

[1] Taken from the official stenographic record produced in *El Mundo*, Havana, December 2, 1961, and March 27, 1962.

On January 1, 1959, Castro saw the opportunity for a quick transformation of the 'democratic' into a 'socialist' revolution. This was bound to lead to a further development of Fidel's Leninism, and to a fusion of the small organizations of the young revolutionaries with the old Communist guard.

(*l*) *The United States and Batista*

Castro's followers claim that the United States helped the dictator in his fight against the revolution. As proof they mention the friendly attitude which leading politicians, members of the government and American businessmen displayed towards Batista, and the arms which he received.

These statements are largely correct: Batista enjoyed considerable sympathy among North American capitalists, senators, ambassadors and army circles. Ambassador Gardner praised Batista so warmly that the dictator himself was embarrassed.[1] In 1957 his successor, Earl Smith, criticized police brutality but tried his best to prevent Castro's victory. In the same year a leading American army officer went to Cuba to decorate the commander of the air force, Colonel Tabernilla, whose aircraft were bombing the population. The American military mission remained in Cuba during the whole period and trained Batista's officers. Until March 1958, the arms which Batista used in his fight against the revolution came from the United States.

On the other hand, American politicians, including Ambassador Smith, and Batista's followers, accuse the American government of having helped Castro to victory. Earl Smith said before the investigation committee that both in the State Department in Washington and among senior members of the embassy in Havana there had been strong sympathy for Castro and that Herbert Matthews and others had succeeded in influencing American policy in Castro's favour. These Americans as well as Batista's followers point out that the rebels regularly received arms from the United States and that the embargo on arms deliveries to Batista, imposed in March 1958, had a catastrophic effect. Some of Batista's supporters, for example Pio Elizalde, claim further that the Americans helped Colonel Barquín with his attempted *coup d'état* and that they were in touch with the rebels of Cienfuegos (in September 1957).

With the exception of the last claim these statements are correct. The policy of the United States was both simpler and more complicated than both sides maintain. Its aims were simple, but it was complicated by tactical changes and differences of opinion among American politicians and officials.

Basically, American policy pursued the following aims: to preserve stability in Cuba, which was very much to the advantage of

[1] Ruby Hart Phillips, *Cuba: Island of Paradox*, p. 325.

American business interests; to strengthen anti-Communist elements; and to avoid as far as possible any direct intervention in Cuban politics.

American relations with the Prío government had been good, and the United States had no reason to welcome Batista's *coup* of which they seem to have known as little as Sumner Welles of the *coup* in 1933. But Batista's anti-Communist and pro-American statements made him acceptable, and the Americans recognized him all the more readily because at the beginning, when opposition to him was weak, he tried to preserve some democratic forms and seemed to be capable of maintaining order.

In 1957, when civil war seemed imminent and the terror spread, the US Government changed its line, partly under pressure from public opinion at home, and Ambassador Smith urged Batista to compromise and to be more democratic. When Batista ignored his advice and mounting Cuban protests found an echo in the United States, the embargo on arms deliveries was imposed. It is not surprising that the United States was in favour of a compromise solution rather than a Castro victory. Smith himself said that only two months after taking office he came to the conclusion that Castro was a dangerous radical: for this reason he regretted not only the sympathy for Castro in his own embassy and in certain sections of the State Department in Washington, but also Batista's refusal to compromise.

The future was to show that responsible US politicians were not altogether wrong to distrust Castro. In one of his essays, Guevara wrote that the victory of the Cuban revolution had been possible partly because 'American imperialism was disoriented and unable to gauge the depth of the Cuban revolution ... When imperialism tried to react, when it realized that the inexperienced young man who had marched in triumph through the streets of Havana knew his duty and was determined to act accordingly it was already too late. Thus in January 1959, the first social revolution in the Caribbean and the most fundamental of all American revolutions was born.'[1]

---

[1] *Verde Olivo* of April 9, 1961, quoted in an English translation in *Monthly Review*, New York, Vol. 13, No. 3-4, July/August, 1961. How little American politicians were prepared for what was to happen later also emerges from the report of Senator George A. Aiken, who after a visit to Cuba in December 1957, said in a memorandum that all was well in Cuba and that 'even if there were to be a change of government in Cuba it is unlikely that any new régime would adopt a hostile attitude to the United States'. (Quoted from John Hickey, 'The Role of Congress in Foreign Policy', *Inter-American Affairs*, Vol. 14, No. 4, Spring 1961.

PART III

THE DEVELOPMENT OF THE CUBAN REVOLUTION

'Revolutionary power is by definition a tyrannical power. It operates in defiance of the law. The duration of the tyrannical phase varies according to the circumstances, but it is never possible to dispense with it—or, more exactly, when it is avoided, there has been reform but no revolution. The seizure and exercise of power by violence presuppose conflicts which negotiation and compromise have failed to resolve—in other words the failure of democratic procedures. Revolution and democracy are contradictory notions.'
(Raymond Aron, *The Opium of the Intellectuals*)

'No revolution ever carries out the programme on which it is sold to the public. It may do more; it may do less; it will certainly do many things that its promoters do not promise and do not want.' (D. W. Brogan, *The Price of Revolution*)

1. The Honeymoon of the Revolution

On January 1, 1959, Cuba left the realm of dictatorial coercion for the realm of chaotic freedom. Oppressive fear had ended and jubilant rejoicing began. Batista's government collapsed and the police disappeared from the streets. Their place was taken by armed 'militia' who dashed about in motor-cars, by bearded, long-haired liberation heroes carrying guns, many of whom—from conviction or for tactical reasons—wore religious medals pinned on their chests, and by young scouts whose duty it was to regulate Havana's traffic.

One might have expected differences between classes to emerge, suppressed political hatred to erupt like a volcano, and widespread murder and looting to break out. Nothing of this kind happened. Instead of fury there was enthusiastic happiness, and instead of violence a feeling of universal brotherhood. Some casinos and a few shops were destroyed, some houses belonging to *Batistianos* were looted, and all parking meters were broken and emptied. There were isolated instances of Batista informers being chased and ill-treated, but otherwise nothing happened which might have recalled the period of Machado's fall. Of course, there were rumours that in the eastern province many opponents of the revolution had been murdered on Raúl Castro's orders—but those were rumours which nobody really believed. Fidel had promised that the guilty would be brought to trial and the people believed him.

The friendly and cheerful nature of these people showed itself during those days, and it was to require increasing conflicts and great efforts of revolutionary re-education to transform the happy, singing, shouting and dancing masses into organized gangs whose catch phrase was *Paredón! Paredón!* (Put them against the wall!)

Castro slowly crossed the country at the head of an ever-increasing procession—surrounded and slowed down everywhere by rejoicing crowds who wanted to see him, to hear him and to touch him. On January 8 he entered the capital. An observer might have thought that the population had suddenly doubled. For miles and miles people were crowding the streets, rooftops and balconies. On television he was seen entering the suburbs with his son, Fidelito, sitting beside him on his tank, and arriving at the presidential palace where he was welcomed by President Urrutia. Viewers saw the crowds outside the palace, in its corridors and halls: men, women and children, armed and unarmed, in uniform and civilian clothes crowded round the celebrated 'Robin Hood'. He sat on a stool talking to Urrutia and others, emptying one bottle of Coca-Cola after another. Then he appeared on the balcony. He was welcomed by an indescribable shout of joy. His speech was short—remarkably short for a man who later spoke almost daily for four to six hours at meetings or on television. This athletic, apparently indefatigable, human volcano was obviously tired. One clearly heard his followers talking to each other and some friends told him to stop so that they could get to their destination, the *Campo Columbia*, where the masses had already been waiting for hours to hear the leader make his main speech. His entourage was heard wondering and asking Fidel how he and they could get through the crowds. He showed them. 'Citizens,' his voice rang out, 'we must move on. I appeal to your self-discipline as free human beings, as patriots ... Where I shall point now two citizens standing beside each other must move away from each other and those behind must follow their example ... Yes, like that ... a bit more. Now that's enough ... Now there are even two corridors. Well, we shall now pass through one of them ...'

On television viewers saw two clearings appear; Castro and his followers passed through one of them.

A few hours later the hero stood on a podium in the heart of the military cantonment that had for so long been the centre of power. Somebody had released some white doves, one of which settled on his shoulder. In that position he made one of his typical speeches, incredibly long, explanatory, exhortatory, repetitive, never appealing only to the emotions but always also to reason; sometimes quiet, then impassioned, sometimes serious, then ironical. The impression was unforgettable; the personality was and remained fascinating. Comparisons with other dictators are difficult. Fidel was never just a power-lusting demagogue (although there is a lot of that in him), never a mystical megalomaniac 'Führer-Duce', appealing to irrational forces in whose name he believed himself to be speaking, never a cruel pseudo-Marxist despot with a contempt for human beings. Could one ever have imagined countless ordinary people calling Hitler 'Adolf', or slapping Mussolini or Stalin on the back? Would Hitler, Mussolini or Stalin have appeared in a village, helped the peasants with their work and discussed their problems with them for hours? Would they have lain down flat on the ground and, with critical comments from the onlookers, sketched out on a piece of paper plans for a new village, school and playing fields—and then really have carried them out, in spite of all the financial experts' objections?

On the whole Castro's first big speech in Havana was peaceful and exhortatory. The first conflicts had appeared shortly before when the leaders of the *Directorio Revolucionario* had settled down in the presidential palace, taken arms from a store and transformed the university into a fortress. These leaders, Chomón and Cubela, apparently did not want to be excluded from power—and they soon received titles and positions. Fidel appealed to everybody: Who still needs arms? Arms—for what? '*Armas para qué?*' What was needed was peace, patience and collaboration. Now there was complete freedom:

'This is the decisive moment in our history. Tyranny has been destroyed—there is general rejoicing: but all the work, all the difficulties lie before us and not behind us. It would be self-deception to think that it will be easy—deception of the people to conceal the difficulties ahead. It is easy to create illusions in a rejoicing people— but to do so would be extremely dangerous, and I think that we must beware of excessive optimism ... Who are the main enemies of the revolution? I think we revolutionaries ourselves ... we must all learn, learn a great deal. We are young and full of good will, but we lack experience. We have a tremendous responsibility towards the people ... It is important to be patient. That is what we young revolutionaries must learn: patience, and yet more patience ... I want to assure the Cuban mothers that no more Cuban blood will be shed through our fault. I want to assure the people that the laws of the land will be respected ... Should the men who form today's government prove unequal to their task the people will be able to replace them by others in free elections ... Public opinion will decide everything—it is an enormous force where there is real freedom ...'

In one of his first television interviews on January 9, Castro said in answer to the question when there would be elections: 'In about eighteen months. The political parties will be reorganized in about eight or ten months. During the first five months after the liberation it would be a crime to bring party politics to the people.'

On January 21 he said: 'Everybody knows how much I respect the civilian institutions of the Republic. Everybody knows that I have not interfered nor shall interfere in the activities of the President of the Republic ... Should the President forbid me to speak in public or tell me not to give even one interview I would unconditionally obey this order.'

On February 6, before workers of the Shell oil refinery, he said:

'This is the first revolution in history which has the support of a ninety-five per cent majority ... In other revolutions revolutionary minorities had to resort to force to retain power and to carry out important social changes ... We shall not do that ... Our methods are based on absolute respect for the individual, on absolute recognition of freedom and human rights. In spite of the revolutionary character of the laws which we shall proclaim we do not want to infringe a single right, nor suspend a single public freedom ... This revolution is unique because it is accompanied by a complete preservation of human rights ... It is a sacrifice for me to accept a position of power. The only sacrifice which I am *not* prepared to make, the only action which would be repugnant to my feelings would be to use force to further the revolution.'[1]

The revolution was to be as 'Cuban' as the palm trees. It was called the 'humanist revolution'. Its place was to be between Western capitalism which provided freedom but no bread, and Eastern socialism which provided bread but no freedom, and it was to give the masses both bread *and* freedom. This was to happen immediately —Castro emphasized repeatedly that he was not prepared to sacrifice the present generation to the interests of future generations and to restrict consumption in order to build factories and machinery.

It was not easy to discern any Machiavellianism in the apostle of freedom, the more so since he undoubtedly believed at least part of what he said. Few could foresee how much tension there would be between the 'democratic' and the 'social revolutionary' elements of the revolution.

There was no opposition to the development of the revolution, no brakes which might have slowed down the revolutionary express: the old government machinery had largely disappeared and its remains were easily destroyed or changed. The old parties were disorganized and most of them had been compromised, except for the Communist 'Socialist Peoples' Party' which was automatically legalized. The Church was weak and, at the beginning, welcomed the revolution like everybody else.

On February 16, Castro became Prime Minister in place of Miró Cardona. This was a realistic move and one which provided opportunities for greater dynamism as Castro became more impatient and more radical. At the end of February, after one of the first ministerial meetings over which he presided, Castro was asked by a minister who until then had not had much contact with the new Prime Minister whether he would like her to resign. Castro replied: 'This train will now start moving fast—probably too fast for you. At some point you will certainly want to get off, but you can choose your own moment.'

The Minister of Finance began to prepare a general tax reform which later became law. Castro was not opposed to it but said ironically: 'The capitalists will try to avoid paying taxes anyway'. He always showed a lack of interest in the doings of the Ministerial Council, which met irregularly, sometimes for several hours, sometimes for a few minutes. Occasionally, at the end of a meeting Castro announced the adoption of a 'law' which had barely been discussed and on which no vote had been taken.

The masses continued to be enthusiastic and many of those who

[1] All verbatim quotations from Castro's speeches in this part are taken from the semi-official pamphlet *Discursos para la Historia*, Vol. I, Havana, 1959.

THE HONEYMOON OF THE REVOLUTION

were beginning to be afraid consoled themselves with the thought that these inexperienced young people would soon learn and settle down. After all, the chaos could not continue for ever. But soon there was ample cause for anxiety:

First of all there were the revolutionary executions, the shootings of 'war criminals', although these aroused more feeling abroad than in Cuba. Officially about 550 people were executed during the first six months of 1959, but in addition there were those who were 'liquidated' during the first weeks after victory at Raúl Castro's orders, apparently without trial. Most of those executed had undoubtedly been guilty of murder and torture and the overwhelming majority of the people were in agreement with the verdicts of the revolutionary courts whose proceedings were sometimes even televised. But some critical voices were heard when at the beginning of March 1959, Castro himself reversed the verdict of a revolutionary tribunal that had acquitted some pilots of the Batista air force because of lack of evidence. A new tribunal, established on Castro's orders, sentenced them to long terms of imprisonment and the president of the first tribunal, the rebel Felix Peña, disappeared from the scene, allegedly committing suicide. To protests from lawyers Castro replied that the interests of the revolution were the supreme law. On May 8, 1959, in a speech in Havana he said: 'We have no need to offend against any laws because we make them ourselves'. Some disquiet was also created by the fact that Castro repeatedly said on television that the objectives of the revolution could only be achieved by radical action: his expression was that it was not a case of disinfecting with mercurichrome but of carrying out a surgical operation.

At the end of March anxieties were increased by developments in foreign policy. On March 22, at a mass meeting, José Figueres, the ex-President of Costa Rica, and a supporter of Castro, gave a warning against exaggerated 'anti-imperialism' and wild attacks on the United States. He was interrupted by protests from the trade union leader, David Salvador, and followed by Castro, who spoke passionately against any links with the western bloc, against participation in the 'cold war' and in favour of a 'neutralist' position.

Events in the sphere of economic policy were equally unlikely to fill 'capitalists' and property owners with confidence in the revolution. On the one hand the country was hit by a wave of strikes in which the workers obtained considerable wage increases, and on the other many laws came into force which sharply reduced profits and seemed to threaten the very existence of a free economy. The government lowered many prices; firms which refused to follow suit or to raise wages were taken over.

Higher taxes were imminent and the old opportunities for defrauding the Exchequer disappeared because of the honesty of the new officials. The houses, businesses, and bank accounts of leading

Batistianos were confiscated, and it was announced that all 'illegally' acquired property would suffer the same fate. A ministry was set up to deal with this question, since no definition of 'illegal' acquisition was given, and there was no appeal against confiscation, everyone was frightened, most of all those whose wealth derived from sinecures, corruption, special payments by former governments, or government contracts. Property worth hundreds of millions of dollars was confiscated and a big heterogeneous public sector established. The former state lottery was replaced by a newly founded 'Institute for Saving and Housing' (INAV) whose lottery was supposed to encourage saving because every ticket could after a certain period be turned back into cash and even earned interest after some years. The state planned to use the profits to build a lot of cheap accommodation. This was all the more necessary because the new régime had cut rents by thirty to fifty per cent; this enactment had put a stop to private building, increased unemployment, and created a mortgage crisis (which was aggravated by other laws reducing the price of land to a quarter of its market value). Meanwhile the government embarked on large-scale public works and provided parks, places of entertainment, sports grounds and splendid sea bathing establishments for the people.

The press was free. Newspaper owners and journalists were no longer subsidized. Castro expressed himself against this form of corruption, as well as against any restriction of the freedom of the press. On April 29 he said on television: 'If one begins to close down *one* newspaper no other newspaper will feel safe—and if one begins to persecute *one* person because of his political views *nobody* else can feel safe.'

But it did not seem entirely safe for the press to criticize the leader of the revolution or his ideas—and that he did not bear criticism gladly became clear as early as February when he complained about a fairly inoffensive caricature which had appeared in the satirical journal, *Zig-Zag*.

While the upper classes were becoming increasingly worried, the enthusiasm of the majority of the population was indescribable, particularly as Fidel occasionally made remarks like the following, which is taken verbatim from the speech which he made on February 16, on the occasion of becoming Prime Minister: 'If we can realize our plans, if we are allowed to carry out our projects you may rest assured that within a few years the Cuban standard of living will be higher than that of the United States or Russia—because those countries spend a large proportion of their national income on the production of armaments.'

In the second half of April Castro visited the United States at the invitation of the American press. In public speeches and in conversations with Secretary of State Herter, Under-Secretary of State

Rubottom, and probably also with Vice-President Nixon, he stressed that he had not come to seek economic assistance but to enlighten American public opinion. He emphasized the humanist character of the revolution and said of the impending land reform that it was necessary, but that it would mainly be unused, or uneconomically farmed land which would be confiscated and distributed, and that the owners would receive compensation. He said that he was fundamentally well disposed towards the United States in spite of its mistaken policy and that 'his heart was on the side of the West': Cuba would continue to recognize existing agreements, in particular the pact of Rio de Janeiro of 1947 by which the American republics undertook to assist each other in the case of attack from another continent.[1]

Castro's trip gave rise to two contradictory interpretations or myths. The first was thought up by Castro-supporters abroad, the second was put forward by Castro himself at the end of 1961.

The pro-Castro myth was created in order to explain Cuba's movement towards the Eastern bloc and communism, and to blame the United States for this twofold development. The theory is that all this could have been avoided if in April 1959 the United States had given Castro generous financial help.

In reply it must be noted that Castro himself repeatedly said, as for example in a speech on 17 April, 1959, to US newspaper publishers, that in contrast to many Latin-American statesmen he had not come to seek financial assistance but only to influence public opinion in the United States. He even forbade the economic and financial experts who accompanied him to mention or ask for financial help. One of his companions, the Minister of Finance, Rufo López Fresquet, wrote:

'When I accompanied Fidel to this country in April 1959, the Prime Minister warned me, as we left Havana, not to take up economic matters with the authorities, bankers or investors of the North. At various times during the trip he repeated this warning. That is why, when I visited the then Secretary of the Treasury, Robert B. Anderson, I did not respond to the American official's indication that the US was favourably disposed towards aiding our country. Also, for that reason, during our stay in Washington, when I exchanged views with the Under-Secretary of State for Latin-American Affairs, Roy Rubottom I feigned a polite aloofness towards his firm statement that the US government wished to know how and in what form it could co-operate with the Cuban government in the solution of the most pressing Cuban economic needs.'[2]

[1] A short objective description of Castro's visit is found in *Hispanic American Report*, published by Stanford University, Vol. XII, No. 4, 1959.
[2] *The Times of Havana*, Miami, September 15/17, 1961.

Felipe Pazos, then Head of the National Bank, and another economic expert from Cuba, Ernesto Betancourt, who both accompanied Castro confirmed López Fresquet's account. Theodore Draper rightly wrote: 'I am intrigued by one aspect of this myth about Castro's allegedly intense desire for American government aid and his reluctant turn to the Soviet Union as a result of frustration: he never complained about this, neither did other leaders ... Yet this charge has become one of the staples of pro-Castro propaganda outside Cuba.'[1]

Fidel Castro himself dealt a mortal blow to this myth in his speech of December 1, 1961. He said that there had never been a possibility of a 'third' position between US imperialism and the Soviet Union and that it had never been his intention to ask for or accept help from the Americans, because, from the beginning, he had been determined to have a socialist revolution and to fight *Yanqui* imperialism. His exact words were:

'When the revolution came to power it had the choice of two courses: either it could remain within the framework of the existing social system or it could go beyond it. One must realize that there are no solutions between capitalism and socialism. Those who try to find a third position are mistaken and suffer from utopian ideas and become the accomplices of imperialism ... There are people who believe that the Cuban revolution should—as they put it—have got money out of the Americans and the Russians. To take money from the imperialists by threatening them with friendship with the Soviet Union is blackmail. There were people who supported this unworthy idea ... This would have meant maintaining the *status quo* and respecting all the interests of imperialism ... There was no alternative: either revolution or betrayal ... We have chosen the only honest way ... the way of anti-imperialist struggle, the way of socialist revolution.'[2]

But Castro's explanations present a false picture of the position in April 1959 and arise from a Marxist-Leninist re-interpretation of his past.

It is a fact that at this time there was considerable anxiety in the ranks of Cuban Communists about Castro's apparent 'pro-*Yanqui*' deviations. His brother Raúl flew to Texas to see him, on his way to Buenos Aires to participate in the Economic Conference of the American States, and asked him angrily if he 'had sold out to the *Yanquis*'. And in his speech of May 2, in Buenos Aires, he made proposals in many ways similar to those later contained in the 'Alliance for Progress': He asked for a sort of Marshall Plan for Latin America, for 30,000 million dollars to be loaned in the course

[1] *New Leader*, New York, October 2, 1961. Letters to the Editor.
[2] *El Mundo*, Havana, December 2, 1961.

THE HONEYMOON OF THE REVOLUTION

of the next ten years by the US for the development of the Latin American subcontinent by fundamental agrarian reform and industrialization which would guarantee the existence of stable democratic régimes combining freedom with bread.[1]

Most interpretations of the Cuban revolution fall into the trap of ascribing to Castro a clearly conceived plan. Although it is true that he was already a 'revolutionary socialist' and in foreign policy a 'neutralist' in 1959, he was still led more by intuition and pragmatism than by any fixed conception. He was certainly more anti-capitalist and anti-American than he publicly declared. It may be that Vice-President Nixon appreciated this better than other people: after his talk with Castro he wrote a memorandum recommending wholehearted support for the anti-Castro forces.[2] Much of what Castro said could not have been proclaimed by a 'Marxist-Leninist'; the glorification of representative democracy, of human individual liberties, and the condemnation of all kinds of dictatorship. However, the rapid radical turn of the revolution could hardly have been avoided even with a different American policy. In any case, it is not plausible to blame Castro's turning towards Communism on 'American pressure'. Draper is entirely right in writing:

'Fidel Castro and his inner circle have never been innocent victims of circumstances; they have always been the engine of this revolution in perpetual motion ... A revolutionary leader does not betray the fundamental character of his revolution because American oil companies refuse to refine Soviet oil or because the United States suspends a sugar quota that has been attacked as 'a symbol of colonialism'. If he is really committed to a new social order different from capitalism and Communism, he does not resist the one by capitulating to the other with the speed of a pushbutton operation.'[3]

There was still no close collaboration between Castro and the Communists. At the end of May the Castroist *Revolución* was still attacking the Communists and Castro himself complained in a speech that the Communists, whom he did not, however, mention by name, claimed to be more radical than the 26th July Movement and that they were encouraging the workers to strike. In his speech on December 1, 1961, he mentioned that in the early days he had regarded the Communists with a certain suspicion which he attributed to misinformation and to the fact that there had been no organized and continuous collaboration between him and the

---

[1] Parts of this speech are available in French translation in 'Fidel Castro parle', *Cahiers Libres*, Paris, ed. François Maspero, 1961, pp. 93–100. This translation contains a misprint: on p. 100 Castro did not ask for 30 million, but for 30 *thousand* million dollars in ten years.
[2] Theodore Draper, 'Cubans and Americans' in *Encounter*, London, July 1961 and 'Castro's Revolution', New York, 1962, p. 62.
[3] Theodore Draper, 'Castro's Revolution', New York, 1962, p. 106.

Communists. Also at the same period the 'Humanist workers' Front' of the 26th July Movement, led by David Salvador, began to fight the Communists inside the 'purged' trade unions. The contrasts had not yet become clear-cut, the illusions continued to exist.

2. The Emergence of Contradictions

The course of the revolution was decided between June and October 1959. In June the contradictions began to become more evident. There were two reasons for this: land reform and the attitude towards Communism. The two questions were closely connected. The agrarian revolution—for it was a revolution—constituted a strong attack on all property owners and also hit American interests. Together with the radical changes already made it amounted to a social revolution which was irreconcilable either with the continued existence of any kind of free economy or with the letter and spirit of the 1940 constitution. This led to growing discord among Castro's followers and to an increase of Communist influence. Any attack on the Communists began to look like an attack on the revolution itself and in fact 'anti-Communism' became the slogan of its opponents.

As we shall deal with the agrarian revolution in a special chapter we shall now concern ourselves only with its political aspect. The radicalism of the law signed on May 17 in the Sierra Maestra went far beyond Castro's original intentions. The Minister of Agriculture, Sorí Marín, a major in the rebel army and former president of the most important revolutionary tribunal, signed it only under pressure. But in fact the agrarian revolution was even more radical than the law. Sweezy and Huberman, the Marxist writers who visited Cuba in 1960, were told that Sorí Marín's original project had neither provided for the establishment of kolkhoz-like co-operatives which formed the centre of the new land reform, nor envisaged the entire direction of agriculture by the state and its omnipotent 'National Land Reform Institute' (INRA). The idea of collectivizing agriculture is said to have been Castro's own.[1]

In his speech of December 20, 1961, Castro said that he had only added the term 'co-operative' to the draft of the land reform law in the aircraft flying to the Sierra Maestra, immediately before the promulgation of the law. At that time it had already become clear that the co-operatives would not own the land which they worked, but for tactical reasons it had been decided to speak of 'ownership'.[2] Manuel Artime, a senior INRA official who fled abroad at the end of 1959, before his departure wrote a letter which circulated illegally describing a meeting of senior INRA members in the late summer of 1959. To many who read this report at the end of 1959 its contents seemed a wicked distortion of the truth—but the future was to

[1] Huberman and Sweezy, *Cuba, The Anatomy of a Revolution*, Routledge and Kegan Paul, London, 1961 and Monthly Review Press, New York, 1960.
[2] *El Mundo*, December 22, 1961.

confirm its accuracy. This circular, from which the following extracts are taken,[1] is an extremely important document for revealing Castro's real thoughts:

Núñez Jiménez (Vice President of INRA) opened the discussion. 'These meetings are private ...' he said. 'Here we shall discuss the real aim of the revolution which the Cuban people cannot yet assimilate. You, the members, represent Cuba's real government. INRA is the real Cuban state—all other government departments act only as a screen ... Each one of you has complete authority within his sphere but must act in accordance with what is said at these meetings.'

Then, after the inevitable delay, Castro, the Prime Minister and official President of INRA, appeared. He began by criticizing measures which had been stupid or costly, though he emphasized that the question of cost was not all-important. He went on:

'It is true that there is not enough money. But when we do not have any more we shall take away the banks' money and put the entire economy under state control ... Soon those who want to invest money will have to be real geniuses to find some way of investing their money. Perhaps in houses? There is a rent law already in force and I have prepared another law which will come into force if the people show signs of dissatisfaction. This law will transform tenants into owners. And INAV is also building houses ... Perhaps they should put their money into land? Now that INRA exists they would be mad to do anything like that. Anyway, the sale and purchase of land is prohibited. They will not invest it in industry—which they could only do over Ché Guevara's dead body. Thus the capitalists must waste their money or put it into banks because they cannot take it out of the country ... About "people's shops" we shall have to be very careful ... If the wholesalers and retailers realize that we intend to push them out we may have great difficulties. It is true that in the end *all* property owners, big, medium, and small, become enemies of the revolution, but it would be silly to make them all enemies at one go ... We must behave as we did during our war: first we shall capture the plain, then attack the towns. On the plain the retailers are weakest and disorganized. We must begin with them. We must explain that the people's shops have been set up only in order to protect the peasants from high food prices ... Later we shall compete with urban traders and force them to lower their prices ... The land itself will belong to the state— but the peasants cannot be told this because it would make them furious. The managers of the co-operatives must be employees of INRA. The ordinary peasant (*guajiro*) lacks the qualities needed for a

[1] Reprinted in Alberto Baeza Flores, *Las Cadenas Vienen de Lejos*, Mexico, 1960, pp. 471–6.

THE EMERGENCE OF CONTRADICTIONS

manager ... He must be educated to work together with others, he must lose his individualism and his ridiculous passion for private property ... The profits of the co-operatives will be restricted by the government.'

In private conversation after the meeting Castro said: 'When the mining law is published we shall have finished with *Yanqui* money here. They will howl with fury when they see what we are going to do with their sugar mills. The *Yanquis* have *one* good quality—they always hope that *I* will change. They are so naïve that it is enough for me to receive Bonsal [the US Ambassador] to make them happy.'

It is questionable whether these are accurate verbatim quotations, since Artime can hardly have taken shorthand notes. But at the end of 1961 the basic truth of this document could no longer be questioned. Because of these remarks Castro can, of course, be branded as a 'cynical traitor to the people', but above all one is conscious of a certain unquestionable 'realism' and of a radicalism going beyond the wishes of the Communists, who were not in favour of rapid collectivization.

In June the commander of the revolutionary air force, Díaz-Lanz, fled to the United States. As reason for his flight he gave the growing influence of the Communists, about which he claimed to have complained to Castro without success.

In the middle of July the Urrutia drama occurred. On July 17 Castro announced suddenly his resignation as Prime Minister. The nation was in despair and demonstrated. He was pressed to give the reasons for his resignation. At first he would only say that it was a question of disagreement with President Urrutia. On July 13 Urrutia had given an interview to Castro's old friend, the radio commentator and journalist, Conte Aguero. Refuting attacks in the Communist daily, *Hoy*, Urrutia had said:

'The Communists accuse me of not being faithful to the revolution ... They do Cuba great harm. For them everything good comes from Russia and everything bad from the United States ... [Their aim is] to make the Cuban people a tool in the cold war. I consider this to be criminal. Therefore I refuse to be supported by the Communists and believe that all true Cuban revolutionaries should reject this support ... I have a moral right to say this: when I was in the United States and appealed to the State Department to stop delivering arms to Batista, the Communist gentlemen here pronounced the policy of insurrection to be wrong. If the Cuban people had listened to them Batista would still be here.'[1]

The interview was televised. Six weeks before, several ministers, including Agramonte, who had been attacked by the Communists,

[1] Quoted by A. Baeza Flores, *op. cit.*, p. 417.

in particular for being pro-American and not sufficiently revolutionary, had left the government. Now it was necessary to go one step further. Urrutia made a direct attack on the Communists, which was contrary to the policy of Castro and Guevara. 'Under popular pressure' Castro agreed to resume the Premiership. On television he began to attack Urrutia, at first quietly and with restraint and then with increasing violence, like a good actor. He accused Urrutia of slowing down the revolution, of putting obstacles in the way of land reform, of splitting revolutionary unity. He also hinted that Urrutia had enriched himself illegally. The masses supported Castro, and the unfortunate Urrutia, who wanted to reply to these attacks on television, was refused the right to do so. He was taken away and then put under house arrest until, in spring 1961, he fled to the Venezuelan embassy where he had to spend several months because the Castro government, contrary to Latin American usage, refused to let him leave the country.

Urrutia was replaced by the former Minister for Revolutionary Laws, Osvaldo Dorticós Torrado, who in the 'forties had been a communist candidate in the elections to the Cienfuegos town council and who had later, for a while, been Marinello's secretary. During the Batista period he had not distinguished himself in any way. On the contrary, the *Gaceta Oficial* of September 15, 1955, had contained a decree of the then Minister of Public Works, signed by him and President Batista (Decree No. 2739) appointing advocate Dorticós Torrado 'legal assessor of the Cienfuegos water-works', a post which was in fact a sinecure.

In August the exposure of a curious conspiracy, allegedly planned with Trujillo's assistance, resulted in mass arrests and momentarily diverted public attention. But the Communist question came to the fore again with the Matos crisis. Hubert Matos was an intellectual from Camagüey Province who became a revolutionary in the Batista era, joined the 26th July Movement, fought in the mountains and became a major in the rebel army. After the victory he was appointed governor of the Province of Camagüey and enjoyed a high reputation in revolutionary circles.

On October 13, 1959, he sent a letter to Castro expressing the wish to resign his post and to return to private life because although he disagreed with the growing influence of the Communists he did not want to make difficulties for Fidel and the revolutionary government. The letter was published by the *Prensa Libre* of Havana at the end of October. It said:

'Compañero Fidel,

'Today I have written to the general staff about my resignation. I consider it my duty to inform you of my reasons . . .

'I do not want to become an obstacle in the way of the revolution.

THE EMERGENCE OF CONTRADICTIONS

Placed before the alternatives of falling into line or of disappearing in order to avoid doing harm, I must consider it more in accordance with my revolutionary honesty to do the second ... Everyone who has spoken frankly to you about the Communist problem has had to leave or be dismissed ... Anyone who wants the revolution to be victorious must say frankly where we are going. It is wrong to treat those who want to discuss serious problems as reactionaries and conspirators. It is disloyal and unjust to suspect people who are disinterested and who did not appear on the scene only on 1st January ... It seems right to me to point out that great men become smaller when they begin to be unjust ... I hope you will understand my reasons and ask you to accept my resignation and to allow me to return to private life, without my sons later being told that their father was a deserter or a traitor ... '

Castro decided immediately to take the offensive against Matos and to unmask him as a counter-revolutionary. He spoke on the radio, flew to Camagüey, mobilized the masses there and set out at the head of an armed band to arrest the alleged counter-revolutionary conspirator, and almost his entire staff, who were in agreement with him. None of them tried to flee and none offered the slightest resistance. Before his arrest Matos wrote a statement which was later circulated illegally. It said among other things:

'I believe that people live in order to defend certain values and that it is better to die than to turn one's back on these values, on truth, reason and justice.

'Yesterday I wrote a letter to Dr Fidel Castro in which I asked him for permission to leave military service because I regard such a resignation as my duty. In reply he accused me of treachery, of collaborating with Díaz Lanz and of wanting to stab the Cuban revolution in the back. It is distressing that such statements should be made in the name of the revolution and by men in whom the people believe. One regrets having been born if one has to witness this sort of thing ...

'All right, Fidel. I am waiting for your decision. You know that I have the courage to spend twenty years in prison—just as today I have the courage to stay quietly at home with my four sons while you gave the order to occupy all radio and police stations and the airport, as though there was a rising.

'I hope that history will judge me—and you too, Fidel, who once wanted the same thing. At that time you defended the people and appealed to them to rebel in the name of reason and justice. But now you are destroying your work, burying the revolution.'[1]

[1] Cf. Yves Guilbert, *Castro L'Infidèle*, Paris, 1961, p. 127 ff.

The arrest of Matos and his officers caused great excitement, particularly among the revolutionaries of the 26th July Movement. It was the decisive turning point, although at the time other events overshadowed it—the so-called 'bombardment' of Havana and the disappearance of Camilo Cienfuegos.

On October 21 Díaz Lanz flew over the Cuban capital dropping leaflets. The revolutionary anti-aircraft organization went into action. Shots were fired from the roofs of police stations and barrack squares, sometimes by mistake at the revolutionary aircraft which had taken off to pursue Díaz Lanz. There were two dead and about fifty injured. At first the police announced that the dead had been the victims of a bomb thrown from a car. But later it was officially stated that Díaz Lanz had bombed Havana. The government published a pamphlet in Spanish and English entitled *Havana's Pearl Harbor*, which compared the attack on Havana with that of the Japanese in 1941 and accused the American government of taking part in the bombing. It also demanded the immediate surrender of Díaz Lanz.

He was in fact arrested in the United States and released after an investigation had proved beyond doubt that the aircraft which he had used was unsuitable for dropping bombs. In fact no bombs were dropped and even if he had been able to bomb Havana it would have been as much in Díaz Lanz's interest as setting fire to the *Reichstag* was in the interest of the German Communists in 1933. The photograph on the title page of the pamphlet showing aircraft fighting over Havana was soon proved to be a photo-montage.[1]

The excitement produced by the alleged bombing and by government propaganda was cleverly exploited in the Matos affair. At a mass meeting on October 27 Castro and other revolutionary leaders accused Matos of treason. The crowd welcomed them enthusiastically and shouted *Paredón! Paredón!*

Some people noticed that the popular rebel leader, Major Camilo Cienfuegos, was not among the speakers at the meeting. For some time he had been considered a firm anti-Communist. On October 28 he boarded an aircraft to fly to the eastern provinces—and disappeared. Soon rumours were heard that Fidel and Raúl Castro had arranged his murder, for which there is evidence but no proof. For days the Cuban people were kept in a state of breathless excitement and mounting tension with reports about the search for the bearded major.

Meanwhile more opposition appeared to be on the way. Elections to a trade union congress in November resulted in a large anti-

[1] That it was a photo-montage became clear from the fact that the 'photograph' showed Havana in broad daylight, but that the sky behind the aircraft was grey. In the Spanish edition of *Life*, Vol. 15, No. 3, February 22, 1960, it was proved that the aircraft were American C54s over New Jersey photographed in 1947.

THE EMERGENCE OF CONTRADICTIONS

Communist majority. At the end of the month there was a Catholic Congress at which anti-Communist shouts were heard and choruses of *Ca-ri-dád! Ca-ri-dád!* in the same rhythm and intonation as the *Pa-re-dón! Pa-re-dón!* of the revolutionaries.

The revolutionary government responded with an intensified campaign against 'imperialists' and their henchmen trying in the name of 'anti-Communism' to weaken the forces of the revolution. The government was reorganized and anti-Communist ministers who had played a big rôle in the 26th July Movement, notably Manuel Ray, Faustino Pérez and Manuel Fernández, were replaced by pro-Communists while at the head of the National Bank Felipe Pagzos was replaced by Ché Guevara. At the trade union congress Fidel Castro intervened personally in order to force the election of a 'united leadership' which before long gave the Communists an opportunity of getting the trade unions under their control.

In December Matos and his officers were court-martialled. There was an embarrassing incident when a number of officers and soldiers of the rebel army welcomed the accused with applause, only to be immediately arrested on Raúl Castro's orders, stripped of their uniforms and expelled from the army.

Castro made an incredibly long speech—as a witness. But neither he nor anybody else could prove real 'high treason' nor the intention to organize a rising. Matos was sentenced to twenty years imprisonment and those tried with him to slightly shorter sentences.

The situation had become clear. In spring 1960 Jean-Paul Sartre and Simone de Beauvoir visited Cuba. On their return to Paris Simone de Beauvoir was interviewed by Claude Julien. The interview appeared, without comment, in Spanish in *Revolución*,[1] She said among other things: 'We asked ... why has the revolution no cadres, no apparatus? The replies received all amounted to the same thing in spite of some differences: the 26th July Movement which fathered the revolution had a lower middle class apparatus which could not keep up with the development of the revolution when the latter started to be more radical. Therefore it was dropped.'

On December 6, 1959, *Revolución* wrote: 'Those who are dissatisfied and therefore join the opposition cannot be regarded as revolutionaries, nor even as opportunists. In times like these opposition is identical with counter-revolution.'

In his speech against Matos, Castro had said: 'We had ideological differences ... I think that Matos and we disagree about the character of the revolution. I am not sure whether Major Matos ever had a clear concept of the character of a real revolution.'

It had now become clear what was really at stake. Castro's 'real' revolution was a 'socialist' revolution which went far beyond what had been planned and proclaimed by the united front which fought

[1] *Revolución*, Havana, April 15, 1960.

against Batista, and which, inevitably, could not be reconciled with the 1940 Constitution, the preservation of a free economy, or representative democracy. Certainly many months were to pass before Castro himself was to speak of 'socialism'. The people had first to be prepared, 're-educated'. But the decision had been made.

3. The Road to Socialism

The change which took place in Cuba had four inextricably interwoven aspects. Economic and social transformation coincided with a reorientation towards the Eastern bloc and, in the sphere of domestic policy, with the destruction of representative democracy, the *gleichschaltung* of pre-revolutionary organizations, the establishment of new institutions and the development of an official ideology. The economic, social, foreign, domestic, and ideological aspects of the revolution are facets of one and the same process, which in Cuba occurred in a highly individual, rather chaotic manner—and tremendously fast. In the interests of clarity we shall start with a brief account of the nationalization of the economy, deal after that with 'foreign policy' and domestic problems, and also then with the most praised 'positive achievement' of the revolution: the steps to improve the position of the lower classes, and, in particular, land reform. Some aspects of the 'ideological' change will be referred to here in connection with other changes, but it will be considered again in the chapter on the situation after the invasion of April 17, 1961. The present chapter is confined mainly to the events of 1960.

(*a*) *The Nationalization of the Economy*

In the April, 1961 number of the Paris journal, *Esprit*, Professor René Dumont—one of Castro's advisers in 1960—wrote that he was worried by the speed of nationalization in Cuba. He preferred the caution of the Chinese Communists, who took seven years (1949–1956) to achieve the change carried out in Cuba in the course of a mere eighteen months. In Cuba, private ownership of the key means of production had in fact been abolished as early as October 1960.

This dynamism was not in accordance with the ideas of the official Communists, who proved to be much more cautious than Castro and Guevara. At the Congress of the 'Socialist People's Party' in August 1960, the revolution had been described as merely a 'national, liberating, agrarian, democratic and patriotic' revolution, and its aims defined as: consolidation of national sovereignty, total abolition of *latifundia*, industrialization, confiscation of all illegally acquired property, reduction of unemployment, raising of the standard of living of the masses, strengthening of the revolution, etc. Most of these measures had already been carried out. There was no 'socialist' demand for the expropriation of industry and trade, which took place only a few weeks after this party congress.

As we saw earlier, the nationalization of the economy had begun in 1959 with the confiscation of firms and estates owned by *Batistianos* and by those whose property had been 'illegally' acquired. By the end of 1959 the value of all the estates confiscated was more than $500 million. The cessation of private building and the initiation of public housing projects was another step in the same direction. In November 1959 a law was passed empowering the state to take over any firm which found itself in difficulties, or tried to cut its losses by curtailing production. Many firms were nationalized under this law, among them most of the big hotels, which had become unprofitable because of the decline of tourism, and which were now taken over by the new state organization for tourism (INIT). Duties on imports had been considerably increased and the export of capital made more difficult even before Ché Guevara took over from Felipe Pazos in November 1959. Now state control of the entire banking system and a virtual state monopoly of foreign trade were introduced.

Land reform had put agriculture under the control of the state, which acquired a growing importance in the domestic market: not only were private retailers in the countryside (though not yet in the towns) replaced by 'people's shops' controlled by INRA, but INRA also acquired a monopoly in the wholesale trade in agricultural products and control of the most important cold storage space and warehouses. At the same time INRA took over fourteen sugar mills confiscated because they had belonged to *Batistianos*, and some rice mills and other concerns. INRA's special 'industrial' department was growing very fast. At the beginning of April all match factories were nationalized. At the same time there was a great 'census' of all employed persons, who from then onwards could get jobs only through the government authorities. Earlier a general wage freeze had been announced—at the request of the workers themselves; there were no more strikes. Jobs, working conditions, and wages were controlled by the state. The separate bodies to which different sections of the labour force had paid their contributions for social insurance and in particular for old age pensions were centralized in a special state bank. This was the position in mid-1960, when the great wave of socialization began.

It started in the oil sector. Prospecting for oil had already been nationalized, as had a small Cuban-owned refinery. A National Institute for the oil industry had been set up under the direction of a Mexican specialist. The Cuban government by this time owed the three big American and British companies, Esso, Texaco and Shell, more than £20 million for crude oil, most of which came from Venezuela. Now, on the basis of a Cuban law going back several decades, which committed the refineries to refine any 'Cuban' oil which might be found, the revolutionary government demanded that the refineries should refine Russian oil bought by Cuba at prices considerably below those paid for Venezuelan oil. When the companies refused to obey the order the refineries were sequestrated.

Shortly afterwards President Eisenhower announced a reduction in Cuban sugar imports to the United States which was regarded as an answer to the latest Cuban measures and as a declaration of economic war. The Castro government replied by nationalizing American firms: the electricity and telephone companies which had long been under government control were completely taken over, together with some of the sugar mills and, on September 17, the American-owned banks. When in October the American government replied with an embargo on all deliveries of American goods, except for medical supplies and foodstuffs, Cuba took over almost all other American concerns, including the nickel mines of Nicaro owned by the American government.

At the same time as foreign concerns—French firms were also taken over by the government—were nationalized, all the big Cuban companies were 'socialized'—textile, tobacco, cement, iron and other firms as well as all banks, large cinemas, department stores and warehouses. Under the law of October 13, no less than 382 firms were taken over by the state. Conservative estimates suggested that by the end of the month the state, through its own enterprises, directly controlled about 70 per cent of the national production. This trend was to continue and to spread to smaller companies; for example, early in August 1961 a decree was published taking over 236 private firms 'because they pursued a policy contrary to the interests of the revolution and of economic development.'[1]

In the course of October 1960 Castro also carried out the housing reform mentioned in Artime's circular of 1959. By an urban reform law all urban flats that were let were expropriated and placed under an institute of urban reform. Henceforth rents had to be paid to the state and were to be regarded as instalment payments: after five, ten or fifteen years their tenants were to become their owners. The former owners of the houses were to receive compensation, which, however, was not to exceed £120 a month. The new 'owners' were forced henceforth to pay 'rent' regularly and punctually, to be responsible for the upkeep of the building and could only change their flats for other flats through the National Institute which markedly restricted freedom of movement.[2]

From the end of October 1960 the Cuban economy must be regarded as 'socialized'.

[1] *Neue Zürcher Zeitung*, August 10, 1961.
[2] It seems as if those whose houses have not fallen down in the meantime or who have not lost their flats because they are 'counter revolutionaries' or 'suspects' apparently must wait much longer before they can become owners than the law seems to indicate. At the beginning of November Fidel Castro said in a speech: 'People's farms will receive preferential treatment over the towns. In the towns it will take *at least* fifteen years before families will pay no more rent while the workers on people's farms receive free housing, free electricity and free services in addition to their wages.' *Obra Revolucionaria*, No. 28, November 9, 1960, p. 26.

(b) Cuba Goes East

Castro could not become a Tito. In the Caribbean the decision to have a socialist revolution could only lead to dependence on the Eastern bloc. At home the radical change presupposed a 're-education' of the masses. For this it was necessary to have an external enemy whose hostility had not only to be exaggerated but even deliberately aggravated by provocative behaviour. Guevara said in 1961 that North America, as a capitalist-imperialist state, could only adopt a hostile attitude towards Cuba[1]. The purpose of the 'myth' of an 'implacable' enemy was to unite the nation behind the revolution. Sartre rightly said that the Cuban revolution would have had to invent the United States if it had not already existed.[2]

Internally the socialist transformation could only take place with assistance from the Eastern bloc. Even if capitalist America had been willing to finance a socialist economic reconstruction it would first have insisted on quick and adequate compensation for its expropriated citizens. But the Cubans were neither willing nor able to pay.

The Cuban revolution was found to provoke growing hostility in the United States by its loudly proclaimed anti-imperialism, its sequestration of American property and its ties with the Soviet Union. In the middle of the cold war, a bastion of the enemy and a centre of anti-imperialist propaganda for the whole of Latin America was being set up a mere ninety miles from the American coast. The Americans could not behave as the Soviet Union had done towards Hungary in 1956, particularly because for a long time Castro succeeded in presenting himself as a victim of the Americans and in disguising the 'Marxist-Leninist' character of his revolutionary aims. To some extent Castro's policy was based on an awareness of those inhibitions which, to use Mao Tse-tung's words, made 'Yankee imperialism' into a 'paper tiger'. But the foreign policy of the Cuban revolution needed the political support of the Soviet Union, which it received.

The situation in Latin America demanded the same foreign policy as the preceding three factors. The anti-Americanism which existed everywhere had to be mobilized against the United States. From the 'Marxist-Leninist' point of view the Cuban revolution could only be victorious if it became 'permanent' by transforming itself from a radical democratic into a socialist revolution covering the whole continent. Castro, the David who fought for social justice against the exploiting Goliath of the North, said on July 26, 1960, that 'the Andes must become the Sierra Maestra of the Continent'.

(c) Relations with the United States

Even after the land reform United States policy was at first

[1] Interview with K. S. Karol, *Express*, Paris, May 18, 1961.
[2] *France-Soir*, Paris, July 12, 1960.

THE ROAD TO SOCIALISM   197

restrained and 'defensive'. This restraint which surprised many people was the expression of both a conscious policy *and* an apparent confusion. The first American diplomatic notes recognized the need for land reform and merely complained about the inadequacy of the compensation promised. But the new Ambassador, Bonsal, appointed in spring 1959, had to wait almost three months before Castro had a full-length interview with him. American press comment on the executions became increasingly unsympathetic after the flight of Díaz Lanz and Urrutia's dismissal and led to Cuban counter-attacks in which the American government was blamed for the 'press campaign' against Cuba, for granting asylum to Cuban counter-revolutionaries, for inviting counter-revolutionaries to appear before the Senate Investigating Committee and for refusing to hand over Cuban 'war criminals' who had fled to the United States. The Cuban campaign grew more violent after repeated 'air raids' on Cuba for which the American government was always held directly responsible and reached its first climax after the alleged 'bombing' of Havana. There was a barrage of propaganda and school children were required to write essays on the subject.[1] At the beginning of 1960 the United States' government was accused of recalling American officials resident in Cuba who had been in charge of the export of fruit and vegetables to the United States. In March Castro said at a public meeting that it seemed as if American agents had been responsible for an explosion on a French ship which had arrived in the harbour of Havana with a cargo of ammunition. Next it was claimed that American warships, for example the cruiser *Norfolk*, had entered Cuban waters; then a sticker issued by the American Embassy, stating that in times of unrest the shops and houses of Americans to which it was affixed were 'under United States protection', was presented as proof of American preparation for an invasion.

To these accusations the American government replied[2] that the American press was independent and not controlled by the American government[3] and that, except for one or two instances, as for example in the case of Díaz-Lanz, the Cuban government had never officially asked for the extradition of individual war criminals; that those who

[1] The essay of a 13-year-old girl was printed approvingly in *Revolución* on March 13, 1960. It said among other things: 'We despise those who bomb our country, who cause the death of many citizens and who set fire to our sugar fields. We despise the Yankee imperialists who welcome war criminals and mercenaries and who try to stop the great march of our revolution ... The contempt of a free people and my own contempt ...'

[2] This was done mainly in two documents: *Responsibility of the Cuban Government for increased tensions in the Hemisphere*, US Information Service, August 17, 1960, and *Facts concerning relations between Cuba and the USA*, US Delegation to the General Assembly of the UN, October 13, 1960.

[3] On February 1, 1960, the publisher of the American daily, *Miami Herald*, offered to publish in his paper a series of articles written by Castro or one of his collaborators. He never received a reply.

misused American territory for air attacks on Cuba were liable to heavy fines, and that at least one of the attacks had been made by an *agent provocateur* with the approval of the Cuban government,[1] but that it was not easy to keep close control over more than 200 private airfields in Florida or to forbid American citizens to use their own aircraft, and that the American government had repeatedly asked the Cuban authorities to say whether they wished the fruit control officials to remain in Cuba but had never received a reply. Castro, it was said, had not provided any proof of the complicity of American agents in the explosion of the amunition ship *La Coubre*; and the cruiser USS *Norfolk* would have gone aground if it had attempted to enter Cuban waters at the place alleged. With regard to the stickers it was maintained that it was customary to use them in countries in which unrest was expected, that if they were meant as protection in case of an American invasion they would not have been in Spanish, and that they dated from the Batista period as could be seen from the fact that they showed a US flag with only forty-eight stars.

None of this was of any avail. The propaganda barrage continued and a flood of accusations of all kinds poured out over the United States: its atom bomb had killed tens of thousands of peaceful Japanese in Hiroshima, in the United States negroes were persecuted and lynched, innocent people like the Rosenbergs had been executed as spies, etc.

By May 1960 the US government had suggested nine times to the Cuban government that they should hold discussions. In a note dated February 22, 1960, Cuba expressed its readiness to take part but demanded that the American government should promise that during the negotiations (of unspecified duration) neither the American government nor Congress should decide on or carry out hostile measures against Cuba.

The revolutionary leaders realized of course that the American government would reject such conditions, if only because under the constitution the executive cannot commit Congress in this manner. But the general public in Cuba was not aware of these 'legalistic' points, and accordingly the manoeuvre served its anti-imperialist purpose. Looking back on the period as a whole, a British journalist remarked with particular reference to liberal American politicians like Kennedy and Stevenson: 'They would have welcomed the original Castro movement. They might have recognized a revolution of the Yugoslav type, independent of Moscow, but they are not prepared to tolerate a régime that is closely associated with Russia and, in their view, acts as Russia's agent in Latin America.'[2]

In any case Castro's policy was successful and the difficulties of

---

[1] The pilot who was later 'caught' in Cuba, a man called Shergales, had been known for some time to have been in touch with Cuban secret agents.
[2] J. D. Pringle, *Observer*, London, May 22, 1961.

THE ROAD TO SOCIALISM

the Americans grew.[1] In official circles it was increasingly felt that firm action must be taken against Cuba.[2] This resulted in the policy which the US pursued between the failure of the Conference of American States at San José in the summer of 1960 and the fiasco of the invasion.

(d) Relations with the Socialist Bloc

The deterioration of Cuba's relationship with the United States was a corrollary of its *rapprochement* with the USSR and its satellites, which officially began in February 1960 with a Russian exhibition and the signing of a trade agreement with the Soviet Union.[3] Mikoyan came to Cuba for this and appeared in a television interview. The Soviet Union promised not only to buy substantial quantities of Cuban sugar, although at a price below the world market price, but also to provide Cuba with goods. At the same time Cuba received the first loan of about £35 million at the very low interest rate of 2½ per cent which is normal for Russian loans. Twenty per cent of Soviet imports from Cuba was to be paid for in dollars and 80 per cent in goods and other forms of aid. Shortly afterwards diplomatic relations between the two countries were restored. Later, relations were also established with the Chinese People's Republic. Numerous delegations and technicians from the Communist countries arrived in Cuba, as well as all kinds of goods, including a variety of arms which soon transformed Cuba into the best-armed Latin American country and for which, according to official statements, no payment was made. The number of Cubans who visited the Eastern bloc countries increased and cultural relations became close: Russian, Chinese and other artists appeared in increasingly large numbers in Cuba and more and more Russian films and books were imported.

As the relations with the United States deteriorated and trade

---

[1] Cf. chapter on 'Castro's Shadow over Latin America'.

[2] The reduction of the sugar quota had some tragi-comic features. Guevara, in March 1960, declared, 'The US citizens have never stopped to analyze what amount of slavery the 3 million tons of our sugar quota which we customarily sell at supposedly preferential prices to the giant of the north has meant, and means, to the people of Cuba'. The US maintained that the cut in the sugar quota was in no way a measure of reprisal. Two North American journalists rightly commented:

'The situation led to perhaps the most absurd argument that developed between the two countries. The United States was claiming that the quota was a generous gift to Cuba but it was threatening to take it away—not to punish the island, but to "assure" sugar supplies. The Cubans were claiming that the quota was "economic slavery" but they indignantly charged that Washington would be practising unfair economic warfare if it should take the quota away.' Karl E. Meyer and Tad Szulc, *The Cuban Invasion*, New York, 1962.

[3] According to Captain Manuel Villafaña, who was at that time Cuban Air Attaché at the Cuban Embassy in Mexico, Ramiro Valdes, later chief of the revolutionary secret Police (G.2), had already visited Mexico in July 1959 to have secret conversations with officials of the Soviet Embassy. See Daniel James, *Cuba—The First Soviet Satellite in the Americas*, Avon Books, New York, 1961, pp. 235–8.

between the two countries declined, the importance of the eastern countries as suppliers, helpers and markets increased. This inevitably caused great problems because Cuba's economy was geared to the American market and it became difficult, for example, to get spare parts. Because the American suppliers had been close at hand and ready to make quick deliveries, Cuba had few warehouses. Now everything had to spend many weeks at sea. Moreover, the Communist countries were not at all dependent on Cuba and not very interested in its main product, sugar: Czechoslovakia and the Soviet Union could produce all the sugar needed for the Eastern bloc. Cuba inevitably had to become much more dependent on the Eastern countries than it had ever been on the United States which, moreover, had paid in convertible currency and not in goods. It was certainly politically important for the Eastern countries to help Cuba, which was both why the Chinese gave Cuba an interest-free loan and why, when the grateful Guevara wanted to make a statement to the effect that China's aid was 'disinterested', Chou En-lai said that this was not the case. The Chinese said that 'their help was by no means disinterested—though they were not interested in financial questions—because Cuba was at present one of the countries in the vanguard of the fight against imperialism and it was in the interest of Socialist countries to help Cuba.'[1]

The reason for giving aid was also explained in the leading organ of the Russian Communist Party: 'Any country, whatever its stage of development, is now in a position to achieve the transition to socialism by relying on economic and political assistance from the socialist system'.[2]

But from an economic point of view this did not seem easy for either party. Guevara in the speech already quoted, pointed out that the Eastern products were designed differently, and that the Eastern systems of measurement were different and had to be adapted to Cuban requirements. 'It is an event unique in the annals of foreign trade that a whole community of countries should change its types of production to help a country like ours.'

But there was another side to the question which Guevara mentioned later in a speech to sugar workers: 'The socialist countries have their own technology and we must change our entire system of production to adapt it to those countries which supply us with raw materials and spare parts.'[3]

There is little doubt that Cuba had to adapt itself more to the Eastern countries than they to her.

More and more Cuban products went to the East and in 1961

---

[1] At the end of December 1960 on television. Text of the speech in *Obra Revolucionaria*, No. 2, Havana, January 6, 1961.
[2] *Communist*, Moscow, No. 13, September, 1960.
[3] *Bohemia*, Havana, April 9, 1961.

when the Americans put a complete embargo on the import of Cuban sugar, the Eastern countries expressed their willingness to buy at least four million tons of sugar at four cents a pound. In return, as early as 1960 more and more Eastern goods appeared or were expected in Cuba: oil and rice (from China and Vietnam), agricultural products (from Poland), telephones (from Hungary), machinery and a variety of tools from Czechoslovakia, Russia and East Germany. These countries also gave new loans[1] and on July 15, 1960, after a visit to the East, Núñez Jiménez announced the impending installation of whole factories and the proposed erection of a steel mill, an oil refinery, and so on.[2]

The 'political' aid which Cuba received is generally known: it is only necessary to recall that Khrushchev himself said in July 1960 that if necessary he was ready to use rockets to protect Cuba from imperialist attacks.[3]

(e) *Beginnings of Totalitarianism*

In January 1959, the revolutionary government had produced a new provisional basic law which incorporated many paragraphs of the 1940 constitution. Paragraph 37 said: 'The formation or existence of political organizations opposed to representative democracy is prohibited.'

One aspect of representative democracy, however, is free elections, which in turn require the existence of a legal opposition. By the end of 1959 it was already clear that there were not going to be early elections and the semi-official *Revolución* had already stated that opposition was identical with counter-revolution. On March 28, 1960, the same paper reported that the former chairman of the Havana hairdressers' association, a certain Raúl Ramón Proenza, had been sentenced to three years' imprisonment for daubing walls with *anti-Communist* slogans. At the same time Castro's former friend, the radio commentator Conte Agüero, had to leave the country because of his opposition to the Communists. Aureliano Sánchez Arango was insulted and threatened at the airport by

[1] A good description of Cuba's economic relations with the East is found in *Der Ostblock und die Entwicklungslaender*, Vierteljahrschrift der Friedrich Ebert Stiftung, Hanover, March 1961.
[2] *Bohemia*, Havana, July 24, 1960.
[3] 'The time of US dictatorship has passed. The Soviet Union is raising its voice and extends the hand of assistance to the people of Cuba ... The peoples of the socialist countries will help their brothers, the Cubans, defend their independence, so that the economic blockade, now declared against Cuba by the US will meet with failure ... It must not be forgotten that now the US is not at such an unattainable distance from the Soviet Union as in the past. Figuratively speaking, Soviet artillerists, in the event of necessity, can with their rocket firepower support the Cuban people if the aggressive forces in the Pentagon dare begin intervention against Cuba.' Address to a Conference of Teachers in the Kremlin on July 9, 1960 (as translated in the Department of State, Historical Office-Bureau of Public Affairs, *Inter-American Efforts to Relieve International Tensions in the Western Hemisphere 1959–1960*, July 1962, pp. 216/217.

Communist demonstrators when he returned from a visit abroad. There were clashes and he too had to go into exile. He was followed by Antonio de Varona and the *Auténticos* were in effect proscribed. Those who tried to set up a 'Christian Democratic' Party suffered the same fate. The 26th July Movement never developed a proper organization and never held a party congress. The 'Socialist People's Party' was the only legal and organized political group and it grew steadily in importance. Leading members of the 26th July Movement disappeared from the scene or went into exile. At first it was said that the elections had been postponed. Then it was announced —with the enthusiastic approval of a specially called mass meeting— that they were unnecessary. 'Representative democracy' was described as a reactionary deception.

At the same time freedom of the press had to go. 'Non-revolutionary' publications were attacked by the government press, radio and television, and at mass meetings at which 'reactionary' newspapers were burned. In addition there was a new method of attack: the unions of journalists and graphic workers, which were largely Communist-controlled, decided to set up a 'Committee for the Freedom of the Press' (*sic*) whose task it was to provide explanatory comments on unpopular articles or new items. These commentaries invariably said that because the press was free the news item, or article, in question had been printed at the request of the newspaper proprietor, but that, because of this freedom of the press, the workers and employees could state that the news item was wrong, corrupting and anti-revolutionary. As time went by, these explanatory notes in heavy type (popularly known as *coletillas*—'little tails') took up more and more space and became stronger and stronger in tone; but the courts refused to deal with complaints from the newspaper owners. Censors who omitted to comment on 'counter-revolutionary news items' were liable to disciplinary action.[1]

[1] *See* for instance *Diario de la Marina*, Havana, February 24, 1960. A reasonably well informed reader can judge the strength of Communist influence in this matter from the following piece which appeared in a 'censored' paper, after the 'censor' responsible for the publication of 'explanatory remarks' had omitted to comment on a 'counter-revolutionary news item':

'Resolution of the Central Committee for the Freedom of the Press.

'A meeting of employees of the *Diario de la Marina*, attended by representatives of the National Federation of Graphic Workers, the National and Provincial Association of Journalists and the Central Committee for the Freedom of the Press discussed the case of a colleague who had omitted to append an "explanatory note" to a news item damaging to the interests of the new Cuba.

'In the course of the meeting the case was analyzed in detail and it was made clear how severely such an action damages the struggle which the graphic workers and journalists lead against counter-revolutionary managements.

'The colleague responsible for the omission admitted himself that his behaviour had caused serious damage.

'After deciding to continue the use of *coletillas*, and after the colleague concerned had given an assurance that he had not acted intentionally and that in future he would do his utmost to see that resolutions were carried out the meeting resolved the following:

At the beginning of January one of the counter-revolutionary dailies, *Avance*, was 'taken over by the staff' and a few months later it ceased publication. Its publisher fled abroad after Castro had produced documentary evidence on television that he had received money from the Batista government. The liberal daily, *El Mundo*, was confiscated on the grounds that its owner had illegally enriched himself. On May 10, 1960, it was the turn of Cuba's oldest conservative daily, *Diario de la Marina*, which for weeks had been the object of violent attacks by the most extreme radio commentator, José Pardo Llada.[1] But the staff of the paper protested against these attacks and the majority decided, in spite of the dangers which this attitude might entail, to print a statement of support for their employers. This had already been set up when an armed gang of revolutionaries and police appeared, destroyed the matrix and allowed a minority to take over the paper. On the next morning, May 11, a 'revolutionary' edition of the paper appeared, containing a resolution of the staff who condemned its reactionary policy and expressed themselves against the continued existence of the paper. This declaration was published over the signature of only 132 out of the 460 workers and employees. The paper stopped publication and the printing press became part of the newly founded 'National Printing Works', together with the presses of *El Pais—Excelsior*, a paper which had already stopped publication. On May 12 a mass march was organized by the university in the course of which the *Diario de la Marina* was ceremoniously 'buried'. Only five days later the widely read 'left-wing', anti-Batista evening paper *Prensa Libre* was taken over by a new, revolutionary editor and the old publishers fled abroad. The non-political mid-day paper *El Crisol* stopped publication at the beginning of June, because of 'economic difficulties'. The same thing happened to some provincial papers. In August the weekly journal *Bohemia*, which had an extraordinarily high circulation of over 600,000 and which was widely read outside Cuba, was taken over by a 'revolutionary' management. Its publisher and owner, Miguel Angel Quevedo, who during the whole of the Batista period had openly proclaimed his friendship with Castro and who had been under constant threat of arrest by the Batista

---

(1) To suspend the colleague concerned for two weeks, from 26th February, from his trade union rights *and* his job. During his absence he shall be replaced by another colleague;
(2) in future to hold the guilty colleague personally responsible for the insertion of *coletillas* and for the execution of the decisions of the Committee for the Freedom of the Press.
(3) all possible future omissions, vacillations and mistakes of the colleague concerned shall result in his permanent removal from his job.
'It is further announced that the colleague whose behaviour necessitated these decisions personally asked for the agreed sanctions to be taken against him.'
He fled from Cuba in March 1961.

police, had unsuccessfully tried to publish a leading article against the growing influence of the Communists; he fled abroad where he soon produced a *Bohemia Libre*. Publication of the daily paper *Información*, which had long been 'tamed', ceased in December 1960. With this act the whole of the press had been brought into line—and the number of papers had been considerably reduced.

At the same time radio and television stations were practically nationalized and formed into a network ironically called *FIDEL* (faithful), an abbreviation of the words *Frente Independiente de Emisoras Libres* (Independent Front of Free Transmitters). The property of the Mestre brothers, the owners of the biggest television network, was confiscated although they had always been 'liberal' and against Batista and although there was no proof that they had acquired their property illegally.

An independent judiciary can exist only in a constitutional state. In Cuba it had to disappear. To begin with the courts were purged and counter-revolutionary judges were removed. The competence of the ordinary courts was reduced by the establishment of 'revolutionary tribunals' which had very considerable powers and were entitled to pass sentence of death, although this was contrary to the 1940 Constitution. Lawyers who were prepared to defend counter-revolutionaries were in danger of being prosecuted themselves. The right of *habeas corpus* was abolished and on October 29, 1959, the Council of Ministers abrogated the right to appeal to the highest tribunal in cases of breach of *habeas corpus* or unconstitutional acts.[1] The importance of the judicature in civil disputes also declined, partly because the public sector was expanding all the time and it was impossible to appeal against 'revolutionary confiscations', and partly because the police would not take action against 'less well-to-do persons' who failed to pay rent or other private debts.

There was growing opposition among the lawyers' and judges associations. Many lawyers sought refuge abroad and the Lawyers' Association was brought into line. The final conflict occurred in July 1960 when the executive committee of the Association joined the Faculty of Law of Havana University in a protest against the new system of justice. *Bohemia* of August 7 contained an account of the 'scandal' and 'general confusion' at a meeting of the Lawyers' Association at which a revolutionary minority took over the leadership. On November 16, 1960, the President and Vice President of the Supreme Court fled abroad and the 'final struggle' began. At the beginning of December the newly-appointed revolutionary public prosecutor, Fernandez Flores, said that 'after failing to turn the university and the lawyers' college into its bastions, the counter-revolution is trying to hoist its flag in the citadel of judicial authority.[2]

[1] *Gaceta Oficial*, November 2, 1959.
[2] *Bohemia*, Havana, January 1, 1961.

THE ROAD TO SOCIALISM

On December 16, Castro himself made an attack on the judges; he said that they had always been on the side of the rich against the poor and that in any case a substantial part of the old legislation and the old legal institutions had become superfluous in the new Cuba:

'Everybody was asking: when will the judicial system be cleaned up? . . . What was civil law concerned with anyway? Usually something that did not affect the people: mortgages, terminations of contracts, inheritance quarrels, legal quarrels between employers, land owners, financiers . . . And today? Is one co-operative likely to sue another? Are tenants going to be sentenced to move out if there are no tenants but only owners? There is no reason why all these courts and judges should exist today.'[1]

As a result of this speech eight judges of the Supreme Court resigned on December 19. On December 22 a new law was passed, enabling the President of the Republic to nominate new judges and to reorganize the judiciary. On February 12, 1961, *Bohemia* was able to report that this task had been more or less completed.

The University of Havana, which had always been the stronghold of all revolutionary movements, had been brought into line earlier.[2] Shortly after the victory of the revolution there had been a 'purge' of *Batistiano* professors. A new student association under Major Cubela then forced other professors to resign and excluded counter-revolutionary students from the university. On May 9, 1960, Cubela said in a television interview that 'the autonomy of the university must be abolished if it stands in the way of the revolution'. At the end of June 1960 a new revolutionary 'junta' of student leaders and revolutionary teachers demanded the resignation of the official university authorities. Those professors who refused to recognize the authority of the junta were relieved of their posts. Their salaries were stopped and disciplinary action was taken against them.

On August 4, 1960 the government retrospectively legitimized the change. In December a 'Supreme Council of the Universities' was set up which since then has controlled all the universities of the country, particularly the two other state universities of Oriente (Santiago) and Las Villas (Santa Clara); in the spring of 1961 the Council took over the private, catholic University of Villanueva. The vast majority of professors had now disappeared, many of them into exile. For example the Rector and Vice-Rector of the University of Santa Clara left in November 1960 and Porfirio Ramirez, the

[1] *Bohemia*, Havana, January 1, 1961.
[2] As late as the summer of 1960 the attitude of the revolutionaries towards the University and its professors was still one of approval. 'Even under Batista the University was a curious island of restricted freedom. The professors who directed it obeyed neither the politicians nor the police. It was the cradle of the revolution.' (C. Wright Mills, *Castro's Cuba*, London, 1961, New York, *Listen, Yankee*, 1960, pp. 40–1.)

leader of the student association of the same university was caught in the mountains of central Cuba and executed as a rebel.

It was obvious too that the unions could not remain independent in a nationalized economy. In November 1959 a trade union congress had taken place attended by freely elected delegates from the various unions. The 'Humanists' of the 26th July Movement under the leadership of David Salvador formed a large majority, and only about eleven per cent of all delegates were open Communists. There were violent clashes and unpleasant scenes between the majority and the communist minority. Although at the opening meeting of the congress Fidel Castro recommended that a unified leadership be established which would include the communists, twenty-five out of the thirty-three federations present adopted resolutions strongly opposing the admittance of communists into the leadership. A representative of the Uruguayan unions who was present as a guest described the hostility of most delegates towards the communists, a hostility which also existed among the workers assembled in the street outside the trade union building.[1] The 'unified leadership' which was finally established under direct pressure from Castro did not contain any of the old familiar communist trade union leaders, but only 'second rank' communists who a year later made way for the 'old guard'. Since 1961, Lazaro Peña, the leading communist trade unionist of the years 1938–46, has again been chairman of the Trade Union Congress.

David Salvador disappeared from the scene in the spring of 1960 after a violent quarrel with the Minister of Labour who had prepared a law (No. 647) which the workers called the 'dagger-thrust law' when it was published. It gave the Ministry the right to 'intervene' not only in all concerns but also in the trade unions and to remove undesirable trade union leaders. Later Salvador tried to flee abroad but was caught and imprisoned. Many trade union officials were relieved of their posts by the Ministry: Manuel Fernandez, Chairman of the Actors' Union, Luis Moreno of the Tobacco Workers' Executive, Luis Panalaz Gonzales, Vice-President of the Building Workers, Mario Fontela of the Agricultural Workers' Union, and many others almost all of whom were 'revolutionary' trade unionists who had only come to the top after the purges in the first months of 1959. Already at the end of 1959 the unions had decided, one after the other, to freeze wages, to ask workers to work harder, to abandon strikes and to give four per cent of their wages to the government as a 'loan' to be used for industrialization. In the spring of 1960 the government published a law to this effect: as the contribution was voluntary workers had the right to refuse to pay it. But if no express declaration was made four per cent was deducted from wages and

[1] Juan Antonio Acuña, *Cuba—Revolución frustrada?* Montevideo, 1960, pp. 28–30.

THE ROAD TO SOCIALISM

salaries.[1] One per cent of the wages was still paid in membership dues to the unions, though they no longer exercised their former functions. In addition there were other more or less 'voluntary' deductions: for the purchase of arms, oil tankers, cows for the co-operatives and so on. One of the main tasks of the trade unions now was to ensure an increase in productivity.[2] Many groups of workers and employees asked the government of their own accord for wage cuts.[3] There was some semi-official propaganda for unpaid overtime, at first in posters of the employees of the 'Public Enterprises'; and organizations of 'voluntary workers' were formed whose members were prepared to work without pay in their free time. Then 'competitions' were introduced between various factories and sectors of the economy. The last conflict between the government and the employees of which news reached the public took place in December 1960. A procession of electricity workers marched through the streets protesting against Communism and against the prosecution of their trade union leaders by the government authorities. (Their leaders had been accused of sabotage.) Fidel Castro made a violent attack on the electricity workers and others workers' organizations saying that they had always been privileged and that they had 'sold the right of primogeniture of the working class, its right to rule and direct the country, for the miserable pottage of special economic privileges.[4]

All remaining social organizations and associations, the lawyers', architects' and teachers' associations as well as private clubs, were purged, reorganized and brought into line, not always without strong protests. Some, for example the association of sugar mill owners and the association of tenants of sugar cane plantations (*colonos*), were dissolved.

Conflict with the Church was inevitable, if only because the atheistic, or at least anti-clerical, character of the revolutionary government, which proclaimed religion to be a private matter but did not build churches or chapels in any of the new settlements, was becoming increasingly clear. The existence of an independent organization like the Church became more and more irritating as the ideology of the revolution moved towards Communism. Nor could the revolution tolerate special Catholic youth organizations or private Church schools. It was also clear that the Church, whether it

[1] The writer of these lines must admit that he too at the time abstained from making such a declaration and preferred to accept the four per cent deduction, although with mixed feelings.
[2] In a speech in August 1960 the leader of the sugar workers, Conrado Beuquér, a non-Communist, said 'Today the task of the unions can no longer be the old one ... They must work together with government officials in order to plan and promote production'. (*Bohemia*, August 21, 1960.)
[3] The first group of workers who demanded a reduction of their own wages were the employees of the nationalized hotel *Sevilla-Biltmore* in Havana who did so as early as the second half of 1959. The sugar workers' union expressed its readiness for similar sacrifices at the beginning of March 1960.
[4] *Obra Revolucionaria*, No. 32, Havana, December 15, 1960.

wanted to or not, would become a centre of counter-revolutionary elements. Both parties started the battle with some hesitation: the Church because of its weakness and because it was compromised by its long-standing 'alliance' with the upper and middle classes, and Castro because he was afraid of creating new enemies, not only in Cuba but in those Latin American countries where the influence of the Church was great and the Christian Democratic parties were sympathetic to the Cuban revolution. Instead of attacks against the Church there were charges against reactionary foreign priests, many of whom came from Spain. The climax of this struggle was only reached in 1961, when private schools were nationalized and many priests (including some of Cuban nationality) expelled.

At the same time as all these institutions were brought into line, the apparatus of the revolutionary government, including the apparatus for oppression, was expanded. Special police units, particularly the feared 'G.2.' (popularly known in counter-revolutionary circles as the *Ge-dos-tapo*) were very active. The navy and air force had to be completely reorganized after increasing numbers of its members had gone into exile. The rebel army was also purged and completely reorganized. Many of the officers from the 'rebel days' fled abroad or tried to organize new rebel movements in the mountains of central Cuba; a number were caught and some of them executed. After the suppression of such a rising, Castro in December made a speech which showed how much still remained to be done: 'Here [the Province of Las Villas] there is still much confusion and suspicion among the peasants and Mujalism [after Mujal, Chairman of the Trade Unions under Batista] in the trade unions and there exist mistaken views in the ranks of the 26th July Movement and counter-revolutionary infiltrations in the public administration and the army. The moment for firm action has come.'[1]

The people's militia became the most important military organization which was used at the same time to re-educate the masses and to keep them in a state of permanent mobilization. Its formation began at the end of 1959. The first units consisted of 'reliable' elements which were given intensive training. Then the militia was expanded to include 'the people' until by the end of 1960 it numbered more than half a million Cubans of both sexes. Training took place after work and on public holidays and being a member of the militia soon became the 'main occupation' of many of the unemployed (although members of the militia received no pay) including those who had come to the towns from the countryside, with the result that there was a labour shortage in the plains. Officially membership of the militia is still voluntary but in practice there is strong pressure to join and anybody who refuses runs great risks, including that of losing his job. The fact that a large section of the population is armed

[1] *Bohemia*, Havana, February 5, 1961.

is regarded by revolutionary circles as proof of mass support and real democracy. But this is questionable: many militiamen have no arms at home; weapons are mostly kept in factories, co-operatives, and so on. In any case nobody can take 'heavy' arms home; the cadres are handpicked and nobody can easily escape the general pressure of discipline.

'Committees for the Protection of the Revolution' were set up in every block in the towns, in every village and every co-operative to act as special organs in the fight against counter-revolution.

In addition the masses were mobilized and politically re-educated through the press, radio and television. As we shall see in the chapter on the cultural revolution there was an ever-growing number of special schools, indoctrination courses and new organizations for women, young people, children and so on; of these the youth organization *Jovenes Rebeldes* played a special rôle as the official organization uniting communist and other youth organizations.

Until 1961 the actual terror was less marked than in other totalitarian revolutions. The emigré newspaper *Avance*, published in the United States, estimated that the number of people shot up to October 1, 1960, was 1,330 and it may be that in spring 1961 the figure did not exceed 2,000. It is impossible to be more specific because there were undoubtedly executions which were not reported. The number of political prisoners was considerable, much greater than ever before; it is estimated that by the end of 1960 there were between 15,000 and 20,000 or even more, but naturally nothing definite is known. There were reports that people were tortured in order to obtain confessions or to intimidate them, but for the period before the spring of 1961 there is no reliable information. There undoubtedly were, and there continue to be, many cases of illtreatment of all kinds, some of these were reported at the beginning of 1960 by the opposition press which at the time was still legal. In January, for example, shortly before it closed down, the Havana *Avance* contained such an account. Since then the refugee press has published some apparently reliable stories of persecutions.

At the end of 1960 the 'International Rescue Committee' in New York estimated the total number of refugees in the United States at a little over 40,000. After that date it increased sharply, although it had become much more difficult to leave Cuba. Every traveller requires police permission and is not allowed to take any money out with him if his return is uncertain, and all emigré property in Cuba is confiscated by the state. No Cuban can buy his air ticket in Cuba but has to have it paid for from abroad. Given these difficulties the number of emigrés is considerable. The International Rescue Committee made an interesting social analysis of the refugees at the end of 1960, according to which 31 per cent were labourers and 30 per cent employees of all kinds. In other words the emigrants came mainly from the 'lower classes'. This may, however, be due to the fact that wealthy emigrants who had means abroad and went to the United States are not included in these statistics. According to official American figures in the spring of 1961 there were over 100,000 Cuban refugees in the United States.

(f) *Castro's Totalitarian Democracy*

'Western' democracy with all its liberal individualist core is the result of a synthesis of opposed ideas and the product of a long historical process. The 'state' which in our era in the 'Western' countries has ceased to be the 'instrument of an exploiting minority' exists for the individual and not *vice versa*. The written or unwritten constitution must guarantee the rights of the individual and of groups of individuals. It contains provisions which prevent the establishment of an omnipotent executive. In totalitarian 'democracy' the individual is subordinated to the whole.[1] The state as the representative of the general interests becomes omnipotent, politics become an all-pervading 'religion' and the 'private sphere' of life is reduced.

Until the second half of 1960, at least, Cuba was undoubtedly a totalitarian democracy. Despite growing opposition the *vast* majority supported 'Fidel'. A charismatic government which is based on faith in and devotion to a leader who is regarded as exceptional and which does not have a strong civil service at its disposal must inevitably be both chaotic and democratic. A French political theorist rightly said: 'Where there are no limbs of government, the rulers, whoever they may be or by whatever name they may go, have no choice but to act with and through the people; where the limbs of government are developed it is possible for rulers to act without and independently of the people.'[2]

The enthusiasm with which the masses supported Castro—whose revolution brought less official terror in its wake than similarly far-reaching and dynamic transformations usually require—an enthusiasm which fascinated so many foreign observers and which characterized the Cuban revolution, arose from the achievements, aims and promises of the government. Unlike other 'socialist' revolutions the Cuban revolution *immediately* and without worrying about the cost or economic consequences of such a policy, provided material improvements for most members of the lower classes.[3] It

[1] *See* J. L. Talmon, *The Origins of Totalitarian Democracy*, London, New York, 1952.

[2] Bertrand de Jouvenel in *Democracy in the New States*, Rhodes Seminar Papers, Congress for Cultural Freedom, New Delhi (India), 1959.

[3] 'The rise of 23 to 30 per cent in real wages was a political feat that enormously enhanced Castro's prestige among the people ... How was it performed? On the supply side it was made possible by the existence of a large margin of unused capacity in the industrial plants that manufactured wage goods, by the consumption of inventories, and by the liberation of foreign exchange through the reduction in the importation of equipment and durable consumer goods ... And it was made possible on the demand side because overall expenditures did not increase; entrepreneurs reduced expenditure on investment and consumption by about the same amount that workers increased theirs.' Felipe Pazos in *Cambridge Opinion*, February 1963.

THE ROAD TO SOCIALISM

increased and extended their freedom (even if, as Erich Fromm and others have emphasized, in criticial situations many people do not regard 'individual freedom' as a blessing). It gave the poor new human dignity. It filled the young, who make up a large part of the Cuban people, with enthusiasm and it offered them an important ideology. With its grand primitive voluntarism it seemed to transcend painful realities and to open up new, unexpected perspectives. This revolution seemed to make little Cuba the centre of America, a thought which stirred the pride of Cubans.

For the masses the years 1959/60 were thus the dawn of happiness. The economic measures crushed the rich—a fact which alone produced understandable satisfaction in many hearts—and led to large-scale redistribution of the national income. For the majority of town dwellers living standards improved, because wages rose while prices and rents were reduced and new parks and places of entertainment or rest were created. But for most of the rural population a veritable heaven on earth seemed to have begun. Small tenant farmers no longer paid rent and many were given 'title deeds' to the land which they farmed; for those who used to live in miserable huts thousands of new, attractive houses were built in the new co-operatives, with tiled kitchens and bathrooms, built-in wardrobes, and front gardens. Schools were built and attractive streets and playgrounds laid out, people's shops sold goods more cheaply than the old private shops, and community centres and clinics were set up. Roads were made, lavatories were built, water and electricity were installed and doctors appeared where misery and undernourishment had reigned before.

In spring 1960 the Institute for Social Research of Princeton University carried out a limited, unofficial opinion poll in Cuba. Of those asked, 43 per cent were enthusiastic supporters of Castro, a further 43 per cent were in favour of the government, and only 10 per cent were definitely in opposition. More women and young people were for Castro than men and people over 25, and his following was naturally greater among the lower than among the upper classes. The following were listed, in this order, as the greatest achievements of the revolution: land reform, honest government, educational advances and greater social justice. After a gap there was also mention of greater freedom. (It must be remembered that those questioned were comparing Castro with the Batista era.) Mentioned *last* were the 'nationalist' achievements: greater national independence and growth of Cuba's international standing. The wishes for the future were mainly of a material nature: an increase in the standard of living was the most important. Sixty-five per cent thought that they were better off than in 1958. In conclusion the American investigators remarked: 'The living standard and chances of work occupied the centre of national and personal worries and hopes . . . The government will be judged by the public primarily on whether it will be able to raise the standard of living and to create more jobs.'[1]

A State Department representative said at a congressional committee meeting on February 18, 1960: 'Well informed observers have reported that so far the Cuban people enjoy relatively more freedom than before. The people seem to have an honest government and enjoy a juster distribution of the national income. The revolutionary government seems to have brought the people political freedom and an improvement of its living standards.'[2]

After spending several weeks in Cuba Theodore Draper wrote with reference to the land reform: 'No matter how the program turns out in practice there is no getting around the fact that for the poor, illiterate, landless outcast "guajiros" the co-operatives represent a jump of centuries in living standards.'[3]

For the first time the poor (*los humildes*) felt that they were really being looked after and had become full 'citizens'. The old, feared army, the country gendarmerie and the police had disappeared and the new 'army'—which was used to build houses, roads and schools —was part of the people. The people themselves were soon given arms and uniforms. The old luxury hotels, restaurants and clubs were thrown open to all. The new popular bathing establishments which sprang up all along the coast were spacious, elegant and comfortable, with cafés, restaurants and playgrounds; there were cabins and weekend cottages with air conditioning and attractive furniture which could be rented for a small sum. The fact that many technicians and experts had fled gave the sons of the lower classes new chances of promotion.

White-collar workers, labourers, peasants' sons and unemployed or underemployed young intellectuals rose to responsible positions in the civil service and the economy. As directors of big sugar mills, which all employed over a thousand workers, a journalist found the following: a 33-year-old ex-employee of the public relations department of a big firm, who had earned £140 a month and who was now enthusiastically running a whole factory for a mere £30 (86 pesos); a 24-year-old former shop assistant; a boy barely 21 years old who used to help in his father's small cigar factory and a still younger boy who had been employed in a furniture factory.[4] They had all volunteered some months earlier to be trained as teachers and because they were 'able, dynamic and revolutionary' they had been

[1] Lloyd A. Free, *Attitudes of the Cuban People towards the Castro Régime*, Institute for Social Research, Princeton, 1960.
[2] Quoted by John Hickey, *The Rôle of Congress in Foreign Policy*, Inter-American Economic Affairs, Vol. 14, No. 4.
[3] 'The Runaway Revolution,' in *The Reporter*, New York, May 12, 1960.
[4] *Bohemia*, Havana, January 15, 1961.—Irving Peter Pflaum met a former pharmacist's assistant at the head of INRA of the province Pinar del Rio and a bank clerk as chief of one large zone of the same province. (*The Tragic Island*, Prentice Hall, N.Y., 1961, p. 126.)

THE ROAD TO SOCIALISM

entrusted by Fidel personally with the running of these factories.

Other opportunities and possibilities of advancement were provided, as we shall see later, by the cultural revolution which also brought foreign and native artists, often of world fame, to the co-operatives.

Many unemployed and underemployed joined the army, the militia and the 'people's farms' where they found permanent employment. The little shoeshine boys who used to hang about the streets were given uniforms and fed in public kitchens by the Ministry of Welfare.

What could 'political freedom' and 'representative democracy' mean in comparison with all this? It was easy to do without them and to believe in the bearded leader who travelled from place to place, who appeared unexpectedly in the most outlandish parts, who spoke to everybody, advised everybody, gave hope to everybody and who for hours on end kept in touch with the people through television.

4. Achievements of the Revolution 1959–1961

(a) *The Cultural Revolution*

The 'Year of Liberation' (1959) and the 'Year of Land Reform' (1960) were to be followed by the 'Year of Education' (1961).

'Culture' had only weak roots in Cuba's national soil. Certainly, there existed dances, popular songs and poems which were indigenous. There was also quite an important Cuban school of painting and some excellent modern architecture. But all this 'superior' culture was confined to the urban upper and middle classes and had little to do with the mass of the population.

Education in school and university was poor in quantity and quality. Officially 24 per cent of the population were illiterate, but this seemed an optimistic estimate. Many children, particularly in the countryside, did not go to school at all. Most poor children who managed to get to school left after about four years. Public education was free, but many schools were over-crowded, and the teachers, whose number was in inverse relationship to their qualifications, were conspicuous for their absences during termtime, particularly in the countryside. In the whole country there were only twenty-one public secondary schools; there was little control over the pupils and the upper forms took more interest in politics than in learning. There were too few specialized schools of all kinds and their ornate exteriors often belied their standards. Those who could afford to do so preferred to send their children to private schools, many of which were run by the clergy. But these schools cost money, and even so were often very bad.

The quality of popular education was no better. The large sums usually allocated to the Ministry of Education in the budget were mainly used for other purposes. Education, including university education, was largely based on learning by rote and *what* was learned by rote had precious little connection with the lives of the pupils or the requirements of the country. As already mentioned, the universities and technical colleges produced many lawyers, journalists and teachers (there were masses of music teachers, handicraft teachers and so on) but hardly any agronomists or engineers.

There was no large theatre in the whole country (though many cinemas) and no opera house. The better concerts were given for members of special societies. There were few museums and they had little to offer. Few books were published—or sold.

The revolutionary government was anxious to influence the cultural life of the country, to extend it, to change it, to widen its basis, to make it more democratic, and to adapt it to the needs of the people.

All this was to be done in the 'Cuban-Castroist' manner, as quickly as possible and without regard to cost. Characteristic of Fidel's attitude was a speech which he made in March 1960 in Havana in order to arouse the interest of the people in the foundation of a university town: 'We must start to build this town immediately. People say that we lack the means. That does not matter because we have the inexhaustible resources of the people at our disposal. It is said that this university town will cost 30 million pesos [£10 million] or more. That is unimportant. What is important is that we need it.'[1]

Reality is nothing, the will is everything.

The revolutionary government wanted to break the educational monopoly of the property-owning classes to make compulsory education a reality, to modernize education, to produce large numbers of new teachers and to train technicians and engineers, partly by sending thousands of young students or semi-qualified technicians together with thousands of children (including Fidelito Castro) and peasants and agricultural workers to the Soviet Union.[2] Above all, the government proposed to eradicate illiteracy in the course of a single year.

In the course of thirty months the revolutionary government opened more classrooms than its predecessors had in thirty years. Almost all barracks were turned into schools, vast school towns were built—one near the Sierra Maestra which was supposed to house (it never reached this number) more than 20,000 pupils. The new teachers were trained 'in the mountains' where they were also given courses in 'physical training' and in 'indoctrination'.

A number of laws were introduced changing the existing school system, the method of teaching and the subject taught. In June 1961 the whole educational system was nationalized, although private schools had in fact already disappeared. New types of schools and new subjects appeared. Boarding schools were set up on confiscated estates (*Centros de Industria y Artesania*) at which technical subjects and handicrafts were taught and there were special schools for book-keepers and agricultural mechanics. In Havana 'peasant schools' (*Escuelas Campesinas*) were set up in about 300 luxury houses confiscated from counter-revolutionaries and the former *Hotel Nacional*. Here several thousand country girls between the ages of fourteen and twenty-one learned sewing and dressmaking

[1] *Revolución*, Havana, March 13/14, 1960.
[2] The results were sometimes unexpected: many Cubans in the Soviet Union were disappointed by the low standard of living and shocked by the fact that they were treated like 'unskilled fools'. In one instance it was explained to Cuban technicians how important it was to build the first cement factory. (Cuba has had three for years.)

as well as reading, writing, arithmetic and 'history'. At the end of the training, which was of course paid for by the state together with all expenses, every pupil was presented with a sewing machine of her own, on condition that she taught others at home in her village.

In general a special emphasis was laid on the schooling and education of women: new teachers' colleges for girls were opened, pre-university courses for peasant-girls were begun, and the percentage of female university students increased considerably. According to a speech by Castro on January 16, 1963, there had never previously been more than 10 per cent of women among the first year medical students, and in 1962 there were 50 per cent.

There were training schools for managers and schools for leaders of the new 'children's circles' which were being set up everywhere; in the middle of 1961 the first 1,300 pupils received their diplomas. Special schools for art teachers (*Escuelas de Instructores de Arte*) were opened with a starting attendance of 3,000 pupils, At the end of a two-year course they were supposed to teach in co-operatives and state farms. A special school in Havana trained domestic servants to be taxi-drivers. Special schools for qualified workers were set up: e.g. in 1962 a school for shoe-makers. According to a speech of Blas Roca, broadcast on October 2, 1962, this institution would train 8,000 unemployed shoe-makers at government expense and they would receive wages during their training. Above all, special political indoctrination schools, *Escuelas de Instrucción Revolucionaria*, were soon set up everywhere. At the beginning of 1961 there were more than 30,000 state stipend holders in Havana—and their number increased in 1962 to almost 80,000. They were all living in requisitioned houses and were clothed and fed at government expense.

The political indoctrination schools became particularly important for the formation of the cadres. Almost from the beginning they taught principles of Marxism-Leninism. The first *Escuelas de Instrucción Revolucionaria* (EIR) began to function regularly at the very beginning of 1961. There was one national school with a term of six months duration and, originally, 60 pupils as well as 12 provincial schools with 700 pupils and terms of 3 months duration. Later in the year six new national schools—one especially for members of the people's farms, another for trade-unionists, and a third for teachers—were established, and a new kind of school for beginners, the *Escuelas Basicas de Instrucción Revolucionaria* (EBIR), was created. A new, higher school, named *Nico Lopez* was opened where the duration of the term was 8 months. At the end of 1961, 18,830 pupils had finished such schools and passed the examinations—in the course of 1962 another 36,487.[1]

[1] Lionel Soto, 'Dos Años de Instrucción Revolucionaria', in *Cuba Socialista*, No. 18, February 1963.

ACHIEVEMENTS OF THE REVOLUTION 1959-1961

A national theatre was opened and the Havana Symphony Orchestra was put back on its feet and sent on concert tours around the country. The museum in the capital was modernized and the number of exhibits increased—mainly by confiscating art treasures of counter-revolutionaries. A special new institute began to produce revolutionary films. The National Library announced that the number of its readers had risen from 25,000 in 1959 to 165,000 in 1960. The University of Havana opened a new Economics Faculty and tried to engage new teachers from abroad to fill the gap caused by the purges. The National Printing Works published a huge amount of literature—from classical works to revolutionary pamphlets and textbooks.

But the main campaign of the year 1961 was dedicated to the eradication of illiteracy. In December of that year, the government proclaimed proudly that Cuba was the first Latin American country without illiterates. According to official statistics, the percentage of illiterates had been reduced from 14 to 3·9 per cent of the *total* population. Only 271,000 adults remained illiterate. Three hundred thousand people had participated in teaching, among them 100,000 pupils of the secondary schools and 35,000 members of the teaching profession.[1] It was this achievement which, together with the apparent success of the Agrarian Reform, helped to create all over Latin America, and even in Europe, enormous sympathy for the Cuban revolution.

Looked at critically, this campaign must be described as a typical 'Fidelista' enterprise, designed to fill the masses with enthusiasm, to indoctrinate them with the communist ideas which filled the official textbooks and to make propaganda for the revolution abroad, rather than to perform the essential, urgent tasks with a maximum of rationality, taking into account the real priorities of economic and social reconstruction.

Cuba badly needed to increase its productivity and production: but instead many millions were spent for instruction and equipment of the *alfabetizadores*. All secondary school pupils attended courses of several weeks duration, living at government expense, mostly in confiscated luxury hotels, were given uniforms, shoes, books and other equipment and a small weekly allowance during their courses. Many workers and employees left their jobs in order to participate in the campaign.

In fact Cuba's illiteracy rate was not a major handicap to its modernization and industrialization. In Great Britain, France, and Belgium some 40 to 50 per cent of the total population had been illiterate in the 1840s;[2] In Cuba, according to the census of 1953, there had been 1,033,000 illiterates representing 23·6 per cent of the

[1] INRA, *Breve recuento de la campana de Alfabetización*, Havana, 1962.
[2] E. Hobsbawm, *The Age of Revolution*, London, 1962, p. 136.

population over 10 years of age and 17·7 per cent of the total population; the above mentioned official figures, supplied in 1961 by the revolutionary authorities, show that some progress had taken place. What Cuba needed above all were technicians of all kinds and levels—and it seemed odd to close all secondary schools for eight months and to draft a considerable proportion of primary teachers into the *alfabetización* campaign.

The results are doubtful. 707,000 adults were taught by more than 300,000 'teachers' and, in the words of an English correspondent, 'The standard of those taught is low, many being able to do little more than sign their names and write a few words they were taught with the instructor holding their hands.'[1]

(b) *The Agrarian Revolution*

'Land reform is a revolutionary step; it passes power, property and status from one group in the community to another. If the government of the country is dominated or strongly influenced by the land-holding group ... no one should expect effective land-legislation as an act of grace.' (J. K. Galbraith)

The following chapter analyses the agrarian revolution only up to 1961. There are three main reasons for this limitation: (1) The claim made for the big successes of the revolution was based on its achievements up to 1961; (2) no comprehensive data have been published for 1962; and (3) according to official declarations, 1962 has been a year of particularly bad climatic conditions. It would be unfair to blame them on the revolutionary government.

The agrarian revolutions in Mexico, Russia and Bolivia were the result of the struggles of the peasants. The Cuban agrarian revolution on the other hand was started and carried out from above. It began with the Land Reform Law signed in the Sierra Maestra on May 17, 1959. The preamble of the law made it clear that it had not been demanded by the rural population: the purpose of the land reform was to diversify the Cuban economy and help the industrialization of the country. A modern, intensive agriculture would provide raw materials for industry and reduce Cuba's dependence on agricultural imports; the improvement in the living standards of the rural population would create an internal market for a national industry.

The ills of the Cuban economy, as defined in the preamble, were: (1) the tenancy system, which put a heavy strain on the farmer and prevented him from introducing modern methods; (2) the fact that the majority of those working in agriculture did not own the land they tilled; (3) the extreme concentration of landed property in *latifundia*; (4) the low productivity and technical backwardness, particularly in animal husbandry, which resulted in excessive depend-

[1] *The Times*, London, March 27, 1962.

ence on imports; (5) the poverty of the rural population; (6) the foreign ownership of much of the land.

To remedy these shortcomings the following main changes were proposed:

(1) The prohibition of *latifundia*: in general private estates would not be allowed to exceed 30 *caballerias*;[1] in the case of exceptionally productive estates the maximum could be increased to 100 *caballerias*. The former owners would receive compensation, The price of the land would be fixed at its rateable value. Compensation would be given in the form of long-term bonds (*Bonos de la Reforma Agraria*), which paid 4·5 per cent interest a year. Agricultural tribunals (*Tribunales de Tierra*) would be set up to decide disputed questions.

(2) Abolition of the tenancy system: all small tenant farmers, including those who had no title deeds would become owners. All payments of rent would stop. This would also apply to tenants of farms owned by proprietors with less than 30 *caballerias*.

(3) Land distribution: all small tenant farmers, including squatters —those without title deeds—would be entitled to a piece of land not less than two *caballerias* per family. This minimum would be distributed free. In addition the new smallholder would be able to buy a further three *caballerias* at a low price. No mortgage could be taken out on the new property nor could it be sold or divided for inheritance purposes. The distribution would start with state-owned land, followed by unproductive private estates and only then by the remainder of the confiscated land.

(4) Foreigners and public companies would no longer be allowed to own land but would receive compensation.

(5) The execution of the land reform would be entrusted to a new State Institution (INRA). The country would be divided into twenty-eight zones controlled by INRA officials. The Institute would give credits and would be partly responsible for the distribution of agricultural products.

(6) Co-operatives would be set up with the assistance and under the direction of INRA. The land and the tools would become the collective property of the members of the co-operative who would farm the land and share the profits.

This law is undoubtedly radical; it is not socialist because it recognizes private property and, in the preamble, refers to the need

[1] According to sworn statements made by the proprietors to the Revolutionary government, the distribution of the land was as follows (one *caballeria* is equal to 33·16 acres):

	extension	per cent	proprietors	per cent
up to 5 caballerias	628,673 cab.	7·4	20,229	66·1
5 to 30 caballerias	1,641,440 cab.	19·3	7,485	24·5
over 30 caballerias	6,252,163 cab.	73·3	2,773	9·4

(J. Chonchol, *Analisis Critico de la Reforma Agraria Cubana*, Mexico, January–March 1963, No. 117.)

for encouraging private initiative in industry. It is true that the smaller farmers are merely given usufructuary rights and do not really completely own the land. But this happened also in other land reforms which are not regarded as socialist, for example in Formosa.[1] The former owners were certainly not going to be satisfied with the compensation because no immediate settlement was envisaged and the arrangement amounted to partial confiscation. But the same is also true of the land reform in Japan carried out by the Americans after the Second World War.[2]

Although the land reform law was not socialist it went far beyond the limits of capitalism and contained socialist elements, such as the introduction of co-operatives combined with the simultaneous establishment of a powerful State Institute for Agriculture. In 1953 Castro had promised the formation of free co-operatives for *special* purposes, but the co-operatives which were in fact set up resembled the Soviet *kolkhozy*, or even *sovkhozy*, from the start, and were intended to develop into basic parts of Cuban agriculture directly or indirectly controlled by INRA. It is true that the United Nations had pointed out in 1951 that it might be necessary for the governments of some countries to establish co-operatives,[3] but these were thought of as more or less free associations. The original draft of the land reform law, prepared by the revolutionary Minister of Agriculture, Sorí Marín, did not contain any mention of 'co-operatives'. They were added at Castro's request. Two pro-Castro authors wrote in 1960: 'He wanted co-operatives and he believed that most Cuban campesinos were ready for them ... That Fidel understood this against his experts and against apparent lessons of history, makes him a political genius and one of the greatest revolutionary leaders.'[4]

On December 20, 1961, Fidel Castro himself said:

'The concept of the co-operative was introduced into the land reform law in the aircraft flying there [to the Sierra Maestra]. There was some discussion as to whether the co-operatives should own the land or merely enjoy the use of it (*usufructo*). We said: [Castro often speaks of himself in the plural] all right, in fact it will come to the same thing, but let us not write down *usufructo*—so that our enemies cannot exploit it—but use 'property' instead. In fact the co-operative only has a usufructuary right, because it cannot sell the land.'[5]

This quotation illustrates the real character of the Cuban revolution and Castro's semantic methods which, after December 1961, he called Marxist-Leninist realism: euphemisms are invented which

[1] Food and Agricultural Organization of the United Nations, *The State of Food and Agriculture*, 1961, p. 98.
[2] United Nations, *Progress in Land Reform*, 1954, p. 63.
[3] Naciones Unidas, *La Reforma Agraria*, 1951, p. 86.
[4] Sweezy & Huberman, *op. cit.*, pp. 115/16.
[5] *El Mundo*, Havana, December 22, 1961.

ACHIEVEMENTS OF THE REVOLUTION 1959-1961

meet the requirements of a particular stage of development and of the political and social situation; this makes it possible to mislead the opponent and to carry out radical measures under harmless names. Castro rightly said in the same speech that nobody could understand the agrarian revolution if he merely read and interpreted the land reform law. The reform was in fact soon transformed into a revolution which brushed aside the spirit and letter of the law.

The Land Reform Law was not socialist: it spoke of confiscating only the land of the big landowners, and promised compensation and the establishment of independent tribunals for the settlement of disputes. It held out the bait of property to smallholders and tenant farmers, completely in accordance with the feelings of those inhabitants of the Sierra Maestra who had fought in the rebel army and of whom Guevera had written—let us repeat the quotation: 'The soldiers that made up our first guerilla army came from that part of this social class which shows its love for the possession of land most aggressively, which expresses most perfectly the spirit catalogued as petty bourgeois; the campesino fights because he wants land for himself, for his children: he wants to manage it, sell it, and make himself rich through his work.'[1]

But Castro from the beginning wanted a revolution, a socialist agrarian revolution, controlled by the state and not merely a reform. In the end it was those very peasants of the Sierra Maestra who had helped him, who became the victims of this revolution.

But Castro's plans, which were speedily put into practice, cannot be taken as proof of the thesis advanced by him after December, 1961 that he had already been a communist at that time. He was to the left of the official Communists who had not begun any agrarian revolution with collectivism: they first distributed the land among the peasants and collectivized it at a later stage. In Cuba it was different. A French agricultural expert who visited Cuba in 1960 wrote: 'In Cuba I found a land reform which differed from all others. By and large it was characterized by the direct transition from *latifundia* to production co-operatives. This did not happen anywhere else. The Communists regard this as heresy.'[2]

Castro's radicalism was not merely the result of his subjective inclinations but arose also from the realities and needs of Cuba. The following facts must be borne in mind:

1. The distribution of many large estates, including sugar and rice plantations, would probably have led to a fall in production. Large agricultural units, which *if well run* are often superior to smallholdings, predominated in Cuba.

[1] *Verde Olivo*, April 9, 1961, quoted in *Monthly Review*, New York, July-August, 1961.
[2] R. Dumont in *Express*, Paris, September 8, 1960.

2. Most of the Cuban rural population were agricultural labourers rather than peasants.

3. There was no tradition whatsoever in Cuba which might have helped the establishment of free, uncontrolled co-operatives. There was nothing corresponding to the Mexican *ejidos*, the Russian *mir* or the Bolivian syndicates.

4. The formation of independent co-operatives would soon have led to a division into rich and poor co-operatives, and probably also to increased exploitation of the rural proletariat working for the co-operatives.

5. The revolutionary government planned to develop a new communal life in the countryside—with new villages, schools, hospitals, clubs and so on. This could most rationally be achieved through collectivization.

6. Most country dwellers lacked any knowledge of modern methods and did not have either the capital or machinery needed to increase agricultural production.

7. If the new individual owners had been given absolute possession of the land it might easily have led to the creation of *minifundia* or new *latifundia*.

The experience of other countries was of no importance to Castro, and personal experience had confirmed him in his nationalization plans. In 1958 the guerillas had captured a large estate which they had handed over to the peasants, dividing the cattle among them. A month later most of the cattle had been sold or eaten.[1] Castro was clearly aiming beyond the alleged reform.

What took place was a chaotic if peaceful[2] revolution, although it did not get into full swing until summer 1960. It was carried out in the individual zones by revolutionary officials, mostly young, inexperienced officers of the rebel army who did what they thought best. All the land which they thought worth confiscating was confiscated. With the land went houses, furniture, machinery and livestock. In most cases there was neither valuation nor inventory. Receipts were hardly ever given. The promised compensation bonds were never printed and the planned tribunals were not set up. No estates of 100 *caballerias* were left in private hands, however productive. The intention of the law had been to delay distribution of private estates until state-owned land had been distributed. But this did not happen either. Although some large estates were not touched in 1959 in order not to interfere with the coming sugar harvest—the law made provision for this—it was generally the best-run private

[1] R. Dumont, *Terres Vivantes*, Paris, 1961, p. 114.
[2] J. Chonchol, of the Food and Agriculture Organization, whom the revolutionary government had called in as an expert, claimed in his report that the confiscations had not met with any opposition. (*La Reforma Agraria Cubana: Realizaciones y Perspectivas. Informe final al Gobierno Cubano*, Havana, August, 1961 (mimeographed).

estates which were confiscated first. It was claimed with some justification that the initials INRA were short for *Instituto Nacional para el Robo Autorizado* (National Institute for Authorized Robbery). INRA soon became the centre of revolutionary power, the real, absolute ruler of agriculture. It organized the agricultural credit system, monopolized the sale of many products and was directly responsible for a growing number of enterprises of all kinds, including even in 1959/60 a dozen confiscated sugar mills and a few rice mills. It established co-operatives, built villages and opened people's shops where goods were sold cheaply. Otherwise the revolutionary measures varied from region to region. Nobody worried whether a measure was advisable from an economic point of view, or how much it cost. One year after the start of the agrarian revolution René Dumont, who was one of the many experts advising Castro, wrote that he had not once been able to discover whether a co-operative was working economically or not, and complained about disorder and waste.[1]

Collectivization took place quickly: at first, co-operatives were set up; later towards the end of 1960, peoples' farms were also established on which farm workers worked as labourers for the state; in other words, *sovkhozy* were set up soon after the *kolkhozy*. Then the small peasants were brought together in a state-run organization (ANAP) of small peasants controlled by INRA, and a beginning was made in combining a number of co-operatives and people's farms in order to establish larger units. As there has never been any real difference between Cuban *kolkhozy* and *sovkhozy* it is better not to make any comparisons with Russia. This was true from the beginning. As early as summer 1960 Sweezy and Huberman wrote that 'the Cuban co-operative appears to be much closer to the state farm than to the collective'.[2]

From the beginning there was no private ownership of fields or cattle. The land and tools were owned communally by the members of co-operatives and the profits were to be distributed regularly. The *cooperativistas* were thus comparable to workers in a profit-sharing system. The co-operatives were established, guarded and administered by INRA. A foreign observer who knew Cuba well describes the foundation of the co-operative *Cuba Libre* in the Province of Matanzas as follows:

'The total area covers 42 *caballerias*. The main crops are sugar cane, beans and potatoes. There are 104 head of cattle, 6 horses, 5 tractors and some other machinery ... INRA decided to con-

---

[1] *ibid.* An excellent description of some instances of the agrarian transformation as it took place in reality can be found in Irving P. Pflaum, *Tragic Island*, New York, 1961—the valuable book of a keen observer who spent several months in Cuba studying the revolution.
[2] Sweezy & Huberman, *op. cit.*, p. 122.

fiscate this farm and to establish a co-operative. An INRA delegation arrived and called a meeting of workers and employees. Altogether there were 70 people. The officials said that the revolution had now come to the countryside; it had been decided to confiscate the estate because it had belonged to a follower of the fallen tyrant. Henceforth it would be administered by INRA. The workers had the opportunity of founding a co-operative. Daily rates would be increased from 2·46 pesos a day to 2·97 pesos. The workers would elect a representative to assist the INRA-appointed manager. A people's shop would be set up in which goods would be available at low prices. At the end of the year there would be profits, but these would not be paid out in cash: INRA would use them to build houses with running water, baths and lavatories which would be much more modern and comfortable than the existing ones. Production surpluses would have to be used for these purposes because the state could not afford to give away such things ... Then the INRA delegate asked those present to vote for or against his proposal. Everybody voted in favour. A document was drawn up and the co-operative was said to have been established.'[1]

The same co-operative is described a little over a year later by an American observer.[2] According to him living standards had improved considerably. Houses were comfortable and attractive, and had cost about £800 each. The people's shop was well stocked and prices were lower than in the old private enterprise shops. All members of the co-operative were given medical care. New crops were grown. Everybody had work all the year round.

During his visit in the summer of 1960 Souchy visited one co-operative which had been founded spontaneously at the request of its members and another, an 'industrial co-operative', founded against the wishes of its members. The workers of the latter belonged to a mechanical repair shop on a big estate near Bayamo in Oriente Province. Souchy was present as a spectator at the foundation:

'The INRA representative outlined the project and suggested the establishment of an industrial co-operative under the direction of INRA. But the workers were interested in other things and asked what wages would be paid. The delegate explained that the wage question was of secondary importance and that the main task was to provide the process of industrialization and asked all workers to make sacrifices for the revolution. This did not arouse any enthusiasm. Finally the delegate said that come what may the co-operative would be founded, with or without the assembled workers.'[3]

[1] Augustin Souchy, *Testimonios Sobre la Revolución Cubana*, Editorial Reconstruir, Buenos Aires, 1960, p. 32.
[2] Samuel Shapiro, 'Cuba—A Dissenting Report', *The New Republic*, New York, September 12, 1960.
[3] Augustin Souchy, *op. cit.*, p. 47.

Other country dwellers showed greater enthusiasm than these workers. Souchy found a group of thirteen women to whom the revolutionary authorities had given sewing machines and who were now making clothes for the people's shops. The women worked eight hours a day and were given only their food but no wages and were quite happy with this arrangement.

Finally he visited a fishing co-operative which was being established in Manzanillo (Oriente). Here a whole little town was being built for the fishermen, with schools, sports grounds and a small shipyard: ' "And where are the fishermen?" I asked. "INRA will bring them when everything is finished. They will fish in new boats, live in modern houses and be free from all economic cares because INRA will buy their fish".'[1]

Soon hundreds of new settlements and co-operatives were set up in this fashion. As far as wage levels are concerned the author knows of cases where they were higher than before, others where they were lower and still others where they remained the same. It seems impossible to generalize, and one must remember that the wages of sugar workers, for example, depended, before the revolution and after, on the world market price. In general the wages of many of those engaged in agriculture had risen sharply. Former tenants no longer paid rent and many who used to work only between three and five months a year were now working the whole year round. In addition there had been an improvement in living conditions, because houses and schools were built, running water was installed, medical care was provided, and so on. Prices in people's shops were lower than they used to be in private shops in the countryside, but differed little from those paid before the revolution in large shops in Havana. The author found this himself in the spring of 1960, and according to F. R. Allemann it was still true in December 1960.[2] It has often been claimed that *cooperativistas* and labourers—because in addition to the actual members of the co-operatives there were many seasonal workers—were not paid in cash but in vouchers. Generally this was not the case, although there is never a rule without an exception in Cuba. What were mistaken for vouchers were often preliminary receipts given by the *cooperativistas* or the labourers to the manager of the people's shops when they made credit purchases. This sum was then deducted from the wages which were paid fortnightly.[3]

---

[1] *ibid.*, p. 50.
[2] *Der Monat*, No. 149, Berlin, February 1961.
[3] But Allemann also reports of a co-operative: 'The *cooperativista* told me that by no means the whole wage was paid in cash. The INRA shop ... sells on credit and after 14 days the whole ... debt ... is deducted from the wage. Other co-operatives pay half the wage in vouchers which can only be cashed in the Tienda del Pueblo.' *Fidel Castro—Die Revolution der Bärte*, Hamburg, 1961, p. 33.

The progress which the agrarian revolution had made by the summer of 1961 can briefly be described as follows:

At the end of May it was announced that 20 per cent of the land was still in the hands of large private owners, that is those who have more than five *caballerias* of land. The remaining 80 per cent was controlled by the state through INRA. At the end of 1960 and the beginning of 1961 'people's farms' (*granjas del pueblo*) were set up primarily in former cattle *latifundia*, in addition to the co-operatives which had been created mainly on the old sugar *latifundia*, and in the spring of 1961 an Organization of Small Farmers (ANAP) was founded; all three were controlled by INRA, which therefore rested on the following foundations:

	Percentage of total area under cultivation	*Number of persons employed*
ANAP	39	about 200,000
Co-operatives	11·8	163,000 (including 45,000 seasonal workers)
People's farms	29·1	105,000

The private sector was decreasing. The other figures varied because, as we shall see, it was possible to move from one group to another. For example, in the INRA report[1] the number of small ANAP farmers in May 1961 was given as 50,000 but, at the end of August, on the occasion of the 'First Production Congress' it was given as 200,000 families.[2] In the summer of 1961 there were about 600 co-operatives and 300 people's farms, which were being made into larger units—a further stage in the socialization of agriculture. This was done, in spite of the opinion of most specialists that the existing co-operatives and people's farms were already too large: the former had, on the average, an area of 2,500 to 3,750 acres, and the people's farm an area of 18,296 acres. Both were rather understaffed: in the co-operatives there was one worker for 12 acres and in the people's farms one worker for not less than 63 acres.[3] *Officially* there was a basic difference between the small landowners of ANAP, the co-operatives and the labourers on people's farms: ANAP was made up of independent landowners and producers who received credits and other help from INRA; the members of the co-operatives owned their land and tools collectively and received a share of the profits; the labourers of the people's farms were workers paid by the state.

But in fact the situation was quite different: ANAP was completely under the control of INRA; its members could hardly be regarded as

[1] *Bohemia*, May 28, 1961.
[2] Jose Ramirez, *Obra Revolucionaria*, No. 30, 1961, p. 57.
[3] J. Chonchol, *Informe de Misión al Gobierno Cubano*, August 1961, pp. 39–42.

ndependent producers, and their produce was rarely sold on the free market, but usually delivered to the co-operatives and people's farms.[1] Up to the end of May 1961 only 31,000 deeds of ownership had been handed out.[2] The small owners retained a certain independence because they were mostly peasants living on individual farms or in small, isolated villages, who worked poor land and whose presence was of value for the economy as a whole because no state investments were needed for houses, schools, and so on. Where there were no such obstacles the government preferred to see the ANAP turned voluntarily into co-operatives, and the small farmers into *cooperativistas*, or better still, into labourers on people's farms. For political reasons no pressure to collectivize has at this time been exerted on the small farmers who were in any case controlled by the state.

In May 1961 Fidel Castro said: 'We have enough land and we have no intention of socializing all the land ... The small farmer is an ally of the working class and he must be helped because he often works in the mountains or on poor soil. There were some small farmers who wanted to join people's farms. Such cases were studied ... Many were rejected because *all* members of a group must agree to such a change.'[3]

As early as December 1960, even before the founding of ANAP, Castro had said: 'If a group of small peasants wants to form a co-operative, a village will be built for them, just as for the co-operatives and under the same favourable conditions. But the revolutionary government will never force a small owner to do this.'[4]

As far as the co-operatives were concerned their 'collective ownership' was of course purely fictitious. As already mentioned, in contrast to the Russian *kolkhozy* the Cuban *cooperativistas* have neither private plots nor private cattle. This is the reason why Sweezy and Huberman likened the co-operatives to state farms. Dumont shared this view and said that the co-operatives 'are much more like Chinese communes than *kolkhozy*.'[5]

In so far as any profits were distributed at all, their maximum for *all* co-operatives was centrally fixed, so that no co-operative would be at a disadvantage. Therefore, even if no cash payments were made, there was no relationship between the real profits of a co-operative and the amounts paid to its members. This was contrary to the expectations of many *cooperativistas*.[6] But in most cases there were no profits which could be distributed, because 80 per

[1] José Ramírez in a television speech. *Hoy*, Havana, August 16, 1961.
[2] *Bohemia*, May 28, 1961.
[3] *Obra Revolucionaria*, No. 21, December 17, 1961.
[4] *Obra Revolucionaria*, No. 33, December 17, 1960.
[5] *Esprit*, Paris, April 1961.
[6] In April 1961, for example, it was announced that in September all co-operativistas would receive fifty pesos per person. (Santos Rios in *Obra Revolucionaria*, No. 30, August 26, 1961).

cent of the surplus was used for the construction of villages. Furthermore, Castro said in a speech that in future the remaining 20 per cent would not be distributed but set aside for cultural purposes, particularly for the work to be done by the newly trained art instructors.[1]

For a time, while the *cooperativistas* expected a share of the profits related to their production, the state preferred the co-operatives to the people's farms, a fact which was openly admitted by Castro: 'At the moment the co-operatives are producing more cheaply than the people's farms because they work for themselves and receive credits from INRA. Therefore the members of the co-operatives try to work as efficiently as possible and to save. Investments in the people's farms are larger than in the co-operatives.'[2]

There was however no basic difference between a *cooperativista* and a farm labourer on a people's farm;[3] in 1962 the 'co-operatives' were indeed all transformed into people's farms, a process which had already begun previously. *Bohemia* for instance reported on April 30, 1961, that the co-operative *Ciro Redondo* had risen to the category of a people's farm (*se ha elevado a la categoria de Granja del Pueblo*) and the fact that the word *elevado* was used, clearly showed what future developments were likely to be.

At the end of 1961 Cuban agriculture *seemed* already more highly socialized than that of many Eastern countries. In Poland collectivization has slowed down markedly since 1956; in Yugoslavia, where there were almost 7,000 collectives in 1950, only 3·4 per cent of land under cultivation is now co-operatively owned; and in the Soviet Union about 40 per cent of the demand for potatoes, vegetables and meat is met from the private sector.[4]

However, the real situation in 1961 (and even in 1962) was so chaotic that the importance of the private sector could not be clearly established. The cultivators organized in the ANAP were either considered as part of this private sector (because officially they were not collectivized and were permitted to sell some of their produce on the free market) or as part of the socialist sector, because they had no full ownership and were—at least on paper—controlled by and utterly dependent on the INRA. But the private sector even extended to the people's farms, the members of which were not efficiently controlled and participated in all sorts of black market operations. Speaking of the bigger farmers (those with more than five *caballerias*),

[1] *Bohemia*, April 2, 1961.
[2] *Obra Revolucionaria*, No. 21, May 29, 1961.
[3] Professor Dumont suggested some changes in the organization of the co-operatives which would give members a feeling of real ownership: 'Ché Guevara accused me ... of having paid attention to the feelings of the owner. He put the main emphasis on the feeling of responsibility, particularly because many of the co-operativistas are not meant to remain in the co-operatives.' *Esprit*, Paris, April 1961.
[4] Food and Agricultural Organization of the United Nations: *The State of Food and Agriculture*, 1961, pp. 88/89.

ACHIEVEMENTS OF THE REVOLUTION 1959-1961

J. Chonchol estimated that, contrary to the official data, not less than some 44 per cent of the agricultural area belonged to this private sector. Most of these farmers were, according to him, 'middle' farmers who each possessed between five and twelve *caballerias* and were poor. He especially complained that this—undoubtedly private—sector had been completely left to its own devices, without getting help, machinery or credits, all of which contributed to the bad results of the first years of agrarian reform.[1]

During the first two years of its existence INRA invested over 400,000 million pesos. In 1960/61 12,500 dwellings were built, most of them comfortable, one-family houses with three or four rooms, bath, kitchen, built-in cupboards, front gardens, running water and electric light. In addition INRA built 500 other buildings: schools, people's shops, clubs, clinics, warehouses and so on. Hundreds of new localities were created with paved streets, sports and playgrounds and libraries. In addition to agricultural co-operatives there were the new fishermen's villages where over 200 boats had already been built. INRA had 2,000 people's shops serving 418,000 customers. It looked after health in the countryside and employed 1,759 doctors and 80 dentists; by May 1961 it had built 35 rural hospitals and started a further 24. It trained specialists, ran agricultural research stations, introduced improved agricultural methods, had the monopoly of the sale of a variety of products, controlled the distribution of the remainder, ran many industries, built roads and gave credits to agriculture.

The head of INRA, Núñez Jiménez repeatedly and proudly pointed out that Cuba's agricultural revolution was the first which led to an immediate increase in production.

The published results were indeed very impressive. The area under cultivation had increased considerably; land which used to lie fallow or was hardly cultivated was now in use. Methods were being modernized, new crops were grown and production rose rapidly.

Year	Rice	Maize	Beans	Onions	Tomatoes	Coffee
		(in millions of Cuban hundredweights)				
1958	4·5	3·2	0·22	0·169	1·2	0·675
1960	6·7	4·6	0·80	0·391	2·52	0·804
1961	9·5	8·7	2·44	0·969	3·37	1·125

Before 1959 hardly any cotton was grown in Cuba because the experts had advised against it. There were only ten *caballerias* under cotton which produced 4,000 Cuban hundredweights: in 1961 there were 3,043 *caballerias* under cotton which produced 1,172,000 Cuban hundredweights!

Production of three widely consumed products, the potato-like

[1] In *Trimestre Económico*, January–March 1963.

malanga root, the sweet potato (*boniato*) and the true potato, also increased:

Year	Malanga	Boniato	Potato
1958	4·9	3·47	1·53
1960	5·58	5·01	3·30[1]

Even in 1963 it was of course much too early to say whether the Cuban land reform had succeeded. But the first results of this attempt to achieve greater social justice and simultaneously to increase agricultural production must be critically examined.

It is undeniable that from the social point of view there has been considerable progress. Everybody must regard the establishment of new settlements with decent houses and schools, the improvement of hygienic conditions and so on as positive achievements, but opinions will differ about the use of authoritarian methods. It is also a fact that the present government shows much greater concern for the agricultural population than any of its predecessors and offers them chances of social advancement and a share in the culture of the country undreamt of before. Further, an attempt was being made to do away with seasonal labour with its insecurity and low incomes.

This problem had by no means been solved. There were still seasonal workers in the co-operatives and even in the people's farms.[2]

According to the estimates of specialists,[3] 860,000 people were employed in agriculture in 1961. If we assume that the proportion of agricultural workers had not changed since 1953, 570,000 of the whole labour force must have been workers. But, according to the official statistics only 122,000 were *cooperativistas* and only 273,000 permanent workers on people's farms, whereas the private sector made up of bigger farms declined rapidly. This meant that for the majority of the labourers the problem of fixed and permanent employment had not been solved. No wonder that so many migrated to the cities and that enthusiasm waned. At the same time many small peasants openly showed their fear of becoming *cooperativistas*. As Castro said in his speech of November 10, 1961: 'The small farmer who causes us such a headache in the province of Matanzas and elsewhere is allergic to co-operatives. He does not want to hear them mentioned—he is frightened by the mere word,'[4] Thereupon

[1] All figures are taken from the INRA report, *Bohemia*, May 28, 1961.

[2] Officially the co-operatives employ 46,000 day labourers. The official journal *Verde Olivo*, No. 34, August 27, 1961, announced that a people's farm in the Province of Pinar employed 500 permanent and 400 seasonal workers. In December 1960 F. R. Allemann found a co-operative which had 1,200 seasonal workers and only 92 *cooperativistas*. René Alleman, *op. cit.*, p. 33. In the report of J. Chonchol it is stated that in 1961 even the 266 people's farms employed 27,300 permanent and 69,000 seasonal workers.

[3] Chonchol Peyrellade & Chao, *Proyecto de Plan Quinquenal para el Desarrollo de la Agricultura Cubana 1961–1965*, Havana, March 1961 (mimeographed), p. 12.

[4] *Revolucion*, November 11, 1961.

Castro decided to solve the difficulty with his characteristic semantic methods: 'As the peasants do not want to hear co-operatives mentioned we are now forming "agricultural societies" ... The peasants liked the name *sociedad agricola* ... These are in fact small co-operatives under a different name.'[1]

Twelve thousand five hundred peasants' houses built in a year— this sounds impressive but was only a little more than the number needed to house the normal annual increase in population. One should not forget that pre-revolutionary governments too built houses for the rural population.[2] According to the census of 1953 there existed in the countryside 289,000 *bohios* (huts) with nothing but earth floors and since then their number had increased. The government promised to build 25,000 houses in 1961/62, but this was impossible. At the Production Congress in August 1961 Castro mentioned that it was planned to build a total of 30,000 rural and urban dwellings for the coming year but doubted himself if this target could be achieved.[3] In November 1961 he complained that new *bohios* had already sprung up, even close to important roads.[4]

A critical examination of the production statistics suggests the following comments:

1. Production figures as such mean little if no figures are given of the expenditure on materials. There was, undoubtedly, a great deal of waste.
2. The figures are not reliable and are sometimes contradictory.[5]
3. Progress cannot be measured by comparing production figures

[1] *El Mundo*, December 22, 1961.
[2] In his book *Piedras y Leyes*, Mexico, 1961, Batista maintains that his government had built 60,000 houses for the rural population—10,000 of them in 1952/53 (pp. 314 and 424).
[3] *Obra Revolucionaria*, No. 30, 1961, p. 217.
[4] *Revolución*, November 11, 1961. In the same speech Castro complained about the strange fact that revolutionary consciousness was particularly backward in those parts of the countryside in which the government had done most for the population.
[5] Besides the examples given later on, it may be interesting to mention the numbers of tractors imported. According to the figures given during the Production Congress of August 1961 (*Obra Revolucionaria*, No. 30, 1961, p. 77), Cuba imported during the first year of the Agrarian Reform 4,177 tractors. But here are the 'confidential' figures contained in the above-mentioned *Proyecto de Plan Quinquenal* by Chonchol Peyrellade Chao (Cuadro Annex XII):

	Number at start of year	Wear and tear	Import	Number at end of year
1957	7,499	2,246	2,484	7,736
1958	7,736	1,409	2,408	8,735
1959	8,735	1,150	1,724	9,309
1960	9,309	1,280	1,182	9,211

According to the FAO *Production Yearbook*, Vol. 13, 1959 (Table 101), Cuba had 13,300 tractors in 1957. The difference between this number and the one given above is difficult to explain, unless one supposes that even the confidential numbers were established so as to hide the 'wear and tear' which occurred in 1959/1960!

for 1958 and 1961. 1958 was a bad year for agriculture because in the last months a state of civil war already existed in eastern provinces. And the figures used for 1961 are those given in the plan, which was only partly fulfilled.

4. The undeniable shortage of almost all foodstuffs which has existed in the whole of Cuba since the summer of 1961 makes official output statistics suspect. The revolutionary leaders openly admit that shortages are only partly due to increased consumption, and that costly mistakes have been made.

Cuba always produced all its *malanga* and *boniato* and imported only about a third of its potato requirements. But at the Production Congress Fidel Castro said:

'Although we have often said that if there is nothing else to eat we should eat *malanga*, we forgot to produce *malanga!* There was no *malanga* anywhere so that of course there was an increased demand for *boniato*. With the result that *boniato* disappeared too. Then, when there were no *malanga* or *boniato*, although there were enough potatoes to cover normal demand, potatoes also became scarce.'[1]

Castro's remark clearly gave the lie to the production statistics. While he claimed that the cultivation of *malanga* had been 'forgotten' the official figures showed an increase of 32·4 per cent. As *malanga* is one of the cheapest foods the demand for it does not increase with a rise in the standards of living—nor has there ever been a *malanga* shortage in Cuba before. The production of *boniato* had allegedly risen by 45·5 per cent. A shortage of *malanga* could therefore easily have been made good by the extra *boniato*. As that was not the case the figures for *boniato* must also be wrong. Finally, according to the statistics there were not only 'enough potatoes to cover a *normal* demand' but far more, because production was claimed to have doubled. Therefore this figure too must be wrong.

One might have thought that the *plan* figures for these three products had been too high, although one of the two annual harvests had already been brought in. But this is ruled out by other figures proudly published in the Cuban press, showing that the plan targets had been substantially exceeded. *Hoy* of July 23, 1961, for example, published statistics of production on people's farms in the Province of Havana. The figures for the three products under discussion were:

	Area under cultivation (in *caballerias*)	
	Plan	Actual Production
Malanga	17·04	39·77
Boniato	15·00	19·05
Potatoes	25·00	29·22

With regard to the production of rice—a product which was not in

[1] *Obra Revolucionaria*, No. 30, August 1961, p. 9.

short supply because of imports from China—INRA announced a production of 4·5 million Cuban hundredweights for 1958 (unpolished rice, equal to about 3 million hundredweights of polished rice). But Núñez Jiménez himself said in his book, published in 1959, that in 1958 Cuba had produced 3·4 million hundredweights of polished rice.[1] He says further that in 1956/57 Cuba's total consumption of polished rice was 7·5 million hundredweights of which 4·5 million (60·4 per cent) were produced in Cuba. According to Santos Rios' statements at the Production Congress[2] total consumption in 1961 was 8·8 million of which 4·8 million were produced in Cuba and 4 million imported from China. A comparison of the import and production figures for 1956/57 published by Núñez Jiménez in 1959 with the official Cuban figures for 1960/61 shows that during these four years rice production increased by only about 6 per cent but imports by almost 25 per cent.[3]

Finally it should be pointed out that so far nobody had tried to explain the lack of black beans which had long been felt in Cuba. Like rice, black beans are a popular food found almost daily on the menu of the average Cuban household. As large quantities had to be imported,[4] yet according to INRA statistics, the production of beans of all kinds had increased tenfold, this shortage must remain mysterious—unless these production figures also were invented.

Not only were some of the official figures manifestly wrong, and others questionable, but the revolutionary leaders also gave statistics which were obviously intended to mislead the uninformed.

Animal husbandry may serve as an illustration. According to the INRA report there were 5,385,000 head of cattle in 1958 and 5,607,000 in 1961. In August 1961 there was a census, the result of which was announced by Castro at the Production Congress. The census listed 5,574,777 head of cattle. But although there were what a speaker at the Production Congress described as 'massive' cattle imports[5] amounting to over 10,000 a year, the increase in stocks must appear remarkable in view of the fact that Castro and other speakers had referred to 'mass slaughter'. If there had really been such an increase one must also wonder why the meat shortage was so great that every Cuban citizen received a ration of only half a pound of beef a week.

[1] *Geografía de Cuba*, Havana, 1959, pp. 230/231.
[2] *Obra Revolucionaria*, No. 30, August 1961, p. 32.
[3] That those figures are wrong also emerges from a sentence in an article by the same Santos Rios entitled 'Tecnificar nuestra agricultura es hacerla mas productiva.' He says: 'In 1961 rice production declined noticeably. This must not happen again'. (*Cuba Socialista*, No. 9, May 1962.)
[4] The Minister of Foreign Trade, Mora, said at the Production Congress that up to the end of August 21,243 tons of beans had been imported and that a further 22,596 would arrive by the end of the year.
[5] Speech by Ing. Julio Serrate, of the Administration of People's farms, *Obra Revolucionaria*, No. 30, August 26, 1961.

But in fact the figure for 1958 was wrong and the figure for 1961 cannot be compared with that for 1958. In 1958 the number of cattle was estimated at 5,700,000 and not at 5,300,000;[1] moreover, earlier censuses included only fully-grown animals. But, according to Castro's statements 1,052,366 of the total number of cattle were less than one year old. The real figures for comparison appear to be the following:

> 1958 approximately 5,700,000
> 1961   4,523,000

This means a reduction of 1,200,000. The same probably applied to fish and poultry. In spite of triumphant accounts of the progress made in fishing and poultry production there was a shortage of fish and even of chickens (which were said to have increased from 20 to 83 million since 1958). At the Production Congress, Salvador Perez, who was in charge of Cuban fisheries said:

'Sometimes one meets comrades who keep on asking one where the fish is. Some put this question cheerfully, others seem pretty furious. Recently I met a colleague who works in the poultry department and he said to me: "Listen old boy, where is this fish?" At that point I couldn't restrain myself any longer and I asked him: "And where might the chickens be?" Now we are quits, and he should not be amused because there is no fish any more than we should laugh because there are no chickens.'[2]

This analysis shows that Cuba was really very different from the rosy picture painted by official figures and revolutionary propaganda. Perhaps as the participants in the debates of the 1961 Production Congress pointed out unanimously, these were growing pains which would soon be overcome. But some degree of scepticism seemed justified because other, similar claims had failed to materialize. When the first serious food shortages appeared in November 1960 Castro himself said that in the next year there would be no more food shortages: 'Remember what I am telling you—the foodstuffs which will be available again by December will never disappear again!'[3] He could not keep this promise and it was doubtful whether the new claims would be borne out by the facts. Many mistakes were undoubtedly being avoided, overall planning had improved, and 'socialist competitions' might provide new incentives for producers. But both the question of costs and the impossibility of carrying out rapid social improvements would become increasingly important. At the same time there had been a noticeable flagging of enthusiasm, so that campaigns for competitions and 'voluntary work' had to be

[1] US Department of Agriculture: *Foreign Crops and Markets*, World Summaries, April 27, 1961.
[2] *Obra Revolucionaria*, No. 30, August 26, 1961, p. 83.
[3] *Obra Revolucionaria*, No. 28, November 9, 1960.

ACHIEVEMENTS OF THE REVOLUTION 1959-1961 235

ordered 'from above'. The smallholders who recognized the illusory character of their ownership, the *cooperativistas* who realized that profits were not being distributed, the farm labourers who continued to have no homes or occupations, would all work less without such campaigns; but experience in other socialist countries has shown how difficult it is to replace spontaneous determination and enthusiasm with authoritarian actions and campaigns. It would of course be premature and unfair to condemn a tremendous transformation like the Cuban agrarian revolution on the basis of the results and experiences of the first two years, or to overlook its great social achievements, because of possibly temporary economic failures. But these achievements depend, in the last resort, on increased productivity. If the prospects for economic development were less favourable than the revolutionary leaders admitted, it was possible that their expectations of social progress would turn out to have been also overoptimistic.

5. Opposition and invasion

(*a*) *Growing Discontent*

In view of the situation in Cuba it was impossible, at the beginning of 1961, to judge the extent of popular support for Castro. There could be no doubt that he had a large following, particularly among the young men, and also that the majority of the rural population was devoted to him. It is probable that he still had the support of a substantial majority of the people, but nobody could discover the size of this majority or the strength of the opposition.

This was impossible just because in a totalitarian system it is impossible to distinguish between spontaneous enthusiasm and enforced or opportunistic conformity. Some foreign opponents of Castro believed that the opposition doubled between the spring and autumn of 1960, so that by the end of September 1960 it comprised a fifth or a fourth of the population.[1] Three months later it was probably considerably larger,[2] though probably not as large as the emigrés claimed. But this opposition was heterogeneous and unorganized. It certainly extended far beyond the injured upper and middle classes. The economic interests of many people, petty bourgeois, peasants and workers, had been or were likely to be affected. Everybody complained about shortages of various goods. Some people felt insecure and constrained. Apart from economic motives there were all kinds of ideological, religious and personal motives.

Officially it was increasingly emphasized that the workers represented the 'leading mass of the revolution'. But not all workers shared this view. During the first phase of the revolution real wages had certainly risen, and many people—mostly seasonal agricultural workers—now had permanent jobs. But wages had been frozen long ago and in some cases cut. In the old days deductions from wages amounted to less than 5 per cent, now they were up to 15 per cent or more if various voluntary contributions were included. The slogan 'more pay for less work' had been replaced by 'more work for less pay'. Voluntary unpaid labour was encouraged everywhere and people found it difficult to avoid their revolutionary duties. After all, the government led by Fidel, set an example of voluntary, often extremely strenuous, manual work in their spare time, when instead of relaxing they cut sugar cane or worked as building labourers. What used to be called exploitation was now called service of the people, but not every worker was sufficiently class conscious to

[1] Sweezy & Huberman, 'Cuba Revisited', *Monthly Review*, Vol. 12, No. 8, December 1960.
[2] *Neue Zürcher Zeitung*, August 13, 1961.

appreciate the difference. There were no more strikes and many of the old extra sources of income had vanished: bus conductors found it difficult to embezzle fares, and dockers were no longer able to postpone their work to the hours when overtime was paid.

The government's inroads on leisure were another cause of discontent. Militia service was officially voluntary, but those who tried to avoid it were regarded as possible enemies of the revolution. An official revolutionary publication said: 'Now Sunday morning is no longer devoted to sleeping late or to private excursions—it is spent in military training ... On working days the *miliciano* starts his service after working hours and receives no pay whatsoever.'[1]

In addition to militia service there were numerous campaigns, organizations in which membership was compulsory, rallies which it was wise to attend. The prying eyes of the newly formed 'Committees for the Protection of the Revolution' were everywhere.

Time and again the revolutionary government promised friendship and protection to the small industrialist, the small trader and the artisan. But many of them felt that in an increasingly socialized economy there would soon be no place for them. Even small tenant farmers had doubts about their future. The author knows of a case where former tenant farmers appeared collectively before their old landlord and offered to continue to pay the old rent. They said that they were not sure how long the present state would last and that, in the event of a change, they would prefer not to lose their rights. They added that the various contributions which they now had to pay amounted to more than their old rent. (This may have been an isolated case, but even so it is symptomatic of the general insecurity.)

The shortage of many goods to which people had been accustomed, soap, nails, toilet articles, medicine and, even as early as 1960, sometimes food, was bound to produce discontent.

Housing was also becoming an increasing problem. The housing shortage began to become noticeable and the ex-tenants who had been transformed into would-be owners and who were forced to pay rent *and* maintain their houses as well were often disgruntled because their freedom of movement had been restricted.

There were also some devout Catholics who anxiously watched the declining influence of the Church and many, by no means always very religious, parents who feared that the state would take their children from them and abolish paternal authority.

There were quite a few people who resented having to fit into a system which restricted their freedom and which reduced the private sphere of life, while others had friends or relations who had emigrated or been arrested.

Among members of the co-operatives too there were occasional instances of discontent. Some had hoped that profits would be shared

[1] *Trabajo*, Havana, December 1960, special edition.

out regularly and waited in vain for this to happen. Then there were instances—only rarely admitted officially[1]—where, contrary to the official policy, peasants were forced to join co-operatives.

Finally, most Cubans are, like everybody else, egoists who think first of themselves and their families. The motto 'public interest comes before private interest' was not always readily observed nor did it invariably receive the enthusiastic support of individual citizens. As a result, there developed increasingly active underground anti-Castro movements, some of them spontaneous and independent, others closely linked not only with counter-revolutionary circles abroad but also with the CIA. Acts of terrorism and sabotage and small-scale guerilla fighting became more frequent.

It was partly because American politicians overestimated this opposition and underestimated Castro's following among the masses and Cuba's military preparedness, that they decided to support an invasion.

(b) *The Invasion of 1961*[2]

At the beginning of 1961 defence against invasion seemed more important to the revolutionary government than any other task. The whole country was mobilized and kept under arms for weeks, although this was bound to have an adverse effect on the economy. The attack was expected early in January, before the Kennedy administration took office. In the event the revolutionary leaders were wrong about the date, though not about the invasion itself. In the spring of 1960 it became clear to most members of the State Department that Cuba had irrevocably become a communist state closely tied to the Eastern bloc. Preparations for an eventual invasion had already been in progress and Cuban emigrants were being trained for this purpose. Slowly the movement gathered momentum: 'Though the decision to invade had not yet been taken preparations went ahead as though it had been taken; like a boulder rolling downhill it became increasingly difficult to stop them.'[3]

At the end of March President Eisenhower seems to have agreed in principle to the preparation of such a plan.[4] While on the diplomatic front the United States opened an offensive aimed at winning the support of Latin American states against the revolutionary island, the CIA was given a free hand to help the preparations for the military action.[5]

[1] E.g., in a speech by Blas Roca to the Heads of Schools for Revolutionary Education, reported in *Hoy*, July 26, 1961.
[2] Cf. *The Cuban Invasion* by K. E. Meyer and Tod Szulc, New York, 1962, which contains useful additional information.
[3] Louis J. Halle, 'Lessons of the Cuban Blunder', *The New Republic*, May 5, 1961.
[4] Cabell Phillips in the *New York Times*, September 12, 1961.
[5] *The Times*, London, June 1, 1961.

OPPOSITION AND INVASION

However, at the Conference of American Ministers in San José, Costa Rica, in August 1960, the political offensive collapsed.[1] The Latin American states were not prepared to take action against Castro. The United States embargo on supplies to Cuba could no more lead to the overthrow of the revolutionary government than the reduction of Cuban sugar imports by which it had been preceded. Direct intervention by American troops was unimaginable, particularly as Secretary of State Herter had solemnly reaffirmed his faith in the principle of non-intervention.[2]

As early as October 1960 the news leaked out that Cuban emigrants were being trained in Guatemala for an invasion. Soon this became a public secret and the Cuban government even learned some details of the plans. At the end of the year photographs appeared in the American press showing Varona, the leader of the Cuban opposition, inspecting recruits. On November 18, 1960, at a meeting of the Commonwealth Club in San Francisco, the Inspector General of the CIA, Mr Kirkpatrick, was asked to what extent these reports were true. The questioner finished with these words: 'If the CIA is really behind this surely it will be a black day for the United States if it is caught red handed?' The Inspector General replied with a smile: 'It would be a black day, *if* we were caught.'[3]

At the beginning of January 1961 diplomatic relations between the USA and Cuba were broken off after a demand by Cuba that the American government should restrict the number of its diplomatic representatives to twelve.

Soon after taking office the new President had to decide what action to take. His advisers were divided: some were against any form of invasion and the majority were against invasion with the open help and participation of America. President Kennedy shared this point of view, thus adopting a different attitude from his predecessor.[4] But he gave his consent to the invasion, provided it was carried out by Cuban emigrants, and expressed his willingness to

---

[1] Cf. the Chapter on 'Castro's Shadow over America.'

[2] 'The most important corner stone in the mutual relations which have developed in this hemisphere is the principle of non-intervention of every American state in the affairs of every other American state. The United States has recognized this principle and has, over the years, become increasingly convinced of its validity.' *Department of State Bulletin*, August 31, 1960.

[3] *Hispanic American Report*, Stanford University, Vol. XIII, No. 10, December 1960.

[4] In a television interview on June 11, 1961, two Republicans, Senator Hugh Scott and Representative W. E. Miller, accused President Kennedy of having forbidden American warships and aircraft to take part in the invasion as planned. (*New York Times*, July 12, 1961.) On September 11, 1961, General Eisenhower denied that he had planned to use American military forces, whereupon a 'well-informed' source declared that the ex-President was wrong and that documents existed proving that there had been such plans. (Cabell Phillips in the *New York Times*, December 12, 1961.) At a press conference shortly before the invasion President Kennedy said that 'in no circumstances would there be an intervention by US armed forces.' (*New York Times*, April 13, 1961.)

continue to assist in its preparation. His attitude was determined not only by his hostility to communism, but also by the argument that preparations for invasion had already progressed too far to be stopped without risking a complete demoralization of the pro-American Cubans and of the opposition inside the country. The CIA claimed that Castro had already lost his majority support in Cuba, and that it would be better not to wait until May when the first Cuban jet fighter pilots would return from training in Czechoslovakia. (The first fifteen MIGs had apparently been delivered in crates in March.)[1]

At the same time the President of Guatemala, under pro-Castro pressure in his own country, seems to have asked that the bases in Guatemala used for training the invaders be evacuated as soon as possible.[2]

On April 4, 1961, Kennedy decided to let the invasion take place.[3] This decision coincided with the publication of a document by the historian, Arthur M. Schlesinger, accusing Cuba of being a Communist state.

Cuba's political emigrés consisted of many antagonistic groups. In general three streams could be distinguished: the *Batistianos*, a left-wing group consisting of former Castro supporters which called itself the 'Revolutionary People's Movement' (MRP) and was led by Manuel Ray, and a 'centre' gathered together in the 'Revolutionary Democratic Front' (FDR), led by the former *Auténtico* leader, Varona. In September there was a split in the centre group after one of its leaders, Aureliano Sánchez Arango, had protested in a secret memorandum against the subjection of the Cubans to the CIA.[4]

In March 1961, under American pressure, Varona's *Frente Revolucionario Democratico* and Manuel Ray's *Movimiento Revolucionario del Pueblo* joined forces; Manuel Ray apparently had the best illegal organization inside Cuba. It was agreed that the illegal movement in Cuba should play the main rôle in any liberation attempt and that no *Batistianos* should take part in an invasion. On the basis of this agreement a Revolutionary Liberation Committee was set up to direct the liberation attempt.

What happened in fact was something quite different. The direction of the invasion lay exclusively in the hands of the CIA, which had confidence in the *Batistianos* but regarded Ray with suspicion. Former Batista officers began to play a leading part in the training camps and recruits who protested against this were removed from the invasion army, or even arrested. The illegal movement in Cuba

---

[1] *Time*, April 28, 1961. This edition of *Time* contains a good description of the history of the invasion; cf. also Theodore Draper's 'Cubans and Americans' in *Encounter*, London, July 1961.
[2] *The Reporter*, New York, May 11, 1961.
[3] Herbert L. Matthews, *op. cit.*, p. 253. Matthews says that by that time only an invasion by American forces could have led to success.
[4] Theodore Draper, *Encounter*, July, 1961.

OPPOSITION AND INVASION

was not kept informed. During the actual invasion the members of the Revolutionary Liberation Committee were put under arrest and held *incomunicado*. The supreme military command of the invasion was given to the inexperienced and unpopular Artime.

The action began on April 16 with a short bombing raid on the military aerodrome of Havana in which seven people were killed. The aeroplanes came from Central America but were not, as stated, piloted by deserters from the Cuban air force. The fact that it fell to Adlai Stevenson to give this piece of misinformation to the United Nations was to prove very detrimental to the popularity of this politician who had hitherto been well liked in Latin America. On April 17 the main body of the invasion army, about 1,300 men, landed on the beach of Girón, in the Bay of Pigs in Central Cuba. Castro was ready, and while suspects were being arrested wholesale all over the country,[1] the army and militia were mobilized. The revolutionary army, equipped with artillery, tanks, bazookas and heavy machine guns defeated the invaders in less than two days. About 90 invaders were killed and 1,214 captured; they were shown on television soon afterwards and interrogated by Castro personally. One month later Castro declared his readiness to release most of them—with the exception of the Batista officers and Artime—in exchange for 500 bulldozers or in return for revolutionaries imprisoned in other countries. Nothing came of this proposal because most Americans regarded it as an attempt at blackmail and because there were no private organizations willing or able to buy the machinery.

On April 20, 1961, President Kennedy made a speech to newspapermen in which he repeated that he did not recognize the communist régime in Cuba and threatened military invasion by the United States, should this be necessary in the interest of the national defence of his country.[2]

The prestige of the United States and of the new President fell everywhere in the world, particularly in Latin America, where sympathy for Castro increased. Both the Cuban underground movement and the emigré organizations began to disintegrate; the utterances of the latter revealing their disappointment and anger against the CIA and against Kennedy's indecisiveness. Castro was triumphant and thought the moment had come to proclaim the socialist character of his revolution. This he did on April 16 in a speech at the grave of the victims of the bomb attack, and again at a mass meeting on May 1. For the first time the masses linked the names of Castro and Khrushchev: '*Fidel-Jruschow—estamos con los dos.*' (Fidel-Khrushchev, we are with both of you.) The Cuban revolution had taken the road of 'totalitarian normalization'.

[1] It appears that over 50,000 arrests were made in Havana alone.
[2] *New York Times*, April 21, 1961.

6. Towards 'Normalization' of the Cuban Revolution

(a) *From 'Humanism' to 'Bolshevization'*

'If ever on earth there has been an unpredictable creature it was
Fidel Castro.'   (Herbert L. Matthews)

'Sukarno: Socialism in Indonesia is not ruthlessly thorough.
Its aim is a good life for all—without exploitation.'
'Khrushchev: No, no, socialism must mean that every minute
counts, a life based on calculation.'
(*New York Times*, March 2, 1960)

Socialism is a system—but the Cuban revolution had hitherto been chaotic and unsystematic. 'If we had an organized political system we could not have done the things we have done in such a short time. Any system would lower the velocity of the revolution', said some of its leaders to C. Wright Mills.[1] As a 'socialist' revolution the Cuban revolution had been abnormal: the proclamation of its socialist character began its normalization. For over two years it had been based on the charisma of its leader and the charisma, to use Max Weber's words, had to become routine. There had been no ruling state party, no firmly organized machinery of government; both now had to be created. There had been no clearly formulated ideology: now 'Marxist-Leninism' replaced the revolutionary 'humanism' and 'pragmatism'. Without worrying about costs or priorities the revolutionary government had provided for the masses: now the leaders began to calculate, to plan, to restrict and to think about the future. The process of normalization or 'bolshevization' could not take place overnight. It had to surmount the obstacles created by the peculiarities of the Cuban situation and by the revolutionary leaders. The Cuban revolution and Cuban socialism would always have their own characteristics—just as there are basic differences between Poland and Czechoslovakia, between the Soviet Union and China, which do not however prevent these countries from belonging to the same type. Cuba was going to conform to this type: the proclamation of socialism could have no other meaning.

(b) *The Ideological Change*

On March 13, 1961, the Cuban Ambassador to the Soviet Union, Faure Chomón, the former leader of the *Directorio Revolucionario*, made a speech in Havana in which he said: 'We communists shall continue to advance ... Anybody who studies our development will see with interest how the whole nation became communist, how even

[1] C. Wright Mills, *op. cit.*, p. 121.

children educated in religious schools became communists. Soon we shall see all Latin American nations achieve communism'.

A pro-Castro American who was present observed that 'these surprising statements pleased the masses. The prolonged applause in presence of Fidel, who was sitting on the rostrum, could only mean that this typically Cuban audience ... had been prepared'.[1] The same author wrote that the demands of revolutionary development and the growing contacts with socialist countries 'appear to have produced a "mass conversion" to Marxist-Leninist ideology'.[2]

Here again the new element was not the admission of such views but the open statement that they were Marxist-Leninist. The child was called by its real name for the first time. On July 16, 1961, Castro rightly stressed that the character of the (first) Havana Declaration[3] had been socialist. At the time the term was not used and even now the Leninist definition of socialism is only mentioned in passing. Communism and the party which represented it had not been very popular either in Cuba or in Latin America. On occasions it had adopted a less radical position than *Fidelism*. The sympathies of many foreign intellectuals were in the last resort based partly on the allegedly original, non-communist character of the Cuban revolution; to destroy this illusion was dangerous. In the sphere of foreign politics an open admission of communism would provide new ammunition for the 'imperialists'. No wonder therefore that the true character of the revolution was kept hidden as long as possible. This too was officially admitted, even if not altogether openly.

At the Party Congress of the Cuban communists in August 1960, the Secretary, General Blas Roca, had said:

'Many things which happen in Cuba are given new, unusual names. This has great advantages. If some things here had been given clear and high-sounding (*con palabras detonantes*) names before our forces had been consolidated, while awareness was still lagging behind, nothing could have been achieved. The astuteness of history, of the people and of the revolution lies in the fact that it finds new names, new methods to fulfil the required tasks.'[4]

The Cuban President, Osvaldo Dorticós, expressed himself in a similar, though more cautious, vein in June 1961: 'It was largely for strategical reasons that no integral revolutionary theory was formulated here ... This would have demanded great efforts and

---

[1] J. P. Morray, *Monthly Review*, New York, July–August, 1961, p. 41.
[2] *ibid.*, p. 37.
[3] Cf. the chapter 'Castro's Shadow over America'.
[4] Epilogue, *VIII Asamblea Nacional del Partido Socialista Popular, Ediciones Populares*, Havana, 1960, p. 388. This is not quoted in the English edition of Blas Roca's speech. (*The Cuban Revolution*, New Century Publishers, New York, 1961.)

ideological indoctrination, which it was possible to avoid until the Cuban people had been educated by the facts themselves.'[1]

The 'radicalization' of the Cuban revolution and its movement towards communism were not due to any insistence on the part of the masses. They were the result of the decisions and activities of the leaders. The ideology of the leaders demanded changes in the economy and social life, and these changes in turn led to a clarification of their views and to an indoctrination of the masses who believed in these leaders. At first, as appears from the interview with the correspondent of *L'Unità* quoted earlier, and from a speech on March 25, 1961, Castro admitted that earlier his ideology had been confused. In the late autumn of 1960, Max Frankel of the *New York Times* wrote that the communist leaders had now convinced Castro of the correctness of the Marxist-Leninist position and quoted remarks made to him by Carlos Rafael Rodriguez—which were immediately denied by the latter. In fact the decisive step in Castro's transformation had probably already been made at the end of 1959; in this connection it is important to point out that after assuming power he never tried to make a clear ideological distinction between himself and the communists: this was taboo because of revolutionary unity. Now Lenin began to be worshipped and the masses began to shout 'Fidel, Khrushchev—we are with both of you'. As far as ideology was concerned 'normalization' was easy.

(c) *Development of State and Party*

It was less easy to put Leninist ideology into practice without friction. A totalitarian society needs an administration with clearly defined spheres of authority, staffed by reliable officials working under the direction of experts.

The control and permanent mobilization of the nation demands the destruction of private life and the transformation of the citizen into a member of numerous organizations which cover every aspect of his existence. The civil service, all organizations, and the propaganda apparatus must be controlled by a single ruling party.

The task was not easy. Not only had the Cuban revolution been characterized by individualism and lack of discipline, there had also sprung up a vast number of authorities and organizations which frequently worked at cross-purposes and without co-ordination. So, in early summer 1961, the JUCEI (*Juntas de Coordinación, Ejecución e Información*) were set up in order to centralize and co-ordinate the work of the revolution. Established at Raúl Castro's suggestion, they were meant to be 'state organs, political and administrative instruments of the revolutionary authority which will cover the whole country'.[2] A provincial JUCEI was formed in each province

[1] *Verde Olivo*. Havana, June 21, 1961.
[2] Speech by Raúl Castro, *Hoy*, July 23, 1961.

with subordinate, municipal organs in towns and villages. The provincial councils had to meet in plenary session twice a year and had to be directed by a Plenum meeting every two months. The Plenum itself was headed by a Permanent Committee of thirteen to fifteen members—representatives of the ministries, state institutions, and mass organizations. The secretary of this Permanent Committee had to be a member of the new revolutionary party (in the process of formation). Soon it became clear that almost all the secretaries of the JUCEI were members of the old Communist party.

There was nothing astonishing about this. The new party, which was started in the summer of 1961, was provisionally called ORI (*Organizaciones Revolucionarias Integradas,* integrated revolutionary organizations). Out of ORI the final *Partido Unido de la Revolucion Socialista* was supposed to arise. Officially the ORI consisted of three groups: the '26th July Movement', the 'Directorio Revolucionario' and the PSP (the Communist Party). But the first two groups never had a programme or collective discipline and real organization, whereas the Communist Party had thousands of members and disciplined cadres. No wonder that old communists tended to become the head and the backbone of the revolution.[1]

The formation of a single Leninist Party could certainly not happen without friction—if only because of the character of Castro himself. But at the end of 1961 it seemed well on the way.

(*d*) *The Threat of Economic Catastrophe*

The economic difficulties began at the end of 1960 and reached threatening dimensions in the autumn of 1961. They made themselves felt in increasingly acute shortages of goods. There was a shortage of spare parts for cars and machinery, a shortage of raw materials and transport, too little soap, too few shoes, textiles, razor blades, needles and bottles: more foodstuffs were in short supply and it was increasingly difficult to find accommodation in the towns.[2] Everywhere customers were met by the two short words *no hay* (there isn't any) and long queues outside shops and at bus

[1] 'In the middle of the remarkable anarchy which exists in Cuba, one occasionally meets islands of some orderliness, for example in the political police and also in land reform. Every time one can detect the presence of communist cadres. Another example is the people's militia. The rebel army which fought in the Sierra Maestra has practically disappeared. Its officers have forsaken it or gone into the opposition... Something else had to be found: hence the people's militia. The militia had to be provided with cadres and this is where the communists came in, not for ideological reasons but because they were the ablest people available.' Max Clos, *Figaro,* Paris, June 15, 1961.

[2] At the beginning of July 1961, Castro announced that there were only 5,000 dwellings for over 150,000 applications (*Bohemia,* July 9, 1961) and at the end of August he said that although the Urban Reform Law had been very sympathetically received the way in which the Institute of Urban Reform had carried it out had aroused much hostility. (*Obra Revolucionaria,* No. 30, August 26, 1961, p. 217.)

stops became part of the scene in Havana and other towns. More categories of foodstuffs were rationed and black market sales flourished.

The causes of this crisis were both external and domestic. Trade with the Eastern countries could not compensate for the American embargo and the suspension of Cuban sugar imports.[1] The socialist countries bought sugar at lower prices than Cuba's northern neighbour, and paid only 20 per cent in convertible currencies. They were unable to provide many of the goods Cuba needed most urgently, including spare parts for American machinery. The physical distances made deliveries slow and necessitated the construction of large warehouses.

The domestic reasons for the crisis included not only the inevitable disorganization which was the result of hasty socialization, the flight of many economic experts, and the lack of experienced administrators and technicians, but also the 'humanist' economy policy of the first phase of the revolution.

On television at the end of December 1960, Guevara had been as frank about the economic problems of humanism as about its political motives:

'We purposely slowed down our development in order to set up workers' clubs, crèches and children's homes, so that all could enjoy the things which some nations only acquired after forty years of hard work. We are building thousands of houses although we know that from a purely economic point of view it would be better to build factories. But we want to strengthen in people the feeling that a revolution like this has taken place for the benefit of all—or at least the big majority.'[2]

While the victorious revolution had no proper administration, political reasons seemed to justify such a policy, which was, moreover, economically possible at first. In the first year of the revolution there was an abundance of everything: 'There were ample stocks of cement and we were faced with the question of what to do with all this cement. There were more than enough girders ... There was everything ... On the other hand many people were unemployed and the building trade was paralyzed. Work had to be created for

[1] The revolutionaries spoke about a 'blockade' of Cuba by the US. Although this expression was also used by Khrushchev on July 9, 1960, it is but another example of the clever semantic game of word substitution which served their propaganda so well. Except for a few days during the rocket-crisis at the end of October 1962, there never was anything approaching the meaning given to the word blockade ('shutting up of a place, blocking its harbour, line or coast, frontier, etc., by hostile forces or ships so as to stop ingress or egress'. *The Shorter Oxford English Dictionary*. This is also the meaning given to the term by the Soviet *Yuridicheskii Slovar*, Moscow, 1956).
[2] *Bohemia*, January 15, 1961.

many people ... Our tradition of unproductive work dates from that period.'[1]

It was inevitable that the policy of raising mass consumption and unproductive public works would not only slow down, but directly impede the future development of the country. Nothing was saved, everything was freely distributed, nothing was invested, everything was consumed. The near future was sacrificed to the immediate present. The effects were even more catastrophic because this irrational policy was carried out in a chaotic fashion, without planning or co-ordination or any consideration of the cost. Against the advice of Dutch and Japanese consultants, millions were spent on a utopian scheme of Fidel Castro's to transform a big swampy peninsula into rice plantations. Houses with tiled bathrooms and bidets were built for farm workers: well-equipped bathing establishments, sports grounds and parks were set up. Innumerable delegations were sent abroad and thousands of foreign visitors were invited and entertained at Cuban expense. The smallest local administrator felt himself called upon to build roads and schools on his own initiative, to confiscate estates and to reorganize the life of his district.

In fact the national product fell and working discipline slackened. Many hours were lost in parades, meetings, military exercises and all sorts of campaigns. Many factories were closed for weeks on end by disorganization and shortages, while the workers and employees continued to receive their pay. The purchasing power of the population increased and productivity declined.

Vast sums were spent on military training, equipment and food, for example, in the first weeks of January 1961, when economic life was interrupted by the mobilization of hundreds of thousands of people to repel the expected invasion. Every officer of the army or the militia regarded it as his right to requisition people, cars and equipment. According to Castro's own calculations,[2] the number of cars driven to destruction by the army amounted to thousands. The waste of enormous funds by the armed forces drew bitter complaints from Guevara at the Production Congress.[3] The campaign against illiteracy for which all secondary schools were closed and hundreds of thousands of teachers were trained, fed, and sent to all parts of the country, contributed to the growing pressure on resources. (Among other things the campaign was considered to have aggravated the shortage of footwear.)[4] There was a big exodus from the countryside to Havana, resulting, among other things, in a shortage of farm labour which in turn made necessary the 'voluntary' help of inexperienced

[1] Fidel Castro at the First Production Congress in August 1961. *Obra Revolucionaria*, No. 30, August 26, 1961, p. 215.
[2] *ibid.*, p. 134.
[3] *ibid.*, p. 127.
[4] *ibid.*, p. 157.

urban employees, students and workers in the sugar harvest, as well as ministers, secretaries of state and officials on Sundays.

It is therefore not surprising that (as Guevara admitted at the Production Congress) none of the nationalized industries managed to reach their targets; if anything it is surprising that in many industries there had allegedly been some, often considerable, increases in production compared with past years. But Guevara himself repeatedly stressed that almost no reliable statistics existed; we have seen how matters stood with regard to agricultural statistics.

It was Carlos Rafael Rodriguez who pointed out, at the Production Congress, that hardly any speaker had mentioned the word 'costs', and who stressed the urgent need of putting the problem of rentability into the foreground. Fidel Castro too had been converted to this point of view some time before. At the end of March 1961 he had said, in a spirit which completely contradicted his earlier utterances, that 'for a country at the outset of such a fundamental revolution it is particularly dangerous to become a victim of illusions and to think that the living standards of the people can be immediately and substantially improved'.[1]

At the Production Congress he spoke of the sacrifices which future developments imposed on the present. Meat consumption would have to be reduced in order to develop animal husbandry and the building of houses would also have to be restricted: 'We need cement —and what should the cement be primarily used for? The answer must be clear: in the first place for the building of factories. Factories and centres of production must have absolute priority.'[2]

The threat of economic catastrophe made it essential not only to increase productivity and to abandon 'humanist' welfare policies but also to reconstruct the economic machinery and to take further steps towards complete socialization.

(e) Towards Complete Socialization

'In Cuba the revolution advanced so fast that the machinery of economic control, administration and planning developed only after the changes had already taken place,' said Professor Regino Boti, the chief planner, at the Production Congress.

During the first months of 1960 when the revolutionary Government already controlled economic key positions there had been no mention of a general nationalization of industry, trade and banking. On the contrary, revolutionary quarters sometimes stressed the importance of private initiative, particularly in industry. When in the autumn of 1960 all big concerns were in fact socialized there still remained a private sector of hundreds of thousands of small farmers, industrialists, artisans and businessmen, which though not very

[1] *Obra Revolucionaria*, No. 11, March 26, 1961.
[2] *Obra Revolucionaria*, No. 30, August 26, 1961, p. 216.

important economically was numerically by no means negligible. Complete socialization seemed neither desirable, nor necessary, nor technically possible.

It was undesirable because an attack on the living conditions of the 'economically independent' sections of the population, which included all medium-size and small farmers and the entire urban lower middle class, would have turned many people into enemies of the revolution. It was unnecessary because in fact the state controlled the private sector whose independence had become a mere illusion. It was technically impossible because 'we have to think hard where we can find 500 factory directors and not a day passes on which we don't have to replace one of them for inefficiency. How then can we find managers for 50,000 food shops!'[1]

In the first half of 1961 new economic institutions were created, the socialist character of the revolution was proclaimed and it was for the first time announced that the private sector would not continue to exist for ever.

Four new ministries were set up: the Ministry of the Interior, headed by Guevara, and the Ministries of Foreign Trade, Domestic Trade and Transport. The intention was that this rapidly expanding bureaucracy should run the economy in conjunction with INRA, the National Bank, and the Ministry for Public Works, while the Central Planning Council (JUCEPLAN) would be the supreme planning authority. Industrial enterprises were combined according to the type of work they did and placed under the sub-departments for heavy or light industry of the Ministry of Industry.

In agriculture, people's farms and later the INRA-directed organization of small farmers (ANAP) were set up. The foundation of the latter meant the beginning of the end of private farming. Many small farmers were selected to become members of co-operatives or workers on people's farms—a process which sometimes aroused resentment. Although the official press reported instances of individual smallholders becoming convinced of the superiority of collective methods and wanting to form co-ooeratives, Fidel Castro said in a speech on November 10, 1961: 'The farmer is allergic to the co-operative. He does not want to hear anything about it; the word frightens him.'[2]

In a speech to trade union leaders Blas Roca said: 'The revolution has started to build socialism and is fighting to eliminate the remains of private capitalism and market production in order to achieve a completely socialized economy'.[3]

In a speech on July 26, 1961, Fidel Castro said that although at the moment the revolution would not interfere with small industrialists, artisans, and traders this would not go on for ever:

[1] Guevara, in *Obra Revolucionaria*, No. 2, January 6, 1961.
[2] *Revolución*, November 11, 1961.
[3] *Hoy*, July 20, 1961.

'Does that mean that there will always be private trade? Private enterprises will not exist for ever. They will disappear in the course of the revolution. Those concerned must know this themselves ... But they must not only know that they (as small businessmen) will disappear gradually—not in a few months, but over the years—but they must also realize that they will not be left in the street without income, without work or without means of support.'

While the inner logic of socialism therefore demanded the disappearance of all elements of private enterprise, the process was speeded up by developments in Cuba which began to give the lie to Castro's promises.

While the independence of private firms was destroyed by growing state control many people were brought near to ruin by shortages of goods which inevitably produced speculation, black marketeering and rising prices, which in turn resulted in increased pressure on traders and in persecution and confiscation.

At the beginning of July Castro complained bitterly that the price of pigs had risen enormously because every small producer and middleman was trying to sell them at the highest possible price behind the back of the authorities.[1]

At the Production Congress the Minister of Internal Trade complained that many articles were only available on the black market, and were either being hoarded or had become objects of speculation so that 'working people and housewives now have to pay four or five times as much in order to be able to buy these goods at all.'[2]

The government promised firm measures. New anti-black market regulations were published, severe penalties were promised, and the 'Committees for the Protection of the Revolution' were called upon to show greater vigilance.

In the countryside and the towns the destruction of the private sector appeared imminent, and given increasing difficulties and growing opposition, it was unlikely to happen painlessly. Democracy was dying and totalitarian pressure growing.

(f) *Socialism from Above—Resistance from Below*

It was inevitable that the worsening economic situation would provoke new disaffection and increase the opposition whose dangers the revolutionary leaders recognized and about which they frequently spoke.

The most dangerous opposition was that of the working class.

The former enthusiasm among agricultural workers had apparently disappeared. One of the speakers at the Production Congress in August 1961 complained about the fact that many managers of

[1] *Bohemia*, July 9, 1961.
[2] *Obra Revolucionaria*, No. 30, 1961, p. 160.

co-operatives and people's farms paid too little attention to the wellbeing of the workers, while 'many *cooperativistas* and workers of people's farms work as though they were employed by private individuals, as though they did not realize that they themselves owned the people's farms and co-operatives.'[1]

The fishermen worked badly and many tried to flee the country—in spite of all that the revolution was supposed to have done for them. 'The fishermen cannot work because sometimes things happen ... There have been cases of death ... Fishermen set out, a militiaman tells them to stop, sometimes the fishermen do not hear the order, and then it happens ...' explained one official. Fidel Castro himself referred angrily to this problem 'Sometimes it is reported that somebody wants to steal a boat and then steps are taken to prevent all boats from going out and the whole harbour is put out of action for weeks ... Such action is quite unjustifiable—how can the fishermen understand it?'[2]

The situation was no better among the proletariat. They were required to make more sacrifices while the new trade unions were transformed. Their most important task was, according to Blas Roca, 'to strengthen the political consciousness of the backward sections of the working class, to mobilize the working masses for the increase of production and productivity and to look after the immediate interests of the workers'. Where the immediate demands of the workers clashed with the interests of the revolution they would have to be sacrificed.[3]

A Marxist supporter of Castro wrote, 'The revolution was confronted with a difficult and potentially dangerous problem in the attitude of the urban workers who succeeded only slowly in understanding their own rôle in the revolution. The initiative for transforming the state into a workers' state came from the bourgeois leaders of the revolution and not from the class-conscious workers. The indifference of the workers became a serious problem as enthusiasm about Fidel's victory declined and new difficulties appeared and began to increase.'[4]

The ideal 'workers' state' seemed very different from that which the workers themselves wanted. Castro asked in desperation 'How is it possible that the nation still has not understood what state of exploitation it was living in before?'[5]

But the workers apparently refused to understand. Indeed the sacrifices imposed on them grew: working hours increased, many of the new managers proved to be as bad, if not worse, than the former capitalist employers, strikes were looked upon with disapproval,

[1] *Obra Revolucionaria*, No. 30, 1961, p. 96.
[2] *ibid.*, pp. 88, 132, and 133.
[3] Speech at the Trade Union Plenum, *Hoy*, July 20, 1961.
[4] J. P. Morray, *Monthly Review*, New York, July-August, 1961.
[5] *Verde Olivo*, No. 40, October 8, 1961.

wages remained the same, though all kinds of 'voluntary' contributions had to be paid. Some of these contributions were official—like those imposed to finance the campaign against illiteracy: 'In some cases a day's pay was deducted per month, in others a certain percentage of the wage.'[1] Other contributions were imposed by overzealous, revolutionary militants. Fidel Castro mentioned them when he quoted instances in which badly-paid rural workers were required to make not only the 'normal' contributions but to buy special trade union bonds, to subscribe to newspapers and then make other payments simply 'because this had been suggested at a meeting by an official, while nobody dared to oppose the idea or to utter any protest.'[2]

Productivity declined and absenteeism increased to such an extent that on October 13 a special campaign against absenteeism had to be started—while at the same time the workers lost more and more of the advantages they had enjoyed under capitalism: for example, the right of every worker to nine days annual sick leave. The introduction of piecework and of 'workbooks' was soon to come, while 'socialist emulation' remained one of the most cherished ways of improving productivity.

Rarely has the tragedy of 'socialism from above' been more clearly expressed than in a speech by Guevara in which he explained that the advisory councils set up 'were not set up under pressure from the workers but created bureaucratically from above in order to give the masses a tool which they had not asked for themselves—and this is where the fault of the masses lies.'[3]

(g) Increased Repression

In view of the general situation official terrorism was bound to increase.

Many of those arrested in April were kept for weeks in prison and discovered on being released that their belongings had been confiscated. Many hundreds took asylum in foreign embassies. The number of officially admitted executions remained low, but among the victims were people whose revolutionary sentiments were not in doubt: as, for instance, Sori Marin, the former Sierra Maestra fighter, a major in the Rebel Army, first President of the Revolutionary Tribunal and first revolutionary Minister of Agriculture, or Eugenio Fernandez Ortega, the former head of the Caribbean Legion, a fighting force against dictatorial régimes. In addition, a number of people seem to have been shot without any public announcement.

[1] *Trabajo*, Havana, No. 13, 2nd half of September, 1961.
[2] *Revolución*, November 11, 1961.
[3] *Obra Revolucionaria*, No. 17, May 15, 1961—Guevara spoke of the *pecado* of the masses, which textually translated would be 'sin' and not 'fault'.

TOWARDS 'NORMALIZATION' OF THE REVOLUTION 253

The death penalty was decreed for sabotage and counter-revolutionary activities, and the revolutionary organs and the people were exhorted to increase their revolutionary vigilance, while responsible leaders frequently warned against mildness towards counter-revolutionaries.[1] Unverifiable reports about the use of torture in the prisons of the G.2 became frequent.

In September 1961, after the invasion, the attack against the Church neared its climax. A religious procession which was to take place in Havana was banned, whereupon thousands began to demonstrate against the government and against communism. Militia units were brought to the scene, there were violent clashes and a member of the Catholic Youth Organization was killed. Shortly after the incident, Bishop Boza Masvidal, a Cuban citizen, together with other Cuban priests, was put on board a ship and expelled. The same thing had happened months before to most foreign-born priests and monks. The Cuban Archbishop had already taken asylum in a foreign embassy, and the catholic schools, together with all private teaching establishments, had already been nationalized.

Symptomatic of the new wave of repression was the fate of the small Cuban Trotskyite group which had up to then been relatively unmolested. The Trotskyites had been the strongest supporters of the Cuban revolution and its socialist development. At the beginning of June the political police occupied their office and smashed the matrices of the next issue of their journal as well as those of the reprint of a book by Trotsky. The Latin American Bureau of the Fourth International protested, in vain, to the Cuban government.[2]

Up to 1961 artists had been entirely free and even 'counter-revolutionary' books were freely sold in the shops. Now a change began. Foreign newspapers and periodicals of western origin began to disappear, and counter-revolutionary publications were no longer on show in the shop windows (although they were still obtainable in some places). The pressure for 'socialist realism' increased. 'The intellectuals began to argue with the communists but found that they had no effective arguments. So they gave way to the communists and imposed a censorship on themselves. They lost because they had neither an ideology nor a policy to put against Marxism-Leninism'—these are the words of a young, pro-communist North American intellectual who lived in Havana at this time.[3]

In June 1961 a national congress of writers and artists assembled

[1] In a speech on July 26, 1961, in Santiago de Cuba, Raúl Castro said 'We must never forget the lessons of the Paris Commune, the first attempt by the proletariat to gain power ... The Commune arrested the saboteurs, the German agents, the agents of the bourgeois government of Versailles—and then let them go. This was the Commune's greatest mistake—this leniency towards its enemies. We must never forget this lesson.'
[2] *Voz Proletaria*, Buenos Aires, 2nd half of June, 1961. Vol. XV, No. 235.
[3] Sam Landau, *New Left Review*, London, No. 9, May–June 1961.

under the chairmanship of the communist poet Nicolas Guillén. Its main object could be inferred from the words of another communist poet printed in *Bohemia*: 'In spite of all the progress made intellecuals have not kept up with the revolution. I believe that the intellectuals are far behind the worst of our militia units with regard to efficiency and service to the revolution.'[1] Something had to be done about it ... Fidel Castro spoke. He reiterated that *formal* freedom would be maintained, but as to the content of their works, the writers and artists would have to pay more attention to the needs of the revolution: 'The revolution must behave in such a way that even those artists and intellectuals who are not deeply revolutionary will have an opportunity of working and expressing themselves within the revolution ... This means: everything within the revolution, nothing against the revolution.'[2] In August, a Union of Writers and Artists was formed. Henceforward there would only be organized intellectuals whose duty it was to serve the revolution. In the declaration of principles it is stated: 'We regard it as absolutely essential that all writers and artists, regardless of individual aesthetic differences, should take part in the great work of defending and consolidating the revolution. By using severe self-criticism we shall purge our forms of expression so that they become better adapted to the needs of this struggle.'[3]

The growth of terrorism could be inferred from the speech of Castro of November 10 which is quoted above. Not only were peasants mistreated and afraid of the mere mention of the word co-operative, not only were workers forced to pay all kinds of contributions without daring to protest, but 'the mere mention of the G.2 frightened many people who regarded it unfortunately as a mysterious body from which injustices must be expected'. Castro stated that many citizens 'are or believe themselves to be in danger of unjustified arrest against which they have no legal redress', that all too many people had become the 'innocent victims of thousands of over-zealous individuals', that many were kept for weeks in prison and often found, upon being released, that their property had been taken away. Although the revolutionary government had, months ago, passed a law imposing severe penalties on the unauthorized confiscation of private cars 'this law has so far, unfortunately, not been applied in a single case'. He gave examples of unjustified persecution, including one tragi-comic instance: After Castro had made a speech attacking the *lumpenproletariat*, a high police chief had given the order *Arrest the lumpenproletariat!* As a result many innocent people had been detained including, in one city, 200 homosexuals...[4]

From a speech that Castro delivered in March 1962 it could be seen how little his criticisms of November 1961 had been heeded.

[1] *Bohemia*, Havana, June 18, 1961.
[2] *ibid.*, June 30, 1961.
[3] *Hoy*, August 23, 1961.
[4] *Revolución*, November 11, 1961.

7. The Year 1962: Unplanned Events in the Year of Planning

(a) *Plans and Realities*
The fourth year of the revolution was named the Year of Planning. In this year 'humanist' chaos was to be finally eliminated, things were to be normalized and the main economic difficulties overcome. Dr Boti announced at the Production Congress in August 1961 that in the four years 1962 to 1965 the gross national product of Cuba was to increase by at least 10 per cent per annum though probably by not more than 15½ per cent.[1]

In the political field it was expected that at home a single revolutionary party would be established, that the revolution would spread to other parts of Latin America, and that collaboration with the Soviet Union would become closer.

On the whole, things turned out differently. Instead of economic progress there was economic deterioration, the social consequences of which would have swept away any non-totalitarian government. Popular discontent grew and there was a political conflict between Castro and a number of leading 'old Communists'. The search for scapegoats and new ideological and psychological differences were mixed up with the struggle for power. In the autumn Cuba became the centre of a conflict between the world powers—and a crisis developed in relations between Cuba and the Soviet bloc.

(b) *Near Starvation*
'This is a revolution which must be ashamed of itself because it is forced to ration *malanga*. And the imperialists are saying to the Latin Americans: "There is your socialism: hunger, shortages, rationing..."'[2]

The failure of agrarian reform could no longer be concealed. The figures triumphantly presented to the public had often represented hopes rather than reality, and statements had been made which owed more to enthusiasm than to measurement. There was not only a shortage of *malanga*, there were no beans or potatoes, and not enough meat, chickens, fish, eggs or milk. It was now also admitted that rice production had fallen. Imports seemed inadequate and transport problems became painfully noticeable.

Three excuses were found: the drought, the *'yanqui'* blockade,

---
[1] *Obra Revolucionaria*, No. 30, 1961, p. 17.
[2] Speech by Fidel Castro on April 10, 1962, in Matanzas (*El Mundo*, May 10, 1962).

and the growth in the purchasing power of the Cuban population.

With respect to the drought Castro himself declared that: 'We should not put all the blame on the drought. We have committed mistakes ... Wrong calculations have been made, numbers have been published on the basis of which we made promises which we could not fulfil. It hurts to be obliged to admit it.'[1]

As for the imperialist 'blockade'—it did not exist. Cuba could import goods from anywhere. She could even buy food (and medicines) from the USA, provided she could pay. True, there were hardly any dollars left. But imports from the USA had already been sharply cut in 1960 at a time when the balance of payments with the USA was favourable.[2]

The argument about growing purchasing power can hardly be taken as valid. There was a reduction of visible unemployment but since 1960 wages had been frozen and 'contributions' of all kinds increased.

Many goods had already been rationed officially, or in fact before general rationing was openly introduced on March 19, 1962; the rations were lower than *per capita* consumption before the revolution.[3]

Citizens were entitled to two pounds of fat, six pounds of rice and one-and-a-half pounds of beans a month. Soap, toothpaste and washing powders were rationed in big towns. In Greater Havana, and apparently also in other towns, meat, fish, eggs and milk were rationed. The monthly ration included three pounds of beef, one pound of fish, a quarter of a pound of butter, one pound of chicken meat, and five eggs. Children under seven years were entitled to one litre of milk a day and five adults had to share one litre or five tins of condensed milk a month. *Malanga*, potatoes, *boniato* and other vegetables were also rationed. Rationing cards were only issued if applicants could provide evidence that they had paid their rent, this had become necessary because many of the tenants whom the

---

[1] *Revolución*, March 13, 1962.

[2] In the first half of 1960 the United States still imported Cuban goods to the value of $274 million whereas Cuba imported only $140 million worth from the United States. (US Department of Agriculture, Economic Research Division, *Agriculture and Food Situation in Cuba*, May 1962.)

[3] The following comparison is based on *per capita* consumption figures for 1958/59 given by the revolutionary authorities. In some cases these figures are much lower than those provided by 'counter-revolutionary' sources:

	1958/59 lb. per annum	after March 1962 lb. per annum
Fats	38	24
Rice	106	72
Beans	25·4	18
Beef	66·8	36

(Chonchol Peyrellade & Chao, *Proyecto de Plan Quinquenal para el Desarrollo de la Agricultura Cubana*, March 1961, Annex VIII.)

urban reform had transformed into 'owners' had not paid rent for two years or more.[1]

'The achievements of the revolution . . . are confined to the establishment of a few small consumer-goods factories and the completion of factories started under the dictatorship'[2] said the Minister of Industry, Guevara, in his speech of March 16, 1962, to trade union officials. He complained about low productivity, opposition from the workers, incompetence on the part of technicians and managers, wholesale absenteeism, and the bureaucratic habits which had replaced the dynamism of the early days and the general decline in revolutionary spirit. Socialist competitions, he said, were going less well than the year before. How could one explain the decline in the quality of goods? Why was it that men's shoes, for example, which were made with the same materials and by the same methods as before, soon lost their heels and that women's shoes often became unusable after being worn for one day, or that Coca-cola now tasted unpleasant and contained all sorts of impurities: 'Does that sort of thing happen under capitalism? No. Why should it happen under socialism? Because it is in the nature of socialism? No, that is a lie! One can say anything but not that! It all happens because of our shortcomings, our lack of revolutionary awareness, the inadequacy of our work, insufficient control, and our lack of revolutionary vigilance.'[3]

The transport situation was even worse. There were no spare parts for American vehicles, the buses imported from the Eastern countries often proved unsuitable for Cuban conditions, tractors wore out quickly, the number of private cars had declined and the railways were badly run.

The housing shortage grew. Many houses were in a state of dilapidation, not enough new houses were built and materials, for example, bathroom fittings, were lacking to complete them. At the end of May Castro said that there were only 5,000 dwellings for 150,000 applicants. Henceforth less elegant and less comfortable houses would have to be built.[4]

(c) Bitter Sugar

The growing worries were increased by anxiety about the sugar which will continue for many years to play a central rôle in the life of the country. Increased imports to overcome the food shortage and future industrialization must be paid for primarily by exporting sugar.

[1] This non-payment of rents partly explains why the purchasing power of the population had increased. On May 31, 1962, Castro complained on television that one-third of all Cubans did not pay their rents to the state. (*Le Monde*, Paris, June 2, 1962.)
[2] *Bohemia*, March 9, 1962.
[3] *Trabajo*, 2nd fortnight of March, 1962.
[4] *Le Monde*, Paris, June 2, 1962.

The value of the sugar crop depends on three factors: the amount sold, the price obtained, and the cost of production.

In 1961 it was decided to cut and refine all the sugar cane. This plan was not carried out, but Cuba had the second largest sugar harvest in its history (6·7 million metric tons). Because of the labour shortage hundreds of thousands of urban 'volunteers', men and women, were mobilized. They were wasteful harvesters, and careless planters. Moreover, the sugar factories were under inexperienced management, and their machinery was wearing out.

Chonchol's Five Year Plan envisaged an annual production of 6 million metric tons and an annual export of 5·5 million, at an unspecified price.[1] Because it was thought that there would be another labour shortage and because at the end of 1961 there was a reserve of over one million tons of sugar the target for 1962 was fixed at 5·4 million. But it soon became clear that the target would not be reached. New volunteers were needed and at a date when the harvest is normally over it was officially announced that only 68·8 per cent of the sugar cane which should have been cut was actually harvested.[2] It was decided to continue cutting during the rainy season, in spite of rising costs and the falling sugar content of the cane. At the end of the *zafra* which went on until the middle of June it was announced that regardless of difficulties and high costs 4·8 million tons had been produced.

This time, by drawing on reserves, it still seemed to be possible to export enough. But the outlook for the future was not bright. In 1960 and 1961 not enough cane had been planted, and in 1962 the situation was even worse;[3] less than two-thirds, perhaps only half the quantity planned was planted. (As we shall mention later on, the quantity of sugar harvested in 1963 fell by another million tons, to 3·8 millions.)

In the three years before the revolution the United States bought over half of Cuba's sugar. On average it paid 5·26 cents a pound, as compared with the world market price of 3·93 cents. In 1957, sugar sales earned Cuba $671 million and in 1958, $613 in convertible currency.[4] In 1959 the world market price of sugar began to fall and at the beginning of 1960 it was only just over 3 cents a pound. The Eastern countries promised to buy 4 million tons at 4 cents a pound and a further 800,000 tons at the world market price. But they paid, at most, only 20 per cent in cash and the rest in goods, technical aid and so on. The Eastern bloc itself decided what the value of this aid should be. On the other hand, in 1962 the world market price of sugar was only about 2·70 cents a pound. In 1963, sugar rose to over

[1] Chonchol Peyrellade & Chao, *op. cit.*
[2] *Hoy*, May 9, 1962.
[3] *ibid.*, April 26, 1962.
[4] *Revista del Banco Nacional*, No. 2, 1959.

10 cents a pound, one of the reasons being the failure of the Cuban sugar harvest. This failure meant that Cuba was hardly able to benefit from the price rise.

Just before the revolution the cost price of Cuban sugar was estimated at about 3·8 to 4 cents a pound. Therefore Cuba could only make a profit because of the higher American price. Lately costs seemed to have risen, not least because of the less efficient agricultural methods of the revolutionaries. They were becoming aware of this. On April 13, 1962, Guevara said to sugar workers: 'This harvest is bad. We are working very inefficiently (*con una enorme ineficiencia*) and if our costs of production are higher than the price at which we can sell, we "decapitalize" ourselves'.[1]

The magnitude of Cuba's sugar problems could hardly be overestimated. It was not just a question of the immediate present. In view of the position in the first half of the 'Year of Planning', there could be no thought of large exports in 1963, which meant the economic situation would not improve in 1963 unless the Eastern bloc provided further considerable credits.

(d) The Paradoxical Labour Shortage

The bad sugar harvest has been blamed on the shortage of labour in the countryside, which in turn was explained by a fall in unemployment figures. But the labour shortage also affected the harvests of coffee, tomatoes, beans, potatoes and so on.[2] For the onion harvest, too, 'volunteers' from Havana factories were mobilized.[3] The labour shortage appeared as early as 1961 when nobody could seriously suggest that unemployment had been abolished; nor could this, of course, be said in 1962. Chonchol, in his plan completed in March 1961, said that after four years of industrialization there would still be some unemployment: 'In 1965 the number of agricultural workers will reach about 960,000. This is a *little* more than will be needed during the main season. At other times of the year, however, there will continue to be considerable underemployment ... But even so the level of employment of the rural population of Cuba will be considerably higher than it is at present.'[4]

The level of employment of which Chonchol and his co-authors speak refers to the year 1961, a period when there was allegedly already a labour shortage.

The report also says that even if industrialization proceeds at a fast rate, there would still, in 1965, be considerable underemployment which would have to be absorbed by the expansion of agriculture.[5] But so far as we have seen, there had been no industrialization, and,

[1] *El Mundo*, April 14, 1962.
[2] *Bohemia*, March 2, 1962.
[3] *Hoy*, May 12, 1962.
[4] Chonchol Peyrellade & Chao, *op. cit.*, p. 140.
[5] *ibid.*, p. 11.

as we pointed out in the chapter on the agrarian revolution, only a few former farm labourers had been absorbed by the co-operatives and state farms. This could hardly have changed during 1961–62 because, according to official figures, the number of workers on state farms had only risen from 96,000 to about 120,000.[1]

The true explanation of the labour shortage lies in the facts that the workers were exasperated, and that many former sugar-cane cutters were 'hiding' inside the people's farms which are much too big to control their workers efficiently, that the whole economy was disorganized and that the rural population was drifting into the towns. The workers were dissatisfied with low wages and with the fact that there was little they could buy with their money. Cuban press comments clearly demonstrated that the will to work was lacking. An article in *El Mundo* of March 28, 1962, for example, complained that there was a general tendency among workers to take days off, and that many sugar workers believed that 'Sunday begins on Friday'.

It was difficult, however, to discover what the rural population now did in the towns. Many factories employed more workers than they really needed; the civil service was greatly inflated; there were many ways of getting a state scholarship to some school or other; although militia service was officially unpaid it was sometimes possible to live on it; finally, it should be pointed out that the system of *botellas*, government sinecures, had reappeared, even if under a different name, as could be seen from the following paragraph from *Bohemia*:

'For the sugar, tomato and coffee harvests and other work there is an acute labour shortage. But for the past two years Cuba has had a sector called *plantilla supplementaria* (approximately 'reserve staff'). Here we have thousands of men and women who do nothing except receive a salary from the state . . . They sit at home and wait until they can collect their cheque at the end of the month. Many of them would like to do something to occupy their time, but others fill their heads with bad ideas.'[2]

(e) Discontent and Terror

In a speech on December 1, 1961, Castro said: 'We lack many material things. But there is something which exists in abundance: a whole revolutionary, scientific doctrine, a profound, deeply interesting theory which we can give to the masses.' Not all Cubans received this somewhat surprising offer of 'ideas instead of butter' with enthusiasm. Hence the growing discontent which was, however, expressed in passive rather than in active resistance. There were many acts of sabotage, which hampered the sugar harvest. There was some guerilla activity, but on a very small scale. There were occa-

[1] *Trabajo*, 2nd fortnight of March, 1962.
[2] Mario Kuchilan, *Bohemia*, March 2, 1962.

sional public demonstrations such as the one in Cárdenas at the beginning of June, and in some other places where people protested against the food shortage.

In November 1961 Castro had complained about the excesses of terrorism. By the spring of 1962 there had been hardly any change. The terror in Cuba was certainly less violent than the emigrés claimed, and less than that which had followed other great revolutions. The real number of executions was probably in excess of the official figures, the prisons were over-crowded and prisoners were often very badly treated, but there was nothing comparable to the 'September Massacres', to the Robespierrian phase of the French Revolution or to the terror in Stalinist Russia. There were no mass-killings and few authenticated cases of systematic torture. Emigration although difficult and unpleasant remained legal, and continued up to October 1962 at the rate of about 2,000 a week. (It also helped to fill the coffers of the revolution, as the property of emigrants was confiscated and they had to pay their fares in US dollars.) There was no systematic censorship of letters. Most foreign correspondents could move unhampered through the country. Official interference with intellectual life was haphazard: the supplement to *Revolución*, *Lunes de Revolución*, which deviated from the official line was stopped on an obvious pretext, but *Bohemia* of March 11, 1962, contained a photograph of Trotsky's widow on her deathbed with a laudatory caption.

The excesses were blamed on the lower cadres but, according to Castro himself, the terror was bad enough. He told how working-class girls had complained to him about all sorts of violent and arbitrary acts.[1] Later he mentioned cases in which peasants who owned small and medium farms were illegally deprived of their farms or arrested and thrown into prison because they had killed a pig.[2] In one case, a revolutionary official had come to a village, declared that everybody there was a counter-revolutionary, and threatened to hang the whole lot.

'Our own mistakes, bad treatment from us, our insolence towards the people—those are the causes of discontent! ... The culminating point is reached if one regards the masses as counter-revolutionary. If the masses are counter-revolutionary we are complete idiots because we made a revolution where no revolution was necessary. But this is untrue: in no other contemporary revolution did the masses give so many proofs of their enthusiasm for the revolution.'[3]

(*f*) *The Political Crisis: Castro and the Old Communists*

The economic difficulties, the terror and the growing discontent were bound to find an echo in the political sphere. The search for

[1] *Bohemia*, March 23, 1962.
[2] *El Mundo*, May 10, 1962.
[3] *ibid.*

scapegoats was bound up with the struggle for power between two factions: the 'old communists' on the one side and Castro and his closer associates on the other. The former had an organization but Castro had his charisma. Without the organization the charisma could not make the revolution work; without the charisma the organization could not preserve the revolution. The old communists could accuse Castro and his friends of subjectivism and ultra-left-wing voluntarism and blame him for the chaos of 'humanist' inexperience. The 'young communists' could accuse the 'old guard' of opportunism, cynicism, and *Batistiano* traditions and could rely on the wide-spread anti-communism which still existed among the people.

Among the 'old guard' there seems to have been some disagreement about the attitude towards the 'leader'—although very little of this ever reached the public. There were probably some who wanted to deprive Castro of real power but retain him as the figurehead of a revolution whose future course they themselves would control. After all, given his past and his personal character, was not Castro a most unreliable fellow, in spite of his conversion to Marxism-Leninism? Where had his irrationality, his ultra-left-wing impatience, his vanity, and the organizational ineptitude of his friends led the revolution? Some members of the old guard were probably more sympathetic to Castro and less dogmatic about the course of the revolution. After all, Castro's belief in Marxism-Leninism was sincere, he himself had recognized the mistakes which had been made under his leadership; to deprive him of real all power would be impossible.

Meanwhile the Communist apparatus went to work: by the end of 1961 it controlled all positions of power. It was directed by Aníbal Escalante, who, with Blas Roca and Carlos Rafael Rodríguez, was one of the three most important Communists. They seemed to be very sure of themselves. After all, in Russia, Stalin's apparatus had been victorious over Trotsky's charisma.

The general deterioration of the situation led to a heightening of all contrasts. The *apparatchiks* not only increased the terror, many of them began to criticize Castro more or less openly, to attack the cult of personality and to bring up the old mistakes of the 26th July Movement.

Castro was undoubtedly aware of what was going on and had probably seen it coming. His open avowal of Marxist-Leninism had legitimized him in the eyes of world Communism and given him the necessary authority to proceed in an emergency against members of the old guard in the name of Marxist-Leninism.[1] In addition the

[1] Draper rightly said about the famous December speech: 'Castro was torn in this speech between the desire to repudiate his past in order to get closer to the Communists, and the desire to salvage his past in order to preserve his revolutionary leadership. His speech was a balancing act, leaning sometimes to one side, sometimes to the other.' (*Castro's Revolution, op. cit.*, London and New York, 1962, p. 146.)

masses were becoming increasingly restive. 'The masses saw all these problems: the transgressions of power, the wilfulness, the excesses, the arbitrary arrests, the whole policy of contempt towards the people ...'[1]

Similar allegations occurred in almost all his speeches against Escalante and the *apparatchiks*. 'How blind we were to see nothing and to suspect nothing,'[2] he said of himself and the other leaders, but the masses had a better feeling for the danger. Castro needed a scapegoat for all the mistakes and for the terror, and he selected Escalante for the part.

On March 9, 1962, the list of the twenty-five leaders of ORI, the preparatory body of the single party of the future, was published for the first time. The members of the old guard included Roca, Rodríguez (who had been appointed Chairman of INRA on February 13) Aníbal Escalante and his brother Cesar, Severo Aguirre, Flavio Bravo, Joaquin Ordoquí, Lazaro Peña, and Manuel Luzardo, who shortly afterwards became Minister of Domestic Trade. Among the old 'Fidelistas' were Fidel and Raúl Castro, Ramiro Valdés (the head of G.2, the secret police), the Minister of Education, Armando Hart, and his wife Haydee Santamaría, Major Dr Sergio de Valle, Major Almeida (formerly chief of the army and then chief of a sector of the army) and Guillermo García, one of the first peasants to join Castro's guerilla force. The Fidelistas also included Major Aragonés and Martinez Sanchez, the Minister of Labour, although these two had been very close to the Communists. In addition there were Dorticós, President of the Republic, Faure Chomón, former leader of the *Directorio* and until then ambassador to Moscow, Osmani Cienfuegos, Minister of Public Works, who as far as is known was a member of the Communist Party (PSP) but could not be counted among the old guard, and Raúl Curbelo reputed to have been a Communist.

On March 12 Castro was asked on television to comment on the composition of the ORI leadership. He said:

'All right. Let me say first of all that the official integration of the national leadership of ORI, the announcement of its composition, forms the epilogue to the whole process of integration of the revolutionary organizations. The list of the comrades who form the national leadership shows that this leadership is really representative of all the forces and factors that participated in the revolutionary process ... It may be—naturally, there are many comrades who have done a great deal—that not everybody has been included, but there really are only few gaps ...'[3]

[1] Speech of April 10 in Matanzas, *El Mundo*, May 10, 1962.
[2] Speech of March 26, *El Mundo*, March 27, 1962.
[3] *Bohemia*, March 16, 1962.

When the issue of *Bohemia* of March 16, 1962, which contained photographs of all the members of the ORI leadership together with extracts from Fidel's television interview, appeared in the streets, the new conflict had already begun. It is interesting to note that the same *Bohemia* contained a speech which Aníbal Escalante had made shortly before to 'revolutionary cells'. He attacked sectarianism and said that it was dangerous to move away from the masses and forget the national heroes of the past, to speak only of Communist heroes and sing only the *Internationale* and not the Cuban national anthem as well. Real revolutionaries should never look down on the masses or think themselves better than others. The revolutionary cells should never interfere in the administrative affairs of the nationalized enterprises and never force their will on the masses.

The conflict broke out and was revealed in four speeches by Castro: the first at Havana University on March 13 on the occasion of a remembrance meeting for those who had fallen during the attack on Batista's presidential palace; the second on March 17 to 'revolutionary instructresses' of the *Conrado Benitez* school; the others on March 26 on television, and on April 10 in the Province of Matanzas.

On March 13, Castro objected to the extreme sectarianism which had manifested itself during the reading of the testament of the student leader, Echavarría, at which paragraphs in which he appealed to God had been omitted. This, said Castro, was a narrow-mindedness which had nothing to do with Marxism and which would mean that all the historic heroes of the Cuban people would be excluded from the revolutionary tradition. He also expressed anxiety about the emergence of a new privileged class, caused by the fact that many young people nowadays quickly obtained leading economic positions in which they earned 500 or 800 pesos a month.

On March 17 he complained that ORI secretaries, revolutionary cells and committees for the protection of the revolution had established a wilful dictatorship in the whole country. Despotic incidents and individual acts of violence had occurred everywhere and honest revolutionaries had been terrorized. 'Those gentlemen who want to force their ideas on others are almost indistinguishable from Batista and his henchmen . . . this is happening at all levels of social life and in all parts of the country. It is happening in cooperatives, state farms and factories.'[1]

He said that many people thought that to belong to the ORI cadres conferred the right to order others about, to interfere in the administration of enterprises and to indulge in favouritism. A complete purge of the apparatus and a change of methods were urgently needed.

On March 26 he was even more outspoken: Aníbal Escalante was

[1] *Bohemia*, March 23, 1962.

responsible for the fact that there had been dangerous deviations from Marxist-Leninism. Escalante's basic mistake was a sectarianism which had expressed itself in suspicion of the masses and of everybody who did not belong to the cadres of the old Communist party. In the early stages of the revolution suspicion had been justified. But now, after the masses had become Marxist-Leninist, and had given proof of their Marxism-Leninism by repelling the invasion of April 1961 and by their enthusiastic approval of the Second Declaration of Havana,[1] such a suspicion was counter-revolutionary, as were all distinctions between 'old' and 'new' Communists. In place of a true *avant garde* party of the masses, Escalante had created a sect of privileged individuals whose provincial secretaries acted like Nazi gauleiters and who indulged in nepotism and terrorism: 'We set up ORI but we excluded the revolutionary masses! What we have created is not a revolutionary party but a yoke, a straitjacket ... When we looked at the result we saw that it was, if you'll excuse the phrase, a dungheap ... How blind we were to the real dangers ...'[2]

He said the much discussed 'cult of personality' was a Russian problem which had never existed in Cuba where none of the revolutionary leaders had become a general, where nobody had given himself or others any decorations, where no towns or streets were named after anybody and where no momuments had been erected to anybody. If there was anything which resembled the cult of the personality it was the cult of Escalante who filled ORI with his supporters. The ORI secretariat had become a second government; there was no factory, no government office, no ministry, where action was taken without first asking for, and obtaining the consent of, the revolutionary cells of the ORI secretariat. The whole life of the economy and administration had been interrupted and chaos had been created everywhere.

An ORI secretary in Oriente Province had said that he did not know people like Hart, García, Aragonés, Haydee Santamaría and so on, that they had no place in the ORI leadership and would soon be thrown out. This gentleman did not know these revolutionaries because he had not taken part in the struggle against Batista, but while others had fought he had hidden under his bed. Others had said that 'Moncada' was a *putsch,* the guerilla fight an adventure,[3]

---
[1] There are remarks by Castro which sound different: 'The most difficult problem of the revolution lies in the fact that to begin with one must understand it ... and comprehend its meaning. At the beginning there were only few who understood the character of the revolution and even today there are many who misunderstand it. That is the struggle—to get an increasing number of people to understand the revolution.' (Speech of March 17, 1962).
[2] Quoted in *El Mundo,* March 27, 1962.
[3] 'How can one be so deaf, so blind, so short-sighted and so idiotic as not to understand the lessons of history?'

and 'History will absolve me' a reactionary document.[1] Many deserving guerilla fighters had been removed from the officers' corps because of their 'low political level' and had been replaced by school leavers who knew the Marxist catechism inside out. The best workers and employees were not admitted to revolutionary factory cells but there were people in them—Castro mentioned one by name—who in 1954 had still belonged to the Batista party, who had been elected town councillors, and who had continued to hold office until December 31, 1958. All this had helped to make Communism more unpopular, the ORI leadership had therefore unanimously decided to expel Escalante from its midst.[2]

In Matanzas on April 10, Castro used even stronger words. The situation was still worse than he had thought at the end of April. Perhaps Escalante should not only have been expelled from the ORI leadership but from ORI itself. Bad things were now being discovered everywhere: disorder, terrorism, illegal arrests, the unjustified confiscation of small farms.[3] Quite out of keeping with the spirit of Marxism,[4] people had been treated with contempt. 'Criticism has become much more necessary still. The people have begun to lose faith in the revolutionary leadership . . . Escalante is not the only one who is responsible for this: there are 500 other Escalantes here . . . The methods which were used have done immense harm to the revolution and have also affected production . . . It is not a question of sectarianism—but of privileges, caste spirit, nepotism and even incipient corruption . . .'[5]

The conflict with the old guard not only brought about a purge of ORI but also led to the postponement of the formation of a final, single party. Castro's idea was to form a new kind of *avant garde* party, which was described in the June issue of *Cuba Socialista* and in a speech by President Dorticós on July 6, 1962. The lower cadres would be elected directly by the workers, who would choose those who worked particularly well and also fulfilled all their revolutionary duties.[6]

[1] 'In all modesty let it be said: "History will absolve me" is the expression of a developing mind, a mind which is not yet Marxist, but which is moving towards Marxism and beginning to be Marxist.'
[2] Escalante was given no more opportunity to defend himself than Urrutia in July 1959. He boarded an aircraft and reappeared some days later in Prague.
[3] 'If the return of illegally confiscated farms is going to give back peace and quiet to thousands of people who must go along with the revolution, then they will have to be given back.'
[4] 'People who say that Marxists have no soul are only repeating what the imperialist, the slanderer, is saying. A Marxist must first of all be a humane being, who values other people, their dignity and their feelings . . . It was his very love of humanity, his desire to fight against the misery of the proletariat, against injustice, against the exploitation of the proletarian that led Marx to Marxism.'
[5] All quotations from the Matanzas speech are taken from *El Mundo*, May 10, 1962.
[6] *Hoy*, July 7, 1962.

It seems most improbable that only a small minority of his close party friends supported Escalante, but at any rate Castro's attack forced the old Communists to retreat. Even those who stood behind Escalante—and it is very difficult to know whether, and to what extent, there were differences within the Party—realized they had gone too far.

After Castro's speech of March 13, *Hoy* (of March 14) published a signed article by Blas Roca in which he expressed himself in complete agreement with Castro and asked everybody to give careful attention to his speech. On March 23 the membership of the new ORI Secretariat was announced in which Blas Roca appeared as the only member of the old guard by the side of the Castro brothers, Guevara and Dorticós. On March 24, *Hoy* welcomed the secretariat: 'Today Fidel is the most responsible Marxist-Leninist in Cuba, the leading representative of the working class and the most reliable of all Communists.'

On the same evening Carlos Rafael Rodríguez spoke on television and announced that on March 26 Fidel would speak on the danger of sectarianism. On March 28 *Hoy* welcomed Fidel's speech and, in a long article criticizing Escalante's whole past, said that he had always been inclined to despise other people and to practise dictatorial and sectarian methods.

On April 11 the Russian Party spoke: in a long unsigned article *Pravda* sided with Castro. For the first time he was referred to as 'Comrade' (while this title was missing from Escalante's name). Castro had been right to criticize Escalante's 'sectarian and dogmatic' practices, and the latter had rightly been excluded from the ORI leadership on the basis of a unanimous decision. It was said once again that the Soviet Union was firmly behind Cuba. The following passages are of special interest: 'The formation of a single Marxist-Leninist Party in a country where the revolution was victorious only three years ago is no easy matter. The Cuban revolutionaries do not regard their task as the mechanical unification of three forces [the PSP, the '26th July' Movement, and the Directorio] but as the creation of a monolithic Marxist-Leninist Party, with one theory and one organization. The foundation of ORI is an important step in that direction.'[1]

The emphasis on the difficulty of establishing a Communist party three years *after* the revolution seems somewhat odd coming from *Pravda*, and can only be understood as a hint in favour of slower progress. The same view appeared in an italicized paragraph which said that the unity of the revolutionary forces had become stronger '... in the course of carrying out the land reform, the nationalization of *imperialist* property, the cultural revolution and other measures which *prepared* the conditions for Cuba's *gradual* transition to the

[1] *Pravda*, Moscow, April 11, 1962.

phase of socialist transformation in town and country.' The article speaks only of the confiscation of *imperialist* property and not of the confiscation of *Cuban bourgeois* property which had in fact taken place soon after the revolution, contrary to the plans and ideas of the Cuban Communists. Nor does the article welcome the socialization which had already taken place; it speaks of preparing the conditions for such changes and says that such preparations should be made *gradually*.

(g) *No Cuban NEP—Liquidation of the Co-operatives and of Small Private Businesses*

In 1920 when the Russian revolution tried to find a way out of the the blind alley of 'War Communism', there was a retreat in the direction of capitalism known as the New Economic Policy (NEP). It may have been no accident that while *Pravda* underlined the necessity of cautious procedures in Cuba, *Cuba Socialista* contained, in its May issue, quotations from articles by Lenin written at the beginning of the NEP period; nor did it seem to be an accident that in his speech against 'Ultra-radicalism' of March 10, Castro mentioned—apparently for the first time—Lenin's *left wing Communism*.

On June 4, 1962, *Revolución* published a speech by Khrushchev given at a farewell meeting for Cubans who had finished a year's training in Russia. He compared the critical state of Cuba's economy with the one Russia had had to face after the civil war. 'There are some who begin to say: "What is this? Fidel Castro calls on us to make a revolution. We follow him, we defeat Batista and now meat is lacking, rice is lacking, milk is lacking. What kind of revolution is this?" The road of socialist construction would be long and difficult. Khrushchev mentioned the NEP and recommended the Cubans to go slow. But there was to be no Cuban NEP, if only because a retreat would have been particularly dangerous while no monopoly party as yet existed. Instead the course was set towards fuller 'socialism'.

In the summer of 1962 the co-operatives, one of the Cuban institutions which appealed most strongly to left-wingers all over the world, disappeared. They were transformed into 'People's farms', the *cooperativistas*, even officially, becoming state workers. Although, as was explained above, they never had been true co-operatives, there had been differences between them and the people's farms. But it was precisely these differences that made them increasingly un-unpopular with both the government and the *cooperativistas*. The latter worked badly and, as control over them was lax, much of their produce found its way on to the black market. The *cooperativistas* did not get the profits they expected, while workers on the people's farms were not even required to pay for the houses and schools the government built or promised. Shortly after becoming head of INRA,

Carlos Rafael Rodríguez declared: 'The co-operatives are dead organisms with hundreds and hundreds of members who want to have nothing to do with them, who have lost their faith in them.'[1] Once the decision to dissolve them had been taken, theoretical arguments were found to support it. These were given by Fidel Castro in an article in *Cuba Socialista*.[2] One of the main progressive peculiarities of the Cuban agrarian revolution, it was explained, was that it did not break up the *latifundia*, but collectivized them. This was good. But the idea of setting up so-called co-operatives was bad, for the small, formerly independent peasant the co-operative is a step towards socialism. But those who worked on the sugar estates were workers, proletarians. To transform them into *cooperativistas* was both unreasonable and reactionary. Castro said this in a speech to the last Congress of the Sugar Co-operatives in August. Carlos Rafael Rodríguez had spoken before and complained about the inefficiency of agriculture in general and of the co-operatives in particular. It was, according to him, scandalous that agriculture was not only unable to feed the towns but did not even produce enough to feed the agricultural population. Irrationality, inadequate methods, lack of controls, and laziness had to stop. The decision to transform the former co-operatives into People's Farms was taken by the delegates with 1,381 votes to 3.

Agricultural workers would no longer be paid by the day, and their incomes would no longer be linked to sugar prices. Norms and piece work would be established. These changes astonished many people. Carlos Rafael Rodríguez answered them: 'A young revolutionary wrote to me recently to say that he was horrified that we are introducing piece rates. But the revolution cannot pay time rates because this encourages slowness and laziness which are infectious ... We shall establish norms and those who work badly will earn less.'[3]

The introduction of piece rates and higher norms were not the only methods used to increase productivity. 'Socialist emulation' was another. Further innovations consisted of the introduction in August 1962, of a 'workers passport' without which nobody could get work and of a decree which abolished the right of every worker to thirty days paid vacation a year. According to the needs of production this time must be reduced to twenty or even ten days.

Successive steps were taken to liquidate the private sector of the economy. This became necessary partly in order to eliminate black marketeering. On March 29, 212 small enterprises (factories producing clothing, shoes, quilts and blankets, bakeries, etc.) were socialized; four days later the same fate befell seven warehouse companies; on

[1] *Revolución*, June 19, 1962.
[2] Alfredo Menendez Cruz, 'La transformacion de las Cooperativas caneras en Granjas caneras', *Cuba Socialista*, October 1962.
[3] *Revolución*, June 19, 1962.

April 7, 107 other enterprises (chemical laboratories, distilleries, hat factories etc.) were taken over by the state. In July, hawking was prohibited and all the small street vendors were promised financial help by the Minister of Internal Commerce until they could be absorbed into the economy. At the beginning of December *Le Monde*[1] reported that many shops, restaurants, grocers, and small perfumeries had been taken over during the autumn without special enactments. Subsequently, the instruments and materials of radio repair shops were confiscated, and at the beginning of December, there were no longer any private shoe-makers. Finally, in December, a new decree socialized all enterprises using hired labour, promising compensation to their former owners.

(h) New Political Institutions

The struggle against the communist old guard, the excesses of terrorism, and growing bureaucratization increased the jacobin tendencies towards totalitarian democracy. Yet many of the excesses of terrorism seem to have been stopped;[2] while 'brainwashing', propaganda, and self-criticism became more important. The political police and the JUCEI apparently became less, and the organs of the Committees for the Defence of the Revolution became more active. At the same time the new party was being created.

(1) The Committees for the Defence of the Revolution.[3] The CDR had been created, in the autumn of 1960, essentially as an auxiliary organ of the G.2 police to ferret out counter-revolutionaries. There were then 7,000 such committees and their number and activity grew: it was the CDR who were mainly responsible for the mass arrests during the attempted invasion in April, 1961.

Two years after their foundation there were about 100,000 such committees—in every streetblock of the big cities, in every town and even village and every people's farm. Some one-and-a-half million Cubans actively participate in their work, and 900,000 of their members were women. They were grouped in thirty-three regions and there was a central leadership at the top. As they were organized territorially many who were not employed in any factory or office found in them their main revolutionary activity—hence the vast number of women, many of whom were housewives. They had become the centres of all revolutionary activity and fulfil some of the functions

---

[1] *Le Monde*, Paris, December 5, 1962.
[2] Counter-revolutionary sources would deny this. However, I think not too much credence should be given to notices appearing in the emigré press like the following: 'Shootings are going on in Cuba. In August more than 40 anti-communist patriots were shot in Camagüey in the course of a few days; towards the end of September more than 100 were executed in the whole island.' (Consejo Revolucionario de Cuba, *Hoja Informativa*, No. 20, October 10, 1962. Florida.)
[3] This paragraph is based on the article 'Dos años de experiencia de los Comités de Defensa de la Revolución', *Cuba Socialista*, No. 15, November, 1962.

of Russian Soviets. The CDR were responsible for the census of inhabitants for the purposes of rationing, and for the distribution of ration cards; they helped the Ministry of Health with a campaign for the vaccination of children; they participated in the allocation of dwellings; they organized battalions of voluntary workers and have been an essential instrument in the struggle against the black market. They also organized indoctrination courses and public meetings at which 'criticism' and 'self-criticism' took place. In the course of the first nine months of 1962 not less than 40 per cent of the whole adult population of Cuba is said to have attended such meetings. Although their activity is strongly reminiscent of Chinese methods, Castro may be right in claiming that the CDR 'constitute one of the essential contributions of Cuba to the fund of revolutionary experience.'[1]

(2) *The Building of the New Party*.[2] No less original were the methods employed from June 1962 to transform the ORI into the '*Partido Unido de la Revolucion Socialista*'. A purge of the former ORI cells, dominated by the Escalante faction, was carried out simultaneously with the creation of new cells ('revolutionary nuclei') combining democracy with centralism. The new party had to be at once an elite and a genuine vanguard of the workers, growing out of the masses themselves.

The whole process of reconstruction could be divided into seven stages: (1) the regional ORI leadership, while cleansing itself of sectarianism, elects commissions responsible for the selection of new militants; (2) these commissions start a long and thorough preparation of staff-meetings in all places of work: factories, offices, people's farms, etc.; (3) assemblies of the workers of these enterprises take place in which, after long debates, accompanied by criticism and self-criticism 'exemplary workers' are elected as candidates for the Party; (4) each of those elected is then called individually before the commission which scrutinizes his former life, his opinions, etc.; (5) a meeting takes place at which all the elected workers join with the commission in criticism and self-criticism; (6) the commission selects those who have passed these tests and adds others who, although not elected, are considered worthy of admission to the cells of the new Party; finally, (7) another assembly of the workers ratifies the choice made. A special bulletin called *Reestructurando* is published by the ORI. It analyzes the experiences of such commissions and lays down rules for their work.

Up to the beginning of September, elections had been held in 3,959 enterprises. 536,000 workers (80 per cent of the total employed) had participated in them and elected 26,000 'exemplary workers', out

[1] *ibid*.
[2] Information based on reports in *Cuba Socialista*, June–November, 1962.

of which only 27 per cent had formerly been in the ORI cells. At the same time, 331 'nuclei' of the new Party had been formed with 2,109 militants. Each party member had to satisfy the following criteria: (1) he must accept the programme as it is laid down in the two 'Declarations of Havana'; (2) he must accept party discipline; (3) he must prove that he has a clean record and that he did not participate in the 'faked' elections of 1958; (4) he must set a good example in his daily life and work; (5) he must contribute to party funds. (The dues are 1 per cent of monthly salary for those earning up to 250 pesos, 2 per cent for those earning between 250 and 350 pesos, 3 per cent for those earning between 350 and 500 pesos, and 4 per cent for those earning more than 500 pesos.)

The whole party was supposed to have eventually between 50,000 and 60,000 militants, and also planned to enrol candidates the most worthy of whom would become full members.

(i) *The Missile Crisis of Autumn 1962*

Early in July 1962 a Cuban delegation headed by the Chief of the Armed Forces, Raúl Castro, went to Moscow to confer with Soviet military and political leaders. Towards the end of August a new delegation under Guevara went to the USSR. Its main concern may have been Soviet economic help for Cuba, especially for the coming industrialization. But military matters were also discussed. The final communiqué, published on September 1st, contains the following passage:

'Views were also exchanged in connection with the threats of aggressive imperialist quarters against Cuba. In view of these threats, the Cuban government asked the Soviet government to help it by delivering armaments and sending technical specialists to train Cuban servicemen. The Soviet government attentively considered this request of the Cuban government and agreement was reached on this question. As long as the above-mentioned quarters continue to threaten Cuba, the Cuban republic has every justification for taking the measures necessary to insure its security and safeguard its sovereignty and independence, while all Cuba's true friends have every right to respond to this legitimate request.'[1]

Cuba already possessed considerable armaments, which were proudly presented in big parades. There were already Soviet and other communist military specialists on the island. The new decision heralded the despatch of heavier armaments and a large number of military personnel.

Since July at least a large number of Soviet and Soviet-chartered ships had come to Cuba bringing, among other things, huge quantities of urgently needed food. Armaments and technicians began to

[1] Moscow Radio in Russian, September 2, 1962.

arrive as early as August. It was highly improbable that the small, rather ridiculous private raids, made twice from small boats by an unimportant Cuban emigré organization, necessitated defensive measures on this scale. On August 20 the emigré *Consejo Revolucionario de Cuba* protested in a declaration against the arrival of 5,000 Russian military technicians, but their number grew quickly. The nervousness of the USA increased when a new Soviet-Cuban agreement was signed towards the end of September, under which the Soviet Union would construct a big fishing port in Cuba: many suspected that the 'fishing port' was a euphemism for a submarine base. The United States' government tried to calm public opinion: there was no evidence of anything more than the installation of defensive weapons in Cuba.

Towards the end of September, Cuban refugees began to report insistently that missile bases were being built, but Soviet representatives, in reply to repeated American enquiries, denied that offensive weapons were being installed on the island. On October 10, North American observation planes for the first time took photographs showing the construction of suspicious military works at different places on the island. On October 14 they brought back proof that missile bases existed: bases for intermediate-range missiles had been built without cover at astonishing speed, and the photographs showed some forty missiles *in situ*. Bases for longer range missiles were rapidly being built and more than two dozen Ilyushin 28 jet bombers able to carry nuclear bombs were observed. On October 22 President Kennedy made his speech to the nation announcing protective measures, including a naval quarantine. He requested Khrushchev to order the destruction of the existing bases, to withdraw the missiles, the other offensive weapons, and the technicians in charge of them, and to stop further deliveries. The notes exchanged between Kennedy and Khrushchev in the next ten days have not been published. But Khrushchev promised to comply with Kennedy's demands and even accepted the idea of international inspection on the spot. Kennedy gave a generally worded promise that when all this, including the inspection, had been carried out, the USA would give a pledge not to invade Cuba. The dialogue was conducted entirely between the North Americans and the Russians. The Cubans were not consulted at all.

In his press conference of November 20, President Kennedy gave a short version of their mutual undertakings:

'Chairman Khrushchev . . . agreed to remove from Cuba all weapon systems capable of offensive use, to halt the further introduction of such weapons into Cuba, and to permit appropriate United Nations observation and supervision to insure the carrying out of these commitments. We, on our part, agreed that once these adequate arrangements for verification had been established, we would remove our naval quarantine and give assurances against any invasion of Cuba.'[1]

U Thant, who flew to Havana in order to arrange matters with the Cuban government, found his task far from easy. Castro refused to behave like an obedient satellite. He insisted on Cuban sovereignty, refusing to permit any inspection of Cuban territory. On November 2 he informed the Cuban people, in a television broadcast, of his discussions with U Thant, and explained the Cuban position. The peace was menaced not by Cuba, but by the imperialism of the USA and its constant acts of aggression. Cuba as a sovereign state had been fully entitled to ask her friends for help and to acquire any weapons capable of deterring the powerful enemy. A distinction between 'offensive' and 'defensive' weapons was impossible: everything depended on the policies they served. Some of these weapons—the missiles—had remained Soviet property and Cuba could not hinder their withdrawal. The other weapons would remain. He did not deny that there were divergences of opinion between Cuba and the Soviet Union, but more important than any such differences was their friendship, the Soviet determination to defend Cuba, and the unity of the socialist camp. Any verbal guarantee given by the imperialist Kennedy Government was worthless so long as it was not backed by acts. The Cuban government would shortly send the United Nations a note defining what these acts must be. The five demands addressed to the USA were: (1) to lift the 'imperialist blockade' of the island; (2) to stop giving aid for subversive activities against Cuba; (3) to put an end to 'pirate attacks'; (4) to put an end to the constant violation of Cuban air and naval space; (5) to withdraw from the base at Guantanamo. These demands were maintained after Castro had accepted the withdrawal of the Ilyushin bombers which he had, at first, included among those weapons which were Cuban, not Russian property, and after he had declared his willingness to accept ground inspection in Cuba provided the USA would accept inspection of the areas used for the training of Cuban counter-revolutionaries and for launching attacks against Cuba. There the matter rested, even after Mikoyan's long stay in Cuba.

The Cuban people at large seem to have been unaware of the existence of Soviet missiles on the island. During the critical days they remained surprisingly quiet, and mobilization proceeded, apparently, in a very orderly manner. There were, this time, no mass detentions: Castro proudly declared that not a single arrest had been made, which proved the absence of any opposition, and the revolutionary patriotism of the Cuban people. Foreign observers confirmed

[1] *New York Times*, International Edition, November 21, 1962.

in essentials what Castro said.[1] Once the Soviet Union had proclaimed its willingness to withdraw, a feeling of being let down arose, and animosity towards the Soviet Union grew. This was inevitable since Castro, Guevara and the other leaders had dismissed United States guarantees as worthless. Ironical songs and couplets could be heard, such as '*Nikita—lo que da no se quita*' (Nikita—one does not take away what one has given). The Havana correspondent of the *Agence France Presse* wrote that the Cubans were extremely dissatisfied with Soviet behaviour and added: 'hence, the Cuban communists, who approved Khrushchev's decision, found themselves in a critical position'.[2] Dissatisfaction was made manifest by the students of the University of Havana and it seems to have been directed especially against the new Rector, the old-time communist Juan Marinello, who was accused, amongst other things, of following the Soviet line too closely.[3] On December 17, *Revolución* not only published a Chinese declaration against revisionism but accompanied it by an editorial supporting the Chinese position. The Warsaw correspondent of the *New York Times* wrote that, according to Polish communist sources, 'a fundamental policy dispute has arisen between Fidel Castro's régime and the Soviet Union'.[4] The Cubans maintained positions very near to those of the Chinese, accusing the Soviet Union of having retreated before imperialism and of sacrificing world revolution to co-existence.

Did the Cubans ask for the rockets or were they persuaded by the Russians to accept them? On this important point we have two contradictory statements each made by Castro to a French journalist. Speaking to Claude Julien, shortly after the crisis, he declared:

'We have, ourselves, envisaged the possibility of asking the Soviet Union to provide us with missiles. But we had not yet come to a decision when Moscow offered them to us. We were told that by accepting them, we would add to the global strength of the socialist camp. Because we are receiving significant aid from the socialist camp, we considered that we were not in a position to refuse them. That is why we accepted them. It was not to secure our own defence, but primarily to strengthen socialism internationally.'[5]

A year later, Castro gave an entirely different account of the matter in a conversation with Jean Daniel. According to the English translation published in *The Observer* of London on December 8,

---

[1] See 'Cuba en état de siège' in *Le Monde*, Paris, November 23, 1962, and also the report of a Canadian correspondent published in the *New York Times*, International Edition, December 1, 1962.
[2] *Le Monde*, Paris, December 19, 1962.
[3] *Le Monde*, December 15, 1962 and January 3, 1963.
[4] The *New York Times*, International Edition, January 3, 1963.
[5] Translation from *Le Monde*, March 22, 1963.

1963, the Cuban leaders had been informed, six months before the arrival of the missiles in Cuba, that the CIA was planning a new invasion of the island. Even before this they had obtained a copy of the report written by the editor of *Izvestia*, Alexei Adzhubei, about a conversation he had had with President Kennedy towards the end of January 1962. Kennedy had, supposedly, repeated that communism in Cuba remained unacceptable to the USA, and reminded the Russians that the USA had not interfered against the Russians when their troops put an end to the Hungarian Revolution of October 1956—thus intimating that the Russians should do the same in the event of a United States intervention in Cuba. 'Of course,' said Castro, 'the word invasion was not uttered and Adzhubei, unaware of the background (*sic!*), did not immediately draw the same conclusions as we did.' But this report was decisive.

'It was this document that provoked the crisis . . . How could we avert an invasion? We found Khrushchev sharing our anxieties. He asked us what we needed. We replied: make sure that the US is aware that an attack on Cuba is an equivalent of an attack on the Soviet Union . . . The Russians told us . . . that they felt that, if they limited themselves to conventional arms, the Americans might risk an invasion . . .'

'As early as June 1962 my brother Raúl and Ché Guevara went to Moscow to discuss the installation of missiles. The convoy bringing them took three weeks. The Americans knew the ships were carrying armaments, but they took two months to discover these were missiles. We never thought it would take them so long, for of course the aim was to intimidate them, not to attack.'

The first conversation, with Julien, took place when the Cubans were aware of the bad press they had had all over Latin America because of the installation of Russian missiles and the transformation of Cuba into a Russian base, and when they were furious because the Soviets had agreed to withdraw the rockets without even consulting them. The publication of Castro's opinion in *Le Monde* aroused, understandably, anger in the USSR and must be counted as one of the causes of Castro's (first) trip to Russia. The second conversation was much more in line with Khrushchev's wishes and took place several months after the visit. Both versions appear not to express the real situation.

We do not know how seriously the Cubans took their information about the possibility of a new invasion, but we do know that they had earlier expressed dissatisfaction with Khrushchev's view that the threat of using Russian missiles to protect Cuba should be considered as 'symbolic'. And it can be surmised that the Chinese warned the Cubans that there was the possibility of a Russian-

American compromise at Cuban expense. Therefore the Cubans were probably not only 'considering among themselves' the installation of Russian missiles in Cuba, but urging the Russians to instal them.

In this respect the second version appears nearer the truth than the first, although it cannot be accepted in its entirety since parts of it are contradicted by known facts. Pierre Salinger, who was present at Kennedy's conversations with Adzhubei, denied that Hungary had been mentioned in the context of the Cuban affair, and bore witness that Kennedy had clearly stated that the USA would *not* attack Cuba.[1] Salinger's testimony is indirectly confirmed by what Castro said; it is indeed hardly credible that if Hungary had been mentioned in that context, Adzhubei would not have understood the significance of the reference. Furthermore, Raúl Castro did not go to Russia in June, but in July, and then without Guevara, who arrived in Moscow on August 27, in order to sign an agreement with the Russians on September 2. If the missiles had been sent immediately after this agreement, they could not have reached Cuba until the end of September, so that it could not have taken the Americans two months to discover them. So the real facts are still to be clarified, although it seems probable that the Cubans and the Russians *both* wanted the rockets in Cuba, although for different reasons, whereas the Cubans were later opposed to their withdrawal, forced on Khrushchev by Kennedy's stand. It was this withdrawal that led to the strain in Cuban-Soviet relations.

In spite of this, and the growing sympathy for the Chinese, there was no prospect of a breach between Moscow and Havana nor, it seems, any lasting decline in Castro's popularity. Contrary to Kennedy's view, Castro proved himself to be anything but an obedient puppet of Moscow. In a very dangerous situation he maintained his own position without regard for the Soviet line, and in spite of his utter dependence on the Soviet economic, political and military help. The Soviet leaders found themselves on the horns of a dilemma: they could continue to help Cuba—and this would need very considerable expenditure as well as acceptance of many of Castro's policies—or they could abandon her, thereby sacrificing almost all their influence in Cuba and in Latin America.

---

[1] The *New York Times*, International Edition, December 13, 1963.

8. 1963: At the Threshold of Socialist Construction

With the year v, the 'Year of Organization' as it was officially called, Cuba was supposed to enter a new era. The first four years—of revolution—had to be succeeded by an epoch of 'Socialist Construction'. This was announced by President Dorticós in an article published by *Cuba Socialista* in January 1963. The new era would be introduced by a three-year period, from 1963 to 1965, in which three main aims were to be achieved: an increase in agricultural production, and expansion and diversification of exports, and preparation for a rapid industrialization during the years 1966–70.

'The creation of the steel, mechanical and chemical foundations of our industry must be the necessary premise for our industrialization from 1966 onwards, when the transformation of our primarily agrarian economy into an agrarian-industrial economy will really begin,' he wrote.

Such a sober picture of the immediate future was far removed from the optimistic expectations of previous years—although less pessimistic than the declarations of Dorticós himself in summer of 1962.[1] But as the year went by, even the modest new aims seemed to founder on the rocks of reality.

In spite of considerable aid from the East, 1962 had ended with a huge deficit. On February 6, 1963, a new trade protocol with the USSR was signed and the new credits began to flow; destined however not for industrialization, or for the construction of socialism but as stop-gaps. Guevara made this quite clear in a speech of February 9:

'Today the newspapers tell of the long-term credits which the Soviet Union has granted us. What are the credits for? Not for building industry, which is the usual reason for extending such credits. They are given us in order to pay for the unfavourable balance which exists in our transactions with the Soviet Union ... because the sugar crops have been so small.'

But the sugar crop went down even more, to 3·8 million tons, while industrialization did not start in earnest and had to be postponed. New restrictions had to be imposed: on clothing, on coffee, even on sugar consumption. The new difficulties forced the Cuban

---

[1] 'Sacrifices and shortages do not end when a revolution takes power. On the contrary, there begins a historical stage in which greater sacrifices are required. ... The revolutionary mission will only be completed when a whole generation ... transmits to the coming generation the developed material basis for the final socialist society.' (*Hoy*, July 7, 1962.)

1963: THRESHOLD OF SOCIALIST CONSTRUCTION

leaders to a dual policy: a retreat and a new offensive. The retreat consisted in giving up any plans to develop heavy industry and to diversify the economy, reverting to sugar and cattle. The offensive consisted of a new, second agrarian law which practically put an end to the private sector, and the introduction of obligatory military service, tantamount to the introduction of forced work. The economic crisis had its political effects: the formation of the new party turned out to be more difficult than anticipated, new conflicts seem to have arisen, so that the PURS did not become a reality even after five years of revolution had passed. The growing dependence on Moscow forced the Cubans, much against their will, to come out in favour of Khrushchev in his struggle with Peking.

The French agronomist and Castro sympathizer, René Dumont, visited Cuba for the first time in May 1960. At that time he was already struck by the dangerous tendency to go all too quickly towards 'socialism' and by the bureaucratic centralization he could observe everywhere, still combined with voluntaristic ideas and disorganization. As he returned to Cuba in August 1960 his disquiet increased. In September 1963 he made his third voyage to Castro's island. He encountered what he called 'bureaucratized anarchy':

'The most realistic Cuban leaders ... have well understood the problems. The dogmatists in the Planning Board and the Ministry of Industries, on the contrary, continue to defend the dangerous thesis of ultra-centralized leadership of the economy, managed by means of budgetary credits. The latter scorn the experience accumulated by the other socialist countries ... Even more serious is the fact that they present the results of their system of government with an over-optimistic slant and continue to make unrealistic, unattainable forecasts of production'.[1]

In one of his speeches Castro complained about the 'economic cretinism' of Cuba's revolutionary economists. It was indeed this 'cretinism', this voluntaristic centralism, imposed from above on a recalcitrant people and put to work without a sufficient number of specialists and technicians which was primarily responsible for the unending troubles.

On July 25, 1963, *L'Express* (Paris) published an interview of Jean Daniel with Guevara, in the course of which the Cuban Minister of Industries declared with his usual candour:

'We have serious difficulties in Cuba—but not because of what you call the blockade. There has never been a complete blockade ... We have not stopped increasing our trade with Great Britain and France, for example ... Our difficulties stem principally from our errors' ...

[1] *France-Observateur*, Paris, October 3, 1963.

Guevara had been even more explicit in a talk he gave in Algiers on July 14, 1963, and which was published by the pro-Chinese monthly *Revolution*.[1] It seems desirable, and even necessary, to quote it at some length:

'We did two contradictory things which were impossible to harmonize; on the one hand, we copied to the slightest details techniques of planning of a fraternal country whose specialists came to help us, and on the other hand, we continued to let spontaneity reign and failed to analyze many decisions, above all political ones, which must be taken every day in the process of governing ... We treated nature subjectively as if we could persuade it by talking to it, leaving aside the experiences of other countries ... The suggestion of having a 15% increase (*sic!*) in agricultural production was simply ridiculous ... In industry, we worked out a plan of development based mainly on the idea of being self-sufficient in a certain range of durable consumer goods and intermediate industrial articles, we could undoubtedly have easily obtained from friendly countries ... In agriculture we made the mistake of underestimating the importance of sugar-cane (*sic!*), our main product, and attempted to carry out an accelerated diversification. The result was a decrease in our stocks of sugar cane. To this fact was added an extraordinary drought ... In the distribution of income, we at first gave too much emphasis to the satisfaction of social necessities, paying more equitable wages and increasing employment, without sufficiently considering the condition of the economy. The absence of basic work norms in industry and agriculture caused a violent change in the general tendencies of the workers, creating in a country where there are still unemployed, the phenomenon in agriculture of a shortage in manpower ... The structure of our economy has still not changed after four years of revolution ...'

It was not to change during the remaining months of the fifth year either. On the contrary: revolutionary Cuba sacrificed the main *idées-forces* which had justified the revolution—rapid industrialization and economic diversification—to return at least provisionally to monoculture in the name of that bugbear of Communist propaganda: the 'bourgeois' theory of international trade, according to which each country had to specialize and to put emphasis on those products it was best able to furnish.

The retreat was announced by Fidel Castro himself in a speech he made on August 10, 1963, before the representatives of the Institute of Hydraulic resources, assembled in the Havana-Libre Hotel in Cuba's capital.

Instead of wasting the country's resources by trying to diversify

[1] *Révolution* (Paris), Vol. I, No. 6, October 1963.

1963: THRESHOLD OF SOCIALIST CONSTRUCTION

and industrialize and to create a heavy industry, Cuba should continue to concentrate on agriculture:

'We are going to develop the cane fields primarily and then the cattle industry. These are going to be the pillars of our economy until 1970'.

Costly plans to build heavy industry would be postponed and priority would be given to the development of hydraulic resources, of a fertilizer industry and to the manufacture of agricultural machinery. During the late 1960s the annual sugar harvests would reach 8 to 9 million tons and the enormous potentialities of cattle-exports would be realized.

'It may well be that we will have to wait until 1970 to develop the steel industry—so why rush to make a mill now when there are other much more important and urgent matters. When our agriculture has reached its peak of development and we have all these resources, then we will begin to develop other branches of our economy.'

It seemed uncertain that industrialization could even start in 1970, if only because of the lack of the technicians required:

'We have good technicians in agriculture [?] Perhaps it will be in the 1970s or the 1980s (sic!) when our turn will come to spur on those branches of the economy that require tens of thousands of technicians.'

The fundamental economic retreat coincided however with a new low in agricultural production as well as new and greater imbalances of all sorts which forced the Cuban leaders to increase socialization and centralization—increasing precisely those ills mentioned by Dumont. Such was one of the causes of the second agrarian law.

In the meantime Castro did not stop attacking those responsible for the present state of disorganization. To quote once more from the same speech of August 10:

'There are people around who are super-radicals in talk, but do not even know that socialism must begin with work, with organization, with the rational use of resources ... We already know that much was stolen under capitalism. There is no stealing in our revolution, but there is waste of money. There are no embezzlers, but there are misspenders.'

By an extraordinary feat of forgetfulness, Castro did not enter into any self-criticism of his own person, although it was he and his like who bore the main responsibility for the errors committed. The 'old communists' were this time not actually mentioned, but it was clear that they were once more considered to be the main culprits. It was, indeed, significant that the Institute of Hydraulic Resources which Castro praised (' ... it knows the exact number of its employees and what each of them is doing') was headed by the veteran leader of the 26th July Movement, Faustino Perez, who had fallen into disgrace because of his opposition to the communist 'old guard' and had so disappeared since 1960 from the political arena.

In the November 1963 issue of the official monthly *Komunist*, published in Moscow, the Uruguayan Communist leader Enrique Rodriguez wrote about the lessons of the Cuban revolution for Latin America:

'The peoples of Latin America have understood that a revolution can only be victorious ... when it is led by an experienced Marxist-Leninist vanguard; in the Cuban case, the United Party of the Socialist Revolution.'

But the reality was quite different. In spite of all the early hopes and endeavours to create the PURS, the party then still awaited its founding congress. In *Cuba Socialista* of April 1963, new details had been given about the party-construction. All in all 36,334 'exemplary workers' had been elected and 2,209 party-cells (*nuclei*) had been established. But the party itself consisted in April 1963 only of 16,002 members (*militantes*) and 2,024 candidates (*aspirantes*). As many of these had not been elected, the great majority of the 'exemplary workers' remained outside the new organization, either because they themselves refused to join or because, in spite of their exemplary qualities, they had not been considered reliable enough. Once more it proved difficult to build a totalitarian élite-party on the basis of democracy.

The slowness of the formation process resulted from technical as well as political difficulties. The former were referred to by Castro in his speech of February 23, 1963, before the members of the PURS of Havana. According to him they arose primarily out of the competition for qualified people which was raging between the economic, administrative and political apparatus of the revolution. The best political cadres were rapidly snatched up by the heads of government departments or economic enterprises which sometimes offered them very high salaries. This, in turn, was corrupting the party. At the time of the Escalante crisis, the party nuclei had become the tyrants of the administration and the economy; now there was the opposite danger, that the nuclei would be broken up by the administration which was taking away the cadres.

There was less talk about the political obstacles. But they had by no means disappeared. On October 15, 1962, Yugoslav correspondents of *Tanjug* had reported that only about 30 per cent of former members of the *Partido Socialista Popular* (the Communists) would be admitted to the new PURS. In Havana alone some 2,000 former Communists and ORI members were purged, because they had participated in the 1958 elections. The divergencies between 'old' and 'new' Communists increased as a consequence of the missile crisis and, within the newcomers, sympathy for the Chinese views were becoming manifest. Not less clear was the conflict of opinions between

1963: THRESHOLD OF SOCIALIST CONSTRUCTION

the Cuban leaders on the one hand and the Russians and their oldtime followers in Cuba and in Latin America on the other. Mikoyan's trip to Cuba did not bring about any real *rapprochement*, but it was probably the publication of Castro's thoughts by Claude Julien in *Le Monde* of March 22 and 23, 1963, which was the last straw and the reason for Castro's invitation to Moscow.

'We cannot be of the same mind as Khrushchev. Cuba does not want to be a pawn on the world chess board. Cuba's sovereignty is a reality for which we have struggled. We are not a satellite ... I have explored the reaction of our people and I found an unanimous feeling that it was necessary to keep the missiles and not to give in to the threat. Some even wanted to prevent their withdrawal by the use of force if need be. Kennedy was using blackmail and should not have been allowed to succeed. The Chinese are right in saying that one must not yield to imperialism. We are well placed here to know that imperialism is not a paper tiger.'

He explained that, in spite of all these disagreements, he was thankful to the Russians for their help and that he had friendly feelings towards Khrushchev although, as he added laughing, he would have had a fight with him if he had come to Cuba (this sentence was mistranslated by US news agencies as 'I would have boxed his ears').

Particularly sharp was Castro's criticism of the official Communist parties:

'What help did we get last October during the blockade when we were at the brink of a major conflict? Where have there been mass demonstrations in our favor? What did the revolutionaries of Europe and Latin America do? Only the Venezuelans reacted. But the big parties which call themselves revolutionary did not stir. They are not revolutionaries, they are bureaucrats, they are satellites. Each time Moscow takes a decision, whatever it may be, the satellites of the whole world applaud it. When Khrushchev takes his missiles away without asking us, the satellites exclaim "Khrushchev has served the cause of peace well". And when Khrushchev criticizes abstract painting in the Riding School in Moscow, the satellites ask me to prohibit abstract painting here. And I tell them that our adversaries are capitalism and imperialism, not abstract painters.'

Even before *Le Monde* had published anything, Castro's opposition to the 'peaceful way to power' propagated by the big Communist parties all over Latin America had been clear. In February 1963 Luis Carlos Prestes had come to Cuba to talk to Castro after he, Prestes, had been in Moscow. There also had been more or less friendly exchanges between Castroites and leading members of the Chilean party. The divergences—of which we shall say more in the last part of this book—remained. But now Castro's criticisms had been published by a leading 'bourgeois' newspaper and vouched for by Claude Julien, who Castro still considered his friend. It is true that the official Cuban news agency published a *dementi* but this merely denied that Castro had given Julien an 'interview' (Julien has never claimed this). *Le Monde*, in its issue of March 24/25, 1963, reaffirmed the authenticity of the statements made by Castro and mentioned that the Cuban leader had expressly authorized Julien to reproduce those of them he considered fit for publication.

Here we see the real causes of the slow progress of the PURS— and here we have the main reason why Castro left on April 26, 1963, for Russia.

The conversations in Moscow took several weeks. The topics treated were political as well as economic, and both were linked. The result was that politically Castro accepted in the main the Russian as against the Chinese line, while the Soviet Union promised further help for Cuba's economy but obliged Cuba to return to economic rationalism, i.e., monoculture.

On May 23 a joint Soviet-Cuban statement was signed by Castro and Khrushchev:

'The two sides are completely unanimous in declaring that, in the present conditions, the struggle for peace is the most important task of mankind... The Soviet and Cuban sides reaffirm that they will fight tirelessly for the triumph of the Leninist policy of peaceful coexistence. In the conditions when states with different social and political systems exist, the principles of peaceful coexistence are the only correct and reasonable basis for international relations... (these principles) are in line with the task of national liberation and anti-imperialist struggle... Peaceful coexistence creates wide opportunities for the rapid economic growth of the socialist states, for the improvement of the welfare of the peoples of these countries... contributes to the growth of the influence of Communist and Workers parties and to the widening of the front of the struggle for socialism. This is exemplified by heroic Cuba, which has embarked on the road to socialism.'

Then comes a mythical description of Cuba's revolution, slanted in favour of Castro's person:

'The people's democratic, anti-imperialist revolution in Cuba was carried out by Cuban workers and peasants under the leadership of Fidel Castro, an outstanding revolutionary and the national hero of Cuba. The workers and farmers fought, arms in hand, against the political tyranny of the exploiters, wrested power from the hands of the national bourgeoisie and foreign monopolies and created the first socialist state in America.'

1963: THRESHOLD OF SOCIALIST CONSTRUCTION

In some way the Leninist tenet about the rôle of the party had to be introduced and the 'old communists' satisfied. This was achieved by ascribing all the achievements to the (not yet formed) United Party of the Socialist Revolution (PURS):

'All these successes were made possible because of the tremendous enthusiasm and cohesion of the Cuban people, who, under the leadership of the United Party of the Socialist Revolution with Comrade Fidel Castro at its head, are building a new life, and thanks to the fraternal solidarity and assistance of the countries of the socialist community.'

Castro expressed his thankfulness to the Soviet Union, stressed the importance of Soviet aid and approved Krushchev's political actions during the missile crisis:

'Revolutionary Cuba carried the banner of freedom and independence high in the grim days of October 1962, when, having prepared a new armed intervention against the Cuban people, the United States, by its aggressive actions, strained the situation in the area of the Caribbean Sea to the limit, as a result of which an international crisis emerged and the world was placed in the brink of a nuclear missile world war. The firm stand of the Soviet Union and the other socialist countries in the cause of defending revolutionary Cuba, the restrained and sober evaluation by the responsible statesmen of the Soviet Union and Cuba of the situation that resulted, and the support for Cuba from all peace-loving states, averted thermo-nuclear war.'

Finally the touchy problem of the road to power in Latin America was settled by a sort of compromise. The Second Declaration of Havana, with its call to immediate revolutionary action, was played down; it was only mentioned in a small section, together with the First Declaration of Havana, and was not presented as being of foremost importance for the overall strategy of Latin American revolutions:

'The two sides point out that the Havana declarations are of historic significance for the national liberation struggles of the peoples of Latin America and correctly indicate the course of events. The question of a peaceful or non-peaceful way to socialism, in one country or another, will be settled, at the final count, by the struggling peoples themselves, in accordance with the concrete correlation of the class-forces, and the extent of the resistance by the exploiting classes to the socialist reorganization of society.'

As important as this declaration, which was obviously drafted by the Russians, was to be for Khrushchev in his struggle with Peking, were for the Cubans the promises of help given by the Soviet Union, especially the promise to buy sugar at a higher price than originally envisaged (although the new price, 6 cents per pound was considerably below the world market price during the first half of 1963) and the permission to divert a part of the Cuban sugar exports towards the world market.

The political consequences of Castro's visit were—for the Russians—rather disappointing and this contributed to his second journey in 1964. Although in July Castro praised the test-ban treaty as an instrument of peace, Cuba refused to sign it. The relations with the Chinese remained close and in November a visiting Albanian was given an ovation. In spite of everything he might have signed, Castro refused to become a puppet of Moscow and the international situation made this relative independence possible. The Russians were well aware of the fact, that they could neither drop Cuba nor openly criticize Castro, without losing out to the Chinese and sacrificing much of their position in Latin America.

The retreat towards monoculture and postponement of industrialization was, as we have noted, followed by a fundamental attack against the remaining 'private' sector of Cuban agriculture and the proclamation of compulsory military service. The former took place on October 2, the latter on November 12, 1963.

In 1961 the 'private sector' in agriculture was officially stated to control 60 per cent of the land—as against 40 per cent in the hands of 'co-operatives', and *granjas del pueblo*. The majority of the 'private' sector was worked by the small peasants with up to five *caballerias* of land each, who were organized inside the ANAP. As already described, the 'privacy' of these peasants existed only on paper. The rest was made up of the properties of some 10,000 larger farmers with between five and thirty *caballerias* each. Since 1961 this part of the private sector had considerably decreased in favour of the state sector, principally through the abandoning of farms by landowners who left the country. Although some independent authorities like Chonchol have maintained that the huge majority of the farmers with more than five *caballerias* of land each, were poor peasants (depending on the quality of the soil and the type of crop, some of the cultivators of very small areas might be considered 'rich') the 10,000 bigger farmers were considered by the revolutionary authorities to belong mainly to the 'rural bourgeoisie', which could not be reconciled to the revolution and constituted one of the main sources of the black market as well as a breeding ground for counter-revolutionary activities.

The Second Agrarian Reform Law, promulgated on October 2, put an end to the bigger private sector. All farms over five *caballerias* were expropriated; the former proprietors who had adequately cultivated their land were to be compensated receiving an indemnity of 15 pesos per month per *caballeria*, payable over ten years. Those lands which had not been cultivated would be simply confiscated. From now on the State would possess from 70 to 75 per cent of the land, the rest being farmed by the small peasants united inside the ANAP. The ANAP itself was however in the process of being transformed into a mere 'transmission-belt', a mass-organization directed from above. Carlos Rafael Rodríguez had indicated this clearly in a booklet printed in English during spring 1963: 'In the process of carrying out this activity, ANAP began assuming administrative functions (in regard to credits and supplies) that have affected its main purpose, that of functioning as a mass organization. The reorganization of INRA [which was transformed into the Ministry of Agriculture] will assign these functions to our central agricultural organization, INRA itself'.[1]

But the new agrarian reform law was not merely the result of 'class-struggle' and another step towards complete socialization. It tried also to introduce some changes which had been considered necessary by foreign observers. J. Chonchol had criticized the Cuban agrarian reality in an article published in Mexico at the beginning of the year.[2] Among the criticisms levelled against the revolutionary changes were that the private sector of farms with between five and thirty *caballerias* had remained in practice unsystematized, being handicapped by not getting any kind of help from the State, whether in the form of credits, or in the form of industrial machinery, fertilizers, etc. This would apparently be remedied now that it was included inside the socialist sector. Another criticism had always been that the agricultural units had been too big, that agriculture itself was all too centralized. In this respect too, certain changes were apparently to be introduced. Greater state-ownership was to be combined with more decentralization, introducing more regional control as well as smaller productive units. Only the future would show how far this plan would be realized.

Compulsory military service had been announced by Castro in his speech of July 26, 1963. It was promulgated in November. Its aim was as much and even more economic and social as military. In his July speech Castro had said that it was primarily a measure to prevent the parasitical element, the potential *Lumpenproletariat*, from developing. Military service was to be a school of discipline and Marxist-Leninism. It was also to be used to solve the problem of the shortage of labour. Indeed; it was in many respects a sort of forced labour, which permitted the state to make considerable economies. Raúl Castro himself made its purpose explicit in November: most of the new recruits would spend three or four

---

[1] Carlos Rafael Rodríguez, *Four Years of Agrarian Reform*, Republic of Cuba—Ministry of Foreign Relations (Havana, [1963]), p. 16.

[2] 'Analisis crítico de la Reforma agraria cubana', in *Trimestre Económico*, Mexico, January–March 1963.

months a year cutting sugar cane or picking coffee-beans. But they would be cheaper than the soldiers or agricultural workers who had done the job before. The average annual soldier's wage had been 803 pesos a year—the new recruits would serve three years, getting only 7 pesos monthly and being obliged to work under military discipline. Their work would not only be less expensive than that of wage labourers but also than that of 'voluntary' workers. Raúl Castro had exemplified it by citing on November 12, the case of fourteen electrical workers who cost 5,800 pesos in salaries and other expenses while picking only 304 pesos' worth of coffee. For many recruits and all those who were considered politically unreliable because of their social extraction, military service would indeed be tantamount to forced labour: indeed, these unreliable elements would not be considered worthy of bearing arms at all and would be exclusively used as labour force and objects of indoctrination.

On January 13, 1959, Fidel Castro had declared: 'We will not establish military service because it is not right to force a man to put on a uniform and a helmet, to give him a rifle and to force him to march'.[1]

As with many other original promises and aims, this pacifist conception had to go down the drain of history.

[1] *Revolución*, January 14, 1959.

9. After Five Years—Past and Future

After five years almost none of the wishes and expectations which had filled the minds and hearts of the revolutionaries of 1959/1960 had materialized. Where, before the revolution Cuba had been dependent on the USA, it was now much more dependent on Soviet Russia. If her economy had formerly been characterized by monoculture, built on sugar (and cattle) she was still dependent on the same products, whose production had sharply decreased. The revolution had promised to give the Cuban people freedom as well as bread. Democratic freedoms had disappeared and national income was considerably lower in 1953 than 1959 or even 1957. Hopes of an increase in 1964 were dashed by the disastrous hurricane 'Flora' which hit the island in October 1963. They would have been problematic even without the storm—as all the hopes of the years before had proved to be illusory.

But it would be wrong to state, that for all these reasons the revolution had 'failed', that there was no prospect of betterment, no stability and that the régime lacked popular backing. This was certainly what the Cuban emigrés wished to believe. But beliefs of emigrés seldom find justice before the tribunal of history.

Five years is a short lapse of time—too short indeed to judge a tremendous social upheaval, with its inevitable failures and the also inevitable mistakes committed by new and inexperienced men put to do responsible jobs for which they were unprepared. They would still commit mistakes in the future—but they would also learn, and improve their work. If the *per capita* income had fallen, there was certainly more social justice in its distribution—much less of the glaring differences between rich and poor. There was no hunger in Cuba and the hitherto poorest had suffered least. Even in 1963 the majority of Cubans lived certainly no worse and perhaps even better, than many millions of Latin Americans in other parts of the continent. There were signs of coming improvement: the price of sugar had gone up, the Russians promised to pay more, the number of new technicians was (if slowly) increasing and the US attempt to cut off the island had totally failed. The 'American blockade' had even its positive aspects: it gave the possibility of blaming many troubles on a scapegoat and so improving the popularity of the revolutionary régime.

The régime was not yet definitively institutionalized or 'normalized': it still remained fundamentally charismatic. But it was also fundamentally stable. Castro's communism was, after all, not imposed from the outside by a foreign power. It had grown out of a genuine national revolution and developed under a popular leader, who was still 'the boss' and could afford to show that he was nobody's satellite, while Russia (and China) had to accept this kind of independence and to go on helping Cuba if they did not want the chances of Communism in Latin-America to crumble.

The system was totalitarian, a fact which by itself made open opposition almost impossible and any inner opposition difficult. It had been, and remained, to a certain extent 'terroristic', although its terror was probably much less pronounced and much less terrible than that of most social revolutions of past and present times. But it was as certainly not just its totalitarian character which explained its stability.

Though the new régime was wasteful and inefficient, it was much less corrupt than the one it had replaced. And it opened perspectives which went beyond the problems of material wellbeing. Moral and psychological factors—hopes, pride, dignity, nationalism, etc., also influence human beings. It could not be a matter of indifference to the average Cuban that his small country had become famous and one of the focal points of contemporary history and that his *líder máximo* had apparently won the contest with the powerful northern neighbour. Havana, formerly the playground for foreign millionaires has been transformed into the Mecca of a new revolutionary faith. If the poor did not rule, they were certainly treated with more care and human respect than before.

Greater social equality has been achieved. 'Vertical' social mobility has become noticeably greater. The new ruling class has not yet crystallized, while tens of thousands have risen into leading positions, most of them from the ranks of the lower classes or from among the formerly frustrated young intellectuals. The rich have gone, their exclusive clubs are open to the people and their elegant homes house new revolutionary dignitaries or are transformed into schools, nurseries, or clubs (if they are not reserved for foreign technicians and specialists). The educational monopoly of the few has been broken. The number of pupils in primary schools has doubled (although the educational level may be very low), tens of thousands of young men and women have been given scholarships or have been sent abroad, and many others hope that their turn will come soon. People who had never heard a concert or attended a theatre are entering into the realm of art. The first steps have been taken to make hospitals and medical attention available to those who had previously been without them.

Inertia has given way to (forced) dynamism, and incessant indoctrination campaigns cannot fail to have an effect, particularly on the young. Those between 10 and 25 years old form more than 40 per cent of the total population, and the huge majority of them back Castro. Even if most of the older people were opposed to the régime, this would still give the revolutionary leaders a mass basis for their régime. Youth plays a much bigger part in Cuba now, and so, apparently, do negroes and women. People with black skin had never been (as the revolutionaries pretended) pariahs in pre-revolutionary Cuba. But their economic and social position had, on the whole, been worse than that of the 'whites'. Now they not only have equal rights, but sometimes even seem to be privileged. Women had always played a minor rôle in economic, social and political life. Now it is different. 'The bourgeois concept of womanhood is disappearing in our country,' declared Castro in his speech to the Women's Congress in January 1963. And so it is—although the concept referred to may be less 'bourgeois' than iberic and pre-capitalist. Women bear arms, enter schools and universities in increasing numbers and get more jobs in the economy. When shoe, clothing and hardware enterprises were nationalized, the Ministry of Internal Trade was instructed to select women as administrators of those firms.

And what is the alternative to Castro? The revolution has gone deep, and so has mutual hatred between revolutionaries and counter-revolutionaries. The position of the latter had become worse since the US administration had begun to cold-shoulder them. The emigrés are split into innumerable hostile factions. The USA had been unable to take effective action against Castro. It is difficult to imagine his enemies obtaining victory without massive outside help, even without a full-scale military invasion by foreign forces. Any counter-revolution could very well lead to the establishment of a dictatorship far worse than that of Batista—a dictatorship which would attempt to undo what has been done, and would permit tens of thousands of Cuban refugees, who have lost everything, to take revenge on the hundreds of thousands who, in one way or another, can be considered beneficiaries of Castroism.

All this does not mean that there are no dangers for Castro. Any change in the international situation combined with growing internal difficulties, or any decrease of Russian aid, could make the situation insufferable. Hopes could disappear and despair permeate the very basis on which the system stands. There is constant danger that enthusiasm will flag, that an 'egotistical' hankering for greater freedom, for individual benefits, for easier life and for more privacy will grow. These desires are deeply rooted in human nature, although Castro considers them to be a heritage of capitalism. An awareness of these dangers accounts for the extraordinary statement made by Castro in the spring of 1962:

'Karl Marx says in his Communist Manifesto that capitalism digs its own grave. But capitalism digs two graves—one for itself and the other for the society which comes after capitalism. What we must do is to fill in the hole quickly, so that the heritage of capitalism may not also destroy and bury socialism.' (Speech in Camagüey, *Hoy*, May 15, 1962.)

10. Analysis of the Cuban Revolution

The revolutionaries who had sought power to restore democracy were using it to build a socialist and totalitarian society.

If one takes socialism to mean an economic order in which private ownership of the most important factors of production is replaced by state ownership and a free market economy by state control, the Cuban revolution has been 'socialist' since 1960. If a political and social structure in which the whole economy has been nationalized, the institutions of representative democracy have been abolished, legal opposition has been made impossible, all social organizations have been brought into line, and the private sphere of individual life has been restricted while the nation has been placed in a state of permanent mobilization through indoctrination and propaganda— if such a society is totalitarian, then Cuba is a totalitarian state.

The Cuban revolution, then, belongs to the class of socialist totalitarian revolutions. If one disregards those that have been forced upon other countries by a foreign power, Cuba is the sixth member of this class which, listed in historical order, comprises Russia, Yugoslavia, Albania, China and North Vietnam. All these countries experienced revolutions made under the banner of Marx, but, contrary to Marx's fundamental conceptions, in them socialism did not arise out of spontaneous tendencies of social development. It did not come about as the result of the inner contradictions of an over-ripe capitalism which had become a fetter on further progress, nor did the objective prerequisites for the higher form of socialism already exist. All these countries were under-developed. In none of them was capitalism 'over-ripe'; in none of them did the majority of the population consist of impoverished proletarians ready to rise against capitalist oppression. In none were the objective preconditions for socialism present.

In all of them revolutionary leaders, recruited predominantly from the intelligentsia, transformed 'democratic' into 'socialist' revolutions. They did it from above, in conflict with the spontaneous tendencies of their respective societies. From this conflict arose totalitarianism. Marxism was thus transformed from the theory of a socialist and democratic workers' movement into the ideology of revolutionary, 'classless' élites.[1] In Russia the élite had been based on

[1] It is interesting to recall the thesis of that long-forgotten Polish anarchist, Waclaw Machajski, who maintained that Marxian socialism was the ideology of the intelligentsia who would use it to get the support of the proletarian masses for the overthrow of private capitalism, and would then establish their own class rule over the people.

the industrial proletariat, in China essentially on the peasantry.

The Cuban revolution had certain distinctive features, both in the first democratic phase of the struggle against the Batista dictatorship, and in the two subsequent socialist phases, the transitional phase of 'revolutionary humanism' and the 'socialist totalitarian' phase.

The Batista dictatorship was overthrown by the activities of small groups helped by the growing hatred of the mass of the people. It was overthrown before the dictatorship had tried to make concessions or compromises; without a *coup* from within the government, without the existence of a profound economic crisis and without an active mass movement. In these respects the revolution differed from other revolutions, including the Cuban anti-Machado revolution of the 'thirties.

The transition from the democratic to the socialist phase took place without civil war and without a change of leadership. It was not directed by a Marxist-Leninist party but by a charismatic leader. It contradicted not only the fundamental ideas of Marx, but also one of the main tenets of Leninism.

In the first 'humanist' phase the leadership was willing and, by sacrificing the interests of the immediate future, able to provide the lower sections of the population with a rapid improvement of their living conditions. The ensuing mass enthusiasm made it possible for the revolution to dispense, at first, with a well organized political apparatus and to do without terror. The bureaucratic transformation of the charisma into a commonplace (as Max Weber called it), the totalitarian normalization of the revolution, its 'bolshevization', was not completed even by the end of 1962.

The development towards socialism was not based on a clearly conceived plan but resulted from the interplay of spontaneous personal decisions of the leader and the consequences of those decisions, which crystallize the ideas of the leadership.

The transition to the 'revolutionary humanist' phase and from there to the 'socialist totalitarian' phase was possible because Cuba was economically more highly developed than other countries in which Marxist-Leninist revolutions had taken place, and because the revolution was able to take over a running economy which has at its disposal unused factors of production—land, labour and capital equipment.

Politically the transition was possible because the masses were enthusiastic and there were no organized forces inside the country which could act as a brake. International considerations deterred the USA from intervention and the Cuban revolution could rely on the sympathy of the Latin American masses and on help from the Eastern bloc.

The Cuban revolution does not conform to the liberal explanation of Latin American Leninist revolutions. According to liberal beliefs such upheavals and transformations result from the activity of communist parties, which are able to exploit popular discontent caused by extreme poverty and economic inequality, they occur mainly in predominantly agrarian countries with archaic and semifeudal structures, in which the middle class is weak, representative democracy lacks popular appeal, and where incipient industrialization causes severe disruption.

This analysis does not fit the Cuban revolution. Cuba was richer than other Latin American countries, the social inequalities were less marked, and the middle class rather bigger than in other parts of Latin America. There was hardly any feudalism, and representative democracy had so much appeal that the whole struggle against Batista was led under its banner. The masses hardly participated in any active manner and the communist party did not direct the struggle.

Neither the democratic nor the socialist phase of the revolution can be accurately analysed with the help of Marxist class concepts.

The Cuban revolution was not a *bourgeois* revolution. This concept has a clear meaning only in connection with concepts like feudalism and absolutism. A bourgeois revolution is one made in the interest of the middle class and in the name of economic and political freedom and legal and social equality. It assaults the remnants of feudal society: a land-owning aristocracy and monarchistic state, and its goal is to permit a free development of capitalism.

In Cuba there was no feudalism. The character of Cuban landownership was mainly capitalist[1] and the landowners had close links with the urban bourgeoisie. The bourgeoisie exerted a strong influence on the government and the social and political institutions were mainly bourgeois in character.

Revolutions can also be regarded as 'bourgeois' if the development of the bourgeoisie is prevented by external forces, that is if they are 'anti-imperialist' revolutions, or if their driving force is the peasantry. Even by these criteria the Cuban revolution was not a bourgeois revolution.

In 1933 the Cuban bourgeoisie was still imbued with the spirit of anti-imperialism; after that date its position and attitude changed. Imperialism made political and economic concessions and a new Cuban bourgeoisie developed whose interests became more closely connected with American business interests. The modern entrepreneurs and technicians in particular became increasingly hostile towards the dictatorship and regarded the government's inefficiency and corruption with growing hatred, and they were at the same time

[1] This fact is recognized even by Marxists. Professor Paul Baran, for example points out that 'the typical Cuban latifundium was not a *feudum* worked by slaves but a plantation owned by companies and worked by paid labour'. (*Trimestre Económico*, Mexico, July/September, 1961.)

strongly influenced by the North American spirit. It was no accident that this particular class was represented in the first revolutionary government and that its members were accused by many radicals of being pro-American. But anti-imperialism was weaker in Cuba than in most other Latin American countries and was widespread only among young intellectuals, in whom it was more a feeling of resentment than a conscious policy.

The Cuban revolution was not a *peasant* revolution. Peasant revolutions take place in countries in which the majority of the population consists of smallholders and tenant farmers, often living in servile conditions, who fight against the big landowners, rural landlords and usurers for a typically 'bourgeois' aim; the free ownership of land. Peasant revolutions cannot be socialist, but can be exploited by revolutionary socialists for aims contrary to those of the peasantry.

Cuba had no 'serfs' and was not a peasant country. Those engaged in agriculture formed a minority of the working population, and among them farm labourers predominated. Frank Tannenbaum rightly said that Cuba's population was typically urban, with urban values and customs; and that a sugar plantation was more like a factory than a farm. Cuba had no 'peasant communes', there had been no *jacqueries* for years and there was no tradition of specifically peasant protest movements. The small peasants of the Sierra Maestra who supported Castro were not at all typical of the Cuban rural population and fought for aims which were, as Guevara admitted, typically petty bourgeois and contrary to the socialist land reforms carried out later.

The lack of revolutionary feeling among the rural population was partly due to apathy and partly to the numerous laws for the protection of tenant farmers passed since 1937, many of which had been enforced.

Neither in its first, nor in its second phase can the revolution be described as *proletarian*: the proletariat, including most agricultural workers, had taken little part in the struggle against Batista and was imbued with the trade unionist spirit. In 1959, the workers welcomed the wage increases, rent reductions, and so on, but resisted all measures to increase productivity and strengthen 'socialist' discipline.

The *intellectuals* cannot be regarded as a social class. They did not form a coherent group as far as their economic interests, social position, or ideology were concerned. Moreover, as almost all modern revolutions have been led by intellectuals the character of a particular revolution is not revealed by the mere fact that it was directed by intellectuals.

There is, however, a Marxist interpretation which evades the pitfalls of class-analysis. Jacques Arnault in his *Cuba et le Marxisme*[1]

[1] *op. cit.*, *La Nouvelle Critique*, Paris, 1962, pp. 53–5.

interprets the revolution, at least in its first phase, as a popular revolution of the type (mentioned by Marx in a letter to Kugelmann) similar to the 1848 revolution, the Paris Commune of 1871, and the Russian revolution of 1905–6. He quotes Lenin's remarks in *The State and the Revolution* in which he explained the differences between popular and other kinds of bourgeois revolutions:

'If we take the revolutions of the 20th century as examples, we will, of course, have to recognize that both the Portuguese and the Turkish revolutions were also bourgeois revolutions. Neither, however, is a "people's" revolution, inasmuch as the mass of the people, the enormous majority, does not participate actively, independently, with its own economic and political demands, in either the one or the other of these revolutions.'

But it is enough to compare the characteristics given by Lenin with the real course of Cuban history to see that this explanation is utterly wrong. Indeed in Cuba, the masses, 'the enormous majority of the people', did not appear on the historical scene in the way described by Lenin either in the first or in the socialist phase of the revolution.[1]

Although it is impossible to answer the question about the 'class character' of the Cuban revolution, there were nevertheless some social groups which were more or less predisposed to favour the revolution and could hope to benefit from a fundamental change. The two most important of these groups were the young intellectuals and the unemployed or rather the underemployed, particularly in the towns. Neither group is a class in the Marxist sense because their position is not determined by their place within the labour market. On the contrary, their social character is the result of the fact that they stand outside the process of production. This accounts for their ultra-radicalism: the rootless have nothing to lose but their rootlessness, and they lack practical experience. It also explains their leanings towards 'anarchistic individualism' and their inability to unite in the furtherance of common interests. They differ fundamentally from the permanently employed workers because they are not concerned to improve their economic and social position within the existing society but to create a new society in which they can take root.

Because the unemployed and underemployed were numerous in Cuba and, together with the underpaid, formed a majority of the population, the national revolution can be regarded as a 'revolution of the rootless'. Its 'anarchistic radicalism' can be used against capitalism but can also be an obstacle to social change.

[1] This in spite of the mythology created by the Castroists about the mass-character of the revolution, and the supposedly violent transition to Socialism. *See* Part IV.

ANALYSIS OF THE CUBAN REVOLUTION

The frustrated young intellectuals naturally played a leading rôle. Impatient, influenced by radical ideologies rather than by facts, they doubted their own economic future and prospects of advancement. They stood for national independence, social justice, and quick modernization of the country. Their impatience led them to favour rapid changes carried out from above and to reject compromises, while their inexperience made them under-estimate the difficulties.

Any far-reaching revolution tends to betray its original aims. At the beginning of the French revolution nobody anticipated the terror, and even Robespierre was in favour of retaining the monarchy. Initially, the eighteenth-century American rebels had no intention of setting up an independent state. The 'free officers' in Egypt wanted to overthrow Farouk and end corruption but did not intend to establish Nasser's 'socialism'. A revolution passes through various phases and changes its character because the seeds of later stages exist already at the beginning and develop under the pressure of conflicting tendencies.

From the beginning, the Cuban revolution contained a mixture of democratic and socialist elements. There was almost universal agreement about the former but not about the latter.

On the basis of past experience it was possible to hold the view that there could be no far-reaching reform if one waited for a legal solution of social problems through the operation of representative democracy. A radical transformation of state and society could not be achieved without profound changes in property relations, a sharp struggle against powerful foreign and local interests, and a change of old customs.

In January 1959 the country was led by a strong-willed and impulsive leader imbued with revolutionary impatience and influenced by Marxist and other radical ideas. He was 'freer' than most historical figures have ever been, because he found himself in a political vacuum, supported by popular enthusiasm. He decided in favour of quick, radical changes. The overthrow of the old realities created new ones which began to dominate him. The stone began to roll with increasing speed towards a socialist, totalitarian solution. Cuba is a classic example of a 'permanent revolution'. The democratic revolution has become a socialist revolution. In its next stage it must transcend the national framework and become a Latin American revolution, or become a frustrated revolution.

In most modern revolutions there has been a period of 'double rule'. During the English revolution in the seventeenth century Cromwell's army was at loggerheads with the Long Parliament. In France in 1792-93 the Paris Commune was at odds with the Legislative Assembly and the Convention. In Russia there was tension between the official government and the Soviets from March to

October 1917. The Marxist-Leninist reinterpretation of the Cuban revolution has produced the theory that there was a similar dyarchy in Cuba in 1959; it is claimed that there was a conflict between the radical peasant rebel army which supported Castro and the bourgeois government under Urrutia and Miró-Cardona.

This theory misinterprets and over-simplifies the facts.

From the first day after Batista's fall Castro was in complete control. The official government was only recognized because it had been appointed by Castro. Less than six weeks after the revolution Castro himself became Prime Minister. The first conflicts between Castro and Urrutia did not arise from a conflict between radicalism and conservatism.

The rebel army could not play the rôle assigned to it: it was numerically very weak, it was socially and politically heterogeneous, it was not a peasant army, it lacked political training and it was no more radical than the government. Although the rebel army had been greatly inflated by latecomers—who were pushed out again shortly afterwards—its real core was formed by less than one thousand men. Such peasants as there were in Castro's guerilla army were, according to Guevara, people with petty bourgeois prejudices who were fighting to enrich themselves and to get land of their own. Many of the rebels, while radical, were at the same time strongly anti-communist—as was shown by the Matos crisis and the numerous purges which became necessary.

If there were elements of double rule they arose from the double rôle played by Castro himself: behind the back of the official hierarchy, with selected rebel officers who were almost all intellectuals, he set up an organization, INRA, in which the communists soon managed to get a foothold.

The growing rôle of the Communists was due to the radicalization of the revolution and the fact that they alone possessed a disciplined organization.

There were various factors which made the socialist transformation in Cuba easier and others which made it more difficult than in other countries where Marxist-Leninist revolutions have taken place.

The favourable factors included the objective need for planning; sound, rapid development was impossible while there was a relatively free market economy. Secondly, Cuba was more developed than other countries which had had Marxist-Leninist revolutions. Its economy was intact and its potential unexploited. Thirdly, the majority of the agricultural population consisted of proletarians working in large enterprises. There was, therefore, little opposition to collectivization. Finally, Cuba was not isolated and could count on economic and political help from the Eastern bloc.

Against this there were several unfavourable factors. Because of its size, its lack of fuel and raw materials, and its concentration on sugar and tobacco, Cuba was very much tied to the world market and was much less capable of autarchy than the other countries had been at the beginning of their revolutions. Cuba was integrated into the Western world and had particularly close ties with the United States. This dependence was not artificial but arose from geographical proximity and economic convenience. The countries of the Eastern bloc, on the other hand, are far away, do not need Cuba's sugar, and have been unable to supply many of the goods which she requires (particularly spare parts for machinery) so that Cuba has been forced to make costly technological adjustments. The Eastern countries have paid less than the North Americans for Cuban sugar; only twenty per cent in convertible currency and the rest in goods, aid, and so on, the value of which they fix themselves. It is doubtful how long they will be willing and able to commit themselves to the extent demanded by the industrialization of the island, and it was still more doubtful whether they will be prepared to maintain a standard of living in Cuba above that of some of their own countries.

The character of the Cuban people, their inclination towards individualism and materialism, the absence of a collectivist tradition in agriculture, the fact that some of them were accustomed to a certain standard of comfort which the lower classes also longed for, the anti-revolutionary, trade unionist attitude of the workers, all this has made the change to socialism more difficult and was bound to cause problems as soon as sacrifices were required.[1]

In those developed countries where all the objective conditions for socialism exist, Marx's prognoses have not come true: capitalism has not collapsed, the forces of production continue to develop without a proletarian revolution, and the workers have not become poorer. Those countries in which the mass of workers and employees have become 'reformist' lack the subjective conditions for revolution. Revolutionary, socialist changes are apparently *no longer* on their agenda.

In the underdeveloped countries the masses are often revolutionary, although the objective conditions for socialism are lacking: here socialism is *not yet* possible, or rather can only be established if it is dictated from above in a totalitarian form.

Cuba stood somewhere between the entirely underdeveloped and the fully developed countries and that position created special difficulties for the revolutionary socialists because on the one hand the country was not yet ready for socialism, while on the other hand there was no revolutionary attitude among the proletariat.

There certainly was—to use Marxist terminology—a conflict

---

[1] In an interview with Leo Huberman in April 1961, Guevara mentioned 'the unwillingness of certain sections of the population to make sacrifices' as one of the main problems of the revolution. *Monthly Review*, New York, September, 1961.

between the development of the 'forces of production' and the 'conditions of production' in pre-revolutionary Cuba. But the conditions of production (that is the social and political institutions) did not represent a complete barrier to all progress, but only obstacles which delayed and made it more difficult. However, these barriers were not the product of overdeveloped capitalism but of a mixture of pre-capitalist, capitalist and 'post-capitalist' factors: the economically irrational attitudes of large sections of the population (including the members of the upper classes who had not yet acquired a 'capitalist spirit'), the free play of world market forces (including the phenomenon of 'economic imperialism'), and premature welfare state measures which strengthened the irrational attitude of the lower classes.

In this situation socialism could not be achieved by democratic means and it was doubtful whether its realization by totalitarian methods could lead to rapid and durable progress.

The objective difficulties of the socialist transformation were magnified by the humanist policy of the first phase. The two main characteristics of this policy were its emphasis on an immediate rise in the standard of living of the lower classes[1] and the chaotic manner in which it was carried out, regardless of cost. The first characteristic destroyed investment and the second produced waste. What capital there was, was distributed, unproductive values were created, and the immediate future of the masses was sacrificed to the present.

Humanism developed in a situation in which there were no organized cadres, too few specialists, and no machinery to carry out a rational economic policy. While the enthusiasm of the masses was kept alive, the leadership was able to maintain itself without an apparatus. 'Humanism' therefore corresponded to political reason but was contrary to economic reason. By increasing hopes and expectations and at the same time making their future satisfaction impossible it produced growing discontent and thus contributed to its replacement by totalitarianism.

As late as the spring of 1961 Guevara had thought that every revolution had some Stalinist characteristics, but that in Cuba these could be reduced to a minimum because industrialization imposed no sacrifices on the Cuban people and would bring immediate advantages, and because the collectivist agrarian revolution did not conflict with the desires of the Cuban rural population.[2]

This prognosis soon proved to be inaccurate and the revolution inevitably developed further in a totalitarian direction. Every step towards the realization of this socialism imposed from above ran

[1] 'The underdeveloped countries today are bent upon creating initial welfare directly out of poverty. To them ... development means primarily rising standards of living for the masses. This cannot, of course, be done.' Gunnar Myrdal, *An International Economy*, 1956, p. 163.
[2] Interview with K. S. Karol, *L'Express*, Paris, May 18, 1961.

counter to the spontaneous tendencies of the country and the wishes of an ever-increasing proportion of the population. The changes desired by the revolutionary leaders might be sensible and progressive, but they conflicted with the desires and modes of behaviour of most Cubans. In Cuba as elsewhere the road to socialism thus proved irreconcilable with an open society and representative democracy.

In spite of its utter dependence on the Soviet bloc, Cuba did not become a satellite but a new centre speaking a new kind of Marxist-Leninist dialectic in the polycentric world of post-Stalinist communism. Hence its attraction for other Latin American countries in search of a future.

Castro promised bread and freedom: he brought austerity and totalitarianism. He spoke of the dictatorship of the workers; but the workers lost their privileges, including that of doing less work. But this may be an inevitable, transitional stage on the way to better things. The historian should not let the present difficulties of the Cuban revolution blind him to its future prospects.

Cuba was one of the few Latin American countries where further progress could have been achieved by means of a free struggle within the framework of representative democracy. Castro decided to achieve it by dictatorial means, to impose it on a reluctant reality. But important and progressive changes have been introduced, although frequently in an irrational and unjust way.

The old parasitical and corrupt state apparatus has been destroyed, together with much of the moral corruption of the underlying society. Capital can no longer be spent on luxuries or conspicuous consumption by a minority, an attempt has been made to use land and labour which were under-used. Greater social mobility and justice are being achieved and the former underprivileged classes can now rise to the top. The spirit of *dolce far niente*, the lottery mentality, has been replaced by an indoctrinated nationalism, an enthusiasm, which will act as the motor of progress and make sacrifices bearable. But, at the same time, new problems and difficulties have arisen. Instead of the old state apparatus a new one has been constituted, in many ways as oppressive as the old, not only larger but more wasteful in the use of resources and inefficient in the direction of the country, and out of which a new ruling class could very well arise. Unemployment has been hidden rather than abolished, land is still used inefficiently, agriculture is in the midst of a crisis and industrialization has not even begun in earnest. It may be considered progressive that workers are forced to work hard and forgo many of the old customs and much of the welfare-state measures and benefits. But this makes essential a degree of control and constraint which is certainly as far from the idea of freedom as Cuba is from the promised abundance of bread.

The picture is full of contradictions. The whole experiment may fail, but many of the radical changes made can hardly be undone or could be undone only by a foreign invasion and the imposition of a new and probably reactionary dictatorship. Unless, of course, the Cuban masses rise; but this is not a likely prospect.

PART IV

THE STRUGGLE FOR LATIN AMERICA

1. The Impact of Castro

'It is not poverty *per se* that leads to revolt; poverty often induces fatalism and despair, and a reliance, embodied in ritual and superstitious practices, on supernatural help. Social tensions are an expression of unfulfilled expectations. It is only when expectations are aroused that radicalism can take hold. Radical strength is greatest ... in societies where awareness of class differences runs deep, expectations of social advancement outstrip possibilities, and the establishments of culture fail to make room for aspiring intellectuals.'
(Daniel Bell, *The End of Ideology*)

For hundreds of years Latin America has been ruled by oligarchies, there has been corruption and oppression and the masses have lived in dire poverty. The poor simply accepted this as a fact. They rebelled rarely, or not at all: people do not become revolutionaries until they feel miserable, until they are *aware* of being cheated of possible well-being. They do not come into political movements until old forms of life and traditional social controls begin to crumble and new contradictions, together with new expectations, arise.

It is a trite but incontestable truth that in Latin America, as elsewhere, this change began to happen under the impact of capitalism and its industrial revolution. As sketched above, these changes came late and are occurring in conditions which are so different from those prevailing in Western Europe more than a century ago, that it is a rather dangerous simplification to write, as a North American author does:

'There is nothing novel about the Latin American phase of capitalism. It is almost precisely the phase through which Europe passed a century ago—and it produces almost precisely the same political results.'[1]

The author seems aware of the fact that this statement is an oversimplification, as elsewhere he writes, 'Social change, in the context of Latin America, involves the possibility, perhaps the probability, that new governments will be established by revolution ... They may change its social system. We must anticipate that, in some countries, social systems will arise or will be imposed wholly different from those to which we are accustomed.'[2]

But the simplification still contains some truth. There are many economic and social phenomena in present-day Latin America which occurred more than a century ago in countries we today consider to be highly developed: the crisis of old forms of life; the coexistence of progressive and backward and of rich and poor in the same society;

[1] A. A. Berle, *Latin America—Diplomacy and Reality*, New York, 1962, p. 36.
[2] *idem*, p. 22.

the increase of income inequalities; urbanization with its slums; the emergence of a huge 'reserve army' of potential proletarians and a relative, and maybe even absolute, pauperization of the masses.

In at least one country of Latin America, Argentina, the beginnings of industrialization go back to the first two decades of the present century. But progress remained extremely modest,[1] soon lost most of its impetus, and did not spread to other countries. The industrialization of Latin America can better be dated from that fateful decade, the 1930s, when under the impact of the world crisis, a new era in the history of the subcontinent began.[2] The first years of this decade were filled by a wave of revolutionary occurrences. In Argentina, the overthrow of the radical government by a military *coup d'état* which inaugurated the period ending in Peronism. In Brazil, the emergence of Vargas and the abortive *Paulista* revolution of 1932. The Chaco War out of which grew the future Bolivian revolution; the anti-Machado revolution in Cuba; and political turmoil including the proclamation of a short-lived socialist republic in Chile. Even Uruguay passed through a period of dictatorship, while in Mexico the revolution reached its peak under Cárdenas.

But the revolutionary wave ebbed, only to reappear with greater force a quarter of a century later. There are several causes which together explain this: an improvement in the economic situation and a degree of industrialization which, though still modest, seemed to show that progress could be made; a certain democratization of political life and the rise of new radical-democratic parties, as well as paternalistic groups and governments, which introduced welfare-state measures, especially for the benefit of the urban population; the Good Neighbour policy inaugurated by Franklin D. Roosevelt, and the international tensions which forced a popular front tactic on the communists, who became the paladins of democracy and, especially from 1941 to 1945, outspoken champions of a Latin American *rapprochement* with the great democracies, including the USA.

The third and biggest wave of Latin American industrialization began in the 1940s, but coincided with an increase in population which, for the first time, reached the dimensions of a demographic explosion.[3] It was accompanied by an urbanization far beyond the

[1] The *per capita* social product had grown, between 1900 and 1930 only by 1·2 per cent per year, Naciones Unidas, CEPAL, *El Desarrollo económico de la Argentina*, Mexico, 1959, p. 3.
[2] T. W. Palmer, *Search for a Latin American Policy*, Gainesville, 1947, thinks that it was around 1930 that Latin Americans awoke to their 'underdevelopment' and the urgent necessity of overcoming it. For the change in ideology which was occurring between the first and the second World Wars, see A. O. Hirschman, 'Ideologies of Economic Development in Latin America', in *Latin American Issues*, New York, 1961.
[3] The effect of the high birth rate and precipitous fall in the death rate has been noted since 1940 and particularly in the 1950's. UN/ECLA, *The Economic Development of Latin America in the Post War World*, E/CN 12/659, April 7, 1964, Vol. 1, p. 140.

possibilities of real economic growth; by the rapid expansion of the media of communication—especially radio and later TV, which presented the effect of 'demonstration' to the masses; by the fall in Latin American export prices from about 1955 on, and the considerable slowing down of economic progress;[1] finally, the cold war by then was in full swing and the East wind filled the sails of growing discontents.

The contradictions arising out of modern capitalism had, during the European industrial revolution, led to sharpened social and political struggles, to the appearance of radical democratic and revolutionary movements and to the birth of Marxism. There is nothing astonishing in the fact that in Latin America similar contradictions led to similar movements and ideologies. Indeed, Marxism is, as a contemporary author puts it,[2] 'the natural ideology of underdeveloped societies in today's world'.

Revolutionary intellectuals in these countries were eager for an ideology which would give them a sense of direction and a set of beliefs; and a simplified Marxism suited them very well. It combined a harsh condemnation of the unsettling effects of capitalism with a positive evaluation of science, modernity and technology; it protested against the alienation of man and provided a rational, 'scientific' basis for chiliastic hopes for a near and 'inevitably' better future. It laid the blame for all miseries on oligarchs, capitalists and imperialists, and allowed a fusion of nationalism with anti-capitalism. So, Marxism could easily become a tremendously powerful weapon in the hands of those 'terrible simplifiers' whose coming Jacob Burkhardt had foreseen.

Given the Latin American reality, there was nothing surprising about the appearance and growth of communist parties. What requires explanation is rather their comparative weakness and unimportance, at least up to the coming of Castro and his acceptance of Marxist-Leninism.

The communist parties of Latin America[3] are by no means recent creations. Most of them began to function in the 1920s and at least one, the Argentinian, is proud of having participated in the founding of the Communist International in 1919. But their importance had

[1] 'There were signs of a downward trend in the rate of development which began to spread from 1955, and by the end of the 'fifties had led to a stagnation in many Latin American countries and in some to a reduction of the absolute levels of real per capita income.' ECLA, *op. cit.*, p. 1. Between 1945–1960 the annual growth of the domestic product was about 5·8 per cent yearly, from 1956 to 1960 only about 4 per cent; and per capita income was growing only at a rate of less than 1·1 per cent yearly.
[2] A. B. Ulam, *The Unfinished Revolution*, New York, 1960, p. 285.
[3] The best comprehensive account of the development of the Latin American communist parties up to 1955 is found in R. J. Alexander, *Communism in Latin America*, New Brunswick, N.J., 1957. For a less objective account of the internal affairs of Latin American Communism, see Eudocio Ravines, *The Yenan Way*, New York, 1951.

never been great. It increased only during the popular front period when the communists ceased to present themselves as radical social revolutionaries and appeared under the banner of democracy. It was during these years, after 1936, that some Communists became cabinet ministers (in Cuba and Chile), and Vicente Lombardo Toledano, the head of the communist-dominated Latin American Trade Union Centre, was fêted by some Latin American governments and appeared occasionally on the same platform as one of the Presidents of the Republics. Even where they were legal, the communists rarely got more than 10 per cent of the popular vote in elections.[1] Their influence in the weak Trade Union movements proved to be small; the same was true of their influence among the students. The total number of organized communists in the whole of Latin America was estimated as being 240,000 in 1958. The strongest party was in Argentina, with some 80,000 members, followed by Brazil and Venezuela with about 40,000 each, Chile with 30,000 and Cuba with 17,000. None of the other parties had as many as 10,000 members.[2]

There are several reasons for the weakness of the communists. Their party structure, politics, way of talking and propaganda run counter to the mood and feeling of Latin American radicals, who are nationalists, express themselves in florid, highly emotional Latin American phraseology, and stand for independence from all foreign powers. The communists are internationalists, they are closely tied to the Soviet Union and speak in badly translated 'Russian'. The young Latin American intellectuals are full of voluntarism and uncompromising radicalism; the communists are guided by a rationalistic theory and by opportunistic considerations. The Latin Americans are individualists, 'personalists', while the Communists have tried to impose on them an impersonal discipline.

The Communists had little contact with the rural population and in the cities and towns they came up against many difficulties. The more or less skilled workers, who enjoyed better working conditions than the majority of the population tended towards what the communists call '*trade-unionism*' and '*economism*', i.e. a preference to struggle for immediate gains rather than to engage in revolutionary action. For the rest there were only impoverished artisans deeply influenced by anarchism and finally a rootless mass which bore a greater resemblance to a *lumpenproletariat* than to an industrial working class, a mass which was easily corruptible but difficult to discipline and to organize. The many changes in the Communist

[1] The highest percentage was in Chile, in 1947, with 16·5 per cent; but in 1961 they only got 11·8 per cent.
[2] Statement by General Cabell (of the CIA): in *Communist Threat to the US through the Caribbean*. Hearings before the Subcommittee to Investigate the Administration of the Internal Security Act of the Committee of the Judiciary. US Senate, 86th Congress, 1st Session, November 5, 1959.

Party's general 'line', which were never the result of internal Latin American events but always of Soviet decisions, did not help to increase the popularity of the communists. During the ultra-left period (1929–1935) they directed their main attacks against the other left-wing groups. They had more success during the popular front period, especially during the Second World War, but they could not avoid antagonizing many workers with their opportunistic policies. To give one example: when they opposed a big strike movement of the Uruguayan meat packers in 1943, because this strike endangered the meat supply to Great Britain, they compromised themselves in the eyes of many radicals by being prepared to support any government, however reactionary, provided it was against Hitler.

Two other factors should also be mentioned to explain the weakness of communist influence: first, the Communist International, up to the cold war epoch, considered Latin America as an area of secondary importance, giving it much less attention than Asia or Europe and the Soviet Union did not yet consider its main enemy the USA. Secondly, the developments in the Soviet Union under Stalin had not been such as to arouse great enthusiasm among the Ibero-American intellectuals, there were as yet no sputniks, the achievements of industrialization appeared doubtful and the unpleasant phenomena of the Stalinist terror were not completely unheard of.

No wonder that revolutionary hopes were pinned, not on the communists, but on the new, autochthonous Latin American parties and movements which were radical-democratic, nationalist, anti-imperialist and vaguely anti-capitalist. Some people call them *Aprista* parties (although they were never very strongly influenced by the ideology peculiar to Haya de la Torre)—some prefer the general term 'populist'. The Peruvian APRA, the *Acción Democratica* of Venezuela, the *Auténticos* and later the *Ortodoxos* in Cuba, José Figueres' *Liberación Nacional* in Costa Rica, the so-called *Febreristas* in Paraguay, the left wing of the Colombian *Liberales* and the Bolivian MNR were all parties of this kind. In Mexico the revolution was pushed forward by Cárdenas and became institutionalized in a state party, which finally took the name of PRI (Partido Revolucionario Institucional). In Argentina, Perón's *Justicialismo* and in Brazil Vargas' paternalism provided hope for the under-privileged and could count on their sympathy and their allegiance. In some countries there existed small, but frequently not unimportant, socialist parties.

All these populist parties and movements played a leading rôle in the upheavals and social changes which occurred after 1930, while the communists played a very minor part and were frequently in opposition to them. In Chile they opposed the 'socialist republic' of 1932 and were constantly squabbling with the socialists. These quarrels did not cease during the period of the Popular Front, which ended in 1946 in an alliance of the communists with the Radical Party, without Socialist participation. For a short while communists became Cabinet Ministers, but could easily be disposed of by their Radical allies. As a Soviet author says: 'the lasting hostility against the socialist party contributed to the isolation of the Communist Party of Chile and deprived it of the support of important proletarian forces.'[1]

In Cuba the communists played a dubious rôle during the struggle against Machado when they attacked the revolutionary government of Grau, and in alliance with Batista, opposed the *Auténticos* in 1944. In Mexico they played no part in the social achievements of Cárdenas, whom they had harshly criticized at the beginning of his administration. In 1945, when Betancourt came to power in Venezuela, the communists were in opposition to him. In Peru they remained sharply opposed to the APRA. In Colombia the radical-democratic tendencies found their main representative in Jorge Eliezer Gaitán, whom the communists opposed. During the presidential elections of 1946 they backed one of his opponents and denounced Gaitán as a fascist. In 1948 Figueres led a successful revolution against a communist-backed régime in Costa Rica. They opposed Perón in Argentina, the MNR in Bolivia and Vargas in Brazil.

But the activity and achievements of the populist parties were such as to lead to new disappointments. It seemed as though the Mexican revolution had ended by giving opportunities to capitalists without alleviating the misery of the poor. The Cuban *Auténticos* proved to be corrupt and unable to oppose Batista's *coup d'état*. Perón's adventure collapsed and, once outside Argentina, he lost most of his prestige and followers. In 1948 the *Acción Democratica* was driven from power without much resistance. The Colombian liberals were unable to prevent the establishment of the conservative dictatorship of Laureano Gómez or the military dictatorship of Rojas Pinilla. The APRA had not been able to win power in Peru and was damaging its prestige by compromising with the ruling oligarchy and toning down its anti-imperialism. The Bolivian revolution seemed to have failed. New disappointments followed the overthrow of Rojas Pinilla and of Perez Jiménez, followed by the reintroduction of a 'democracy' which held out little hope of improvements. Anti-*Yanqui*-ism had become stronger after the overthrow of Jacobo Arbenz in Guatemala, but the Communists had to suffer a new loss of prestige because of the suppression of the Hungarian Revolution in 1956. The economic and social tensions were growing, so too were the revolutionary pressures, but it seemed as if all revolutionary

[1] N. W. Myatchin, *Borba Kommunistischeskoy partii Chili in Borba sa edinyi rabotschii i antiimperialistitscheskii front w stranach Latinskoy Ameriki*, Moskva, 1963, p. 144.

THE IMPACT OF CASTRO

movements had failed. Then Castro arrived, and a new era began.

The Castro revolution was an autochtonous product of the Continent. It had not been imported from outside. Here, and here alone, was a Latin American David who dared to defy the northern Goliath. The enthusiasm which he had aroused in his own people spread to other Latin American countries.

The Chilean Socialist leader and former presidential candidate, Senator Allende, wrote in 1960: 'Cuba's fate resembles that of all Latin American countries. They are all underdeveloped—producers of raw materials and importers of industrial products. In all these countries imperialism has deformed the economy, made big profits and established its political influence. The Cuban revolution is a national revolution, but it is also a revolution of the whole of Latin America. It has shown the way for the liberation of all our peoples.'[1]

The Mexican intellectual, Noyola, who had worked in Cuba with Boti, made a speech at Mexico University on January 4, 1961, which was warmly welcomed by the economic journal *Trimestro Económico*.[2] 'The Cuban revolution,' he said, 'is the common heritage of all Latin American nations. At the present moment it is our most valuable heritage.'

In the towns there was universal enthusiasm: it spread from the intellectuals to the workers and employees. The new gospel soon penetrated to the most distant parts: 'At peasant meetings in the Andes, a new shout: "A la Cubana" (the Cuban way) is heard echoing through the chill mountain night'.[3] Doubts began to arise, it is true, even before the proclamation of the socialist and Marxist-Leninist character of the Cuban revolution; but they were quickly suppressed.

There were executions and mass arrests; but was not this terror less cruel than that of preceding revolutions? Were not its victims former torturers, former exploiters, and counter-revolutionary saboteurs? Did not the mass of the Cuban people approve of the terror?

There was no rule of law, no freedom of the press; but had not the laws been used by the oligarchy to exploit the people, had not the press been a venal tool of the rich?

There were no elections; but had not past elections been squabbles between political thieves over the division of spoils? Had not the right to vote—even on the occasions when elections had been free and fair—meant only that people could choose every few years which politicians should rob them? Was it not a fact that most Cubans were unwilling to be diverted from more important matters by unnecessary electoral campaigns?

[1] Preface to J. Tabares del Real, *La revolución Cubana*, Havana, 1960.
[2] *Trimestre Económico*, Mexico, 1961, July/September, 1961.
[3] *Time*, June 16, 1961.

There seemed to be less and less individual freedom, but, it was argued, freedom for most people had meant the right to starve. Other apologists went further: 'What did you do in your industrialized countries in the nineteenth century while you were industrializing and setting up a capitalist economy?' students asked a Western writer. 'Did you really respect human beings when you sent children down the mines and forced workers to work twelve or fourteen hours a day and forbade them to form trade unions?...'[1]

These words raised the question whether rapid modernization could be combined with the preservation of individual freedom or whether the latter ought not to be curtailed in the interest of the former.

All doubts were cast aside and the Cuban revolution became the hope of the underprivileged and the banner of the dissatisfied, the frustrated, the anti-imperialists and the radicals. Latin American delegations were received and entertained in Cuba, Cuban delegations went to all countries of the subcontinent. The Cuban government began to increase its propaganda. It set up its own press agency, the *Prensa Latina*, gave moral and financial support to pro-Cuban movements and organizations, produced radio programmes and made the Cuban embassies into centres of revolutionary activity.

In Mexico, it seemed that the stationary revolution might begin to move again:

'Under President Miguel Alemán, Mexico was patiently transformed into a country after the US image, in which businessmen and the profit motive became dominant forces. At the same time, in a rather empty gesture of respect for the revolutionary traditions of Mexico, politicians continued to talk as though they were carrying on a permanent revolution. This make-believe was suddenly shaken by the hard reality of the Cuban revolution. Mexican politicians were confronted with the simple question: "Did they believe in revolutions or didn't they?"'[2]

Members of parliament, artists, students and workers demonstrated their sympathy for Cuba, and a pro-Castro movement with its own organ, the journal *Politica*—which was apparently financed by Cuba—grew up round ex-President Cárdenas. In 1961 these activities culminated in the foundation of the *Movimiento de Liberación Nacional*. In March of that year a big international Congress for National Sovereignty and Peace assembled in Mexico. It was attended by delegations from many countries and much attention was devoted to the Cuban revolution. (The Chinese delegate, particularly, stressed the central importance of this revolution, whereas

[1] Raymond Scheyven, *De Punta del Este à la Havane*, Brussels, 1961, p. 52.
[2] *Hispanic American Report*, Stanford University, Vol. XII, No. 8, August, 1960.

the Russian delegation confined itself to general expressions of sympathy).

President López Mateos found it necessary to emphasize that he was 'on the extreme left inside the Constitution'. His government became one of Castro's most energetic protectors and introduced revolutionary measures of its own. Foreign companies, for example the electricity company, were nationalized, and the government pushed ahead with the distribution of land: in the first three years of Lopez Mateos' Presidency, 16·8 million acres were confiscated and given to peasants. This was about 5·7 million a year, as compared with an average of about 1·48 million a year for the period 1948–1958.

In Venezuela, Castro's influence strengthened the opposition against Betancourt's reformist, anti-revolutionary government. In the summer of 1960, after Betancourt turned against Castro, his foreign minister, a member of the URS, had refused to sign the declaration of San José and had to be replaced. The *Acción Democratica* split, a large number of Castro-sympathizers were expelled and, together with others who had left the party in April, formed a new organization, the Movement of the Revolutionary Left (MIR) which was to become the main spearhead of Castroist influence and the organizer of terrorism and guerilla warfare. The leader of the URD, Jovito Villalba, protested against the signing of the San José Declaration which he denounced as an imperialist manoeuvre directed against the sovereignty of Latin American nations. Two ministers belonging to his party left the government and in November 1960 the coalition was ended. From now on, the URD found itself in a common front with MIR and the Communists. Violent street demonstrations, terrorist acts and clashes between revolutionaries and government forces became common.

It was of little use to Betancourt that he seemed to have the support of the peasantry, as was shown by a mass demonstration in September 1960. In the towns the left appeared to predominate, while the extreme right attacked Betancourt as a revolutionary and supported disaffected groups in the army. In a period of serious economic difficulties the President thus found himself between two lines of fire. Time and again he found it necessary to declare a state of emergency and suspend the constitution.

In Brazil, the fast-growing peasants' leagues in the north-east expressed enthusiastic sympathy for Cuba. Castro's picture hung in their central office above the head of their leader, the socialist deputy Francisco Julião. Most students, many trade union leaders, and members of parliament of different parties came out in support of Cuba. The anti-*Yanqui* mood grew. The new President, Quadros, who had visited Cuba as presidential candidate in order to increase his prestige, took a firm stand against all anti-Cuban suggestions by the Americans. His action in conferring the highest Brazilian decoration on Guevara contributed to the crisis which led to his resignation. Civil war threatened and the army was divided. A compromise was found which enabled Vice-President Goulart to become Quadros' successor. Goulart had more than once firmly expressed his sympathies for Castro. His brother-in-law, Brizzola, governor of Rio Grande do Sul, formed a 'National Liberation front' with Julião and others, which, supported by the semi-legal communists, many union leaders, politicians of the Workers' Party (Goulart's own party) and many intellectuals, seemed to be developing into the bastion of Castroism.

Of particular importance were the changes which occurred inside the Brazilian trade union movement. It had previously been dominated by government appointed and controlled leaders who were closely linked with ORIT (Inter-American Regional Organization of Workers) to which the most important Brazilian trade union confederations belonged, and which was strongly influenced by its most important member, the AFL-CIO of the USA. Under Quadros and Goulart changes took place which became apparent at the Workers Congress in August 1960. The old leaders were expelled and a left group composed of *Trabalhistas*, socialists and communists took charge. The most important trade union organizations, especially the Confederation of Industrial Workers (CNTI) became standard-bearers of anti-imperialism, pro-communism and Castroism.

In Argentina the aged Socialist leader, Palacios, was elected a senator for the first time, primarily because he had supported the Cuban revolution. When in summer 1961, he changed his mind there was a split in the Socialist party in which the pro-Castro wing retained the majority. President Frondizi's brother formed a pro-Castro 'revolutionary left'. A united front of Castroists, Peronists, communists and left-wing Socialists began to develop, and in July 1960 the bourgeois, anti-Castro *Unión Civica Radical del Pueblo* made public its view that Castroism was having a favourable effect on the Latin American policy of the United States. In this situation President Frondizi had no choice but to adopt a policy of benevolent neutrality in the quarrel between the United States and Castro. In spite of increasing pressure from the right, particularly the army, he refused to take any action against revolutionary Cuba.

In Uruguay the Castroists controlled the university and managed to gain a foothold in the unions. Their influence was particularly strong in the large party of the *Colorados*, which was in the government and managed to frustrate the anti-Castro intentions of their *Blanco* colleagues. In July 1960 the congress of Socialist and Popular Parties of Latin America, which took place in Uruguay, had expressed itself in favour of protecting the Cuban revolution. In 1961 when

THE IMPACT OF CASTRO

anti-Castro feeling increased there were demonstrations and bloody clashes in Montevideo.

In Chile Castro became a symbol for the entire left in its struggle against President Alessandri's stabilization programme. Until late 1960 the important Christian Democratic Party also viewed Fidelism sympathetically. The most important trade union organization, CUTCH, controlled by communists and socialists and led at the time by an ardent Castroist, Clotario Blest, became the champion of the Cuban revolution. Pressure from below was so great that the government—consisting of conservatives, liberals and radicals—which normally pursued a right-wing policy, opposed the anti-Castro policy of the United States.

In Bolivia the Cuban revolution aroused enthusiasm among the masses and sympathy among the government. In July 1960 the powerful trade union organization, COB, which monopolized the workers and peasant movement, sent a telegram to the United Nations protesting against the threat to Cuba and saying that Latin America would not permit a repetition of the Guatemalan affair. The Communists represented only a small minority, and Bolivia was dependent on economic assistance from the United States, but both houses of parliament adopted almost unanimous resolutions in the summer of 1960 urging the government to protect the Cuban revolution.

In Peru, the Castroists were able to entice a section of the APRA away from Haya de la Torre. An APRA *rebelde* was founded which later changed its name to MIR (Movement of the Revolutionary Left). They won the support of the majority of the students at San Marcosa University which up till then had been a bulwark of APRISM. Together with the communists they infiltrated into the Popular Action Party of Belaunde Terry, the future president, and could count on the active sympathy not only of the tiny socialist party but also of two new movements: the *National Liberation Front* of General Cesar Pando, a known fellow-traveller, and the *Social Progressive Movement*, presided over by Alberto Ruiz, yet another pro-communist who was to run for President. While the communists were able to establish their control over some sections of the trade union movement, peasant-leagues arose in distant parts of the country and at their rallies there were shouts of 'Viva Castro!' All these movements were united against the APRA, now accused of being pro-*Yanqui* and in collusion with the oligarchy. Because the army regarded APRA as its traditional enemy, leftist, including Castroist and pro-communist ideas, influenced a part of the officer corps, which up to then had always been considered a prop of the ruling classes.[1]

[1] After the army *coup d'etat* in 1962, the story was told of how the generals of the Junta explained to the representatives of the ruling oligarchy that they should be thankful to them for having rebelled because if they had not done so,

In Ecuador on the other hand Fidelism managed to make capital out of the fact that a Latin American mediation commission (with the blessing of the United States) had decided in favour of Peru in a frontier dispute. President Velasco Ibarra made anti-imperialist speeches and strongly opposed any intervention in Cuban affairs. But for many people he did not go far enough. Among his left-wing critics were Vice-President Arosemena and the Minister of the Interior, Araujo Hidalgo, who left the government to become one of the leaders of Fidelism in Ecuador. When Vice President Arosemena returned from his visit to Russia in the summer of 1961 the masses welcomed him with shouts of *'Cuba si! Yanqui no!'* and 'long live Castro'. In the autumn of 1961, a political crisis took place and there were strikes and street fighting; the armed forces split, Velasco Ibarra fled and Arosemena took his place. The causes of the upheaval were mainly domestic but the problem of their attitude towards the Cuban revolution played a part in Ecuador, just as it did in Brazil.

In Colombia the Castroists exploited the conflict within the Liberal Party. The pact between the Liberals and the Conservatives, which had led to the fall of Rojas Pinilla's dictatorship and the restoration of democracy, laid down that for the next sixteen years there would only be two parties, Liberals and Conservatives, which would hold the Presidency in turn. This arrangement prevented any other party from getting into power but resulted in bitter internecine struggles within the two legal parties. A left-wing movement developed in the Liberal Party which, although led by millionaire López Michelsen, was strongly influenced by Castroism and Communism. In addition there were other openly pro-Castro organizations, for example, the Gaitanists, and regional parties like the *Moviemiento Popular Revolucionario* in Medellin.

The situation was the same in other countries. Fidelism had become a mass movement and the more it was attacked by the United States the stronger its influence grew. The Cuban revolution became the leading opponent of imperialism, and anti-imperialism is the deepest political sentiment in Latin America. Even before Castro's victory Eudocio Ravines rightly wrote, 'One can discuss the

---

the colonels would have—and the colonels were Nasserists, while the majors were Fidelistas. Aníbal Ismoderes Cairo, 'La conducta de los militares peruanos', in *Panoramas*, Mexico, No. 2, March–April 1963. In his report on *The Peruvian Elections of 1962 and their Annullment* (American Field Services Staff, West Coast South America Series, Vol. IX, No. 6), Richard W. Patch writes that many generals, among them all the members of the Junta which took power in 1962, attended the meetings and participated in the discussions of the Peruvian Center for Advanced Military Studies. Among the civilian consultants who act as teachers in this institution are intellectuals known for their communist sympathies, although some of them are scions of oligarchic families. 'The militarists active in the Center for Advanced Military Studies are impressed by the arguments of these men who seem to be preaching a new social doctrine while springing from irreproachable families and backgrounds.'

existence or non-existence of imperialism, but what one cannot deny is the existence of a militant anti-imperialism directed against the USA which determines the policy pursued, without exception, by all Latin American countries'.[1]

In the summer of 1960 at the Conference of Foreign Ministers of the Organization of American States at San José in Costa Rica, the State Department—which is always inclined to underestimate the pressure of public opinion on Latin American governments— presented a resolution condemning Castro.

It was based on the decisions adopted as a result of the Guatemalan revolution at Carácas in 1954. In Carácas it had been laid down that 'the domination or control of the political institutions of any American State by the international communist movement, extending to this hemisphere the political system of an extra-continental power, would constitute a threat to the sovereignty and political independence of the American states, endangering the peace of America and would call for a meeting of consultation to consider the adoption of measures in accordance with existing treaties.'

The Americans regarded Castro as an agent of world communism, and Khrushchev had announced that the Soviet Union would help Cuba militarily, if need be by using its rocket power against the US.

The State Department had reason to hope that the Latin American states would condemn Castro, if only because he had abolished representative democracy, thus going contrary to the Santiago Declaration which, together with the other American republics, Cuba had signed in 1959.[2] In addition, the State Department had furnished the other American states with a memorandum which provided evidence of the growth of communism in Cuba.[3]

The US experienced a disappointment: the pro-Castro mood of the Latin American peoples as well as the deep suspicion with which Latin American governments regarded anything that could be interpreted as intervention in the affairs of a sister republic proved stronger than US pressure and antipathy to communism.

A resolution was adopted with nineteen votes in favour and none against[4] strongly condemning 'intervention or the threat of intervention' by an extra-continental power as well as all attempts by the 'Sino-Soviet powers to exploit the political, economic or social situation of American states for their own ends, and pronouncing

[1] Eudocio Ravines, *America Latina—Un Continente en Erupción*, 1959, Havana edition, 1959, p. 151.
[2] The Santiago Declaration supported the rule of law, strict division of power, free elections, individual freedom and freedom of the press and of public opinion. See: *Department of State Bulletin*, September 7, 1959.
[3] *Department of State Bulletin*, August 19, 1959.
[4] The Dominican Republic, which was also under attack and against whose dictatorship economic sanctions were taken, was not represented, and the Cuban delegation ostentatiously left the meeting.

any form of totalitarianism to be irreconcilable with the inter-American system. But at the same time the principle of non-intervention of every American state in the internal and external affairs of every other American state was restated—and neither Cuba nor Castro were referred to by name.[1] Two delegates refused to sign even this 'platonic' document and had to be replaced by their deputies, while the Mexican delegate claimed that the resolution was not aimed against Cuba.

Castro's reply to the Declaration of San José was the first Declaration of Havana which was enthusiastically received by a mass meeting of the 'Plenary Assembly of the Cuban People' on September 2 and has become the basic document of the revolution. The preamble says: 'True to the spirit of authentic, revolutionary democracy, the revolutionary government has assembled the Cuban people for a meeting at the José Martí memorial in order to reply to the decisions of the Conference of San José and to oppose aggressive manoeuvres against the revolution and the Cuban people'.

The declaration condemns the 'open and criminal intervention policy of American imperialism' which 'has repeatedly attacked' the people of Latin America in the past century. (Mention is made of the annexation of Texas, the creation of a Panamá State in order to build a canal under exclusive North American sovereignty, the occupation of Puerto Rico, the numerous landings of North American troops, the exploitation of Latin American countries and so on.) The Latin American governments which do not oppose *Yanqui* imperialism are accused of betraying their people. The declaration rejects the Monroe Doctrine as a cloak for a greedy, hypocritical imperialism, but at the same time proclaims Cuba's feelings of friendship towards 'the American *people*, the people of lynched negroes, persecuted intellectuals and workers who are forced to accept gangsters as their leaders'. Thanking the Soviet Union for its offer of help, the Declaration promises that the Cuban revolution will be defended with the aid of Russian rockets against intervention. It states that the Cuban revolution is the work of the Cuban nation itself and that it is a reply 'to the crimes and injustices of imperialism'. The Cuban people intend to establish diplomatic relations with the Chinese People's Republic at once, and proclaim that true democracy is irreconcilable 'with the rule of a financial oligarchy, discrimination against negroes, the activity of the Ku-Klux-Klan, and the persecutions to which intellectuals like Oppenheimer are exposed'.

'The National General Assembly of the Cuban people', the document continues, 'expresses the conviction that democracy does not consist only of using the right to vote—a right which almost always

[1] The complete text is found in the *Department of State Bulletin*, September 12, 1961.

THE IMPACT OF CASTRO

remains a fiction and is misused by latifundists and professional politicians—but also of the right of citizens to decide their own fate, as this meeting is doing now. Democracy will only become a reality in America when the poor (*los humildes*) are no longer condemned to . . . hunger, powerlessness and illiteracy.'

The Declaration

'condemns *latifundia*, the root of peasant misery . . . starvation wages and the exploitation of the workers . . . illiteracy . . . the lack of any measures for the care of the old . . . discrimination against negroes and Indians . . . military and political oligarchies . . . the concession of the natural wealth of our countries to foreign monopolies . . . the systematic poisoning of public opinion by a press obedient to the oligarchies . . . the exploitation of man by man, and the exploitation of underdeveloped nations by imperialist capital.'

It proclaims

'the right of the peasant to the land; of the worker to the product of his labours; of the child to education; of the sick to medical care; of the student to free education; of negroes and Indians to full human dignity; of woman to real equality with man; of the elderly to [a] secure old age; of the intellectual to participation in the struggle for a better world; of states to nationalize imperialist monopolies; of nations to full sovereignty; of the people to the transformation of garrisons into schools; the right of the workers, peasants and intellectuals to arms . . .'

This declaration, published all over Latin America, was intended to be the spark which would start the fire of South American revolutions.

The increasingly obvious authoritarian, socialist tendencies of the Castro régime—the nationalization campaign in the autumn of 1960, the drive to bring the trade unions into line, growing conflicts with the Church—were bound to reduce Castro's appeal. Opposition to him, once practically confined to the oligarchs and soldiers, spread to sections of the middle classes, and even to the workers. Some trade unionists who had originally been pro-Castro began to take a stand against him.

At the beginning of 1961 only the first signs of such a change could be discerned. While Fidelism still looked different from communism, while it was possible to assume that the mass of the Cuban population enjoyed a higher standard of living than before, Castro's popularity remained more or less intact.

The abortive invasion of April 1961 gave Castroism a new impetus throughout Latin America. The critical voices became weaker and anti-imperialism increased. A French author rightly remarked that this 72-hour adventure did more for the success of communist propaganda in Latin America than hundreds of propagandists in months of work.[1] A wave of protest meetings swept the whole continent. There were mass demonstrations in Carácas and Bogotá, in La Paz and Lima, in Santiago, Recife, Rio de Janeiro, São Paulo, Montevideo, Buenos Aires, Mexico and even Guatemala.

Months passed before Fidelism began to wane again. It became clearer that Castro's socialism was identical with communism. The rapid socialization of the economy, the showdown with the Church, the proclamation of the need for a single monopolist party of which the communists would form the core, and the increasing economic difficulties contributed to this. The majority of the Christian-Democrats and of other leftist movements began to turn against Cuba; the alliance between Peronistas and Castristas in Argentina passed through a crisis. Some leading socialists made known their disenchantment with the Cuban revolution, as for instance, Palacios and Arévalo. Anti-Castroism began to grow among the students, as was shown by the preponderance of the anti-Fidelistas at a Latin American Student Congress in Brazil in October 1961. Castro's open espousal of Marxist-Leninism in December 1961 caused consternation and a certain disorientation on the left.

The decline of Castroism even towards the end of 1961 should not be exaggerated. The economic crisis in Latin America was becoming, if anything, more acute. Cuba's difficulties could very well be explained by 'imperialist' activities. If the Cubans living conditions were much worse than expected, they still lived better than tens of millions of their Latin American brethren. Besides, except for devout Christians, there seemed to be no valid ideological alternative to Castroism. Most socialist and radical movements had enthusiastically accepted Fidelism as an alternative both to ineffectual, bourgeois democracy and to old-line communism—and they would cling to it. Anti-Americanism remained stronger than anti-communism.

But many Latin American governments felt that they could safely break relations with Cuba. Peru, followed by Colombia, pressed, with the approval of the United States, for another conference of the OAS and for some sanctions against Cuba. The Alliance for Progress had been proclaimed and seemed to provide a favourable background for a sharper anti-Communist and anti-Castroist policy.

The Conference of Ministers of the Organization of American States which took place in Punta del Este in January 1962 was convened to discuss measures to be taken about a state which now officially professed Marxist-Leninism.

The proposal to call the conference was made by Colombia. But

[1] G. Friedmann, *Signal d'une troisième voie*, Paris, 1961, pp. 63/64.

behind Colombia stood the United States, whose aim was described in a leading article in the *New York Times*: 'A clear condemnation of Cuban communism with an agreement to take sanctions against the Castro régime would be a victory for the United States. A weak resolution, accompanied by a serious split of the OAS, with Brazil, Argentina, Chile and Mexico refusing to join in the denunciations and in the proposed sanctions against Cuba would be a defeat for us and a victory for Havana.'[1]

Juan de Onis, the correspondent in Uruguay of the *New York Times* wrote: 'A minimum of sixteen or seventeen votes is considered necessary to avoid the impression of disunity that would arise from a bare two-thirds majority'.[2]

The North American delegation, headed by Secretary of State, Dean Rusk, laboured unceasingly to win over the vacillating Latin American states. Congressmen in the US delegation hinted that Congress might refuse all financial aid to states adopting a neutral position.

The United States must have been disappointed by the result. The conference decided that 'Cuba has voluntarily placed itself outside the inter-American system', and that the incompatibility of Marxist-Leninism with the democratic foundations of the OAS 'excludes the present Government of Cuba from participation in the inter-American system'. But the last paragraph of the resolution merely required 'the Council of the OAS and the other organs and agencies of the inter-American system to adopt without delay the measures necessary to implement this resolution.'[3]

Cuba was therefore not really 'excluded', it had left of 'its own free will'; the measures against Cuba were not specified and no sanctions were taken. Only fourteen delegations—exactly the required two-thirds majority—voted in favour of the resolution while the representatives of six states (Argentina, Bolivia, Brazil, Chile, Ecuador and Mexico), inhabited by two-thirds of the Latin American *population*, abstained. The governments of these countries agreed with the condemnation of Marxist-Leninism but were opposed to a complete break with Cuba and claimed that the statutes of the OAS did not provide for the expulsion of an American state.

The legal arguments concealed the real motives: fear of internal unrest in their own countries and reluctance to take any step which might be interpreted as intervention in the affairs of a sister state or as giving way to *Yanqui* imperialist pressure.

The Punta del Este conference immediately contributed to an increase in political tensions. Pro-Cuban mass demonstrations occurred in many Latin American towns. There was unrest and

[1] The *New York Times*, January 22, 1962.
[2] *ibid.*, January 23, 1962.
[3] *ibid.*, February 1, 1962.

strikes, as well as increased counter-pressure from the right. Violent controversies split the Uruguayan government. The Christian Democratic party of Ecuador expelled the Foreign Minister, who had taken up a neutralist position at Punta del Este.

After the conference, 'Washington tried, not without success, to convert its partial defeat into a modest victory'.[1] Under pressure from his own army Frondizi was forced to break off diplomatic relations with Cuba. Bolivia and Ecuador were in an economic situation which made it difficult for them, in the long run, to resist United States pressure. At a meeting of the Council of the OAS in the middle of February the representatives of these three countries voted with fourteen others in favour of Cuba's expulsion.[2]

But in Havana a Conference of the Latin American Peoples was called to protest against American imperialism and its aggressive intentions. The conveners included Cárdenas from Mexico, Allende from Chile and Julião from Brazil. On February 4 the second General Assembly of the Cuban People met in Havana. Castro read a Second Declaration of Havana, which rejected as illusory any hope of solving the social crisis of the subcontinent through reforms, and without communist revolutions.

This was Castro's reply to the basic change in the Latin American policy of the United States which had found expression in Kennedy's 'Alliance for Progress'.

---

[1] *Le Monde*, Paris, February 18/19, 1962.
[2] One wonders whether the modest victory of the United States was not a Pyrrhic victory. The break-off of diplomatic, and even of economic, relations between the Latin American states and Cuba could not bring Castro to his knees. Many people regarded such measures as simply the preparation for later direct military intervention which, even if crowned by quick success, would only lead to greatly increased anti-*Yanquism* in Latin America. All this was to Castro's advantage; the North Americans would be made responsible for the hardships of the Cuban people and denounced for preparing an open attack.

2. The United States Between Monroe and Moscow

In the 1820s Tsar Alexander of Russia had granted the monopoly of trade in certain north-west regions of the North American continent to a Russo-American company. About the same time Spain, with the help of the Holy Alliance, seemed to want to reconquer its former colonies.

These encroachments drew from President Monroe his declaration of December 1823 that henceforth the American continent could no longer be regarded as an object of European colonization, and that the United States would regard any attempt by a European power to extend its system of government to the western hemisphere as a danger to its own security. Monroe explained that his government had no intention of disputing the right of European powers to their surviving colonies, but that it would regard as an act of hostility to the United States any attempt to reconquer those Latin American countries which had already achieved independence.

This unilateral statement was made in answer to an ephemeral and largely imaginary threat. Russia soon and without much difficulty expressed itself prepared to limit its demands. Spain was unable to carry out its plans if only because Britain, which controlled the seas, was opposed to them. 'There is no evidence that Monroe was in any degree aware that he was enunciating maxims which should govern *in perpetuo*, or at least for a long time to come, the foreign policy of the United States. The language of the message related to a specific situation ... it was fashioned to meet a concrete, though it turned out, an imaginary, danger.'[1]

During the 1840s the land hunger of United States settlers began to make itself felt. Territorial expansion started during which the state of Texas—which had already broken away from Mexico—was incorporated into the United States. Then after a successful war against Mexico, large areas formerly under Mexican suzerainty, were annexed. Some European powers, particularly France, were opposed to this extension of the American sphere of influence and tried to prevent it by diplomatic means. In reply the United States proclaimed that it was its 'manifest destiny' to control the whole *north* American continent. Monroe's words were brought out again and interpreted to suit the occasion. US claims to hegemony were combined with an 'isolationist' attitude towards the old world. This revised 'Monroe Doctrine' found expression, for instance, in a

[1] Dexter Perkins, *A History of the Monroe Doctrine*, Boston–Toronto, 1955, p. 68.

diplomatic note handed by the American ambassador, Horatio J. Ferry, to the Spanish government in June 1861 in which the US government demanded that European powers should refrain from any intervention in American affairs, just as they, for their part, would refrain from interfering in European affairs.[1]

The Monroe Doctrine thus became the expression of domination long before the era of modern imperialism. The hatred which it aroused in Latin America, and continues to arouse today, is shown in its interpretation by a contemporary apostle of anti-imperialism, the ex-President of Guatemala, Arévalo. In his fable of the shark and the sardines, written in typical Latin American Spanish prose, but published in the United States in an English edition in 1961, he says: 'No shark on the other side of the sea will have the right to interfere in the life of the Latin American sardines unless they accept all that I, cisatlantic shark, shall do with them.' And since France pretended not to be listening, the American shark shouted in the language of a *banlieu* [sic] '*Ici c'est moi qui commande*'.[2]

In the 1890s, after the beginning of the era of modern imperialism, the Monroe Doctrine was reinterpreted once more. It was used to justify expansion beyond the frontiers of the *north* American continent. On the occasion of a conflict between the United States and the United Kingdom over their respective spheres of influence in Venezuela the then Secretary of State, Richard Olney, said in 1895, in a note addressed to Lord Salisbury that 'the American states of the northern and the southern subcontinent, in consequence of their geographical proximity, their natural sympathies and the similarity of their constitutions are the friends and allies of the United States and also that to all intents and purposes the United States has sovereignty over the continent'. The British government energetically contested this view.[3] The same Secretary of State, Olney, emphasized that the United States had a 'vital interest' in the cause of popular self-government on the continent, and that the Monroe Doctrine could not be interpreted to mean that the United States would prevent any Latin American Republic from changing its system of government according to its own free will (Pro-Castro lawyers tried at the beginning of 1962 to use Olney's statements against the anti-Cuban policy of the United States.)[4]

The main interest of the United States was to secure control over Central America, particularly the Caribbean, an activity in which economic interests were by no means always the main motive for

[1] *ibid.*, p. 141. When in February 1962 the USA approached its European allies to persuade them to boycott Cuba, *The Times* on February 19 published an article with the ironical heading 'US Reversal of Monroe Doctrine over Cuba—Old World called on to put Pressure on Dr Castro'.
[2] J. J. Arévalo, *The Shark and the Sardines*, New York, 1961.
[3] Dexter Perkins, *op. cit.*, pp. 174-8.
[4] A. Krock, 'The Limitations of the Monroe Doctrine' in the *New York Times*, February 16, 1962.

imperialist expansion.[1] Here they came up against European competitors. In fact disputes had already occurred between west European capitalists and Latin American governments, primarily because many of the latter did not pay their debts or proved unable to protect the lives and property of foreigners. Such conflicts were bound to lead to intervention from the states whose citizens felt themselves threatened. The United States, which at the turn of the century had already established its protectorate over Cuba, annexed Puerto Rico and set up an 'independent' Panamanian republic in order to make sure of controlling the Panama Canal, could not tolerate such interference by extra-continental powers. President Theodore Roosevelt therefore announced that the United States alone must take over the rôle of policeman in Central America. This was the Roosevelt corollary to the Monroe Doctrine which inaugurated a period of constant intervention in the affairs of the states of Latin America. Diplomatic, economic and military means were used to achieve US objectives.

This policy reached its climax under President Wilson who, full of moral indignation about Latin American corruption and brutality, employed force to teach his southern neighbours democracy. The recipients of this education naturally refused to take the civilizing, educational intentions of the US at their face value. These methods were even less likely to achieve the desired results because in fact US foreign policy was obviously heavily dependent on the profit interests of American capital and was usually carried out by inexperienced lawyers whose legalistic attitude made them blind to historical forces. 'Dollar diplomacy', the open use of military force and the view firmly held by North Americans, that their form of society should serve as a universal pattern, all increased the hatred of Latin America for the *Yanquis* and their Monroe Doctrine. There were also psychological and moral factors which still operate today: 'Our conflicts with the Latin Americans', writes an American professor, 'are not only of an economic or a political, but also of a moral nature. We treat them as inferiors and can neither avoid nor disguise this fact.'[2]

---

[1] 'In many cases the intervention of American capital in Central America and the West Indies was not undertaken at the instance of American capitalists seeking outlets for their funds. It was undertaken at the direct instance of the American government, and the motive appears to have been the fear that European capital, affected by European politics, might find a foothold on this side of the Atlantic. An example may be found in the occupation of Haiti and S. Domingo. In each case American banks had purchased the control of the banks previously serving those island countries, but the documents today make it clear that the American financiers did so rather unwillingly at the direct urging of the Department of State.' A. A. Berle, *The Policy of the US in Latin America*, May 3, 1939. Department of State Press Release XX, No. 501, Publication 1328, quoted in Samuel Flagg Bemís, *The Latin American Policy of the US*, New York, 1943.

[2] Frank Tannenbaum, 'Estados Unidos y América Latina', *Cuadernos*, Paris, October 1961, No. 53.

The policy of the United States towards Latin America began to change in the thirties, under President Hoover. Then Franklin D. Roosevelt proclaimed a 'Good Neighbour' Policy. Haiti and San Domingo were evacuated and the Platt Amendment was repealed. In 1933, at the Pan-American Conference in Montevideo, the United States for the first time unequivocally proclaimed the principle of non-intervention. In 1936 an additional protocol was ratified according to which all American states regarded as inadmissible direct or indirect interference by any one of them in the internal or external affairs of any other.

A Latin American author speaks of the 'deep emotion, the profound joy with which we all welcomed the recognition of the non-intervention principle as the dawn of a new era, as the second liberation of America'.[1]

But a North American historian wrote:

'The Republic of the North was now committed to the doctrine of non-intervention in its most absolute form. It is true that *joint* intervention might still be possible, because the parties ... had declared inadmissable only intervention by any *one* [state]. There might still be differences of opinion as to what constituted intervention or as to what was meant by indirect intervention ... but any such dispute was left to eventual settlement by conciliation, arbitration or judicial settlement.'[2]

On paper at least, therefore, absolute non-intervention, the 'sacred cow' of Latin Americans, had been victorious over the Monroe Doctrine of North Americans. But this was not a victory for realism. Henceforth any state could discriminate against foreigners, nationalize their property (which hardly helped to attract foreign capital), abolish any constitutional order to enter into close contacts even with extra-continental powers, and resist any attempt by a foreign power to exert influence as 'indirect intervention'. But the shark was stronger than the sardines, and the fact still remained that the national interests of the United States did not always permit complete non-intervention. Moreover dictators could also benefit from this principle, as any action against dictatorial rule would infringe the principle of non-intervention, and this form of non-intervention would provide another opportunity for anti-imperialists to accuse the *Yanquis* of tolerating and supporting dictators.[3]

---

[1] A. Gómez Robledo, *Idea y experiencia de América*, Mexico, 1958, p. 182.
[2] S. F. Bemis, *op. cit.*, pp. 292, 293.
[3] Soon there were 'deviations' on this question. In 1945 for example, Haya de la Torre found that there could be 'good' and 'bad' intervention. 'Within the system of Inter-American relations there must be a right of democratic intervention ... Just as the home of the citizen is inviolable while no crime is committed within its walls, so a country must be regarded as sovereign while no crimes against humanity or democratic principles are committed in it.' Haya de la Torre, *Y despues de la guerra—qué?* Lima, 1946, p. 97.

The Roosevelt corollary finally collapsed in 1938 when the US government refused to support British claims against Mexico which had just nationalized the oil industry.[1]

No wonder that most Latin Americans continue to look on Roosevelt's Good Neighbour era with approval, although Roosevelt by no means always behaved as a firm opponent of dictators.[2] This almost unanimous praise is explained by the fact that at that time the communists too were in favour of close ties between Latin America and the United States.

After the second world war the loose Pan-American Union with its congresses[3] transformed itself into an autonomous regional organization of the United Nations: the Organization of American States (OAS).[4] It was based on the Inter-American Treaty of Reciprocal Assistance, concluded in 1947 in Rio de Janeiro which, officially at least, transferred from the United States to the twenty-one members of the OAS the responsibility for protecting the Western hemisphere. The preamble to this treaty contained a confirmation of the 'manifest truth' that lasting peace must be based on 'justice and moral order', on the 'recognition and the protection of the rights of freedom of man' and that it presupposes an interest in the welfare of the people and the preservation of democracy. The Latin American oligarchies and dictatorships readily paid lip-service to these noble principles.

In 1948 the Charter of the OAS was drawn up in Bogotá. Article 15 says that 'no State or group of States has the right to intervene directly or indirectly for any reason whatever in the internal or external affairs of any other state'.

This time intervention was forbidden not only by individual American states but by any group of states, and it included any action committed in the interests of democracy or human rights. However, *one* possibility for intervention was expressly left open:

[1] 'In this way the corollary of the other Roosevelt disappeared for ever which had made the United States into financial agents of the European powers.' Gómez Robledo, *op. cit.*, p. 184.
[2] In 1933 and afterwards Batista enjoyed the benevolent protection of F. D. Roosevelt. 'Roosevelt attacked European and Asian dictatorship, but the United States supported the most blood-thirsty dictatorships in Latin America.' E. Ramirez Novoa, *América Latina y Estados Unidos*, Lima, 1958, p. 10.
[3] The first Inter-American Congress which gave birth to the Pan-American Union took place in Washington in 1889/90. It was followed by International Conferences of American States in Mexico in 1901/02, Rio de Janeiro in 1906, Buenos Aires in 1910, Santiago de Chile in 1923, Havana in 1928, Montevideo in 1933 and Lima in 1938. In between there were special congresses dealing with questions of peace and war. One such conference took place in Rio de Janeiro in 1947. At the Ninth International Conference in Bogotá in 1948 the new Organization of American States was officially set up.
[4] A survey of the development of the OAS is found in the *Encyclopaedia Britannica* under 'Pan American Conferences' and also in the section on this organization prepared by North Western University for the US Senate. *US–Latin American Relations*, Compilation of Studies prepared under the Direction of the Sub-Committee on American Republics Affairs of the Committee on Foreign Relations. US Senate 86th Congress, 2nd Session, Document 125, 1960.

Article 19 of the Charter says that 'measures adopted for the maintenance of peace and security in accordance with existing treaties do not constitute a violation of the principles set forth in Article 15 . . .'

This meant there was no principle of absolute non-intervention, any proposed intervention merely needed to be justified differently.

Article 6[1] of the Treaty of Rio de Janeiro had said that joint measures for the protection of peace must be taken not only in the case of an open attack on one of the American republics but also if the inviolability, integrity, independence or sovereignty of an American state was threatened from outside without direct military attack. This is obviously a reference to the danger of communist infiltration.

It is this interpretation which forms the basis of the 1954 Declaration of Carácas referred to above: the infiltration of communism into Guatemala was regarded as an indirect attack by the Eastern bloc and therefore not only as a threat to the independence of an American state, but also as a danger to inter-American peace.

The Mexican Gómez Robledo, expressing the general Latin American view, regarded the declaration of Caracas as a direct breach of the principles of non-intervention,[2] Colonel Castillo Armas' invasion, encouraged and assisted by the US, was taken as proof that *Yanqui* imperialism would attack left-wing governments, whose popular measures endangered the interests of American big business, and would support more amenable dictatorships. Latin American politicians and authors even went so far as to declare that 'dictatorships exist because the United States wants them',[3] and some North American liberals seemed to share this view.

After 1955 the prices of most Latin American exports began to fall and economic development encountered new obstacles. The United States continued to be more interested in Europe and Asia than in events south of the Rio Grande. Latin America was far off the Russian 'beat' and less in need of help than many other areas. Only a fraction—barely 4 per cent—of the aid distributed by the United

---

[1] The texts of the treaties and agreements can be found in *Documents on American Foreign Relations*, published annually by the Council on Foreign Relations, Harpers, New York. Paragraph 6 of the Treaty of Rio de Janeiro says: 'If the inviolability or the integrity of the territory or the sovereignty or political independence of any American State should be affected by an aggression which is not an armed attack or by an extra-continental or intracontinental conflict, or by any other fact or situation that might endanger the peace of America, the Organ of Consultation shall meet immediately in order to agree on the measures which must be taken in case of aggression to assist the victim of the aggression, or, in any case, the measure which should be taken for the common defense and for the maintenance of the peace and security of the Continent.'

[2] *op. cit.*, pp. 205/6.

[3] E. Ramirez Novoa, *América Latina y Estados Unidos*, Lima, 1958, p. 10.

States since the end of the Second World War has gone to Latin America. At the same time, protectionist measures were introduced to help US producers, and the US government worried less about their detrimental effects than about the effect of similar steps in other parts of the world.[1] In other respects too, Latin America was neglected. The cream of the diplomatic service was sent to Europe and Asia and the brightest members of the universities concentrated on Asian and European problems. The Latin Americans were not taken seriously, they were misunderstood and little was known of what went on in their countries. It needed the mass, anti-*Yanqui* demonstrations which Vice-President Nixon encountered in 1958 to arouse the United States from its complacency and ignorance.

Then came Castro, and his victory which resulted in a complete reorientation of the Latin American policy of the United States, and which at the same time, inevitably showed up the difficulties of such a reorientation.

In the United States, as in any democratic, pluralist society, foreign policy at any given moment is the result of the interaction of many, often contradictory, forces. Once the general line has been decided it passes through the filter of constitutional institutions and is finally carried out by people belonging to different and often competing departments. Any simplification of this highly complicated process merely distorts the facts.

The President acts on suggestions made by his advisers, who may be badly informed, are subject to all kinds of pressure, and run the risk of being publicly criticized before a Congressional Committee.

Congressmen are not, as a rule, well-informed in questions of foreign policy and are under pressure from various groups whose support they need.

In the Executive, different departments are often at loggerheads with one another: the State Department, the Pentagon and the Central Intelligence Agency work as often against, as with, each other.

Because civil servants are paid less than senior executives in private industry, and do not enjoy a status which might compensate for the inequality in pay, their quality is frequently not all it might be. Many ambassadorial posts are filled without regard to qualifications, and diplomats usually have contacts only with government supporters and the upper class of the country in which they are stationed.

The pressure groups which influence foreign policy naturally include representatives of big business. They represent not merely small 'exploiting minorities', but millions of shareholders, workers

[1] This was also the view expressed by the National Planning Association in its report to the Subcommittee on American Republics of the US Senate, January 31, 1960.

and employees. They do not speak with a single voice. Different business interests fight each other, without paying any attention to the effects of their actions on the rest of the world.

In addition to the monopolists, inaccurately described in communist propaganda as 'Wall Street', there are many other groups; big and small farmers interested in protective measures, trade unions which, for example, protest against the influx of cheap labour, and the press which often plays an independent part.

US foreign policy can therefore never be as single-minded as that of a totalitarian state. Policy towards some countries vacillates under pressure from various forces. This has been particularly true of the Latin American policy of the United States since the Second World War.

'The explanation for the inconsistencies in our politics towards Latin America seems ... to be the fact that lacking any overall policy to follow in the area, the State Department and other officials charged with conducting our affairs ... have been subject to an infinite variety of pressures. They have tended to give wherever the pressure was hardest at any particular moment.'[1]

But in spite of some ambiguity, US foreign policy was based on two main principles: the defence of capitalism and the fight against communism. The protection of American business interests appeared much more important to American politicians and diplomats than the existence of democratic forms of government. This was why North Americans resident in South America who were interested in profits used to show some sympathy for dictators, provided they were better able to maintain peace and order than democratic governments. If these dictators took an anti-communist line then American politicians would also regard them as allies.

It was therefore not surprising that the *Yanquis* became unpopular.

As defenders of a free economy they came into conflict with those who believed in planning as the only solution to underdevelopment.

As friends of dictators they appeared hypocritical in their defence of the 'free world' and aroused the hatred of democrats.

As exporters they competed with South American industrialists and opposed the industrialization of the subcontinent.

As investors they contributed to a state of affairs where too many Latin American industries were owned by foreigners who were earning big profits.

As protectors of their own producers they came into conflict with Latin Americans interested in the sale of their goods on the North American market.

[1] Charles O. Porter & Robert J. Alexander, *The Struggle for Democracy in Latin America*, New York, 1961, p. 186.

As propagandists of capitalism they became the target of all its emotional opponents.

As wealthy self-important representatives of a developed industrial society they aroused feelings of resentment and hatred.

The agonizing reappraisal of US policy towards Latin America began under President Eisenhower and was provoked by the incidents which had marred the trip of Vice-President Nixon to South America in May, 1958. The initiator of the new era was Brazil's Juscelino Kubitschek. In June 1958 he sent President Eisenhower a letter in which he indicated that the deplorable incidents during Vice-President Nixon's voyage had made it imperative to take steps to reinforce inter-American solidarity by measures designed to overcome Latin America's basic difficulties. Eisenhower replied: 'While your Excellency did not suggest any specific program to improve Pan American understanding, it seems to me that our two governments should consult together as soon as possible with a view of approaching other members of the Pan American community . . .'

In August Kubitschek, in an identical note to all Latin American governments and to the US Government, formulated a plan *Operation Panamerica*. This proposal

'called for an integrated, hemisphere-wide development program consisting of increased public and private investment, stepped up technical assistance and measures for the stabilization of commodity prices . . . The aim of Operation Panamerica . . . was to achieve a rate of economic growth of 5 to 6 per cent a year with the ultimate objective of making Latin America self-sustaining by the end of the 1970s.[1]

In September 1958 the Foreign Ministers of the OAS met in Washington to consider these proposals and decided to set up a special Committee of twenty-one to study the measures to be taken. In January 1959 a specialized commission of government representatives began the discussion of a draft for the creation of an Inter-American Bank, which was sent to the governments in April of this year.

The discussion of measures like the stabilization of commodity prices, the elaboration of an integrated programme for Latin America which included some fundamental economic and social reforms, as well as a greater degree of public financing, showed a change in the attitudes of the North Americans who at the Economic Conference of the OAS in Buenos Aires in autumn 1957, had rejected similar proposals put forward by Latin American representatives. But there

[1] Department of State Historical Office, *Inter-American Tensions in the Western Hemisphere*, 1959–1960, Washington, July 1962, Department of State Publication 7409, pp. 90/91.

was still no sense of urgency. This was apparent at the second meeting of the Committee of twenty-one at the end of April, 1959. It took place in Buenos Aires and Fidel Castro was there to make his own proposals.

'No significant decisions were taken, however. The US delegation confined itself to reviewing the complex of measures it had already undertaken to stimulate economic development in Latin America and stressing the responsibility of each country to intensify and improve its own measures in this field. It opposed a proposal of Cuban Prime Minister Fidel Castro . . . that the US undertake a vast aid program in the order of 30 to 40 billion dollars over a ten year period to underwrite the economic development of Latin America.'[1]

The Latin Americans were disappointed and this became obvious to President Eisenhower when in February 1960, he made a goodwill trip to South America, during which he had conversations with responsible leaders of different countries. 'The result of the President's trip was a clear realization on the part of the US Government that broader and more vigorous co-operative efforts were necessary if adequate economic progress was to be reached in freedom.'[2]

On July 11, 1960, President Eisenhower announced that the US was prepared to extend its co-operation in promoting social progress and economic development in Latin America, and mentioned the necessity of agrarian reform and of an improvement in housing and education. He declared that he had already requested Secretary of State Herter to consult with the Latin Americans and prepare specific recommendations, and that he would seek from Congress authorization for additional public funds amounting to $600 million. The Congress approved this sum on August 31, 1960.

In September 1960, representatives from all Latin America, except from the Dominican Republic, met with the North Americans at Bogotá. Although most of the fundamental ideas expressed in the decisions taken at Bogotá stemmed from Latin American sources, especially those connected with Raúl Prebisch and the ECLA (UN Economic Commission for Latin America) the Cuban representative stated that the proposals were elaborated by the USA in order to stifle the revolutionary awakening of the Latin American peoples and to prepare aggression against Cuba. He left the conference and refused to sign its decisions, which can be resumed under four headings: measures for social improvement, the setting up of a special fund for social development, measures for economic development within the general framework of President Kubitschek's original proposals and the setting up of institutional framework for inter-American co-operation. Such was the history of the Alliance

[1] Department of State, *Inter-American Efforts, op. cit.*, p. 91.
[2] *op. cit.*, p. 92.

for Progress proclaimed by President Kennedy in March 1961 and confirmed at the Conference of Punta del Este in August of the same year. It found expression in two parallel forms of action: direct opposition to the Cuban revolution, and encouragement of extensive social reforms which would take the wind out of revolutionary sails. The parallelism was obvious, perhaps too obvious. After the offers of help in Bogotá came the reduction of the Cuban sugar quota and the condemnation of Castro at the Foreign Ministers' Conference in San José. The proclamation of the Alliance for Progress was followed by the invasion of Cuba in April, 1961, the Alliance was set up at Punta del Este in August, 1961, and in January 1962, a Conference of Ministers assembled in the same place found Cuba's communism irreconcilable with the principles of the inter-American system.

The threat of communist revolutions arose from the poverty of the masses. It could only be removed if living standards were raised. This presupposed economic development based on comprehensive planning and was impossible without extensive social reform. The United States not only abandoned the principle of a free economy but pressed for social changes which went against the direct interests of the oligarchies. It was prepared to provide assistance which was not primarily concerned with profits but only those countries which could prove that they were serious about economic development and social reform were to benefit from this aid.

In his message to the Punta del Este Conference President Kennedy said:

'Self-fulfilment for the developing nations means careful national planning, the orderly establishment of goals, priorities and long range programs. It means expanded export markets, closer economic integration within Latin America and greater market stability for the major primary products. It means the dedication of a greatly increased proportion of national resources and capital to the cause of development, and it means full recognition of the right of all people to share fully in our progress.'

He specially mentioned the need for land reform, for reforms of the fiscal and educational systems, and for an improvement in health and housing conditions. He said that the achievement of progress presupposed the collaboration of the people, workers, peasants, businessmen, intellectuals and youth. The United States promised aid to the value of $1,000 million a year, mainly in the form of long-term, low-interest or interest-free loans, to be supplemented by private investment, likely to amount to another $1,000 million a year.

Secretary of State Dillon explained that, with such foreign assistance and on the assumption that there would be a corresponding investment of local capital, the national income of Latin America

could grow at an annual rate of not less than 2·5 per cent *per capita*
The aims of the alliance are:
1. To strengthen democratic institutions.
2. To speed up economic and social development by a continuous and considerable increase in average incomes, aimed at narrowing the gap between living standards in South America and the developed countries.
3. To provide rural and urban housing.
4. To embark on an extensive land reform which would put an end to the unjust distribution of land and would replace *latifundia* and *minifundia* by a more productive organization of agriculture.
5. To eradicate illiteracy.
6. To improve hygienic and sanitary conditions.
7. To carry out tax reforms in order to achieve a juster distribution of national incomes and to encourage saving and investment.
8. To elaborate a sound financial policy which would stabilize prices and promote development.
9. To promote private enterprise.
10. To stabilize the prices of Latin American exports.
11. To speed up the economic integration of Latin America.

The United States promised to make available over the next ten years the major part of a sum of not less than $20,000 million, mainly in the form of long-term loans, as well as technical assistance, while the Latin American countries agree to devote a steadily increasing share of their own resources to economic and social development and to make the reforms necessary to assure that all would share fully in the fruits of the Alliance for Progress.

Finally, it became the duty of every country to draw up an extensive, well-conceived reform programme.[1]

This then was the outcome of the agonizing reappraisal of US policy begun in 1958. In its fundamental conceptions it was not only different from, but even contradictory to, the whole free enterprise philosophy which predominated in North America. As a matter of fact, the US government had accepted most of the Latin American tenets it had for such a long time opposed Raúl Prebisch was right in stating that:

'The basic ideas ... were conceived and gradually developed over a period of years in Latin America ... In times that are not yet far behind, some of these ideas encountered very strong resistance, which was frequently couched in intractable and dogmatic terms. Now they are recognized as sound and valid and are largely em-

[1] For the full text of the Conference resolutions *see* the *Department of State Bulletin*, Vol. XLV, 1159, September 11, 1961.

bodied in the Charter of Punta del Este. However, there has developed a rather peculiar tendency to present these ideas as having been conceived in the United States ... I am really concerned about this trend, for not only is it contrary to the facts, but its political implications are highly detrimental to the Alliance itself and to the broad popular support it requires in Latin America.'[1]

From present-day economic and technical trends there arises the tendency of the world towards the unification, the transformation of every territory into a dependent part of the whole. This tendency is counteracted by ideological and political differences which lead to the division of mankind into an ever-growing number of independent nations and to its polarization into two power blocs.

The tendencies towards unification and polarization both contribute to the disappearance of separate states. Concepts like independence and sovereignty become relative.

In order to avoid economic catastrophe, the underdeveloped and politically weak states of Latin America must be involved in more or less close collaboration with their powerful northern neighbour. The United States, for its part, cannot pursue a policy of isolation towards its southern neighbours. Such a policy would transform the Latin American subcontinent into a political vacuum which would be filled by the influence of the Eastern bloc.

Hence the problem of the policy of non-intervention. The principle of absolute non-intervention is unrealistic; it also becomes pointless when applied to dictatorships because it derives its moral force from the principle of popular self-determination. Only because it is postulated that every nation has the right freely to determine its own life can intervention from outside be condemned on moral or legal grounds.

The right of self-determination cannot exist without democratic institutions. We may find the concept of self-determination unclear, we may criticize representative democracy for being inadequate, we may question whether it can be achieved at all in some countries, or we may claim that it merely disguises the rule of a minority. All this is irrelevant to our problem because without the free expression of opinion, a legal opposition and free elections, there is no possibility of discovering what citizens want. Totalitarian dictatorships render the concept of self-determination meaningless by making irremovable the ruling minority, the only interpreters of the 'general will'. Where self-determination can no longer be empirically verified it ceases to exist and the moral objections against intervention automatically collapse.

Most Latin Americans refuse to admit this truth and the United

[1] Raúl Prebisch, 'Economic Aspects of the Alliance', in *The Alliance for Progress* (ed. John C. Dreier), Baltimore, 1962, pp. 24–5.

States *cannot* point it out because emotions are stronger than reason, because the dreams of past generations fill the minds of the living, and because politics and logic are not synonymous. The principle of non-intervention remains sacrosanct because it is in accordance with nationalist and anti-imperialist feelings. But in reality the question is not whether the United States, as the strongest power, should interfere in their internal affairs, but only how it should interfere, to what extent, with what aim, and what methods it should use. The Latin American nations will welcome or condemn intervention depending on whether it corresponds to or conflicts with their basic interests. From the point of view of the United States there should be no intervention which looks like blackmail or which could be interpreted as an imperialist attack on a Latin American state.

The Alliance for Progress, despite the fact that its main ideas are derived from Latin America, represents an indirect intervention by the United States in the internal affairs of the Latin American countries. It puts pressure on Latin American statesmen and makes conditions and demands. 'Dollar diplomacy' has come alive again but its novelty lies in the fact that the United States urges constitutional reforms which taken together amount to a social revolution. Presently, American political leaders frankly admit that the Alliance for Progress is a race between a social-democratic revolution supported by them and a communist revolution promoted by Russia. As Adlai Stevenson put it: 'We learned . . . that a social revolution in some cases is a precondition of political stability and economic growth'.[1]

---

[1] *New York Times*, October 17, 1961.

3. 1962–1963: Years of Indecision

1962 began with Punta del Este and Castro's answer: the Second Declaration of Havana. 1963 ended with the assassination of President Kennedy and the Castroists defeat in Venezuela. In between fell the missile crisis of October 1962. The struggle between the two opponents—Democracy and Communism remained undecided and the perspectives, on the whole, unclear.

The development of the Alliance for Progress turned out to be disappointing, in the economic as well as in the social and the political sphere. Certainly, there were some thousands of houses and classrooms, some hundred of hospitals, built in Latin America, but this was not more than a drop in the ocean. There was not enough capital pouring into the region, because of difficulties made by the US Congress, of the unwillingness of other countries to contribute more; because of the lack of a favourable climate for investment by private persons, because of unfavourable terms of trade, which however began to improve towards the end of 1962. There was some progress in a few countries (Venezuela, Mexico) but on the whole the picture was rather that of economic stagnation. The modest rate of a *per capita* increase of 2·5 per cent per year was not achieved.

The social aspect was even less encouraging: hardly a serious step was done towards the realization of basic reforms. All attempts in this direction were met by resistance or inertia. No more was achieved than some partial and modest improvements in a few countries, some more or less platonic declarations, and the elaboration of more or less perfect plans, which tended, as always, to remain on paper. The revolutionary spirit which the originators of the Alliance had tried to inspire disappeared. Nowhere did the masses of the people become inspired by a movement towards peaceful and fundamental change.

Nor did the political developments work out according to the hopes. While Cuba remained a bastion of Communism and a beachhead of the Latin American revolution, democracy went from crisis to crisis in the rest of the continent. Military dictatorships replaced constitutional governments in Argentina, Peru, Ecuador, the Dominican Republic and Honduras. In the first two countries the rule of the army was provisional and was replaced by democratic régimes whose future looked dubious. The government of Illia in Argentina seemed to lack any drive and to be destined to produce disenchantment. That of Belaunde in Peru found itself confronted with an opposition oddly composed of an alliance between the APRA and Odría, which had the majority in parliament and seemed decided to make efficient government impossible.

The *coup* in Ecuador could have been considered as necessary, in so far as it put an end to the rule of a President who was manifestly unfit for his job. The new Junta promised to modernize the country. But it soon became obvious that no serious reforms were forthcoming, while the army seemed unwilling to permit any return to constitutional government. Worse was the case of the two other countries of Central America, where democratic governments were deposed under the eternal flag of 'anti-Communism'. The rapid and violent end put to the rule of Juan Bosch could only serve to support the Castroist contention that peaceful reforms were impossible, and that the utter destruction of the old state apparatus was the prerequisite for any deep social change.

In spite of all the economic help and sympathy it had received from the USA, Bolivia's revolution appeared to be failing. In order to progress, the country had to improve the productivity of its economy and especially of its mines. This proved impossible above all because of opposition by the miners. The resulting social and political crisis led to divisions within the ruling party. The earlier split, when a 'moderate' wing under Guevara Arze had founded a new opposition party, was followed during 1963 by the Lechin crisis. This was even more serious, because, as leader of a prospective radical opposition party, Lechin was backed by many workers, especially the miners, as well as by the numerous if small communist and protocommunist groups. The '*co-gobierno*' of the leading party (MNR) and the Trade Union Centre (COB) broke asunder. Inside the rump of the MNR there was a growing struggle between several factions. Even the former President, Hernan Siles, showed his opposition to Paz Estenssoro. Eventually, in November 1964, the military Junta under General Barrientos, seized power and Paz Estenzorro went into exile in Peru.

In Brazil, the inflation and disorder that had begun even before the resignation of Quadros grew alarmingly under the presidency of Goulart, who turned out to be a vacillating politician rather than a statesman. Towards the end of 1963 he seemed inclined to lean increasingly on the extreme left, composed of the friends of his brother-in-law Brizzola, some radical members of his own party and of the Trade Unions, protocommunist Christians, Castroists such as Julião, and the communists of the Moscow and the Peking persuasions. This finally led to his overthrow and the establishment of the new régime headed by Castello Branco.

In Chile, the Alessandri government, although it had built a considerable number of houses and tried to stop economic deterioration, proved unable to cope with inflation and social disorganization. 1964 was to be a year of presidential elections and it was almost sure, at the close of 1963 that the 'Democratic Front' of Conservatives, Liberals and Radicals was doomed, and that Chile's future government would hardly conform to the ideals of 'free enterprise'. The alternatives were either Eduardo Frei, President of the 'leftish' and vaguely pro-socialist Christian Democrats, or Allende, the candidate of the Communist-dominated FRAP, where the communists' allies were, in some respects, even more radical than they.

No decision seemed near in Colombia. There the future of democracy was doubtful, although the opinion of a British Marxist historian, Hobsbawm, who after a visit wrote about the 'revolutionary situation in Colombia',[1] might have been considered as somewhat exaggerated. Violence in the countryside continued and a new form of violence, visibly inspired by Cuba, appeared: namely, urban terrorism. Encouraging signs of economic growth, which appeared in 1961, disappeared later, while the cost of living began to climb to an accompaniment of growing social discontent and strikes. There was hardly any sign of vigorous social reform. On the contrary, the new Agrarian Reform Institute (INCORA), formed in 1961, played a constantly diminishing rôle. The general disenchantment with the government of the Conservative-Liberal Coalition was reflected by the growing percentage of 'abstentions' in the national elections (some 52 per cent of the electors had cast their vote in the Congressional elections of March 1962, some 44 per cent in the presidential elections of May 1963, but only 33 per cent participated in the elections of March 1964). New groups on the extreme left appeared and the former dictator of Colombia, Rojas Pinilla, enjoyed an increasing prestige.

The only two countries in which development seemed favourable were Mexico and Venezuela. But even here qualifications were necessary. Mexico's economy had passed through a period of stagnation in 1961 when the rate of growth of the GNP, 3·5 per cent, was hardly greater than that of demographic increase. True, it recovered. But the increases of 4·8 per cent in 1962 and some 5·5 per cent in 1963 could hardly be considered satisfactory. A considerable part of the population still stood outside the scope of monetary economy, the huge majority were still destitute, most intellectuals remained 'disaffected' and profoundly influenced by Marxist ideas, while there was an almost constant unrest in the countryside, frequently harshly dealt with by the authorities.

In Venezuela Betancourt's government achieved a considerable success, against enormous odds, especially the terrorism and guerilla activities inspired and helped from Havana. Its main success consisted in being able to maintain itself in power and to hold elections, in which the huge majority of electors participated, in spite of all the attempts by the Castroist communists to make them impossible. While progress in the educational domain was considerable, that of the agrarian reform seemed to be exceedingly modest.

[1] Eric Hobsbawm, *World Today*, June 1963.

In view of these developments, the prospects of the 'Alliance for Progress' looked unpromising. The general disenchantment found a clear expression during the meeting of the Economic and Social Council of the UN in November 1963 in São Paulo. It was doubtful if the creation of a new organ to supervise the Alliance or the appointment of Thomas Mann, considered a 'conservative' and an avowed friend of free enterprise, would help very much, and the assassination of Kennedy could well be considered as the tragic epilogue to failure.

The Second Declaration of Havana—hailed with enthusiasm by Peking—was a call to violent revolution throughout the subcontinent. Latin American democracy was a sham not a reality, it claimed; peaceful roads to liberty were closed; revolutionary situations existed in most, if not all, countries and it was the duty of revolutionaries to make use of them.

'Where the repression against laborer and peasant is fierce, where the domination of *Yanqui* monopolies is strongest, the first and most important thing to understand is that it is neither just nor correct to mislead the peoples with vain and comfortable illusions of snatching power by legal means . . . a power which the monopolies and oligarchies will defend by blood and fire . . . The duty of a revolutionary is to make a revolution. The revolutionary outburst of the peoples is inevitable . . .'

While the peasants remained unable to conquer power without being led by the workers and intellectuals, they remained the main revolutionary force: 'No matter how hard the living conditions of the urban workers are, the rural population lives under even more horrible conditions . . . it also constitutes the absolute majority . . . of the Latin American populations.'

It was among these rural masses that guerilla groups were to be organized, which had to conquer the sympathies of the peasantry:

'Armies, organized and equipped for conventional warfare, constitute the power on which the exploiting classes depend; when they have to face the irregular struggle of peasants in their habitat, they are rendered totally impotent; they lose ten men for one revolutionary fighter and demoralization spreads quickly among them when they must fight against an invisible and invincible enemy who does not give them a chance to employ their professional tactics . . . The initial struggle of small groups of fighters is unceasingly strengthened by new forces, the mass movement begins to spread, the old order slowly cracks into a thousand pieces and then the moment comes when the working class and urban masses decide the battle . . .'

The authors of the declaration were careful to avoid heretical ultra-left formulations and accusations of *putschism*. It was not denied that the 'national bourgeoisie' could participate in a revolution, but only that it could lead it. The working class was considered as the vanguard and leader of the whole process while the possibility of a peaceful acquisition of power was not excluded. 'Whether this takes place peacefully or comes to the world after painful labor, does not depend on the revolutionaries; it depends on the reactionary forces of the old society'

Even if this document could in principle be accepted by all 'communists', its meaning and its implications were of a definite kind. Hence it was applauded by the Chinese much more than by the Russians. The Second Declaration of Havana should indeed be seen in the whole context of development which includes the former opinions of Castro and those which were expressed by Guevara in his book on guerrilla warfare, as well as the later utterances of the Cuban leaders, the criticism of the 'official' Communists, treated as impotent satellites of Moscow in Castro's conversations with Claude Julien; or the declarations made by Castro to the Women's Congress on January 16, 1963:

'We do not deny the possibility of a peaceful transition, although we are still waiting for the first such case ... The theoreticians of imperialism may preach conformism; the theoreticians of revolution should fearlessly preach revolution. This is what we think, and that is what we have said in the Declaration of Havana, a declaration which in some brother countries received the honor, by some revolutionary organizations, of being "honorably shelved", instead of being publicized as it deserves ... If we tell the masses that such and such is the situation, we also have to tell them what road to take, and to lead them into the battle, and this road is much easier in many countries of Latin America, than it was in Cuba ... This is the duty of the revolutionary leaders ... to get the masses to march, to launch the masses into battle.'

Castro admitted that each country had its specific conditions, and that in some of them revolutionary situations might not for the present exist—but they existed, according to him, in the vast majority of Latin American countries. Far from considering 'bourgeois democracy' as favourable, a real revolutionary had to recognize it as a form of bourgeois dictatorship and struggle against it. Changing his former opinions, Guevara, in an important article on guerilla warfare published in the September 1963 issue of *Cuba Socialista* (and in English translation in *Peking Review* of January 10, 1964) wrote: 'A dictatorial régime always tries to maintain its rule under conditions where it may not need to use violence on a large scale; one must force it to appear undisguised, that is to say, force it to appear for what it is: a violent dictatorship of the reactionary class.'

During 1963 the inner meaning of Castroism became clearer. This, together with Peking's influence, contributed to split the ranks of the communists in almost all Latin American countries. The leaders of the 'official' pro-Moscow parties were accused of being traitors, reformists, revisionists by newly founded pro-Castro or pro-Chinese organizations all over the continent.[1]

While it cannot be our present task to describe these developments, it seems possible to sketch schematically the essence and background of the split.

The 'official' communists had as already stated always been close followers of the Kremlin, and therefore were suspect to genuine revolutionary nationalists. Their leaders were fundamentally opportunistic politicians, *apparatchiks*, and bureaucrats—a human type quite different from the young and impatient intellectual so characteristic of Castroism. Their strategy and tactics were directed towards the formation of a 'popular front' formed with the participation of all 'progressive' social groups, including the so-called 'national bourgeoisie', and then making the utmost use of legal means. Although as communists they always maintained that illegal methods had to be used, and violent revolution had to be considered as a possibility, their real policy was that of the 'peaceful road'. The Castroists and pro-Chinese held that the national bourgeoisie was never to be trusted, that the patient efforts to build 'popular fronts' were condemned to failure, and that the ideological and political concessions made 'to win friends and influence people' were tantamount to a betrayal of the revolution. The 'official' communists denied that a revolution was possible without an objectively revolutionary situation; whereas the 'left' communists maintained that a potentially revolutionary situation was in existence and that it could be actualized, if not created, by the action of determined minorities. The 'official' communists considered the urban working class to be the decisive force and its mass movements to be the prerequisite for any revolutionary progress. The 'left' saw the main force of the revolution in the peasantry and considered guerilla warfare and urban terrorism to be the principal means of struggle. While the most important 'official' parties—the Chilean above all, but also the Brazilian and Argentinian—had intellectuals among their leading strata, the majority of their cadres were of working-class background. The 'Castroists' were recruited among young intellectuals and among the 'marginal population' of un- and underemployed

[1] For an excellent analysis of the divergences between Castroism and 'official' communism as represented, above all, by the Chilean Communist Party, see the three contributions by Ernst Halperin, *The Sino-Cuban and the Chilean Road to Power*, *Castro and Latin American Communism*, and *The Ideology of Castroism and its impact on the Communist Parties of Latin America*, published 1963 by the Center for International Studies, Massachusetts Institute of Technology, Cambridge, Mass.)

1962-1963: YEARS OF INDECISION

of town and country—those who, lacking roots in the economic and social framework of their countries, had nothing to lose but their rootlessness and who had enough free time and spirit of adventure to engage in terroristic activities and become guerillas.

It would be wrong to think that Peking or Havana created these splits artificially. They grew out of widespread disillusionment with the activities of the official communist parties, which in more than forty years of existence had nowhere been able to attain power or even to become important factors in the political life of their subcontinent. It was obvious that newly strengthened suspicions about Soviet foreign policy would increase this disillusionment. If everything depended on the 'peaceful competition' between Russia and the USA, if the interests of the Russian consumer became more important than those of the world revolution, if—especially after the missile crisis—the Soviets seemed to be interested in improving their relations with 'North American imperialism'—what should Latin American revolutionaries do but try another way? The first pro-Chinese (and therefore pro-Cuban) heterodox party formed in Latin America, the *Partido Comunista do Brasil*, was born at the beginning of 1962, when—according to its leaders—the 'revolutionary' communists did not yet understand the importance of the Chinese-Russian conflict. One year later their organ, *A Clase Operaria*, wrote: 'The revolutionary struggles in Latin America have proved the correctness of the Chinese Communist party's thesis concerning the national liberation struggles of oppressed nations and the rôle of these struggles in the world situation as a whole. The peoples of Latin America cannot afford to wait for their liberation by "peaceful competition".'

4. Reform or Revolution?

Only in a very crude sense can we call 'reformists' those who favour the way of the 'Alliance for Progress' and 'revolutionaries' those who profess some kind of communist creed. But we can start by enquiring how the prospects for each appeared five years after the victory of the Cuban revolution.

From its very inception, the 'Alliance for Progress' was full of paradoxes. To begin with, it is based on the belief that communist revolutions arise out of the revolt of the masses against poverty. This view is questionable. There is, as the Cuban case has shown once more, no clear correlation between mass misery and communism, and communism can be victorious even without the active participation of the masses. Even where the masses do play a bigger rôle, they are always prepared and led by élites, mostly composed of intellectuals.

The Charter of the Alliance emphasizes that social reform must take place within the framework of representative democracy. Even if the meaning of this term is conveniently reinterpreted to cover such cases as that of Mexico, one should not forget that few of the developed countries reached 'take-off' inside such an institutional framework. Economic growth implies sacrifices and therefore a certain amount of coercion.[1] This coercion may be internal or external to the human being, but if there is no 'inner policeman' in the individual conscience, there must be an external policeman to guarantee satisfactory behaviour. The 'internal policeman' arose in many developed countries out of traditions which are absent in most underdeveloped societies of today. Coercion may be based on economic or on other means, but it must be there, and the economic incentives were certainly stronger in North America than they are south of the Rio Grande. Representative democracy has worked rather badly in Latin America, but even if it were improved, the numerous pressure groups and an inevitable amount of social demagogy might hinder rather than encourage rapid progress.[2]

[1] 'The absence of political democracy and of an independent union movement compelled the worker to accept the verdict of the market with respect to the distribution of income. Industrial capitalism thus developed amidst institutions which prevented the investment surplus from being dissipated in additional consumption.' K. de Schweinitz, 'Economic Growth, Coercion and Freedom', in *World Politics*, 1957, Vol. IX, No. 2.

[2] 'No more than a quite limited welfare state is compatible with a high rate of economic growth in present underdeveloped lands. For this reason, a multi-party system is not compatible with economic growth, it is too likely to give in to ever present demands for liberal "welfare state" provisions.' J. J. Spengler, 'Economic Development—Political Preconditions and Political Consequences' *The Journal of Politics*, August, 1960.

Finally, representative democracy, as practised in most countries, is based on the passivity of the citizens in relation to problems of more than local importance. But with respect to rapid economic progress there is an essential truth in the remark made by Asoka Mehta: 'The basic thing is not democracy but the ability to stir the people, to realize their energies, their *elan*, their enthusiasm'.[1]

Proposed reforms are offered in the interest of development—but even their successful execution will not necessarily contribute to greater political stability. The conservative elements will defend themselves with all their might, while the masses, encouraged by the prospect of speedy improvement, may consider the pace of transformation too slow. Stagnating societies fall prey less easily to communist revolutions than societies which are developing in a contradictory fashion and with an unsatisfactory rhythm. The planned annual rise of 2·5 per cent per annum in *per capita* income in the first two years after the beginning of the *Alliance* has not been achieved, but it is not likely in any case to narrow the gap between Latin America and the developed countries[2] nor to satisfy the masses, or to immunize them against communism, particularly as they realize that they owe the new reform policy to the pressure of Castro's revolution.

It is true that each country must rely mainly on its own resources and that foreign financial aid can do no more than supplement a country's own investments. In the 'fifties, in fact, only about 15 per cent of all capital invested in Latin America came from abroad.[3] But a supplement from outside remains essential. To many people the proposed sum of $20,000 million over ten years seems insufficient and the United States itself regards this as the minimum. But it is doubtful whether even this minimum can be achieved.

Private investors in Latin America have had experiences which are unlikely to encourage substantial new investments in this part of the world. As far as public funds from the United States are concerned, it is doubtful whether Congress is prepared to make substantial long-term loans, thus giving up its traditional means of exerting pressure on the executive. Moreover, it is by no means certain that Congress—and the US taxpayer—will always be prepared to find the

---

[1] *Democracy in the New States*, Rhodes Seminar Papers, New Delhi, 1959, pp. 20-1.

[2] 'In 1958, a North American economist, G. L. Bach, had calculated that if the total Latin American output would rise at a rate of 2·5 per cent per capita, it would take the peoples of the subcontinent 40 years to reach one-third of the US per capita of 1957. But if the US income continued to grow at around 2 per cent per year, it would take more than 250 years before Latin American incomes would reach one-third of the then current US income levels.' Quoted in Robert L. Heilbroner, *The Future as History*, New York, 1959, p. 163.

[3] University of Oregon, Problems of Latin American Economic Development, *US–Latin American Relations, A Compilation of Studies*, US Senate 86th Congress, 2nd Session, 1960, Document 125, p. 581.

money to help states whose governments demonstrate their independence by pursuing policies which the US dislikes.

The majority of United States politicians should certainly not be identified with the Kennedy Administration. Senators and Congressmen are more influenced by the immediate interests of their constituents and by pressure groups than by long-term, international considerations. Nothing would be more dangerous for the government than to appear as appeasers and to be attacked for excessive leniency towards communism and, as experience has shown, the term 'communism' can be very widely interpreted. Nor should it be forgotten that most US politicians are conservative in outlook and view extensive social reforms with suspicion.

This brings us to the greatest difficulty: the double paradox on which the Alliance for Progress is founded: a state in which most politicians continue to swear by the preservation of a capitalist economy suggests to the ruling classes of Latin America that they should carry out a social revolution and commit suicide for fear of murder.

It is true that in many Latin American countries something like a modern-minded bourgeoisie of entrepreneurs, professionals, and technicians has arisen. But they still form a small minority inside the ruling class of most of them. And as a whole this class is unwilling to realize the programme of the Alliance. Their resistance became manifest quite early: in January 1962, one of the leading US officials, Teodoro Moscoso, complained that the upper classes and governments of most Latin American countries had still not understood the need for the proposed reforms. Commenting on this speech the correspondent of the *New York Times* remarked: 'Mr Moscoso's estimate represented the gloomiest forecast of prospects for the Alliance for Progress since the program was adopted'.[1]

The ruling circles and classes of Latin America will not openly oppose the Alliance for Progress programme, but will rather try to sabotage it. They might be in favour of representative democracy, but only in so far as it may enable them to maintain some of their privileges. They gladly accept loans and gifts from the USA—to enrich themselves. They may even be prepared to agree to welfare state measures, wage rises for the workers, and may put up with inflation; but they will then attack the USA because it demands a healthy financial policy.

The task of putting the Alliance programme to work was certainly not facilitated by its history. For many Latin Americans it was, indeed, extremely doubtful if the reappraisal of US policy had really been 'agonizing'. They doubted, not without reason, whether there really had been any profound change of mood. Even if the North Americans had accepted some Latin American ideas, they had only

[1] The *New York Times*, January 26, 1962.

done so after Castro's victory and because of the threat it implied. To very many of them the whole programme appeared as nothing but the intent to defeat Cuba and to prevent any deep social transformation. They saw the programme against the background of US policy towards Cuba, and this reminded them more of the 'bigstick' policy of the first, than of the 'good neighbourliness' of the second, Roosevelt. This image was not entirely correct; it had been created by the extraordinary skill of Fidel Castro himself. The continent witnessed a cat and mouse game, but with the Cuban mouse tricking the *Yanqui* cat into one blundering move after another.

Hardly anyone took seriously the sweet-sour professions of approval which the North Americans made in 1959. The shooting of 'war criminals' was greeted with all too great a show of moral horror. And even if Castro did not ask for financial help in April 1959, it could and should have been offered. Instead his request, made at Buenos Aires, for 30 billion dollars to be shared amongst the countries of the subcontinent, was ridiculed. Official American approval of agrarian reform was coupled with legalistic demands for adequate and rapid compensation which would have emasculated the revolution. Cuban refugees, even the most reactionary of them, were fêted in the USA. Washington was unable or unwilling to check piratical air incursions, while leading politicians repeated their paternalistic recommendations in favour of private property and representative democracy. The expropriation of the oil companies, which could only arouse sympathetic emotions in the breasts of all anti-imperialists, was followed by the suspension of the Cuban sugar quota. The hypocritical declarations explaining this measure were not likely to improve Washington's standing with Latin Americans. When in July 1960 a prominent Mexican parliamentarian made a pro-Castro and anti-*Yanqui* speech, the State Department summoned the Mexican ambassador to demand an explanation. The television debates between the two presidential candidates in the autumn of 1960 could only pour oil on the anti-imperialist fire. Kennedy upheld the Monroe doctrine and criticized the economic measures taken against Cuba as 'too little and too late', recommending collective, direct OAS intervention. Nixon declared such proposals to be irresponsible, while secretly backing the coming invasion attempt. He hoped that economic pressure would bring about Castro's downfall and referred to the example of Guatemala where the people had, supposedly, driven out the pro-communist régime. Everyone in Latin America knew that this version was untrue, and that Arbenz had been toppled by the intervention of a reactionary colonel backed by the US. Both candidates maintained that communist régimes in America could not be tolerated. Neither of them gave any thought to the fact that the revolutionary government of Cuba had not been imposed by Russian fiat, and that régimes which would be characterized as 'communist' by North Americans, could well be backed by popular majorities; in which case intervention would be contrary to the principle of self-determination.

Up to the end of 1961, the Castro régime was not communist in the eyes of Latin American radicals. 'Communism' was introduced little by little, through deceit and with the help of semantic subterfuges. But even then, many if not most Cubans seemed to back it, as happens in every totalitarian régime. To many of them the Alliance for Progress appeared to be an instrument in the struggle against the Cuban revolution, waged under the banner of the Monroe doctrine. The developments of the years 1962 and 1963 did little to improve the prospects of the reformers in Latin America. It is true that the communists have suffered several setbacks since then, but social and economic problems have not been tackled as vigorously as the situation demanded. Their solution, whatever the political developments may be, can only be a long-term process, so that political stability in Latin American countries is, in any case, likely to remain precarious.

In 1956, Z. Brzezinski wrote:

'In the present epoch non-democratic forces enjoy a definite advantage over the democratic countries in being able to export their political structure to the newly liberated peoples not only through conspiratorial action, but also through the dynamics of the situation, given the economic and political aspirations of these peoples. As a result, the totalitarian pattern of political and social organization is more likely than not to engulf an even larger portion of mankind. If this happens it will be exceedingly difficult for these new totalitarian systems to avoid following the communist model and they will tend to gravitate towards the Soviet orbit.'[1]

These words were written with reference to newly independent and economically backward countries. But they are also relevant to Latin America, which is becoming one of the main arenas of 'peaceful competition' between the two world systems, and the alternative methods by which they propose to overcome underdevelopment.

The Cuban revolution, the deepening of the economic and social crisis, and the obstacles and difficulties in the way of the Alliance for Progress have apparently increased the chances for the communists. In many central and south American countries, the masses are far more wretched and the revolutionary ferment much more voilent than in the Cuba of Batista. This is particularly true of the peasants, who have benefited least from economic progress, while their expectations have soared. One of the clearest social thinkers of

[1] 'The Politics of Under-Development,' *World Politics*, Princeton, October, 1956.

Brazil pertinently observed that 'the only reason for the possibility of a revolution of a Marxist-Leninist type is the persistence of an anachronistic agrarian structure'.[1] This, he said, results from the fact that whereas even miserable urban workers live in a more or less 'open' society and have the chance of bettering their lot and of achieving certain reforms through their trade unions and political parties; agrarian society remains rigid, and life, for the majority of peasants and labourers, hopeless. The Indian peasants of Peru and Colombia are stirring, the intellectuals mock the reformist plans backed by '*Yanqui* imperialism', and revolutionary groups have increased in number and influence. Socialists like the Brazilian Julião[2] and the Chilean Allende do not object to Marxist-Leninism. The leader of the Uruguayan Socialists, Vivian Trias,[3] attacked the Alliance for Progress whose aim, he said, 'is not to overcome backwardness but to increase it' and which 'represents a false alternative, an unacceptable substitute for the way which Castro has taken'. The 'democratic' groups are, as we saw, in difficulties, and the Christian Democratic or Christian Socialist groups, although opposed to Communism are also opposed to the oligarchies, are doubtful about the Alliance for Progress and are (as a sympathetic European observer noted)[4] 'much farther to the left' than similar groups in Europe.

The communist gospel is simple, and its simplicity enhances its appeal. The only way out is to mobilize the masses for a radical social revolution which would uproot the oligarchies and confiscate their wealth, dissolve the parasitic armies, break up the corrupt civil service, drive out the imperialists and their agents, expropriate the capitalists, give land to the peasants, offer a new faith and a worthwhile career to the young intellectuals, and break the educational monopoly of the rich. It would replace the capitalist 'anarchy of production' by a planned economy and form close ties with the Eastern bloc. It would indoctrinate the people, fill them with a quasi-religious ideology which would give them spiritual security and increase their will to work. The programmes of the Alliance for Progress are based on rigorous economic calculation and may

[1] Celso Furtado, 'Reflexiones sobre la prerevolución Brasileña,' *Cuadernos*, Paris, August, 1962.

[2] In his propaganda, Julião mixed primitive Christianity with Castroism and the Chinese brand of Communism, as the following extract from one of his manifestos shows: 'It is you, who kill our hunger while you die of hunger. You clothe us and you yourselves are clothed in rags ... The Church asks you to be resigned—in the name of Christ. But Christ was a rebel, and therefore he was crucified. Like Christ and the good St Francis of Italy, I stand by your side and two men who are now alive, Mao Tse-Tung of China and Fidel Castro of Cuba. They achieved victory because they were with you and you with them,' *O Semanario*, No. 253, April, 1961.

[3] Vivian Trias, *El Plan Kennedy y la Revolución Latinoamericana*, Montevideo, 1961.

[4] Raymond Scheyvan, *op. cit.*, p. 11.

commend themselves to administrators and experts. But the communist alternative propagated by enthusiastic and, mostly, passionately honest radicals, can inspire the masses. Utopian enthusiasm is an asset in itself:

'It is this passion of the politicians which is crucial, more than savings, more than foreign aid and more than technicians ... If the passion and understanding are not there, the rest will turn to dust ... For a society to develop, it must want to develop; for a society to want to develop its politicians must dream dreams of development. If the politicians are bad, the economic development will not happen, as there is the whole history of Latin America to prove.'[1]

Does this mean that a communist solution to the Latin American crisis is probable, or even inevitable? Hardly, and for a number of reasons which, taken together, constitute an obstacle no less formidable than the one barring the way of the Alliance for Progress.

The first difficulty consists in the weakness of the Communist parties, which, in spite of all the revolutionary potentialities and their long history, remain unimportant in most countries. The faction-ridden Marxist-Leninists of Mexico have never been more than a sect; the impotence of the Ecuadorian party—which was supposed to be the leading force of the trade union movement there—was proved by its utter inability to resist the military *coup* of 1963. The parties of Colombia and Peru, debilitated by 'leftist' splits, are still far from having become centres of power in their respective countries, or from being able to influence the rebel movements going on in the countryside.[2]

The Argentinian party—characterized by a Trotskyite critic as 'not a revolutionary party, not even a party, but rather an organizational and financial machine, immune to the historic process'[3]—which participated in the free election of 1958, did not get more than 2·5 per cent of the vote and has proved since powerless to break the influence of the *Peronistas*. The Uruguayan party, as already noted, received by 3·5 per cent of the votes in the elections of 1963, and that not even by itself, but only in combination with other 'radical' groups. The only important parties were—towards the end of 1963—the Brazilian and Chilean ones. While the party of Prestes seemed to play a growing rôle in the chaotic process of radicalization going on under the rule of Goulart, it remained, however, quite incapable of preventing his overthrow. In an article on occasion of the forty-first

[1] Maurice Zinkin, *Development for Free Asia*, London, 1956, p. 75.
[2] The Peruvian writer Víctor Villanueva is entirely right in stating that the communist party is 'absolutely innocent with respect to the agrarian rebellions which constitute a real danger for the landowners of Peru', *El militarismo en Peru*, Lima, 1962, p. 275.
[3] Jorge Abelardo Ramos, *El Partido Comunista en la Política argentina*, Buenos Aires, 1962, p. 255.

anniversary of the party one of its leading members complained bitterly about 'the contradiction between the extraordinarily favorable objective conditions on the one hand and our own weakness on the other . . . between the growth of the proletariat and the small number of party-members'.[1] The Chilean party, despite its influence, lost the elections of 1964 and the communist-led FRAP coalition proved unable to win the presidency. It is also not clear how the communists would have fared once they had won it.

As weak as the parties themselves are the 'proletarian' mass organizations they are supposed to influence and lead. The Latin American trade union movement, important when and where it gets official government support, is much smaller than is thought by those who take seriously the mythical membership figures claimed by the different organizations.[2] These 'trade unions' include, in many countries, social strata which can by no means be characterized as 'proletarian': small peasants, university students, even small independent tradesmen. The majority of the 'members' neither participate in the inner life of their organizations nor pay dues in so far as these are not automatically deducted from the wages. The strongest organization is probably the Argentinian CGT, which is dominated by the Peronists. The Brazilian and Chilean Confederations and Federations include but a small proportion of the workers and employees of their countries.[3]

Communist efforts to infiltrate the trade unions have proved disappointing. The pro-communist faction of MUCS in Argentina remains small, and the same is true for Bolivia, Colombia, Peru, Mexico and Venezuela. The communist-led trade union centre of Ecuador collapsed with the victory of the military junta. Communist efforts to form a new 'independent' Latin American Confederation of Trade Unions to replace the moribund CETAL failed in 1963. Brazil and Chile are (apart from Cuba) the only countries where communists play an important rôle in the trade union movement. But their influence is more apparent than real. This is clearly so in Brazil, where radical 'fellow travellers' belonged to Goulart's party and before his overthrow, they and not the communists stood in the forefront of the trade union movement, having formed the *Comando Geral dos Trabalhadores*.

[1] Moises Vinhas in *Novos Rumos*, April 19–25, 1963.
[2] The author has tried to describe the reality of Latin American trade union movements in an, inevitably very deficient, book published in 1963 in Germany.
[3] The official *Anuário Estatístico do Brasil*, 1962, gave the total membership of all trade unions as 1,217,665. A more recent *Cadastro Sindical Brasileiro* showed total membership to have grown by December 1961 to about 1·7 million. The most important trade union, Confederation of Chile, the CUT, had, in 1963, not more than 400,000 affiliates. For a very good objective analysis of their numerical development up to 1959, *see* Universidad de Chile–Instituto de Organización y Administración, *Afiliación y Finanzas sindicales en Chile, 1932–1959*, Santiago, 1962.

It was then by no means clear whether the 'official' communists could be considered to be 'genuine' revolutionaries. Trotskyites and Castroites doubted it.[1]

But even if we do consider them as revolutionaries—which in a sense they certainly are—their strategic conception, imported from outside, hardly conforms to Latin American realities. According to it, Latin American development is rendered impossible by fetters which are inherited from a combination of feudalism and imperialism. The first task, then, is to promote a 'democratic, anti-feudal, anti-imperialist', i.e., a *bourgeois* revolution, which should grow out of a 'popular front' led by industrial workers and supported by the peasants and the 'national bourgeoisie'.

Now the existing 'fetters' cannot be classified as 'feudal'. They result from a peculiar combination of pre-capitalist, capitalist, and 'post-capitalist' elements. The pre-capitalist elements—those that so frequently but so inappropriately are designated by the cliché 'feudal'—consist not only of the archaic parts of the agrarian structure but also of habits and behaviour patterns prevalent in the normally 'capitalist' population. The 'capitalist' aspects arise especially out of the dependence of Latin America on the world market; the 'post-capitalist' ones out of the inefficient but omnipresent governmental '*dirigisme*' and the premature introduction of elements of the welfare state.

The industrial workers of Latin America are hardly to be considered a revolutionary force, even when and where their representatives use wildly revolutionary language. A considerable part of them are a 'workers' aristocracy' enjoying much better living conditions than the huge majority of their countrymen. This is particularly the case with most workers employed in big foreign-owned enterprises, whose 'anti-imperialist' tendencies seem—to say the least—to be not quite genuine.

The anti-imperialist 'national bourgeoisie' is largely a myth. The rather small but well-established stratum of modern enterpreneurs know that they can come to terms with foreign capitalists and frequently acquire greater strength with their help. The most 'anti-imperialist' bourgeois are objectively the most reactionary and inefficient industrialists, and tradesmen who fear foreign competi-

---

[1] Among the doubters we may include Ernst Halperin and the radical Argentine intellectual Rogelio García Lupo, who writes about the 'counter-revolutionary rôle of the Latin American communist parties' in *La Rebelión de los Generales*, Buenos Aires, 1963, p. 35; the Peruvian Villanueva, the Argentinian *Peronista* Alberto Belloni, who writes *inter alia* that the official communists 'bear the responsibility of too many errors, many of which are in reality betrayals of the interests of the working class', in *Peronismo y Socialismo Nacional*, Buenos Aires, 1962, p. 47; and many others. John Scott of *Time* was told by Chilean Socialists in 1963 that their party was in many ways more radical than the Communists. 'Here in Concepción particularly the Communists are trying to be moderate because they are very rich.' *How much progress? A report to the publisher of Time*, by John Scott, 1963, p. 49.

tion. The whole bourgeoisie is closely connected with the so-called 'oligarchies', if only because most of the richer bourgeois own land. And all of them tend to favour the *status quo*.

The peasants constitute in many countries a revolutionary force. But its revolutionary potential cannot be realized without outside leadership, and the aim of the peasant is to acquire private property, and not to become a unit of collective agriculture. Many of them are quite suspicious of communist aims, even when these are adroitly masked. How can the Communists acquire power in Latin America? The Cuban example can hardly be repeated. In no other Latin American country do we find the combination of a dictator backed by a corrupt and inefficient army and, at the same time, hated by the majority of the population, a revolutionary *caudillo* pretending to be nothing more than a radical democrat and counting on widespread sympathies inside the whole population, including the upper classes, together with the absence of organized social forces opposed to a socialist transformation of the democratic revolution. In most countries of Latin America the state apparatus, the armies and the Church are stronger than they were in Cuba, and many have learned a lesson from the Cuban experience.

There seem to exist only two roads to power: either the 'peaceful' one, propagated by the official parties or the 'violent' one of the Castroist-Trotskyite-Peking wing. Both are strewn with obstacles.

'Popular front' tactics have frequently been tried, always without success. It is doubtful if next time it will be different. In 1962/63 there were, as a matter of fact, only two countries on which the communists pinned their hopes: Brazil and Chile. But the Brazilian party was, as events have shown, quite weak; the 'front' it tried to form suspiciously wide[1]. Its allies were hardly dependable, while the anti-communist forces were stronger than they appeared on first sight. The chances seemed brighter in Chile, where the social and political crisis was sharpening, the Communist party was better organized and where it could count on the collaboration of the socialists, who, on the whole, were rather more radical than the communists themselves. From the purely electoral standpoint it seemed rather improbable that the (communist-directed) FRAP and its candidate Salvador Allende would win, but even if this happened, the real difficulties would only just begin. The radical changes wanted by the FRAP could not be accomplished within the framework

[1] One of the leading members of the Brazilian Party, Gorender, explained that the popular front should not be limited so as to include only 'left wing' forces. 'In our conditions the correct way is to build a nationalist and democratic united front (which) permits the inclusion in it of those sections of the bourgeoisie and petty bourgeoisie which today do not belong to the left. . . . Nor do we close our eyes to the possibility of an alliance with other non-revolutionary forces . . . They can include even the *comprador* bourgeoisie and the latifundists.' Exchange of views on 'Building a United Anti-Imperialist Front', *World Marxist Review*, January 1963.

of the constitution. If Allende were to try to remain *inside* this framework he would have to moderate his policies, provoking disillusionment and splits inside his own camp. If he were to transgress it he would call into play all the possible counter-revolutionary forces, including the hitherto non-political (and very efficient) Chilean army. Then the 'peaceful way' would be transformed into a violent one, in which the probabilities of victory would lie rather with the enemies than with the friends of the FRAP. As it happened, Allende was beaten by his competitor, the leader of the Christian Democrats, Eduardo Frei, and Chile became the second country, after Brazil, in which front tactics brought no success to the communists.

Elsewhere the chances of the 'peaceful road'—which hardly existed outside the two above mentioned countries—seemed dim, a fact which, to some extent, explains the growing influence of Castroist and pro-Chinese tendencies on the radical left.

The latest formulation of the 'Castroist' concept can be found in Guevara's article mentioned above, published in *Cuba Socialista* of September 1963.

The Latin American revolution he claims, will be violent, protracted and continental in character ('it is very difficult for a single country to achieve victory and consolidate it'). The 'national bourgeoisie' cannot be considered a revolutionary force ('The majority of the national bourgeoisie is in league with US imperialism and want to throw in their lot with it in every country'). The main revolutionary potential is constituted by the peasantry ('Our peasants have dormant, untapped sources of strength and it is necessary to use this strength for the liberation of America') which, however, needs the leadership of workers and intellectuals. The objective conditions for revolution obtain all over Latin America ('there exist everywhere in this continent the objective conditions which compel the masses to oppose the governments of the bourgeoisie and the landlords by violent acts') and 'it is criminal not to take action to seize state power in those countries where all these conditions obtain'. The main road to power is guerilla warfare. Only thus can a 'people's army' be born, able to vanquish and destroy the official army, the main bulwark of counter-revolutionary power. Only through guerilla warfare can experienced cadres be formed and the germ of the future state be established in 'liberated' areas. The formation of a guerilla nucleus in the countryside 'will ensure the security and continuity of the revolutionary command'. While guerilla warfare may start with acts of self-defence and with the struggle of small groups of revolutionaries, it must acquire mass character. 'Guerilla warfare is a kind of people's war, a kind of mass struggle. The attempt to carry out this form of war without the support of the local population means certain defeat.'

It is interesting to note that Guevara does not mention the importance of acts of terrorism—which play a very important rôle in the tactics of all 'Castroist' groups; that he seems only to pay lip-service to the hegemony of the workers without analysing how this is to be established ('the peasantry is a class which ... requires the revolutionary and political leadership of the working class and the revolutionary intellectuals'), and that, while declaring that 'in general' Latin America is ripe for revolution and guerilla warfare, he still implies that this is not the case in all countries, without any concrete and clear specification of what constitutes a revolutionary situation. Now it is precisely here that the main contrast between the 'left' and the 'official' communists becomes apparent. The latter tend indeed to deny that any acutely revolutionary situation obtains in Latin America. And they are by no means alone in their opinion. It is particularly interesting to quote the opinion of two writers who are particularly close to the Chinese and Castroist views—Huberman and Sweezy—who, after a prolonged trip to Latin America, wrote in February 1963:

'Does this mean that we can expect a rapid spread of revolutionary processes in one or more regions of Central and South America? Many people, including ourselves, have in fact entertained such expectations ever since the victory of the Cuban Revolution four years ago. Unfortunately, we have now come to the reluctant conclusion that this revolutionary optimism was, and still is, based more on wishful thinking than on a sober estimate of possibilities. Our present view is that further successful revolutions are not likely to take place in Latin America in the near future.'[1]

But, when revolutionary situations do not exist, guerilla warfare and terrorism acquire inevitably the character of *putschist* activities, which may disrupt the normal life of a country but are unable to lead to a seizure of power. This is precisely what has happened in Venezuela, where the Castroist formula has suffered a (maybe provisional but still real) defeat as heavy as any of the 'official' communists. This in spite of the fact that the Venezuelan 'official' communists participated in the protracted guerila and terrorist activities which were helped and encouraged from Cuba. The radical groups proved not only unable to seize power but even to influence the line of the Betancourt government and to force it to make any concessions. (This fact was clearly recognized in an article published in the Parisian *Voie Communiste* in January 1963, in which the author spoke of innumerable errors committed by the Venezuelan radical left and stressed the 'mythical character' of the peasant guerillas. The guerilla groups of Venezuela are isolated, they experience more defeats than victories, the peasants show them their hostility or, in the best case, their indifference.)

[1] 'Notes on Latin America', *Monthly Review*, No. 11, New York, March 1963.

Thus, although a final judgment about failure or success of any kind of Communist strategy and tactics can not yet be given—the Communist chances in Latin America seem at present not much brighter than those of the protagonists of the 'Alliance for Progress'.

Behind the alternative, Alliance for Progress or communism, looms the dichotomy: reform or revolution?—the problem whether the changes considered necessary for Latin American development can only come about through violent upheavals or may be realized by more or less 'piecemeal' forms of social engineering.

Unfortunately the term 'revolution' is highly ambiguous. 'Revolution' is a catchword in Latin America. Its constant and emphatic repetition frequently substitutes for thought and serious analysis. Almost everyone claims to be 'revolutionary': the communists and the socialists, radical democrats and populists of all descriptions, *Peronistas* and Christian Trade Unionists, many protagonists of the Alliance for Progress and even some groups which rather appear as 'counter-revolutionary'.

It does not help to distinguish revolution from reform by the use made of violence, because, on the one hand, official communists proclaim the possibility of a 'non-violent road' to power, whereas world history is full of examples where reforms could only be realized by more or less violent means. Nor does the pseudo-marxist definition help, according to which a social revolution implies change in governing classes, the progressive development of Latin America presupposing the rule of the proletariat, principally, because it is by no means clear which clearly definable social class rules in each country or in the whole of the subcontinent;[1] secondly because it is rather misleading to classify the social struggles going on as *class* struggles;[2] thirdly because only a simplifier and falsifier can claim that the seizure of power by radical intellectuals or a party machine is identical with the establishment of proletarian rule; fourthly, because no single social class of Latin American society can be considered as the scapegoat responsible for underdevelopment.

Still, there is some meaning behind the dichotomy. Taking 'revolution' to mean a rapid and radical change of the political and social set-up, a breach of constitutional continuity usually requiring mass movements and a considerable amount of more or less centralized

---

[1] There is much to be said for Benjamin Higgins' statement: 'It is not so much a matter of a firmly established political power élite being opposed to development, but rather that it is not altogether clear who the power élite are.' *Social aspects of economic development in Latin America*, I, UNESCO, p. 165.

[2] An author writes about Brazil: 'The social conflicts in our country are not so much struggles between classes as conflicts between the dynamic and the static, the productive and the parasitic sectors within each class.' Helio Jaguaribe, *Burguesia y proletariado en el nacionalismo brasileño*, Buenos Aires, 1961, p. 38.

violence.[1] We may ask if the reforms essential for progress do not *presuppose* a revolution. Most of those reforms imply shifts in property and power which are resisted by those who are or will be their victims, and the history of the last decades shows clearly the force of this resistance.

But even if reformulated in this way, the question remains difficult to answer in general terms which would have validity for all countries from Haiti to Argentina and from Uruguay to Mexico. It may, also, still be misleading, for there are many who still consider a revolution to be the midwife of a progressive society already existing in the womb of the old one and waiting to come to life. This is simply not the case in Latin America. It is not true that there exists, below the chains and fetters imposed by oligarchies and imperialism, the complex of material and human conditions and relations to guarantee a quick and painless development. There is no adequate infrastructure, not enough capital, an insufficient number of well-prepared peasants, workers, technicians, administrators and managers. Nor are those habits and the behaviour pattern generally prevalent without which a rapid general progress is impossible.

Those elements and factors have to be created—and this will take a very big amount of time and effort, while a violent revolution may and can provisionally increase the difficulties. To take only the agrarian problem; which is by no means the same in all countries and all parts of each country. Even if '*latifundism*' were the only, or even the main defect of Latin American agriculture, it certainly would not be sufficient to distribute all the big properties among the land-hungry peasants. 'Agrarian reform' includes the building of roads, houses, hospitals and schools, the introduction of modern methods and adequate implements, the opening up of new lands, the creation of credit-institutions and co-operatives, and last but not least, the re-education of the farmers. While it *might* be true that agrarian reform will not really be launched without an initial revolution, the process of fundamental reform can also come about through pressures exercised by reformist groups and movements on the ruling strata, if they are able to exert pressure on them and to take, at the same time, advantage of the conflicts of interest existing among them.

Now, this could not even be imagined if the overall situation were entirely hopeless and if Latin America were nothing but a mass of backwardness and misery, in which no progress had ever occurred.

[1] Albert O. Hirschman writes in his latest work, which I consider to be one of the most important books ever published about Latin America: 'even if violence is a necessary condition for revolution, it is not a sufficient one, and it is also a common element of reform. To qualify as revolutionary, violence must be centralized; it must attack and conquer the central seats of political and administrative power.' *Journeys toward Progress*, New York, 1963, p. 257.

But although the black certainly outweighs the white, this would not be a true and complete picture of the subcontinent.

Though most countries of Latin America must still be classified as 'underdeveloped', development has taken place, and in some parts rather quickly. The present tensions and contradictions are indeed as much an outcome of progress, and of the growing expectations it has produced, as of the obstacles which delay it. 'The region as a whole has developed at a sufficiently rapid rate, in fact more rapidly than most of its counterparts in the western world.' This statement by a leading Latin American economist[1] is rather too optimistic and does not take into account the years 1961-62, in which progress has notably slowed down, but nevertheless reminds us of the overall picture of the previous decades. Even during the last years, *per capita* income of Latin Americans has at least continued to rise—if at a desperately low rate—in spite of the demographic explosion. Latin American industrialization has been impressive; one has only to compare the southern regions of Brazil, Mexico and Venezuela with what they were some three decades ago. Not only consumer goods but also intermediate and heavy goods are being manufactured at an increasing rate. Steps have been taken in the direction of building markets, the first of which has been successful in Central America at least and which, in time, may give a decisive stimulus to further development. Although progress has been uneven and highly developed segments and districts coexist side by side with backward ones, one should not forget that most processes of industrialization have begun in this way and to mention that progressive changes are happening even in some of the most miserable regions, as for example, in the Brazilian North-east.

The slowness of the development process has produced dissatisfaction not only in the masses, but also inside the strata which can be considered as belonging to the upper class, among the entrepreneurs and technicians. These last are still scarce, but their scarcity must be considered in its proper setting and not unduly exaggerated.[2] Too much entrepreneurial talent has been wasted in dubious speculations, or been diverted to finance and commerce, and not enough has gone into the field of production proper; but these strata exist.

'During the last few decades and in the more advanced countries of the region, the presence of thriving complexes of entrepreneurial capacity is undeniable ... In the majority of these countries the commercial enterprise has prevailed over that of a strictly industrial

[1] Jorge Ahumada in UNESCO, *Social Aspects*, I, p. 115.
[2] With respect to Mexico, Frank Brandenburg writes that there is no shortage of competent technicians and administrators. On the contrary, there are too many of them in relation to the number of jobs available. 'A Contribution to the theory of Entrepreneurship and Economic Development. The Case of Mexico', in *Inter-American Economic Affairs*, Vol. XVI, No. 3, Washington, Winter 1962.

nature, and above all, the political or conjunctural type of entrepreneur has predominated, thanks to the vicissitudes of power. In several countries the entrepreneurial type described as the public manager may be said to have made its appearance.'[1]

That a stratum of bourgeois entrepreneurs exists and that it is playing in part a rôle in industry too, is seen also by Russian, communist authors: 'The rôle of the local bourgeoisie has changed and at present it cannot any longer be considered as intermediary or comprador or commercial bourgeoisie of the old type ... the bourgeoisie itself organizes production.'[2]

Even if many 'bourgeois' invest in land and try to climb into the aristocracy, while almost all of them are afraid of revolutionary upheavals, their fundamental interests are still not identical with those of the landowning oligarchs. It is precisely the menace of revolution which may make them favourably disposed toward the lesser evil of reform. Even more reform-minded are most of the new specialists and technicians whose future depends on a rapid development of their countries. Some of them are working in state-owned enterprises, which—as the example of Pemex shows—are not always hotbeds of corruption and paragons of inefficiency. There are also signs of greater organization and clearer consciousness of their interests among the working classes. In some countries trade unions are appearing which are neither anarcho-syndicalist nor communist, nor government-managed institutions.

There are also some trends in the political sphere which must be mentioned and rated as positive. The traditional Latin American 'establishment' is cracking. Mass-pressure makes itself felt and forces politicians to proclaim the necessity of changes. Leading politicians are beginning to understand the necessity of radical reforms, precisely because they are afraid of revolution. Some reforms have indeed been launched—for example in Venezuela. They may be termed modest, but are still real. The rôle of the armed forces can no longer be simply classified as reactionary. New ideas penetrate the officer-corps, ideas which are technocratic rather than democratic, and which sometimes appear in the form of 'kemalism' or 'Nasserism', with its anti-feudal, nationalistic and/or anti-capitalist connotations. The Church has begun to adopt a new attitude and to demand social transformation. Radical reform movements are born under the sign of Christian Democracy or Christian Socialism, which offer the people an ideology able to compete with communism and which—and this is especially true of the Christian Democrats of Chile and their leader Eduardo Frei—are much more serious, informed and realistic than the old 'populist' movements and groups.

[1] Joé Marisa Echevarría, in UNESCO, *Social Aspects*, I, p. 93.
[2] W. Myatchin, *Borba za edinyii rabochii i antiimperialisticheskii front*, Moscow, 1963, p. 130.

Here are, then, some factors and aspects of present-day Latin American reality whose importance should not be overstressed but which exist and make the prospect of evolutionary change possible—at least in some, if not in all countries. Yet even evolutionary change has revolutionary implications and will hardly occur without popular struggles and constant pressure on those who will have to give up privileges and power. Even in the developed countries of the West essential reforms have often required violent social action. In Latin America the obstacles are greater, the solutions more difficult to find, the masses more impatient, the intellectuals more disaffected. They are hardly prepared to wait much longer or to remain forever passive. Nor should they. It will only be if they appear on the political scene that the barriers obstructing progress will be overcome. It will be through their active participation that the masses will cease to be amorphous, acquire a clearer consciousness of their tasks, shed their old habits and become full citizens. It is also only if well organized and responsible radical reform movements arise and strengthen themselves, that Latin America will be able to avoid the Charybdis of critical underdevelopment as well as the Scylla of chaotic rebellion or totalitarianism.

BIBLIOGRAPHY

Acuña, Juan A. *Cuba ¿Revolución Frustrada?* Montevideo, 1960.
Adams, Richard N., et. al. *Social Change in Latin America Today.* New York, 1960.
Akienis y Urosa, J. *Características Fundamentales de la Economía Cubana.* Havana, 1950.
Alba, V. *Le Mouvement Ouvrier en Amérique Latine.* Paris, 1953.
Alexander, Robert J. *The Peron Era.* New York, 1951.
—. *Communism in Latin America.* New Brunswick, N. J., 1957.
—. *The Bolivian National Revolution.* New Brunswick, N. J., 1958.
—, and Porter, C. O. *The Struggle for Democracy in Latin America.* New York, 1961.
Allemann, F. R. *Die Revolution der Bärte.* Hamburg, 1961.
Almeyda, C. *Reflexiones políticas* Prensa Latinoamericana, Chile, 1958.
Anuario Azucarero de Cuba de 1959. Havana, 1960.
Arango, R. *Política Agraria.* Havana, 1958.
Arciniegas, G. *Entre la Libertad y el Miedo.* Buenos Aires, 1957.
Arévalo, J. J. *The Shark and the Sardines.* New York, 1961.
Arnault, J. *Cuba et le Marxisme.* Paris, 1962.
Arredondo, A. *Cuba: Tierra Indefensa.* Havana, 1945.
Avarin, B. Ya, and Danilevich, M. V. *Natsionalno Osvoboditelnoe Dvizhenie v Latinskoi Amerike na Sovremennom Etape.* Moscow, 1961.
Baeza-Flores, A. *Las Cadenas Vienen de Lejos.* Mexico City, 1960.
Bagú, S. *Economía de la Sociedad Colonial.* Buenos Aires, 1949.
—. *Estructura Social de la Colonia.* Buenos Aires, 1952.
Barahona-Jimenez, L. *El Ser Hispanoamericano.* Madrid, 1959.
Batista, R. *Respuesta.* Mexico City, 1960.
—. *Piedras y Leyes.* Mexico City, 1961.
Belloni, A. *Del anarquismo al Peronismo.* Buenos Aires, 1960.
—. *Peronismo y Socialismo Nacional.* Buenos Aires, 1962.
Bemis, S. Flagg. *The Latin American Policy of the United States.* New York, 1943.
Benham, F., and Holley, H. A. *A Short Introduction to the Economy of Latin America.* London and New York, 1960.
Benton, W. *The Voice of Latin America.* New York, 1961.
Berle, A. A. *Latin America—Diplomacy and Reality.* New York, 1962.
Betancourt, R. *Trayectoria Democrática de una Revolución.* Carácas, 1948.
—. *Venezuela: Política y Petróleo.* Mexico City, 1956.

Beteta, A. E. *Apuntes Socio-económicos del Perú y Latinoamérica.* Lima, n.d.
Bledel, R. *América Latina en su Actual Encrucijada Económica.* Buenos Aires, 1956.
Bosch, J. *Cuba: Isle Fascinante.* Santiago, 1955.
Brennan, R. *Castro: Cuba and Justice.* New York, 1959.
Brogan, D. W. *The Price of Revolution.* London, 1951.
Brown-Castillo, G. *Cuba Colonial.* Havana, 1952.
Castro, F. *Discursos para la Historia.* Vol. I. Havana, 1959.
—. *Political, Economic, and Social Thought of Fidel Castro.* Havana, 1959.
—. *Fidel Castro Parle: La Révolution Cubaine par les Textes.* Paris, 1961.
Casuso, T. *Cuba and Castro.* New York, 1961.
Cereceda, R. *Las Instituciones Políticas en América Latina.* Bogotá, 1961.
Chapman, R. *A History of the Cuban Republic.* New York 1927.
Chonchol, J., Peyrellade, and J. Chao, C. *Proyecto de Plan Quinquenal para el Desarrollo de la Agricultura Cubana 1961-1965.* Havana, 1961.
—. *La Reforma Agraria Cubana.* Havana, 1961.
Cline, H. F. *Mexico: From Revolution to Evolution.* London and New York, 1962.
Congress for Cultural Freedom. *Democracy in the New States.* New Delhi, 1959.
Cordoza y Aragon, L. *La Revolución Guatemalteca.* Mexico City, 1955.
Corredor, B. Torres, S. *Transformación en el Mundo Rural Latinoamericáno.* Bogotá, 1961.
Cuadra, J. de. *Prolegómenos a la Sociología y Bosquejo de la Evolución de Chile Desde 1920.* Santiago, 1957.
Cuba, Republica de. *Anuario Estadístico, 1956.* Havana, 1957.
—. *Banco Nacional: Programa de Desarrollo Económico, Informe No. 3.* Havana, October, 1957.
—. *Informe del Ministerio de Hacienda al Gobierno Revolucionario al Consejo de Ministros.* Havana, September, 1959.
—. Consejo Nacional de Economía. *Encuesta Sobre Empleo, Subempleo y Desempleo.* Havana, 1958.
—. Tribunal Superior Electoral. *Censo de Población, Vivenda y Electoral.* Havana, 1955.
Curtis-Wilgus, A. (ed.). *The Caribbean.* Vol. I to VII. Univ. of Florida, Gainesville, 1950-1957.
Danilevich, M. V., and Shulgovski, A. F. *Problemy Sovremennoy Latinskoy Ameriki.* Moscow, 1959.
—. *Rabochii Klas v osvoboditelnom dvizhenii narodov Latinskoy Ameriki.* Moscow, 1962.

Davis, H. E. (ed.). *Government and Politics in Latin America.* New York, 1958.
Debuyst, F. *Las Clases Sociales en América Latina.* Bogotá, 1962.
Dell, S. S. *Problemas de un Mercado Común en América Latina.* Mexico City, 1959.
Draper, T. *Castro's Revolution: Myths and Realities.* New York, 1962.
Dreier, John C. (ed.). *The Alliance for Progress.* Baltimore, 1962.
Dubois, J. *Fidel Castro: Rebel = Liberator or Dictator.* New York, 1959.
Dumont, R. *Terres Vivantes.* Paris, 1962.
—, and Coleou, J. *La Reforme Agraire à Cuba.* Paris, 1962.
Fitzgibbon, R. F. *Cuba and the USA 1900–1935.* Menasha, Wisc., 1935.
Foreign Policy Association. *Problems of the New Cuba.* New York, 1935.
Friedmann, G. *Problèmes d'Amérique Latine.* Paris, 1959.
—. *Signale d'une Troisième Voie?* Paris, 1961.
Friedrich, C. J., and Brzezinski, Z. K. *Totalitarian Dictatorship and Autocracy.* New York, 1961.
García Lupo, R. *La Rebelión de Generales.* Buenos Aires, 1963.
Gómez, R. A. *Government and Politics in Latin America.* Rev. ed. New York, 1962.
Gómez Robledo, A. *Idea y Experiencia de América.* Mexico City, 1958.
Grubbe, P. *Im Schatten des Kubaners.* Hamburg, 1961.
Guerra y Sánchez, R. *Azúcar y Población en las Antillas.* 2nd ed. Havana, 1953.
—. *La Industria Azucarera de Cuba.* Havana, 1940.
—, et. al. *Historia de la Nación Cubana.* Vols. VIII and IX. Havana, 1952.
Guevara, E. ('Che'). 'Guerrilla Warfare,' in *Che Guevara on Guerrilla Warfare.* New York, 1961; *Mao Tse-tung and Che Guevara, Guerrilla Warfare.* London, 1962.
Guilbert, Y. *Castro l'Infidèle.* Paris, 1957.
Gutiérrez, G. *El Desarrollo Económico de Cuba.* Havana, 1952.
Halperin, E. *The Sino-Cuban and the Chilean Road to Power.* Cambridge, Mass., 1963.
—. *Castro and Latin American Communism.* Cambridge, Mass., 1963.
—. *The Ideology of Castroism and its impact on the Communist Parties of Latin America.* Cambridge, Mass., 1963.
Hanke, L. *Modern Latin America.* Vols. I and II. New York, 1959.
Hanson, S. G. *The Economic Development of Latin America.* Washington, D.C., 1951.

Haya de la Torre, R. V. *El Antiimperialisme y el APRA*. Santiago, 1936.
—. *¿Y Despúes de la Guerra qué?* Lima, 1946.
—. *Treinta Años de Aprismo*. Mexico City, 1956.
Herring, H. A. *History of Latin America*. New York, 1955.
Hirschman, A. O. (ed.). *Latin America Issues*. New York, 1961.
—. *Journeys towards Progress*. New York, 1963.
INRA (Instituto Nacional de Reforma Agraria). *Informe Technioeconómico sobre la Reforma Agraria*. Havana, 1959.
International Commission of Jurists. *Cuba and the Rule of Law*. Geneva, 1962.
Iscaro, Rubens. *Origen y Desarrollo del Movimiento Sindical Argentino*. Buenos Aires, 1958.
James, D. *Cuba, The First Soviet Satellite in the Americas*. New York, 1961.
James, P. E. *Latin America*. 3rd ed. New York, 1959.
Jenks, L. *Our Cuban Colony*. New York, 1928.
Johnson, J. *Political Change in Latin America*. Stanford, Calif., 1958.
Julien, C. *La Révolution Cubaine*. Paris, 1961.
Kantor, H. *The Ideology and Program of the Peruvian Aprista Movement*. Berkeley, Calif., 1953.
Kuba: Istoriko-etnograficheskie Ocherki. Moscow, 1960.
Latinskaia Amerika v Proshlom i Nastoiashchem. Moscow, 1960.
Lazacano y Mazon, M. *Las Constituciones de Cuba*. Madrid, 1952.
Lieuwen, E. *Petroleum in Venezuela*. Berkeley, Calif., 1954.
—. *Arms and Politics in Latin America*. Rev. ed. New York, 1961.
López Aparicio, A. *El Movimiento Obrero en México*. Mexico City, 1952.
MacGaffey, W., and Barnett, C. R. *Cuba: Its People, Its Society, Its Culture*. New Haven, Conn., 1962.
MacEoin, G. *Latin America: The Eleventh Hour*. New York, 1962.
Martz, J. D. *Central America*. Chapel Hill, N. C., 1959.
Máspero, E. *América Latina: Hora Cero*. Buenos Aires, 1962.
Matthews, H. L. *The Cuban Story*. New York, 1961.
Mejía Fernández, M. *El Problema del Trabajo Forzado en America Latina*. Mexico City, n.d.
México: 50 Años de Revolución. Vols. II and III. Mexico City, 1961.
Meyer, K. E., and Szulc, T. *The Cuban Invasion*. New York, 1962.
Mills, C. Wright. *Castro's Cuba*. (Published in the United States under the title *Listen, Yankee*.) London and New York, 1960.
Myrdal, G. *An International Economy*. New York, 1956.
Nelson, L. *Rural Cuba*. Minneapolis, Minn., 1950.
Nuñez Jiménez, A. *Geografía de Cuba*. Havana, 1959.
OAS. *Financing of Economic Development in Latin America*. Washington, D.C., 1958.
Osborne, H. *Bolivia*. 2nd ed. London, 1955.

Partido Socialista Popular: VIII Asamblea Nacional. Havana, 1960.
Pendle, G. *Argentina.* London, 1955.
Perkins, D. *A History of the Monroe Doctrine.* Boston, 1955.
Perón, J. D. *La Fuerza es el Derecho de la Bestias.* Lima, 1956.
Pflaum, I. P. *Tragic Island: How Communism Came to Cuba.* New York, 1961.
Phillips, R. Hart. *Cuba: Island of Paradox.* New York, 1959.
Pinto-Santos, O. *El Imperialismo Norteamericano en la Economía de Cuba.* Havana, 1961.
Pinto-Santa Cruz, A. *Chile: Un Caso de Desarrollo Frustrado.* 2nd ed. Santiago, 1962.
Portell-Vilá, H. *Historia de Cuba en sus Pelaciones con España y los Estados Unidos.* Vols. III and IV. Havana, 1941.
Portuondo del Prado, R. *Historia de Cuba.* Havana, 1957.
Prebisch, R. *The Economic Development of Latin America.* New York, 1950.
Ramírez-Novoa, E. *América Latina y Estados Unidos.* Lima, 1958.
Ramos, J. Abelardo. *Revolución y Contrarevolución en la Argentina.* 2nd ed. Buenos Aires, 1961.
—. *El partido communista en la politica argentina.* Buenos Aires, 1962.
Ravines, E. *The Yenan Way.* 4th ed. New York, 1951.
—. *La Gran Estafa.* Santiago, 1957.
—. *América Latina: Un Continente en Erupción.* Havana, 1959.
Roca, B. *Los Fundamentos del Socialismo en Cuba.* Havana, 1943.
Roig de Leuchsenring, E. *Cuba no Debe su Independencia a los Estados Unidos.* Havana, 1960.
Rostow, W. W. *Stages of Economic Growth.* New York, 1960.
Ruiz-Garcia, E. *Iberoamérica entre en Bisonte y el Toro.* Madrid, 1959.
Salazar, R. *Líderes y Sindicatos.* Mexico City, 1953.
Sánchez, L. A. *Historia General de América.* Vol. II. Santiago, 1944.
Sauvage, L. *Autopsie du Castrisme.* Paris, 1962.
Scheyven, R. *De Punta del Este a la Havana.* Brussels, 1961.
Schneider, R. M. *Communism in Guatemala.* New York, 1959.
Scott, J. *How much progress?* (A Report to the Publisher of *Time*), *Time* Inc., 1963.
Seton-Watson, H. *The Pattern of Communist Revolution.* 2nd ed. London, 1950.
—. *Neither War nor Peace.* London and New York, 1960.
Shonfield, A. *The Attack of World Poverty.* London and New York, 1960.
Simpson, L. B. *Many Mexicos.* Berkeley, Calif., 1959.
Smith, E. T. *The Fourth Floor: An Account of the Castro Communist Revolution.* New York, 1962.
Smith, R. M. *The U.S. and Cuba: Business and Diplomacy.* New York, 1960.

Souchy, A. *Testimonios Sobre la Revolución Cubana.* Buenos Aires, 1960.
Staley, E. *The Future of Underdeveloped Countries.* New York, 1954.
Strachey, J. *The End of Empire.* London, 1959; New York, 1960.
Sweezy, P. M., and Huberman, L. *Cuba: Anatomy of a Revolution.* New York, 1960.
Tabares del Real, J. *La Revolución Cubana.* Havana, 1961.
Tannenbaum, F. *The Mexican Agrarian Revolution.* New York, 1929.
—. *Mexico: The Struggle for Peace and Bread.* New York, 1950.
Toriello, G. *La Batalla de Guatemala.* Mexico City, 1954.
Tovar, G. I. *Visión Breve de Iberoamérica.* Bogotá, 1956.
Trias, V. *El Plan Kennedy ya la Revolución Latinoamericana.* Montevideo, 1961.
Ulam, A. B. *The Unfinished Revolution.* New York, 1960.
Union Panamericana (Pan American Union). *Materiales para el Estudio de la Clase Media en Américalatina.* Vols. I–VI. Washington, D.C., 1950.
—. *Financing of economic development in Latin America.* Washington, D.C., 1958.
—. *América en Cifras.* Vols. I–VIII. Washington, D.C., 1961.
—. *Integración Económica y Social del Perú Central.* Washington, D.C., 1961.
United Nations
  Department of Economic and Social Affairs. *Report on the World Social Situation.* New York, 1961.
  —. *Progress in Land Reform.* E/2526, ST/ECA/21; Sales No. 1954. II. B3. New York, 1954.
  —. *Progress in Land Reform.* E/2930, ST/ECA/42; Sales No. 1956. II. B3. New York, 1956.
  ECLA. *Economic Survey of Latin America 1955.* E/CN. 12/421/Rev. 1; Sales No. 1956. II. G1. New York, 1956.
  —. *Economic Survey of Latin America 1956.* E/CN. 12/427/Rev. 1; Sales No. 1957. II. G1. New York, 1957.
  —. *Economic Survey of Latin America 1957.* E/CN. 12/489/Rev. 1; Sales No. 1958. II. G1. New York, 1958.
  —. *Economic Survey of Latin America 1958.* E/CN. 12/498/Rev. 1; Sales No. 1959. II. G1. Mexico City, 1959.
  —. *Economic Survey of Latin America 1959.* E/CN. 12/541. New York, 1960.
  —. *Economic Survey of Latin America 1960.* E/CN. 12/565. New York, 1961.
  —. *The Economic Development of Latin America in the Post-War Period.* E/CN. 12/659/Rev. 1; Sales No. 1964. II. G6. New York, 1964.
  Food and Agriculture Organization. *The State of Food and Agriculture 1961.* Rome, 1961.

United Nations—*cont.*
International Bank for Reconstruction and Development. *Report on Cuba.* Baltimore, Md., 1951.
International Labour Office. *The Landless Farmer in Latin America.* Geneva, 1957.
UNESCO. *Basic Facts and Figures.* Paris, 1961.
—. *Urbanization in Latin America.* Paris, 1961.
—. *Social Aspects of Economic Development in Latin America.* Vol. I. Paris, 1963.
United States of America
Department of Commerce. *Investment in Cuba.* Washington, D.C., 1956.
—. *U.S. Investments in the Latin American Economy.* Washington, D.C., 1957.
—. *U.S. Business Investments in Foreign Countries.* Washington, D.C., 1960.
Department of Labor. *Foreign Labor Information: Labor in Cuba.* Washington, D.C., May, 1957.
Department of Labor. *Foreign Labor Information; Latin American Labor Legislation,* Comparative Summaries [Cuba], Washington D.C., December, 1956.
Department of State. *Interamerican Efforts to Relieve International Tensions in the Western Hemisphere 1959–60.* Washington, D.C., 1962.
Congress. *Communist Threat to the United States through the Caribbean.* Hearings before the Subcommittee to Investigate the Administration of the Internal Security Act. United States Senate, 86th Cong. 1st and 2d sess. Washington, D.C., November 1959–August 1960.
—. Committee on Foreign Relations. *US—Latin American Relations. Compilation of Studies.* (Doc. No. 125.) United States Senate, 86th Cong. 2d sess. Washington, D.C., August 31, 1960.
—. *Economic Developments in South America.* Hearings before the Subcommittee on Inter-American Economic Relationships of the Joint Economic Committee. 86th Cong. 2d sess. Washington, D.C., 1962.
Universidad de Chile. Instituto de Organización y Administración. *Afiliación y finanzas sindicales en Chile 1932–1959.* Santiago de Chile, 1962.
University of California. Center of Latin American Studies. *Statistical Abstract of Latin America 1960.* Los Angeles, 1960.
Urquidi, V. L. *The Challenge of Development in Latin America.* New York, 1964.
Uslar-Pietri, A. *Sumario de la Economía Venezolana.* Caracas, n.d.
Veitia, P. H. *Presente y Futuro del Agro Cubano.* Havana, 1959.

Vicens-Vives, J. (ed.). *Historia Social y Económica de España y América*. Barcelona, 1959.
Villanueva, V. *El militarismo en el Perú*. Lima, 1962.
Wallich, H. C. *Monetary Problems of an Export Economy*. Cambridge, Mass., 1950.
Weyl, N. *Red Star Over Cuba*. New York, 1960.
Whitaker, A. P. *Argentina Upheaval*. New York, 1956.
White, E. *Azúcar Amargo*. Havana, 1954.
Worcester, D. E., and Schaeffer, V. G. *The Growth and Culture of Latin America*. New York, 1956.
Woytinsky, W. S. *The U.S. and Latin America's Economy*. New York, n.d. (1958).
Ycaza-Tigerino, J. *Sociología de la Política Hispanoamericana*. Madrid, 1950.
—. *Originalidad Hispánoamericana*. Madrid, 1952.
—. *Hacia una Sociología Hispanoamericana*. Madrid, 1958.
Zubok, L. I. *Imperialisticheskaia Politika S. Sh. A. v Stranakh Karibskovo Baseina*. Moscow, 1948.

INDEX

AAA, 147
ABC, 104–7
Acción Democratica (Venezuelan), 19, 92, 94, 95, 309, 310
Acción Revolucionaria Guiteras, 149
Adzhubei, Alexei, 276–7
Agriculture: in Latin America, 32–3, 58, 65, 66, 80, 83–4, 88; Cuban, 121–2, 124–5, 128, 134; monoculture, 27, 128, in Cuba, 279, 280, 286, 289; crops, 229–30, 232, 233; animal husbandry under Castro, 233–4, 248, 279, 281; agrarian discontent with Castro, 250–1; difficulties, 281, 301; labour, 269. *See also* Land Reform
Agramonte, Prof. Robert, 110, 111, 187–8
Alemán, Miguel, 63, 312
Alessandri, President, 315, 338–9
Alfabetización campaign, *see* Education (illiteracy)
Allende, P. H., 322, 339, 349, 354
Alliance for Progress, 320, 322, 333; Kennedy on, 333; aims, 333–6; development, 337–40; prospects, 344–6; resistance to in Latin America, 346–8, 349
ANAP, 226–7, 228, 249, 286–7
Anticlericalism, 49, 50, 61, 101. *See also* RC Church
APRA, 53, 309, 310, 315, 337
Aprista parties, 309
Araña, Major Francisco, 67, 68
Arbenz, Capt. Jacobo, 67–70, 72–3, 310, 337
Arévalo, Juan, 67, 68, 320, 324
Argentina, 23; economy, 29, 75, 80–1; land ownership, 32; society, 39, 75, 76; armed forces, 48, 76–8; Church, 49, 77, 80–2; education, 51, 52, 54, 55; government (1916–30), 74–5; political parties, 75–8; Communist Party, 76, 80, 307, 308, 310, 350, 351; government (1930–43), 76–7; 1943 military dictatorship, 77, 306; industrialization, 76, 306; Trade Unions, 75–8, 82, 351; under Perón, 77–83; incomes, 92; Castroism, 314; military dictatorship (1962), 337
Armas, Colonel Castillo, 73–4, 328

Arosemena, Dr. Carlos, 316
Artime, Manuel, 185, 187, 195, 241
Audit, Court of (Cuban), 109
Auténticos, the, 107, 109–11, 112, 115, 116, 118, 147; opposed to Batista, 156–7; & Pact of Caracas, 161; proscription of, 202, 240; as populists, 309, 310

Barcena, Garcia, 147
Barquin, Colonel Ramón, 154, 161, 163, 170
Barrientos, General, 338
Batista, Fulgencio: *coup d'état* of, 106, 310; régime of, 107–9; return of, 110, 111–13; & Communist Party, 117; & Castro, 143–4, 151; opposition to, 146–7, 151, 153, 154, 156–7, 160–3, 293; & RC Church, 157; & USA, 107, 170–1; collapse of, 175
Batistianos, 240 *et passim*
Bay of Pigs incident, 241
Bayo, Alberto, 154
Belaunde Terry, 315, 337
Betancourt, Ernesto, 182
Betancourt, Rómulo, 91, 94, 95, 313, 339
Black Market, 250, 268. *See also* Economy under Castro
Blas Roca, 117, 118, 145, 216, 243, 249, 251, 262, 263, 267
Blest, Clotario, 315
Bohemia, 111, 113–14, 144, 156, 203–4, 228, 254, 260
Bolívar, Simon, 23
Bolivia, 23; army, 47, 48, 53, 85, 86; Church, 49; intelligentsia, 53; people, 83, 84; Indian population, 83–4, 86, 88; incomes, 83; agriculture, 83–4, 88; minerals, 84, 88; tin mining, 84, 87, 88–9; & Chaco War, 84, 306; Revolution, 84–9; Trade Unions, 85, 88–9, 315; land reform, 87; industry, 84, 87–9; & USA, 89; MNR, 309; Communist Party, 319, 351; Castroism, 315; & Punta del Este Conference, 322; failure of Revolution, 338

Bonsal, Philip Wilson, US Ambassador to Cuba, 197
Bosch, Juan, 338
Braden, Sprualle, US Ambassador to Argentina, 79
Brazil: early history, 19–23; economy, 26; industrialization, 29, 35; railway, 30; land ownership, 32; coffee production, 36; people, 39, 53; army, 47, 53; Church, 49; *Paulista* Revolution, 306; Communist Party, 308, 310, 343, 350–3; Vargas' régime, 306, 309; Castroism, 313–14; Trade Unions, 314, 351; discontent under Goulart, 338
Busch, Lieut.-Col., German, 85

Cabildos, 19–20
Cacigazos, the, 18
Cacique, the, 18
Caffery, Jefferson, 107
Caldera, Rafael, 94, 95
Calles, P. E., 61, 62
Camacho, Avila, 63
Caracas, Declaration of, 317, 328
Caracas, Pact of, 160–1
Cardenas, Lazaro, 57, 60, 62–3, 306 309, 310, 312, 322
Cardona, Miró, 161, 178
Carranza, Venustiano, 59
Casa del Obrero Mundial, La, 59
Castro, Fidel: legend of, 143–4; early programme, 144, 152–4, 160–1, 178, 183; youth of, 147–50; & *MSR*, 49; & *Ortodoxos*, 150, 151, 153; his landing, 113, 154–6; 'Manifesto of the Sierra Maestra', 157, 158, 163–4; campaign, 159–63; & 'Pact of Caracas', 160–1; economic programme, 164–5; & Communists, 161, 165–70, 183, 185 (*see also* Communist Party, Cuban); his popularity, 180, 210, 211–12, 236, 289, 293, 319; his visit to USA (1959), 180–1, 277; & Urrutía affair, 187–8; & Matos, 189–91; & Trade Unions, 206; living conditions under, 211–13; opposition to, 236–8, 250–4, 262, 319, 320; his Moscow visit, 286; his attainment to power, 297–8; & *Operation Panamerica*, 332
Castro, Fidel, foreign policy of: relations with USA, 179, 181–3, 196–201; & Eastern bloc, 181–2, 196–201; & USSR, 279, 289; 1961 invasion, 238–41; missile crisis, 272–7; & test ban treaty, 286
Castro, Fidel, ideology of, 163–5, 191–2, 201 ff., 210 ff., 220–1, 242 ff., 248–54, 279, 290, 292–3, 300–1, 320
Castro, Fidel, speeches of: 'History will absolve me', 151; in Havana (1959), 176–8, 179; on international position, 182–3; on land reform law, 185, 186–7, 220, 227, 230–1; on education, 215; to Women's Congress (Jan. 1963), 216, 291, 341; on food scarcity, 232; after Bay of Pigs incident, 241; on dangers of optimism, 248; on agriculture, 249; on private sector, 249–50; on Trade Unions, 252; on censorship, 254; on doctrine, 260; on discontent, 262–3; on ORI, 263; reveals split in Revolutionary Party, 264–6; on cooperatives, 269; on missile crisis, 276; on economic cretinism. 279 on monoculture, 280–1; on PURS, 282; on political position, 283–4; on military service, 288; on capitalism, 291
Castro, Raúl: on the Cuban Revolution, 144; part played in Revolution, 155, 175, 179 & Communist Party, 161; & JUCEI, 244; as member of secretariat of ORI, 263, 267; leads delegation to Moscow, 272, 276–7; on military service, 287–8
Castroism, in Latin America, 312–17, 319–20 *et passim*
'Catholic Action', 51, 147
Catholic Youth Organization, 253
Censorship, 253, 261
Centros de Industria y Artesania 215
Céspedes y Quesada, Carlos Manuel de, 105–6
Céspedes, Carlos Manuel de, 99–100
Chaco War, 84, 306
Chibás, Eduardo, 104, 110, 115
Chibás, Raúl, 153
Chile, 23; land ownership, 32; army, 47; Church, 21, 49; Trade Unions, 51, 315, 351; rural education, 51; socialist republic, 306; Communist Party, 308, 350–1; populist party, 309–10, 353–4; Castroism, 315; difficulties, 338–9
China, Communist Party of: relations with Cuba, 199, 275–7, 282, 318, 340–1; is represented at Peace Conference in Mexico, 312; attacked by

INDEX

China, Communist Party of—cont.
  USA at San José Conference, 317–18; influence in Latin America, 342–3
Chomón, Faure, 176, 242–3, 263
Chonchol, J.: his Five Year Plan, 258, 259; on agriculture, 287
Christian Democratic Party, 51
Christian Social Party, 51
Christian Socialism (in Argentina), 81
'Christian Working Youth', 51
Church, Roman Catholic: in Latin America, 17–21, 49–51, 359–60; in Cuba, 49, 101, 132, 157, 191; & Castro, 207–8, 237, 253; organizations of, 51, 147, 253
CIA, 238–41, 276
Cienfuego, Major Camilo, 190
CLASC, 51
CNTI, 314
COB, 315, 338
Codigo de Trabajo, 68
Coffee, 35–6 *et passim*
Colombia, 23; coffee production, 36; society, 39; army, 48; Church, 49; Trade Unions, 51; schools, 51; populist party, 309; Communist Party, 310, 350, 351; *coups d'état*, 310; Castroism, 316; anti-Castroism, 320; difficulties of revolution, 339; agrarian reform, 339
Comando Geral dos Trabaldahores, 352
Committees for the Protection of the Revolution, 237, 250, 270–1
Communism, Latin American, 307–11, 348–56; & Popular Front, 306, 308, 309–11, 313, 353; weakness of, 350; & Trade Unions, 351; tasks of, 352–4. *See also various countries*
Communist International, 309
Communist Party, Cuban, 104–11, 112, 113–19; influence on workers, 145; & Castro, 146, 182, 183, 191; 1960 Congress, 193, 243; as a legal group, 202; & Trade Unions, 206; & JUCEI, 245; & ORI, 245; split over Castro, 261ff.; takes control of positions of power, 262, 308; & PURS, 282; growing role of, 298; its role in pre-revolutionary Cuba, 310
Compania Minera de Bolivia, 87
Confederation of Industrial Workers, 314
Confederación Latino Americana de Sindicalistas Cristianos, 51

Conquistadores, 17–20
Conte Aguero, 187, 201
Contreras, General Lopez, 90
COPEI, 92, 95
Corregidores, 18
Costa Rica, 23; coffee production, 36; army, 47; Trade Unions, 51; populism, 309; Revolution, 310
Cuba, pre-Revolutionary: army, 47, 154; education, 52; war of independence, 99–100; period of US domination, 100–4, 105; Liberal party, 104–5; Constitution of, 108–9; people, 131–5; culture, 214–18
CTC, 112, 117
Cuban Trade Union Confederation, 112, 117

'*Descamisados*', 76, 78
Díaz, Porfirio, 57–8
Díaz-Lanz, 187, 190
Directorio Estudiantil, 104
Directorio Revolucionario, 156, 157, 159, 161, 176–7, 245
Dominican Republic, 23, 337
Dorticós Torrado, Osvaldo, 188, 243–4, 263, 266, 267, 278
Draper, Theodore, on Castro, 182, 183, 212
Dulles, John Foster, & Guatemala, 72, 74

Echeverría, Esteban, 155, 156–7
Economic & Social Council of UN at São Paulo, 340
Economy, Cuban, early, 27–8, 34–6; pre-Revolutionary, 100, 120 ff., 126–31, 134, 135–42
Economy, Cuban, under Castro, 179; nationalization, 193–9; trade restrictions, 194; socialization, 194–5; relations with USA, 194, 199–201; & USSR, 199, 200–1; loans from Chinese People's Republic, 199, 200; improvements in, 210–11; threats to, 245–8; shortages of commodities, 232, 234, 237, 245–6; sugar embargoes, 239, 246; rationing, 255–7, 278; blockade of, 256; & NEP idea, 268; fuller socialization of, 268–70; difficulties of, 278 ff.; summary, 299–300
Ecuador, 23; society, 38; Church, 49; Castroism, 316; after Punta del Este Conference, 322; military dictatorship, 337–8; Trade Unions, 351

Ecuador—cont.
Education, colonial, 22; pre-Revolutionary reform, Cuban, 101, 109
Education, Cuban: as factor in Revolution, 52-6; reform under Castro, 209, 211, 214 ff., 290; illiteracy, 214, 215, 217-18, 247; schools, 214, 215-16; teachers, 214-217, 247; indoctrination, 215-17; nationalization of system, 215; e. of peasants, 215, 216; e. of women, 216
Eisenhower, Dwight, 73, 195, 238, 331-32
Ejidos, 53, 58, 60, 61, 64
El Salvador, 23
Emigration, 209-10, 261
Emigrés (from Cuba), 238, 239, 240, 241, 289, 291
Employment, 132-3, 230, 259, 260; conditions, 194, 211-13; wages, 236-7, 256, 259
Enlightened Despotism, Latin American, 21-2
Escalante, Anibal, 118, 123, 262-7
Escuelas Basicas de Instrucción Revolucionaria (EBIR), 216
Escuelas Campesinas, 215-16
Escuelas de Instrucción Revolucionaria (EIR), 216
Escuelas de Instructores de Arte, 216, 238
Estrada Palma, Tomás, 100, 103

Farell, General, 78
Febreristas, see Paraguay
Federación Estudiantil Universitaria, 154
Fernández, Manuel, 191
Figueres, José, 179, 309, 310
Finance: productive capital, 31, 33; taxation, 31-2, 44, in Cuba, 130; income distribution, 36, in Cuba, 120-4, 289; taxation under Castro, 178, 179; 'Cubanization' of, 126
Fishing, 225, 234, 251
Fortuny, Manuel, 69, 71-2
Frei, Eduardo, 339, 354, 360
Frondizi, Dr. Arturo, 82, 314, 322
Fuentes, Ydigotas, 74

G.2, 253, 254, 270
Gaitán, Jorge, 310
Gallegos, Rómulo, 91

Gardner, Arthur, US Ambassador, 170
Gómez, General Juan Antonio, 90
Gómez, Laureano, 310
Good Neighbour Policy, *see* Roosevelt, F. D.
Goulart, J. B., 314, 338
Grau San Martin, Ramón, 106-7, 109-10, 116, 118
Guatemala, 23; land ownership, 32; Church, 49; Revolution, 65-74, 317, 328; Indians, 65-7; economy, 66; Constitution, 68; Trade Unions, 68; political parties, 68; education, 68; Communist Party, 69-74; & USA, 70-4; land reform, 69-70; & invasion of Cuba, 239, 240; & overthrow of Arbenz, 310, 347; & Declaration of Caracas, 317, 328
Guevara Arze, 338
Guevara, Ernesto ('Che'): on past economic development of Cuba, 137; on US sugar quota system, 139; on peasant element of Revolution, 145-6; & Castro's landing, 154-5, 162-3; & Communist Party, 161; on causes of the revolutionary victory, 171; as head of National Bank, 191, 194; on US policy, 196; on 'Humanism', 246; as Minister of Interior, 249; on labour problems, 252; on achievements of Revolution, 257; on sugar industry, 259; & ORI Secretariat, 267; his visit to Moscow, 272, 277; on economic errors, 279-80; decorated by Quadros, 314; on guerrilla warfare, 341; on Castroism, 354-5
Guillén, Nicolas, 254
Guiteras, Antonio, 107-8, 151
Gutierrez Menoya, Carlos, 156-7

Haciendas, the, 20, 23-4, 58
Haiti, 22
Hart, Armando, 263
Havana Declarations, 243, 272, 285, 318-19, 322, 340-1
Herter, Christian, US Secretary of State, 180-1, 239, 332
Hevia, 110-11
Hidalgo, Aranjo, 316
Honduras, 23, 49, 337
Housing, under Castro, 180; reform of, 195, 211, 229, 231; as problem, 237, 248; shortage of, 257

INDEX

Hoy, 117, 118, 166, 187, 232, 267
Huerta, General, 58–9

Ibarra, President Velasco, 316
ICFTU, 51
Illia, Dr. Arturo, 337
INAV, 180
INCRA, 339
Indians, 17–22, 24, 49; in Mexico, 53, 58, 60
Industry, colonial, 21, 26–8, 33–5
Industry, Cuban: American interests in, 102, 104, 126; expansion of, 122; 'Cubanization' of, 126; difficulties of, 137–42; Castro's programme for, 152, 193, 194; difficulties of under Revolution, 259, 278–81, 301; in Latin America, 305–7
INIT, 94
INRA, *see* National Land Reform Institute
'Institute for Rural Education', 51
'Institute for Saving and Housing', (INAV), 180
Inter-American Regional Organization of Workers (ORIT), 314
Irigoyen, 76

Jesuits, 21–2, 51
Jiménez, Pérez, Marcos, 48, 90, 92, 93, 94, 310
Joven Cuba, 107
Jovenes Rebeldes, 209
JUCEI, 244–5, 249, 270
JUCEPLAN, 249
Julião, Francisco, 313–14, 322, 338, 349
Juntas de Coordinación, Ejecución è Información, *see* JUCEI
Justicialism, 83, 209, *and see* Peron

Kennedy, John F.: & Cuban invasion, 239–40; & missile crisis, 273–4, 276–7; Cuban policy, 347. *See also* Alliance for Progress
Khruschev, Nikita: on Cuban economy, 268; & missile crisis, 273–4, 275–7; announces aid to Cuba, 317
Kirkpatrick, Inspector-General of CIA, 239
Kubitschek, Juscelino, 331

Land reform in Cuba: necessity for, 33–4, 109; situation at the Revolution, 124–5, 129; Law (1959), 185–7, 194, 211, 212, 218–21; problems, 218–19, 221–2; new wages, 225; cooperatives, 219–20, 222, 223 ff., 237–8, 249, 268–9; course of land reform, 222 ff.; collectivization, 223; private sector, 219–20, 226, 228–9, 230, 249, 269, 279, 286; People's farms, 226, 249, 268–9; socialization, 226–8; production results, 229, 231–4; employment, 230, 259, 260; 2nd Law, 279, 281, 286–7. *See also* Military service
Language, 38
Larrazábal, Admiral Wolfgang, 94, 95
Law reform under Castro, 204–5
Lechin, Juan, 85, 338
Liberacion nacional, 309
Lombardo Toledano, Vicente, 308
López Fresquet, Rufo, 181–2
López Mateos, President, 313
López, Michelsen, 316
L'Ouverture, Toussaint, 22
Luzardo, Manuel, 263

Machado, Gerardo, 104–5, 115, 306
Madero, Francisco, 58
Magoon, Charles E., 103
'Manifesto of the Sierra Maestra', *see* Castro, Fidel
Marinello, Juan, 117, 143, 165, 166, 275
Marti, José, 100, 151
Martinez, Sanchez, 263
'Massacre of Oruru', 86
Matthews, Herbert, 156, 170
Matos, Hubert, 188–91
Medina, General Isaias, 90
Mendieta, Carlos, 104, 107–8
Menocal, President, 104
Mestizos, 18, 23–4
Mexico, 22, 23; industry, 35, 58, 63–4; income distribution, 36, 64–5; population, 38; army, 47, 62; Church, 49, 61; education, 52, 54; Indians, 53 (*see also Ejidos*); Revolution, 57–65; agrarian affairs, 58, 62–4; political parties, 61; business expansion, 61, 63–5; oil, 62–4; Trade Unions, 62; Revolutionary Party (PRI), 309; Communist Party, 62, 310, 351; Cuba's influence on, 312; Castroism, 312; Alliance for Progress, 337; development of Revolution, 339

Mikoyan, A. I., 199, 274, 283
Military service, in Cuba, 279, 286, 287
Militia, in Cuba, 208–9, 237, 247, 260
MIR, 313, 315
Mora, Menelao, 156–7
Morelos, 22
Movement of the Revolutionary Left (MIR), 313, 315
Movimiento de Liberacion Nacional, 312
Movimiento Nacional Revolucionario (MNR), 85–7, 89, 147
Movimiento Popular Revolucionario, 316
Movimiento Revolucionario del Pueblo (MRP), 240
MSR, 149
Mujal, Eusebio, 109, 110, 112

National Bank of Cuba, 109, 141, 249
National Land Reform Institute (INRA), 185–7, 194, 219, 220, 223–6, 228, 249; public achievements of, 229, 230; reorganization of, 287; Communists in, 298
National Socialist Party, Bolivian, 85
Nationalization of Labour, Law of, 106
Nicaragua, 23, 47
Nixon, Richard, 181, 183, 329, 331, 347
Núñez-Jiménez, 186, 229, 233

OAS, *see* Organization of American States
Obregón, Alvaro, 59, 61
Odria, General, 337
Oil, Cuban, 194–5. *See also* various
Operation Panamerica, 331–2
Organización Auténtica (OA), 147
Organizaciones Revolucionarias Integradas (ORI), 245; publication of leaders, 263–4; purge, 266–7; new secretariat, 267; transformation, 271–2; & PURS, 282
Organization of American States: Conference at Punta del Este, 320–2; Council meeting of, 322; Charter of, 327–8; & *Operation Panamerica*, 331–2
ORIT, 314
Ortodoxos, the, 110–12, 150, 151, 153, 161, 309

Pacto de Zanjón, 100
Pais, Frank, 154, 155, 157

Palacios, 311, 320
Panama, Republic of, 23
Pan-American Conference (1933), 326
Pan-American Union, 327
Pando, General Cesar, 315
Paraguay, 21, 23, 43, 47, 84; *Frebreristas* in, 309
Paris, Treaty of, 100
Partido Communista do Brasil, 343
Partido Revolucionario Institucional, 61
Partido Socialista Popular, see Communist Party, Cuban
Partido Unido de la Revolucion Socialista (PURS), 245, 271, 279, 282
Paz Estenssoro, Victor, 85, 86, 87, 338
Pazos, Felipe, 164, 182, 191, 194
Pelayo Cuervo Navarro, Senator, 147, 157
Peña, Felix, 179
Peña, Lazaro, 206, 263
Pérez, Faustino, 191
Perón, Evita, 80
Perón, Colonel Juan, 48, 77–83, 310
Peru, 22, 23; army, 47; Church, 49; education, 52–4; Communist Party, 310, 350, 351; Castroism, 315; anti-Castroism, 320; military dictatorship, 337. *See also* APRA
Peurifoy, John M., US Ambassador to Guatemala, 73
Plan de Ayala, *see* Zapata, Emiliano
Platt Amendment, 102–4, 107, 326
Popular Front, *see* Communism
Press, under Castro, 180, 202–4
Prío Socarras, Carlos, 104, 109–13, 147, 154; & USA, 171
Private sector, *see* Land Reform
Production Congress, First (Cuban), 226, 231, 233, 234, 247, 248, 250
Property under Castro, 109, 179–80, 193–4. *See also* Housing
Public works under Castro, 180, 211

Quadros, Janis, President of Brazil, 313–14

Racial prejudice, 290–1
'Radepa', 85–6
Radio, 204, 307
Radiophonic schools, 51
Rationing, *see under* Economy
Ray, Manuel, 158, 191, 240
'Razón de Patria', 85–6
'Red Trade Union International', 62

INDEX

Rice, 121, 194, 233, 255 *et passim*
Rio de Janeiro, Treaty of, 327, 328
Rodriguez, Carlos Rafael, 117, 161–2, 166, 244, 248, 262, 263, 267, 269, 287
Rojas, José, 85, 87
Rojas Pinilla, General, 48, 93, 310, 316, 339
Roosevelt, F. D.: Good Neighbour Policy of, 74, 306, 326, 327; & Cuba, 105, 106
Roosevelt, Theodore, 103, 325
Rubottom, R. R., US Assistant Secretary of State, 181
Ruiz, Alberto, 315
Rural missions, 51

Saladrigas, Dr Carlos, 109, 118
Salvador, David, 158, 179, 184, 206
Sánchez Arango, Aureliano, 112, 147, 201–2, 240
San Domingo, 47
San José, Conference in, 239, 313, 317–18, 333
Santamaria, Haydee, 263
Sindicato Campesino de Ucurena, 85
Slavery, 18–19, 21
Smith, Earl T., 157, 170, 171
Sorí Marín, 185, 220
Souza, Ireneo Evangelista, 24–5
Stevenson, Adlai, 241, 336
Suazo, Hernan Siles, 85, 338
Sugar industry: improvements of with US money, 102; collapse of market (1929), 104; under Batista, 112; as mainstay of Cuba, 121, 137; protection of, 125, 138–9; expansion of, 127–9, 298–9; US restrictions on, 139, 195, 200–1, 239, 246, 256, 289, 291, 333, 347; under INRA, 194, 212; its reliance on voluntary help, 248; problems of, 257–9, 278–9; Five Year Plan for, 258; & Eastern bloc, 199, 258, 286
Summapaz, 39

Tamborini, 79
Technology, developments in, 200, 215–18, 289, 299
Tequendama, 39
Terrorism, in Cuba, 208–9, 252–4, 260 ff., 270
Toledano, Vicente Lombardo, 61–2
Toriello, Jorge, 67, 73
Torre, Haya de la, 309, 315
Tourism, in Cuba, 194

Trade Union Centre (of Latin America), 308
Trade Unions, in Cuba, 107, 108, 112, 157, 161, 184–7; suppression of, 206, 251; & Castro, 206; attitude to Communism, 206
Transport, 27, 30–31, 62; in Cuba, 129, 255, 257. *See also* various countries
Trias, Vivian, 349
Trotskyites in Cuba, 253
Tupac Amaru, 22
Twenty-sixth July Movement: foundation of 146; & Moncada attack, 150–1; independence of, 153; & Castro's landing, 154–9; aims of, 164, 191; & Communist Party, 166; & Humanists, 184, 206; organization of, 202; & ORI, 245. *Refer also* Castro, Fidel

Ubico, Jorge, 67
Unemployment, 246–7, 256, 259, 301
Union Civica Radical del Pueblo, 314
Union Insurrecional Revolucionaria, 149
United Provinces of Central America, 23
United Fruit Co. (of Guatemala), 66, 70
Universities, 52–4; under Castro, 205–6, 214–15, 217
Urbanization, 39–40, 306–7
URD, 92, 95, 313
Uriburu, General, 76
Urrutía, President, 163, 175, 187–8
URS, 313
Uruguay, 23; army, 47; Church, 49; students, 52; dictatorship, 306; Castroism, 314–15; split after Punta del Este Conference, 322; Communist Party, 350
USA: & Guatemala, 70–4; & Bolivia, 89; & pre-Revolutionary Cuba, 100–4, 105, 107, 126, 136–42, 170–1; & 1961 invasion, 238–41; break-off of diplomatic relations with Cuba, 239; & missile crisis, 273–7; & Cuban Revolution, 293; policy towards Castro, 317, 321–2, 347; & Monroe Doctrine, 323–5; 'Dollar diplomacy' of, 325, 336; non-intervention policy, 326–7; policy towards Latin America, 328–9, 335–6; foreign policy, 329–31, reappraised, 331–5; & Alliance for Progress, 333–4; *see also* Sugar industry

USA—cont.
  US Standard Oil Co., 81, 82, 85
  USSR: relations with Cuba, 196–201, 267–8, 283–5, 293; as training ground for Cubans, 215; & missile crisis, 272–7; trade protocol with Cuba, 278; & Cuban sugar industry, 286; Cuban dependence on, 289, 301; represented at Peace Conference in Mexico, 312; attacked by USA at Conference of San José, 317–18; & Havana Declarations, 318
U Thant, & missile crisis, 274

Valdés, Ramiro, 263
Valenilla, 92
Vargas, G. D., 306, 309
Varona, Antonio de, 101, 147, 202, 239, 240
Venezuela, 23; railway, 30; incomes, 36, 92; army, 48, 53, 89–91, 94; Church, 49, 94, 95; Trade Unions, 51, 91, 92; Revolution, 89–96; oil, 90–3; economy, 90–3, 95–6; education, 53, 95–6; industrialization, 90–1; political parties, 91, 92; land reform, 91, 95; Communist Party, 91, 94, 95, 308, 310, 351; population, 92, 95; Castroism, 313; & Alliance for Progress, 337; revolutionary developments, 339; defeat of Castroism, 355–6
Villa, Pancho, 59
Villalba, Jóvito, 94, 313
Villaroel, Major, 86

Welles, Sumner, 105, 106, 171
Women, emancipation of, 216, 291
Wood, General, 102
Workers: & Cuban Revolution, 144–5, 295–6, 301; opposed to Castro, 251–2; attitude to Communism, 308–9; drift to towns, 260
Writers and Artists, Union of, 254

Zapata, Emiliano, 57, 58, 59, 60; & *Plan de Ayala*, 58